AFTER GAMES, WHAT?

"For certain fortunate people there is something which transcends all classifications of behavior, and that is awareness; something which rises above the programing of the past, and that is spontaneity; and something that is more rewarding than games, and that is intimacy. But all three of these may be frightening and even perilous to the unprepared . . ."

From the conclusion of *Games People Play*

BEYOND GAMES AND SCRIPTS

Beyond Games and Scripts

by Eric Berne, M.D.

Selections from His Major Writings

Edited by Claude M. Steiner
and Carmen Kerr

Introduction by Claude M. Steiner

BALLANTINE BOOKS • NEW YORK

Library of Congress Catalog Card Number: 76-14558

ISBN 0-345-30053-X

This edition published by arrangement with Grove Press, Inc.

Printed in Canada

First Ballantine Books Edition: April 1978
Fifth Printing: December 1983

First Canadian Printing: April 1978

To the many people,
students, teachers,
clients, and friends,
who provided Eric Berne
with the raw material
with which he created
Transactional Analysis.

CONTENTS

THREE: Group Dynamics

BEYOND GAMES AND SCRIPTS

PREFACE

A Living Problem: "The Gordon Knot"
by Cyprian St. Cyr

Once there was a man called Gordon. When he was a little boy, his parents tied a monkey on his chest. Every day they made the knot tighter and more complicated, until the monkey was almost a part of Gordon's body. With this handicap, Gordon found it difficult to have any fun or play with other children, and it interfered even more with his life when he grew up. So he decided to go to a doctor and get rid of the monkey.

The first doctor he went to said: "Well, if you will lie still and don't give me any back talk, maybe we can do something." So week after week Gordon lay still while the doctor tried to unravel the knot. At the end of a few years, there were some loose ends, but the knot still held firm. Then Gordon got tired of going to that doctor and stopped.

The next doctor looked at the knot carefully and said: "That's awful. It's not just a knot, it's a double knot." He was a good doctor, but he couldn't get the knot untied.

Gordon then went to a third doctor. This doctor looked at the knot carefully, took out a sword, and with one blow cut right through the centre of Gordon's knot, so that the rope fell off and the monkey ran away.

When the first doctor heard about this, he came to look. He said: "That's not fair. You're supposed to unravel it. And besides, Gordon has a big white spot where the monkey used to be." And he said to the second doctor: "Don't worry, it's not gone for good anyway. Gordon will soon be back for more treatment." And Gordon said to the third doctor: "He's right. That was cheating. You were supposed to unravel it. And I do have a big white spot where the monkey used to be. And besides I miss my monkey."

So the third doctor said: "I'll tell you what. Let's have some fun. We'll paint designs on the white spot where the monkey used to be." So they painted pictures and designs on the white spot. At first Gordon didn't like the idea, but he soon began to enjoy it. "They're only watercolors," said the third doctor, "and they'll wash off any time. And in any case, after a while the white spot will go away and you'll look just like everybody else." But Gordon's friends, when they heard about Gordon having fun like that, said: "Disreputable. Disgusting. Cynical. Everybody knows you're not supposed to have that kind of fun. Why can't he stick to standard methods of having fun?"

Question: Why is it usually considered unethical to cut a knot instead of unravelling it?

INTRODUCTION

Eric Berne, *ne* Eric Leonard Bernstein, alias Cyprian St. Cyr, alias Eric Leonard Ramsbottom Gaudalae Bernstein, was a brilliant thinker, innovator, and therapist. But these gifts would probably not have sufficed to bring him fame within his lifetime had he not had a wonderful wit which made it possible for him to present the most radical ideas to what is probably the most skeptical, competitive, and discounting audience in the social sciences.

I am sure that most of his writings, just like his last public statement, brought out the same approximate response with its creative and funny approach: laughter on one hand and huffy indignation on the other, followed by thoughtful consideration.

I witnessed Eric Berne's last public speech, given on June 20, 1970, at the luncheon of the Golden Gate Group Psychotherapy Association's yearly conference where he was the keynote speaker. I remember him as clearly as if it was today, with his back to a panoramic view of San Francisco and the Golden Gate, facing a room filled to overflowing, as he did for the last time what he did so well throughout his lifetime—speak openly and freely about what he thought of psychiatry. He was earnest as well as entertaining, the audience laughed many times on that occasion, and I, as usual, walked away with a number of new insights. He died a few weeks later; this speech therefore represents his absolute latest thoughts as he was willing to share them with an audience of fellow psychotherapists. It contains his wit, his thoroughness, his playfulness, his interest in people and their well-being, all of which characterized him throughout his writings and his life. His wit was present in all of his writings. One of his very first published articles, "Who Was Condom?" is an exploration of the possible existence of a man called Condom who popularized or improved the "machine" about which Berne includes an eighteenth-century panegyric which begins: "Hear, and Attend: In Condom's nightly praise I sing, for sure, 'tis worthy of a Song. . . ."

—C.S.

1. Away from a Theory of the Impact of Interpersonal Interaction on Non-Verbal Participation

Okay, today I'm going to talk very seriously; this is sort of a "give them hell" speech. At the time that I thought out the title two years ago, I had some idea of what I was going to say but I've forgotten so I'll just talk and say whatever comes into my head.

The problem is that in spite of everything there are still half a million or possibly a million patients in state hospitals, so there has been a great demand for psychiatry resulting in one million vegetables walking around taking phenothiazines, and estimates are that there are a hundred and twenty million people who need psychotherapy. So the problem is how are we going to cure patients, which is what I want to talk about. And I have some questions like: How many cured patients do you know? Have you ever cured a juvenile delinquent by psychotherapy? How many? Have you ever cured a schizophrenic and if not, why not?

The basic thing I'm going to talk about is that psychotherapists, like poker players, are winners and losers. If you have permission to be a winner from your parents you can cure patients, in which case you might not be in psychiatry, you might be a surgeon or a real doctor of some kind. Maybe the reason that people go into psychiatry is that they're not required to do very much except to have staff conferences to explain why they can't do very much. The analogy with poker is that you can tell, in about three hands, who's a winner and who's a loser by the way players react to what happens. And I think patients can tell in about three hours which therapist is a winner and which is a loser. And since most patients don't really want to get well they're very likely to stay with the losers, but if they do want to get well they may find a winner.

I'm going to try to talk about how people make themselves into losers, particularly in the social sciences where there seems to be a tremendous resistance against knowing anything. The one thing that you can't say in any kind of a social science meeting is that you really know something because the reaction will not be, "tell us what you know," but it will be, "I'm going to show you that you don't really know anything," which doesn't occur in any of the other sciences.

The title of this talk, as you may have already figured out, is a put on. If you didn't figure it out you're lucky you're here. "Away from a theory of the impact of interpersonal interaction on non-verbal participation"—I think we got everything in there except "toward." We figured we'd leave out "toward" and put in "away from" just for fun. There are lots of papers coming out called "Toward" and you wonder when they're going to get there. And if you ask toward people when they're going to get there, they say, "Well, we don't know how to get there, and we don't even know where we're going." Well, I think real people know where they're going. One example is an airplane pilot. I once got on an airplane, and the pilot came over the loudspeaker and said: "This flight is going toward New York." I said: "Let me out of here, I want to go to New York." Then I went to the hospital to have my tonsils out, and the surgeon said: "I am going to take some steps toward taking out your tonsils." In other words: real people don't say "toward." They say, "That's where I'm going and that's where I am going to get." Well that takes care of toward and away from, and maybe away from is even better than toward. At least if you get away from, you can look at it more clearly.

About theory; a theory is one of two things: It's either a bright idea, like—I don't mind being specific—the kind of thing they do in psychology at the Rand Corporation where somebody sits down with a little

computer or very sophisticated adding machine and
makes a theory of human behavior without ever having
looked a human being in the eye, possibly. Or it's a
real theory which is an abstract from experience. The
more thousands of patients you see, the better your
theory is going to be, or the more hours you spend
with one patient and the less time you spend with the
adding machine the better your theory is going to be.

Then the word impact is very fashionable. Everybody wants to make an impact. Now an impact, to me,
is not a dull thud. Bang! Bang! That's what you should
be doing with your patients, not making dull thuds.
The phrase "interpersonal interaction" to me is usually
the mark of a jerk. I just don't see any point in that
expression at all—just the opposite: an impersonal
interaction, an interpersonal superaction, or infraction.
Actually this is sort of a chicken phrase because it
means: "If I use a lot of big words I don't really have
to find out what's happening, and it sounds good." Of
course, my tendency is to propose the term transaction.
The value of the term transaction is that you're committed to something; you're saying that something is
exchanged. Whereas if you use interaction you're saying, "I don't know, I'm only going toward it." Transaction means: "At least I got to the first stage. I know
that when people talk to each other they are exchanging
something, and that is why people talk to each other."

The fundamental question in social psychology is:
Why do people talk to each other? Interaction essentially means no action, in most cases. People who are
really going to do something do not use words like
interaction. That reminds me of an old joke of mine
about the way that patients are diagnosed in the average
clinic; the person who has less initiative than the psychotherapist is called passive-dependent. The person
who has more initiative than the psychotherapist is
called a sociopath.

Non-verbal, of coure, is very fashionable. The thing
that bothers me personally about non-verbal is using
it as a kind of shibboleth. There are lots of things people
do with their faces and their bodies, but as soon as
you call it non-verbal it makes it sound a little phony.

Also, people don't understand the verbal. There's still plenty of work to be done in the field of verbal activity so don't be discouraged if you are not going along with the non-verbal crowd.

Participation usually means talking my way. I ran across a very interesting example of that. I was feeling very good one morning, and I walked into the group therapy room at the hospital, and somebody had piled up a lot of coffee tables. So instead of going around them I sort of leaped over all the coffee tables, and the patients cheered. I thought it was neat and so did they. Later on in the session a man said: "I don't have any feelings. I never get angry." This guy had been in many kinds of therapy groups so after a while I said: "Well, you look as though you're feeling good now. Isn't that a feeling?" And he was really surprised because it had never occurred to him that feeling good was a feeling. So that's one of the problems with participation. Another very interesting thing is that laughing is not considered an expression of affect. In certain parts of the East which have a cultural lag of twenty or thirty years, the only thing that counts in groups is expressing anger. If you go and visit their big city you can see why they're all pretty mad at each other. If somebody has a group meeting and everybody laughs for a whole hour then the therapists go out looking very gloomy and say: "Nobody expressed any feeling. That was a bad group meeting, and a good group meeting is a group meeting where somebody expresses anger."

I once visited a clinic and passed through a group meeting, and at the staff conference afterwards everybody was saying, "Gee whiz, that was a good group meeting," except one nurse who looked sort of glum. I asked, "Don't you think it was a good group meeting?" She said no, and I asked why. She said, "Well, I was just transferred here from the medical service, and in the medical service patients are supposed to get better. I don't see why they're calling it a good group meeting because nobody got better." Which I thought was a very acute observation, but obviously she's going to be rapidly couchbroken so she'll soon think like all the others.

Properly played by the right people—played seriously—poker is one of the few really existential situations left in the world. Now here's what I mean by existential: Everybody's on their own. Nobody's going to feel sorry for you. You're fully responsible for everything you do. Once you put the money in the pot, you've put it in the pot. You can't blame anybody else. You have to take the consequences of that. There's no copping out. You can't talk your way into being a winner or a loser. All that counts is how much money you've got in your pocket when you hit the sidewalk, and that determines whether you're a winner or a loser, and nobody has to have a conference about it. It's really existential, and I think that's why people like it, and why a lot of people are quite devoted to it.

Another thing about it is you don't get any grants to play poker. Now grants are good in the physical sciences where people want to build an accelerator, and they have to go to the hardware store and need some money. In the behavioral sciences a grant is usually something you get when you don't know what you're doing. If you know what you're doing you usually don't need money. I never understand why people need money to do research unless they've got to go to the hardware store and buy something. And not a computer because I don't understand why people use computers in the social sciences when they're dealing with a few cases because you can do it yourself in an hour without bothering with a computer.

So in a way therapy should be like a poker game. In other words, the result is what counts. You're responsible for what you say. You shouldn't cop out and go and cry on somebody's shoulder at a staff conference. And if it is like a poker game, then there are certain unique features about it. For example, if you're a straight therapist then all your cards are up, while the patient has the privilege of keeping at least one of his cards turned down, so you're at a disadvantage. Of course you're supposed to be a professional and he's an amateur; that's why he's allowed to have that advantage. And another thing about therapy is that the patient always has the joker. In other words, no matter how well it's going, how well you understand each other, the patient always has a thing that he can do that will really upset the apple cart and there's nothing you can do about it. You can have the most beautiful therapeutic situation in the world and all the patient has to do is reach into his pocket, and he can destroy the whole thing or one of you. There's no towarding in poker. You either win or you lose. Your theory had to be based on practical things. All the armchair theories, like the rhythm theory, don't work in poker. There really isn't any rhythm to it. You've got to know what's happening with each hand. Also, nobody in poker ever ends the evening by saying, "We sure had some nice interpersonal interaction tonight, didn't we?" They say, "Well, that was a good game"—they use one-syllable words. Another thing is there's lots of non-verbal stuff in poker. In fact a lot of the game depends on getting to know the other guys and what they are doing. So maybe what I'm saying is that big words are hiding the reality of what's going on between people.

Since we got poker into this, let me talk a little more about it. How you win at poker: First, it's a game of skill, not luck, in which you're dealt cards, and if you lose a hand that's not luck that's skill—you shouldn't have been in the hand if you lose the hand. So that's pure skill. And it's the same way, I think, in psycho-therapy. If the therapy doesn't come out right you shouldn't have been in it or the cards weren't right, and you should have waited around a little longer or something should have been done. A lot of therapy is not scientific and is regarded as a matter of luck. Like people hold things called encounter groups. Now this may hurt your feelings. I don't understand encounter groups. They're purely empirical. Nobody really knows what they're doing. Nobody really offers to do anything, actually. But you do get good results. And that applies to a lot of therapy. In other words roughly speaking most of the group therapy done in this country—by most I mean 51%—could probably be just as well done by a sophisticated scout master. You know we all have a lot of education, and we use our degrees probably even less well than a good scout master would use his group skills. So if we took the trouble to go to all that college we should use that knowledge and not be trusting to luck or the fact that being in a room together is good for people in any case, so that an encounter group makes people feel good. Which brings me to another name for encounter groups, which is sensitivity groups. My definition of a sensitivity group is a group where sensitive people go to get their feelings hurt, and I'm not sure that's all that good for them.

Another thing about poker is you've got to know what you're there for. You're there to win money, and that's all you're there for. And if you're not there to win money you're not going to have any fun and neither are the guys you're playing with. Then you have to know certain facts. You have to know the rules of the game. You have to know what the stakes are. And that's something you have to know in therapy as well. Another sort of analogy is that you can always tell a loser in poker, as I say, by the first three hands because he says "I should" or "If only" or "I want to see the next card." "I want to see the next card" is a staff conference. In other words, "If I had done it differently or if I had stayed in, what would have happened?" So after the patient's quit you go to the staff conference to see why he quit which is like seeing the next card, and the other guys will tell you what you should have done, but they don't know either so it's just sort of a mutual stroking situation. I can think of several conversations I've had lately. I called a very, very well trained therapist about a patient, or rather he called me. For some reason those people always want to do a lot of talking about the patient when anything comes up. Well what happened is that he's seeing the wife five times a week and I'm seeing the husband once a week, and he wanted to have a long conversation. And I said, "Well, the husband looks a little paranoid to me, and I'm afraid to cure paranoids because in my experience when you're just about to cure paranoids they often get a very serious physical

disorder like a perforated ulcer or diabetes or a coronary." When I talk about being about to cure a
paranoid I mean when he has talked about his anal-
sadistic fantasies. About the word "sadistic." Sadistic
means hurting people and getting erections—that's
sadistic. Masochistic is being hurt and having sexual
pleasure. But sometimes people use sadistic or masochistic symbolically. So now anytime you don't like
somebody you can say they're sadistic. But I like to
stick to the original definition. Sadistic means somebody is getting pleasure out of inflicting physical injury.
Otherwise the word is sort of useless. Well, paranoid people have sadistic fantasies, anal-sadistic fantasies. Now anal doesn't mean "I don't like you so I'm
going to call you anal or compulsive or something," it
means anal. So a paranoid has fantasies of sticking
traumatic objects up people's rectums, like billy clubs
—that's what he has. That's anal-sadistic fantasies,
there's nothing symbolic about it. Now, if the paranoid
patient gets so that he can talk about those—and I
don't mean you just say, "Hey man, let's hear your
anal-sadistic fantasies." Say the relationship or the
transference or whatever it turns out to be is good
enough so that he is willing to tell you those fantasies,
he's about ready to give them up and start living
decently. And at that point, in my experience, he often
gets physical illness, all of a sudden. There's nothing
more sudden than a perforated gastric ulcer, for example. So I said to this psychotherapist, "Whenever
you try to cure paranoids . . ." and he said, "Oh, you
don't want to cure them, just make them feel good or
make them feel comfortable, make them able to live
with it." Which I thought was rather typical of the
common therapeutic attitude that you're not supposed
to cure anybody.

And to another intensive psychotherapist I said,
"Wow. I've just started with the brother and you've
been seeing the sister for five years—you must know a
lot about them. When is she going to get better?" And
he said: "I'm in no hurry." And here's this woman with
three little kids, and the therapist isn't in any hurry.
Well, I'm in a hurry. I want to cure people. And I'm

not interested in progress—progress is like trying. When a patient says, "I'm going to try to stop drinking," you know he isn't going to stop drinking, and that's that. So progress doesn't help anything. You get the patient well or you've got to win the pot.

And here I want to say something real dirty which is about psychoanalytic therapy. Now there are two different things—one is called psychoanalysis and the other is called psychoanalytic therapy. And, of course, everybody in the Psychoanalytic Institute knows, and a lot of other people agree with them, psychoanalysis is the real thing. The psychoanalyst says, "I can cure people," but if you learn psychoanalytic therapy you're not supposed to cure anybody because you don't know as much as the analyst and you're only supposed to make progress. So in a way the whole business of psychoanalytic therapy sounds to me like a joke laid on the residents by the instructors in which they're saying, "We'll teach you to do little things around the operating room but when it really comes to taking out the appendix you have to be like me." Well, surgeons don't teach their pupils that way—they tell them how to take out an appendix.

Another thing which is allied to that is the problem of comfort. "I'm not comfortable doing that kind of therapy." My reaction to that is if you're not comfortable why don't you be something else other than a psychotherapist. You have no business there. You're not there to be comfortable. You're there to cure patients. And the analogy is that if you're a surgical resident and you say to the chief surgeon, "I'm uncomfortable in the operating room with gloves on," the chief surgeon doesn't say, "Well, of course we can't have our residents being uncomfortable, you just come in the way you are—you don't even have to put a gown on." He says, "If you're not comfortable doing it right then go into some other specialty, like psychiatry."

Another one is: "You can't help anybody, they've got to help themselves." Now that is sheer baloney. People who are working in organizations don't really have to do anything as long as they follow the rules of the organization and play the game and don't cure too many patients (that really bugs the hell out of the people in such organizations; you will literally get fired, as we know from experience). But if you're in a private practice and you're getting large fees for doing psychotherapy, you have got to produce. You can't sit around saying to a sensible person, "I can't help you. You've got to help yourself." You can say that to a jerk or somebody who has been couchbroken by previous therapy, but with real people you can't say that. If a guy who really knows his own job comes for psychotherapy and you say, "I can't help you; you've got to help yourself," he'll just walk out. And I don't blame him.

For instance, you know very well that you can talk people into killing themselves. You know you can talk people into getting drunk. Therefore, you talk someone out of killing himself and out of getting drunk. But you've got to know how to tell him, what to do, and what to tell him. You can say to a patient: "Don't kill yourself." Now, if you say it wrong, you can then prove that you can't tell people anything because you said it to three patients and they all jumped off the bridge. They didn't jump off the bridge because you told them not to kill themselves, they jumped off the bridge because you told them wrong in order to prove that you can't help patients.

Another way that we get out of doing anything is the fallacy of the whole personality. "Since the whole personality is involved how can you expect to cure anybody, particularly in less than five years?" Okay. Well, here's how. This has to do with a splinter in the toe. Now, if a man gets an infected toe from a splinter, he starts to limp a little, and his leg muscles tighten up. Then, as he keeps walking around, in order to compensate for his tight leg muscles, his back muscles have to tighten up. And then, in order to compensate for that his neck muscles tighten up; then his skull muscles; and pretty soon he's got a headache. He gets a fever from the infection; his pulse goes up. In other words everything is involved—his whole personality including his head that's hurting and he's even mad at the splinter or whoever put the splinter there, so he may spend a lot of time going to a lawyer. It involves his whole personality. So he calls up this surgeon. (The same surgeon who said: "If you're not comfortable you may come in and operate in your street clothes without wearing gloves.") He comes in and looks at the guy and says, "Well this is a very serious thing. It involves the whole personality as you can see. Your whole body's involved. You've got a fever; you're breathing fast; your pulse is up; and all these muscles are tight. I think about three or four years—but I can't guarantee results—in our profession we don't make any guarantees about doing anything—but I think in about three or four years—of course a lot of it is going to be up to you—we'll be able to cure this condition." The patient says, "Well, uh, okay. I'll let you know tomorrow." And he goes to see another surgeon. And the other surgeon says, "Oh, you've got an infected toe from this splinter." And he takes a pair of tweezers and pulls out the splinter, and the fever goes down, the pulse goes down; then the head muscles relax and then the back muscles relax and then the feet muscles relax. And the guy's back to normal within forty-eight hours, maybe less. So that's the way to practice psychotherapy. Like you find a splinter and you pull it out. That's going to make a lot of people mad, and they'll prove that the patient was not really cured, or they'll prove that the patient was not completely analyzed. And it's not cricket to say, "Okay, doctor, how many patients have you completely analyzed?" Because the answer to that is: "Are you aware of how hostile you are?" So everybody's writing papers. And there's only one paper to write which is called "How To Cure Patients"—that's the only paper that's really worth writing if you're really going to do your job.

Let me talk about a couple of other things—sort of anecdotal. I have a friend in Czechoslovakia who was a creative writer and was publishing books. Now she writes me and asks for two things: One is American short stories, so I send her the *New Yorker*, and I get Grove Press to send her some books of short

stories. And the other thing she wants is a sedative.
So that's what there is to do in Czechoslovakia. There's
nothing they can do except take sedatives or get killed,
so that if you're not ready to get killed you take a
sedative. So that's how politics fits into psychiatry
which I'm sure my friends in radical psychiatry will be
interested to hear. So it's very much the same as giving
your patients pills; it's great, but it doesn't sound to
me like a very nice idea to have patients walking
around vegetating. Running through this I think you
will hear the dread medical model of psychotherapy,
which scares the hell out of people—gives them night-
mares. But I think it's a very good model. That's because it works for other conditions, and if you are
going to cure people's heads I think you should use the
medical model.

Personally I'm a head mechanic—that's all I am.
Like you come in with wheels wrong in your head, and
I'll say, "Okay, we'll try and fix your head. What goes
on outside your head belongs in a different department
from what I deal with, and I might be interested in
dealing with it but I don't feel that that is my primary
job." And if you're going to do that, then the first
thing you have to learn is simple, pure psychotherapy.
In other words: there's a patient sitting there in a chair
and you're sitting there in a chair, and there's no
gadgets. There's just two people—that's all there is.
And two chairs for comfort. Some people don't even
use the chairs. So a real psychotherapist's problem is:
What do I do when I'm in a room with a person who
is called a patient if I am called the therapist? Absolutely no gadgets—no note papers, no tape recorders,
no music, nothing. That's how you learn to do psychotherapy. Now once you learn how to do that and are
an expert at that, then you can start introducing trimmings. But to me the introduction of devices and
trimmings into any kind of psychotherapy usually means
that the therapist doesn't know what he's doing. It's
pretty hard to know what you're doing in psychotherapy because most of it is about at the level of the
University of Paris faculty of medicine in the sixteenth

century when people were using a lot of big words and they were having a lot of staff conferences, but none of the patients were getting better. Okay. I guess that's it.

ONE ○ ○ ○

Ego States, Transactions, and Games

Introduction

Carmen Kerr and I have selected from Eric Berne's prolific writings a series of pieces which would give both an historical perspective on Eric's development and a comprehensive coverage of it. We approached the task from two very different perspectives: I from the perspective of a colleague, close associate who was intimately and emotionally involved with the development of his theories; and Carmen, with the perspective of a writer, journalist, and psychotherapist who appreciates and uses Berne's theories from a more detached, objective perspective. Our aim is to show to the best extent possible Eric Berne's brilliant theory of personality as well as the subtleties of his emotional makeup.

Eric Berne and I met in 1958 when I was an undergraduate in psychology. He was having weekly meetings of his Tuesday evening seminars, then called the San Francisco Social Psychiatry Seminars. Our relationship, which later turned into friendship, lasted for twelve years until he died in July 1970. I was totally fascinated by his ideas and thinking and never tired of hearing him speak about any topic no matter how many times I had heard him speak on it previously. He always managed to put an interesting, novel, and unexpected twist on old material. In a way, going over his writings has been a similar experience in that he repeated many of his thoughts in his different works, each time with a different emphasis or with a subtle new development. As we selected the different portions which to our mind best represented his views, we tried to pick the most clear and most poetic that we could find. From an historical point of view whenever possible I picked the latest and most developed exposition. Many of his ideas changed, not very dramatically, but

they did change and I avoided including in this book
thoughts which he clearly abandoned or repudiated in
his later years, or intricacies which were temporary and
never to be picked up again either in writing or otherwise. I also have to take personal responsibility for
avoiding the inclusion in this book of portions of his
writings which I found personally distasteful and sections which I felt are contradictory with the main-
stream of his ideas. For instance, I have avoided in-
clusions of overly sexist and heterosexist material and
I also specifically excluded from this book a very brief
but very dramatically significant section from *What
Do You Say After You Say Hello?*, "The Little Fascist," which, to my mind, represented a reversal of
what to me is the core of his theory, namely, that people are born, at base, OK. This section—puzzling, unexpected, and in my mind theoretically unwarranted—
is, I believe, an expression of what Eric Berne calls the
demon, who in the last minute whispers a defeating
course into Jeder's ear which, in one fell swoop, wipes
out all of his former accomplishments. I never knew of
the little fascist until I read *Hello* after Eric's death.
Readers who wish to pursue the little fascist may do so
on their own.

EGO STATES, TRANSACTIONS, GAMES

One is struck, when reading Eric Berne's theories,
with the similarity that they have to some aspects of
Freudian theory: the ego, the superego, and the id.
Berne was a psychoanalyst by training, though he never
received the final seal of approval of the psychoanalytic
brotherhood. In fact, it is probably true that his development of Transactional Analysis was spurred by
a competitive urge that was generated in him by the
continued refusal of psychoanalysts to accept him in
their society. He tried to operate within the confines
of psychoanalysis for some time but did not find it
adequate and so he struck out on his own and did very
well indeed.

The theory of ego states has its roots in psychoanalysis only in that it deals with one aspect of psycho-

analysis, the ego. Otherwise, ego states were generated by Berne's interest in psychic phenomena: seances, telepathy, and clairvoyance. While a psychiatrist for the army, he thought that he might be able to guess the professions of servicemen being discharged by the mere use of his intuitive powers. He performed a number of informal experiments along these lines and concluded that intuition was indeed a capacity which he possessed and that with it, he was able to guess with better than chance results certain of the dischargees' occupations.

Encouraged by these results, he began to use his intuition in his work as a psychotherapist. He found that with certain of his patients, his intuition generated what he called "primal images." These primal images, similar to the intuitive images which enabled him to guess people's occupations, were useful in making "primal judgments" about people. Primal judgments about people revealed important states of mind related to their childhoods such as "this man feels as though he were a very young child, standing naked and sexually excited before a group of his elders. . . ." These childhood images he called "ego images."

The therapist's intuitive ego images, Berne reasoned, corresponded to a child ego state in the patient. Following, I quote at length Eric Berne's classic "cowpoke example."

Apparently it was with this example that Berne's decade of interest in intuition (1945–1955) crystallized into the ideas which are the cornerstones of Transactional Analysis—Child and Adult ego states.

An eight-year-old boy, vacationing at a ranch in his cowboy suit, helped the hired man unsaddle a horse. When they were finished, the hired man said: "Thanks, cowpoke!" To which his assistant answered: "I'm not really a cowpoke, I'm just a little boy."

This story epitomizes something which has to be understood in regard to a patient (or anyone else) to maintain rational insight into the interpersonal relationship when that is desirable. The patient who told it remarked: "That's just the way I feel. Sometimes I feel that I'm not really a lawyer, I'm just a little boy." Everything that was said to this patient was overheard by both people: the adult lawyer and the inner little boy. To anticipate the effect of an intervention, therefore, it is necessary to know not only what kind of adult one is talking to, but also what kind of little boy. This man came from Nevada, and he had a special system for avoiding depression when he was gambling. If he won, he would feel duly elated. If he lost, say $50, he would tell himself: "I was prepared to lose $100 tonight and I've lost only $50, so I'm really $50 ahead and I needn't be upset." Often, especially if he was winning, he would take a shower, after visiting one casino, before he visited another, as if to wash away his guilt so he could feel "lucky" once more.

It is evident that there were two kinds of arithmetic employed here: When he was winning, that of a rational adult; when he was losing, that of a child with an archaic method of handling reality (denial). The taking of the shower represented a lack of confidence on the part of the "child." He did not trust the rational, well-thought-out, and rather effective gambling system of the "adult." The shower was part of a primitive, autistic contract the "child" made with the powers of gambling, in order to obtain license to win again.

It was difficult to deal effectively with this patient without understanding these two different aspects of his personality. They were both conscious and both belonged to the ego system. One part of his personality faced reality as a whole, the other took it bit by bit and, by convenient manipulation, managed to find comfort in distressing situations, and anxiety in comforting ones. One part handled reality rationally, the other exploited it in an archaic way. There was no immediate question of the conscious versus the unconscious, or of ego versus id, in the sense of parapraxis or egodystonic behavior. Each approach made good sense in its own way: One was appropriate for the mature ego, the other was appropriate for a more primitive one. Conscious and unconscious, ego and id, were all involved somehow; but what was observed directly and what was most apparent to the patient and to the observer was the existence of two different conscious ego states: one that of an adult, the other that of a child.

The selections here in Part One include writings in the early period of development of Transactional Analysis theory, which culminated in two articles appearing in the *International Journal of Psychiatry* (one of which is included here) and later presented in a book, *Transactional Analysis in Psychotherapy*. In that book, Eric Berne mentions games rather briefly; a few years later he wrote a thesaurus of games that he called *Games People Play*, which became an astonishing success by staying on the best seller list for 101 consecutive weeks. During this period of early development of Transactional Analysis theory, Berne also wrote *Principles of Group Treatment* and *The Structure of Dynamics of Organizations and Groups*. We have selected pieces from both to use in later sections of this book.

—C.S.

2. What Is Intuition?

The matters related in the following sections will have to be accepted for what they are worth as true accounts of personal experiences. Similar occurrences have been demonstrated to fellow psychiatrists and before groups of doctors, and of course the patients and others involved can verify what happened, but there is no way of demonstrating the veracity of these events to the individual reader.

Intuition is the acquiring of knowledge through sensory contact with the object, without the intuiter being able to explain to himself or to others exactly how he came to his conclusions. In other words, intuition means that we can know something without knowing how we know it.

Intuition is a fragile and personal thing, and its study has been discouraged by those who cling strictly to scientific principles and refuse to admit that such a faculty exists unless its effects can be produced and reproduced at will. Unfortunately, at present intuition can be exercised only at such times and under such circumstances as the intuiter himself feels are correct. He is either "on the beam" or he isn't, and until someone can discover how to control intuition so that it can be brought into play at will and investigated under proper laboratory conditions, we shall have to accept people's word for what happened, just as we did during the "anecdotal" stage of animal psychology, in the days of the good and learned Reverend J. G. Wood.

Now let us study some examples of intuition from the writer's experience.

When on night duty in various hospitals, I used to gather social pleasure and bits of knowledge by passing the time with the patients in the wards whenever opportunity offered. One evening I walked into the office of a ward in a large hospital and found one of the patients sitting on the desk. Knowing that he should not have been there, he got up to leave, but since I felt that I was in an intuitive mood, I invited him to stay. We had never seen each other before and did not know each other's names. The incident took place in a part of the hospital far from the pychiatric section where I worked during the day, on a ward which was completely strange to me.

Before the man had a chance to say anything, I asked him to be seated again, and inquired:

"Does Philadelphia mean anything to you?"

"Yes," he replied. "I was brought up there."

"Well," I said, "but you left home when you were fifteen."

"That is correct," he replied, beginning to wonder what was going on.

"If you will permit me to say so," I continued. "I believe your mother disappointed you."

"Oh, no, doctor. I love my mother very much."

"Nevertheless, I think she disappointed you. Where is she now?"

"She's at home. She's not well."

"How long has she been ill?"

"Most of her life. I've been taking care of her since I was a young fellow."

"What's her trouble?"

"She's always been nervous. A semi-invalid."

"Then in that sense she disappointed you, don't you think? She had to take emotional support from you rather than give it to you, from your earliest years."

"Yes, doctor, that's correct, all right."

At this point another man entered the office, and was invited to sit down. He sat on the floor with his back against the wall and said nothing, but he listened with great interest.

"You give me the impression that your father was ineffective from the time you were about nine," I continued with the first man.

"He was a drunkard. I believe about the time I was nine or ten, he began to drink more heavily."

This conversation took more time than its description does, since it was punctuated by frequent groping silences on my part. The second man now requested that I tell him something about himself.

"Well," I replied, "I think your father was very strict with you. You had to help him on the farm. You never went fishing or hunting with him. You had to go on your own, with a bunch of rather tough fellows."

"That's right."

"He began to scare you badly when you were about seven."

"Well, my mother died when I was six, if that had anything to do with it."

"Were you pretty close to her?"

"I was."

"So her death left you more or less at the mercy of your tough father?"

"I guess it did."

"You make your wife angry."

"I guess I did. We're divorced."

"She was about sixteen and a half when you married her."

"That's right."

"And you were about nineteen and a half when you married her."

"That's right."

"Is it right within six months?"

He stopped to figure for a moment and then replied: "They're both right within two months."

There was another long silence, but by this time I could feel the intuitive feeling slipping away so I said:

"Well, fellows, that's as far as I can go."

"Doctor," said the second man, "could you guess my age?"

"I don't think I'm in the groove for guessing ages tonight."

"Well, try, Doc!"

"I don't think I'll get this, but I'll try. You were twenty-four in September."

"I was thirty in October."

These two cases are selected out of a large number, mainly because these men later consented to appear at the regular weekly meeting of the staff doctors of the hospital, where they bore witness to the authenticity of the observations. (At this meeting I was attempting to demonstrate how the early emotional adventures of the individual leave their marks not only on his later personality but also on his muscular set, particularly in the face, and these two men seemed ideal for such an occasion.)

Most of these observations were the results of "intuition," specifically, what doctors call "clinical intuition." Just as the old family doctor could diagnose typhoid fever "by the smell" because of his vast experience with this disease, so nowadays the observant psychiatrist learns to judge many things about his patients "by intuition." Since he is continually seeing patients and inquiring about their ages, marital status, home life, parents' characters, and so on, it is to be expected that after some years he should acquire the ability to make pretty shrewd guesses on sight.

Such shrewdness is not confined to psychiatrists, nor to the medical profession. Any professional becomes pretty "intuitive" about his own business. Professional age-guessers and weight-guessers at fairs and carnivals make their living through such intuition, which they cultivate by practice and experience. The average person can judge ages and weights fairly accurately, yet perhaps no one could put into words exactly how he makes such judgments. Not even portrait painters, who are accustomed to copying intuitively the very visual clues from which such information is derived, can explain how they tell the difference between a man of twenty-three and one of twenty-six.

It is important to realize, then, that we can know something without being able to put into words exactly how we know it; but we can know it surely, nevertheless. This was clearly shown in the first case above, where I knew that the man's mother had "disappointed" him. So sure was I of this knowledge that when he denied it I insisted upon my judgment, and it finally turned out to be correct. On the other hand, the gross error I made in guessing the second man's age, after I had guessed all the "more difficult" things ac-

curately, but after my intuition had worn itself out,
shows that without intuition to aid him, even an experienced observer can be easily led astray.

These impressions are not ruled by the laws of
chance. It is not a question of being right part of the
time through coincidence. When one has "that feeling,"
one rarely makes a mistake. When one doesn't have the
feeling, one's guesses do follow the laws of chance.
Guessing the age when fifteen men left home and being
right in two or three cases would be one thing; guessing
different things about fifteen men and being right almost a hundred per cent of the time is another. That
is why it is so difficult to study these things properly.
They cannot be done by request. The feeling of being
"on the beam" comes only at certain times, and then
it is gone.

HOW DOES INTUITION WORK?

To understand intuition, we have only to rid ourselves of the belief that in order to know something we
have to be able to put into words what we know and
how we know it. This belief is the result of an over-
development of the modern scientific outlook, which
has taken us in some ways too far in the direction of
testing reality, and away from nature and the world of
natural happenings. By chaining the Child in us, we
have imprisoned much that could be useful and beneficial. Those with enough control should be able to
allow intuitive faculties to develop without endangering
their necessary contact with reality. As Freud says, "All
this is highly speculative and full of unsolved problems,
but there is no need to be alarmed by it." Intuition is
simply induction without words. When we are able to
put into words what we intuit and how we came to our
conclusions, we have verbalized induction, which is
commonly called Science.

An admirable opportunity for studying the intuitive
process at work was offered in interviewing 25,000
men for the United States Government at the rate of
two hundred to five hundred per day. Under such pressure, the individual "psychiatric examinations" were a

matter of seconds rather than of minutes. With such a strict time limit, one's judgments had to be based more on intuition than on examination. In order to study the problem, two stock questions were first devised. An attempt was then made to predict by intuition what each man's answer to these questions would be. The intuitions were recorded, and then the questions were asked. In a surprisingly large percentage of cases (over 90 per cent), the intuitions were found to be correct. The two questions were: "Are you nervous?" and "Have you ever been to a psychiatrist?" After much study, the grounds for making the predictions in each case could be put into words, so that eventually, instead of using intuition to predict the answers, they could be predicted by applying certain rules which could be written down.

After confirming these rules in several thousand cases, another study was undertaken. An attempt was made to guess each man's occupation before he spoke, simply by watching him come into the room and sit down. The men were all clothed alike in a maroon bathrobe and cloth slippers. Again it was found that the guesses, or intuitions, were surprisingly accurate. On one occasion, the occupations of twenty-six successive men were guessed correctly by this method, ranging through farmer, bookkeeper, mechanic, professional gambler, salesman, warehouseman, and truck driver.* Once more the grounds for making the prediction in each case were studied until some of them could be put into words, so that eventually, for at least two occupational groups, instead of using intuition to predict the answers, they could be predicted in a large percentage of cases by applying certain rules which could be written down.

---

* In this situation there was no fatigue, such as occurred in the hospital, because the "examinations" were the writer's sole occupation during this period and he arrived fresh each morning, whereas the hospital scene took place after a hard day's work with heavy responsibilities. It is also easier to see a lot of people in a given time than to spend it with one person, since in the former case there is no personal involvement such as develops in a longer interview.

After the rules upon which the predictions were based were discovered, an interesting observation came to light. The conscious intention in the second experiment was to diagnose occupations. It was found, however, that it was not occupations which were being diagnosed at all, but ways of handling new situations! It was found in the two occupational groups that were most clearly understood, that it just happened that those men who handled the examination situation in one way (passive waiting) were nearly all farmers, while those who handled it in another way (alert curiosity) were nearly all mechanics. Thus it turned out that intuition did not diagnose occupations, but emotional attitudes, even though the conscious intention was to diagnose the former.

This was an important discovery. It meant that since intuitions are not known through words, the Ego doesn't really know what it is that is known. All the Ego can do for the intuiter and those around him is to try to put a very subtle feeling into words as best it can, and it often merely comes close to the truth rather than actually hitting it. Secondly (really another aspect of the above), intuition cannot be asked any specific question but can only be guided in one or another general direction; it presents us with an impression and then we have to look for the answer in the material which it puts at our disposal.

It was further found that with each new rule that was written down, the accuracy of guessing by conscious observation went up, but was always less than the intuitive accuracy. It thus seemed evident that the feeling of "things arranging themselves without conscious control" which had been observed during intuition had to do with a large number of factors which were being noticed and arranged without being put into words, by something below the conscious level. Since all of these factors could not be put into words, the intuitive accuracy was always greater than the accuracy obtained by applying consciously those rules which could be written down.

Thus a psychological definition of intuition can be stated. Intuition is subconscious knowledge without words, based on subconscious observations without words, and under the right circumstances it is more reliable and accurate than conscious knowledge based on conscious observation.

As we have seen in the last section and in this section, intuition deals with at least two different aspects of the personality. The first is the early childhood emotional relationships between the individual and those around him, such as his parents and relatives, and the adult representatives of those relationships: emotional attitudes toward various people who are important to the individual. These are based on ungratified Id tensions. The second is the individual's way of experiencing and handling new situations. This, though based on Id tensions, actually relates to the attitude of the Ego, and its reaction to reality. We can say roughly that we may have intuitions about Id tensions, and about Ego attitudes.

Careful study during the experiments led to the tentative belief that intuitions about Id tensions are mostly formed by watching the mouth of the subject, while intuitions about Ego attitudes mainly come from observing the eyes. Thus we may tentatively venture to say that in a certain sense the muscles about the eyes serve chiefly to express Ego attitudes, while the muscles about the mouth serve chiefly to express Id tensions. In the classical anal erotic, this idea is strikingly illustrated. In the cold eyes of such a person we read his consciously suspicious approach to the world and its new situations, while in his tight-cornered mouth we read his constipation, his stubbornness, his stinginess, his orderliness, and his cruelty, the classical symptoms derived directly (as his suspiciousness is indirectly) from his anal interests.

It is worth noting that much intuitive knowledge may depend upon the sense of smell. The odor of a person's breath and sweat can change with his emotional attitude. Some people are more aware of smells than others, and the distance over which smells can influence emotions is incredible; certain moths can detect sexual odors a mile away. The fact that we are not aware of a smell does not mean that it is not affecting our emo-

tional attitude. Smells can change dreams without being
perceived as smells.

Further study of intuition from the point of view of
Transactional Analysis indicates that this faculty belongs to the Child ego state. If the Child is left free
of influences from the Adult and Parent ego states,
intuition is at its best. The moment the Adult comes in
with conscious reasoning, or the Parent with its prejudices and preconceived ideas, intuition is impaired as
the Child retreats before these superior forces. Intuition
also fails if the Child is corrupted by an offer of rewards
or a threat of punishment. In other words, this is a
fragile faculty which can be easily disturbed or distorted
by external pressures, which is one reason it is not
forthcoming on demand.

3. The Structure of Personality

Mrs. Primus, a young housewife, was referred by her family physician for a diagnostic interview. She sat tensely for a minute or two with her eyes downcast, and then she began to laugh. A moment later she stopped laughing, looking stealthily at the doctor, then averted her eyes again, and once more began to laugh. This sequence was repeated three or four times. Then rather suddenly she stopped tittering, sat up straight in her chair, pulled down her skirt, and turned her head to the right. After observing this new attitude for a short time, the psychiatrist asked her if she were hearing voices. She nodded without turning her head, and continued to listen. The psychiatrist again interrupted to ask her how old she was. His carefully calculated tone of voice successfully captured her attention. She turned to face him, pulled herself together, and answered his question.

Following this, she answered a series of other pertinent questions concisely and to the point. Within a short time, enough information was obtained to warrant a tentative diagnosis of acute schizophrenia, and to enable the psychiatrist to piece together some of the precipitating factors and some of the gross features in her early background. After this, no further questions were put for a while, and she soon lapsed into her former state. The cycle of flirtatious tittering, stealthy appraisal, and prim attention to her hallucinations was repeated until she was asked whose voices they were and what they were saying.

She replied that it seemed to be a man's voice and that he was calling her awful names, words she had never heard before. Then the talk was turned to her family. Her father she described as a wonderful man, a considerate husband, a loving parent, well-liked in the community, and so forth. But it soon came out that he drank heavily, and then he was different. He used bad language. She was asked the nature of the bad language. It then occurred to the patient that she had heard him use some of the same epithets that the hallucinated voice was using.

This patient rather clearly exhibited three different ego states. These were distinguished by differences in her posture, manner, facial expression, and other physical characteristics. The first was characterized by tittering coyness, quite reminiscent of a little girl at a certain age; the second was primly righteous, like that of a schoolgirl almost caught in some sexual peccadillo; in the third, she was able to answer questions like the grown-up woman that she was, and was able to demonstrate that in this state her understanding, her memory, and her ability to think logically were all intact.

The first two ego states had an archaic quality in that they were appropriate to some former stage of her experience, but were inappropriate to the immediate reality of the interview. In the third, she showed considerable skill in marshaling and processing data and perceptions concerning her immediate situation: what can easily be understood as "adult" functioning, something that neither an infant nor a sexually agitated schoolgirl would be capable of. The process of "pulling herself together," which was activated by the business-like tone of the psychiatrist, represented the transition from the archaic ego state to this adult ego state.

The term "ego state" is intended merely to denote states of mind and their related patterns of behavior as they occur in nature, and avoids in the first instance the use of constructs such as "instinct," "culture," "super-ego," "animus," "eidetic," and so forth. Structural analysis postulates only that such ego states can be classified and clarified, and that in the case of psychiatric patients such a procedure is "good."

In seeking a framework for classification, it was found that the clinical material pointed to the hypothesis that childhood ego states exist as relics in the grown-up, and that under certain circumstances they can be revived. As already noted in the introduction, this phenomenon has been repeatedly reported in connection with dreams, hypnosis, psychosis, pharmacological intoxicants, and direct electrical stimulation of the temporal cortex. But careful observation carried the hypothesis one step further, to the assumption that such relics can exhibit spontaneous activity in the normal waking state as well.

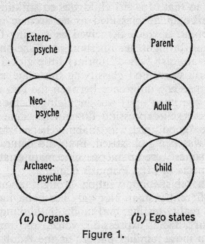

(a) Organs   (b) Ego states

Figure 1.

What actually happened was that patients could be observed, or observed themselves, shifting from one state of mind and one behavior pattern to another. Typically, there was one ego state characterized by reasonably adequate reality-testing and rational reckoning (secondary process), and another distinguished by autistic thinking and archaic fears and expectations (primary process). The former had the quality of the usual mode of functioning of responsible adults, while the latter resembled the way very young children of various ages went about their business. This led to the assumption of two psychic organs, a neopsyche and an archaeopsyche. It seemed appropriate, and was generally acceptable to all individuals concerned, to call the phenomenological and operational manifestations of these two organs the Adult and the Child, respectively.

Mrs. Primus's Child manifested herself in two different forms. The one which predominated in the absence of distracting stimuli was that of the "bad" (sexy) girl. It would be difficult to conceive of Mrs. Primus, in this state, undertaking the responsibilities of a sexually mature woman. The resemblance of her behavior to that of a girl child was so striking that this ego state could be classified as an archaic one. At a certain point, a voice perceived as coming from outside herself brought her up short, and she shifted into the ego state of a "good" (prim) little girl. The previous criteria warranted classifying this state also as an archaic one. The difference between the two ego states was that the "bad" girl was indulging in more or less autonomous self-expression, doing what came naturally, while the "good" girl was adapting herself to the fact that she was being chastised. Both the natural and the adapted states were archaeopsychic manifestations, and hence aspects of Mrs. Primus's Child.

The therapist's intervention brought about a shift into a different system. Not only her behavior, responsiveness, reality-testing, and mode of thinking, but also her posture, facial expression, voice, and muscle-tone took on a more familiar pattern as the Adult ego state of the responsible housewife was reactivated. This shift, which was brought about repeatedly during the interview, constituted a brief remission of the psychosis. This implies a description of psychosis as a shift of psychic energy, or, to use the commonly accepted word, *cathexis,* from the Adult system to the Child system. It also implies a description of remission as the reversal of this shift.

The derivation of the hallucinated voice with its "unfamiliar" obscenities would have been evident to any educated observer, in view of the change it brought about in the patient's behavior. It remained only to confirm the impression, and this was the purpose of turning the discussion to the patient's family. As anticipated, the voice was using the language of her father, much to her own surprise. This voice belonged to the exteropsychic, or parental system. It was not the "voice of her Superego," but the voice of an actual person. This emphasizes the point that Parent, Adult, and Child represent real people who now exist or who once existed, who have legal names and civic identities. In the case of Mrs. Primus, the Parent did not manifest itself as an ego state, but only as a hallucinated voice. In the beginning, it is best to concentrate upon the diagnosis and differentiation of the Adult and the Child, and consideration of the Parent can be profitably postponed in clinical work. The activity of the Parent may be illustrated by two other cases.

Mr. Segundo, who first stimulated the evolution of structural analysis, told the following story:

An eight-year-old boy, vacationing at a ranch in his cowboy suit, helped the hired man unsaddle a horse. When they were finished, the hired man said: "Thanks, cowpoke!", to which his assistant answered: "I'm not really a cowpoke, I'm just a little boy."

The patient then remarked: "That's just the way I feel. I'm not really a lawyer, I'm just a little boy." Mr. Segundo was a successful courtroom lawyer of high repute, who raised his family decently, did useful community work, and was popular socially. But in treatment he often did have the attitude of a little boy. Sometimes during the hour he would ask: "Are you talking to the lawyer or to the little boy?" When he was away from his office or the courtroom, the little boy was very apt to take over. He would retire to a cabin in the mountains away from his family, where he kept a supply of whiskey, morphine, lewd pictures, and guns. There he would indulge in childlike fantasies, fantasies he had had as a little boy, and the kinds of sexual activity which are commonly labeled "infantile."

At a later date, after he had clarified to some extent what in him was Adult and what was Child (for he really was a lawyer sometimes and not always a little boy), Mr. Segundo introduced his Parent into the situation. That is, after his activities and feelings had been sorted out into the first two categories, there were certain residual states which fitted neither. These had a special quality which was reminiscent of the way his parents had seemed to him. This necessitated the institution of a third category which, on further testing, was found to have sound clinical validity. These ego states lacked the autonomous quality of both Adult and Child. They seemed to have been introduced from without, and to have an imitative flavor.

Specifically, there were three different aspects apparent in his handling of money. The Child was penurious to the penny and had miserly ways of ensuring pennywise prosperity; in spite of the risk for a man in his position, in this state he would gleefully steal chewing gum and other small items out of drugstores, just as he had done as a child. The Adult handled large sums with a banker's shrewdness, foresight, and success, and was willing to spend money to make money. But another side of him had fantasies of giving it all away for the good of the community. He came of pious, philanthropic people, and he actually did donate large sums to charity with the same sentimental benevolence as his father. As the philanthropic glow wore off, the Child would take over with vindictive resentfulness toward his beneficiaries, followed by the Adult who would wonder why on earth he wanted to risk his solvency for such sentimental reasons.

One of the most difficult aspects of structural analysis in practice is to make the patient (or student) see that Child, Adult, and Parent are not handy ideas, or interesting neologisms, but refer to phenomena based on actual realities. The case of Mr. Segundo demonstrates this point fairly clearly. The person who stole chewing gum was not called the Child for convenience, or because children often steal, but because he himself stole chewing gum as a child with the same gleeful attitude and using the same technique. The Adult was called the Adult, not because he was playing the role of an adult, imitating the behavior of big men, but because he exhibited highly effective reality-testing in his legal and financial operations. The Parent was not called the Parent because it is traditional for philanthropists to be "fatherly" or "motherly," but because he actually imitated his own father's behavior and state of mind in his philanthropic activities.

In the case of Mr. Troy, a compensated schizophrenic who had had electric shock treatment following a breakdown during naval combat, the parental state was so firmly established that the Adult and the Child rarely showed themselves. In fact, he was unable at first to understand the idea of the Child. He maintained a uniformly judgmental attitude in most of his relationships. Manifestations of childlike behavior on the part of others, such as naiveté, charm, boisterousness, or trifling were especially apt to stimulate an outburst of scorn, rebuke, or chastisement. He was notorious in the therapy group which he attended for his attitude of "Kill the little bastards." He was equally severe toward himself. His object, in group jargon, seemed to be "to keep his own Child from ever sticking his head out of the closet." This is a common attitude in patients who have had electric shock treatment. They seem to blame the Child (perhaps rightly) for the "beating" they have taken; the Parent is highly cathected, and, often with the assistance of the Adult, severely suppresses most childlike manifestations.

There were some curious exceptions to Mr. Troy's disapproving attitude. In regard to heterosexual irregularities and alcohol, he behaved like an all-wise benevolent father, rather than a tyrant, freely giving all the young ladies and men-about-town the benefit of his experience. His advice, however, was prejudicial and based on banal preconceptions which he was quite unable to correct even when he was repeatedly proven wrong. It was no surprise to learn that as a child he had been scorned or beaten by his father for occasional exhibitions of naiveté, charm, and boisterousness, or trifling, and regaled with stories of sexual and alcoholic excesses. Thus his parental ego state, which was protectively fixated, reproduced his father's attitudes in some detail. This fixated Parent allowed no leeway for either Adult or Child activities except in the spheres where his father had been skillful or self-indulgent.

The observation of such fixated personalities is instructive. The constant Parent, as seen in people like Mr. Troy; the constant Adult, as seen in funless, objective scientists; and the constant Child ("Little old me") often exemplify well some of the superficial characteristics of these three types of ego states. Some professionals earn a living by the public exhibition of a constant ego state: clergymen, the Parent; diagnosticians, the Adult; and clowns, the Child.

The cases presented so far demonstrate the theoretical basis for structural analysis, which comprises three pragmatic absolutes and three general hypotheses. By a "pragmatic absolute" is meant a condition to which so far no exceptions have been found.

1. That every grown-up individual was once a child.
2. That every human being with sufficient functioning brain-tissue is potentially capable of adequate reality-testing.
3. That every individual who survives into adult life has had either functioning parents or someone *in loco parentis*.

The corresponding hypotheses are:

1. That relics of childhood survive into later life as complete ego states. (Archaeopsychic relics.)
2. That reality-testing is a function of discrete ego states, and not an isolated "capacity." (Neopsychic functioning.)
3. That the executive may be taken over by the complete ego state of an outside individual, as perceived. (Exteropsychic functioning.)

In summary, the structure of personality is regarded as comprising three organs: the exteropsyche, the neopsyche, and the archaeopsyche, as shown in Figure 1a (p. 37). These manifest themselves phenomenologically and operationally as three types of ego states called Parent, Adult, and Child, respectively, as shown in Figure 1b (p. 37).

BIBLIOGRAPHY

Berne, E. "Ego States in Psychotherapy." *Amer. J. Psychother.* 11:293-309, 1957.

Berne, E. "Primal Images and Primal Judgment." *Psychiat. Quart.* 29:634-658, 1955.

Freud, S. *An Outline of Psychoanalysis.* W. W. Norton & Company, New York, 1949.

4. Transactional Analysis: A New and Effective Method of Group Therapy

There is need for a new approach to psychodynamic group therapy specifically designed for the situation it has to meet. The usual practice is to bring into the group methods borrowed from individual therapy, hoping, as occasionally happens, to elicit a specific therapeutic response. I should like to present a different system, one which has been well-tested and is more adapted to its purpose, where group therapists can stand on their own ground rather than attempting a thinly-spread imitation of the sister discipline.

Generally speaking, individual analytic therapy is characterized by the production of a search for material, with interpersonal transactions holding a special place, typically in the field of "transference resistance" or "transference reactions." In a group, the systematic search for material is hampered because from the beginning the multitude of transactions takes the center of the stage. Therefore it seems appropriate to concentrate deliberately and specifically on analyzing such transactions. Structural analysis, and its later development into transactional analysis, in my experience, offers the most productive framework for this undertaking. Experiments with both approaches demonstrate certain advantages of structural and transactional analysis over attempts at psychoanalysis in the group. Among them are increased patient interest as shown by attendance records; increased degree of therapeutic success as shown by reduction of gross failures; increased stability of results as shown by long-term adjustment; and wider applicability in difficult patients such as psychopaths, the mentally retarded, and pre- and post-psychotics. In addition, the intelligibility, precision, and goals of the therapeutic technique are more readily appreciated by the properly prepared therapist and patient alike.

This approach is based on the separation and investigation of exteropsychic, neopsychic, and archaeopsychic ego states. Structural analysis refers to the intrapsychic relationships of these three types of ego states; their mutual isolation, conflict, contamination, invasion, predominance, or cooperation within the personality. Transactional analysis refers to the diagnosis of which particular ego state is active in each individual during a given transaction or series of transactions, and of the understandings or misunderstandings which arise due to the perception or misperception of this factor by the individuals involved.

I have discussed elsewhere the nature of ego states in general, and of their classification according to whether they are exteropsychic, that is, borrowed from external sources; neopsychic, that is, oriented in accordance with current reality; or archaeopsychic, that is, relics fixated in childhood. These distinctions are easily understood by patients when they are demonstrated by clinical material, and when the three types are subsumed under the more personal terms Parent, Adult, and Child, respectively.

As this is a condensation in a very small space of a whole psychotherapeutic system, I can offer only a few illustrative situations, choosing them for their relative clarity and dramatic quality in the hope that they will draw attention to some of the basic principles of structural and transactional analysis.

STRUCTURAL ANALYSIS

The first concerns a patient named Matthew, whose manner, posture, gestures, tone of voice, purpose, and field of interest varied in a fashion which at first seemed erratic. Careful and sustained observation, however, revealed that these variables were organized into a limited number of coherent patterns. When he was discussing his wife, he spoke in loud, deep, dogmatic tones, leaning back in his chair with a stern gaze and counting off the accusations against her on his upraised fingers. At other times he talked with another patient about carpentry problems in a matter-of-fact tone, leaning forward in a companionable way. On still other occasions, he taunted the other group members with a scornful smile about their apparent loyalty to the therapist, his head slightly bowed and his back ostentatiously turned to the leader. The other patients soon became aware of these shifts in his ego state, correctly diagnosed them as Parent, Adult, and Child, respectively, and began to look for appropriate clues concerning Matthew's actual parents and his childhood experiences. Soon everyone in the group, including the patient, was able to accept the simple diagram shown in Figure 2 as a workable representation of Matthew's personality structure.

In the course of Matthew's therapy, he asked the physician to examine his father, who was on the verge of a paranoid psychosis. The therapist was astonished, in spite of his anticipations, to see how exactly Matthew's Parent reproduced the father's fixated paranoid ego state. During his interview, Matthew's father spoke in loud, deep, dogmatic tones, leaning back in his chair with a stern gaze, and counting off on his upraised fingers his accusations against the people around him.

It should be emphasized that Parent, Adult, and Child are not synonymous with superego, ego, and id. The latter are "psychic agencies," while the former are complete ego states, each in itself including influences from superego, ego, and id. For example, when Matthew reproduced the Parental ego state, he not only behaved like a stern father, but also distorted reality the way his father did, and vented his sadistic impulses. And as cathexis was transferred from the Parental ego state into that of the scornful Child, the planning of his attacks and the accompanying guilt-feelings had a childlike quality.

In therapy, the first task was to clarify in Matthew's mind what was Parent, what was Adult, and what was Child in his feelings and behavior. The next phase was directed toward maintaining control through the Adult. The third phase was to analyze the current conflicts between the three ego states. Each of these phases brought its own kind of improvement, while the ultimate aim in this pre-psychotic case was to enable all three ego states to cooperate in an integrated fashion as a result of structural analysis.

There were two contra-indications in this case. The first was the universal indication against the Child to grow up. One does not tell a two-year-old to grow up. In fact, from the beginning it is necessary in every case to emphasize that we are not trying get rid of the Child. The Child is not to be regarded as "childish" in the derogatory sense, but childlike, with many socially

MATTHEW

Figure 2. Structural analysis.

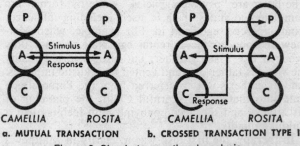

CAMELLIA   ROSITA   CAMELLIA   ROSITA
a. MUTUAL TRANSACTION   b. CROSSED TRANSACTION TYPE I

Figure 3. Simple transactional analysis.

P = Parent
A = Adult
C = Child

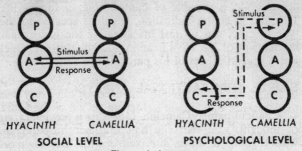

Figure 4. A game.

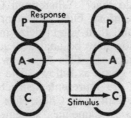

MATTHEW   ANOTHER MEMBER
Figure 5. Crossed transaction type II.

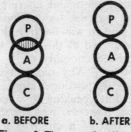

a. BEFORE   b. AFTER
Figure 6. Therapeutic effect.

valuable attributes which must be freed so that they can make their contribution to the total personality when the confusion in this archaic area has been straightened out. The child in the individual is potentially capable of contributing to his personality exactly what a happy actual child is capable of contributing to family life. The second contra-indication, which is specific to this type of case, was against investigating the history and mechanism of his identification with his father, which was a special aspect of his parental ego state.

SIMPLE TRANSACTIONAL ANALYSIS

A patient named Camellia, following a previous train of thought, said that she had told her husband she wasn't going to have intercourse with him anymore and that he could go and find himself some other woman. Another patient named Rosita asked curiously: "Why did you do that?" Whereupon Camellia, much to Rosita's discomfort, burst into tears and replied: "I try so hard, and then you criticize me."

This transaction may be analyzed according to the diagram in Figure 3. This figure was drawn and analyzed for the group as follows. The personalities of the two women are represented structurally as comprising Parent, Adult, and Child. The original *transactional stimulus* is Camellia's statement about what she told her husband. She related this in her Adult ego state, with which the group was familiar. It was received in turn by an Adult Rosita, who in her response exhibited a mature, reasonable interest in the story. As shown in Figure 3a, the transactional stimulus was Adult to Adult, and so was the *transactional response*. If things had continued at this level, the conversation might have proceeded smoothly.

Rosita's question ("Why did you do that?") now constituted a new transactional stimulus, and was intended as one adult speaking to another. Camellia's weeping response, however, was not that of one adult to another, but that of a child to a critical parent. Camellia's misperception of Rosita's ego state, and the shift in her own ego state, resulted in a crossed transaction and broke up the conversation, which now had to take another turn. This is represented in Figure 3b.

This particular type of crossed transaction, in which the stimulus is Adult to Adult, and the response is

Child to Parent, is probably the most frequent cause of misunderstandings in marriage and work situations, as well as in social life. Clinically, it is typified by the classical transference reaction, which is a special case of the crossed transaction. In fact this particular species of crossed transaction may be said to be the chief problem of psychoanalytic technique.

In Matthew's case, when he was talking about his wife, the crossing was reversed. If one of the other members, as an Adult, asked him a question, expecting an Adult response, Matthew instead usually answered like a supercilious parent talking to a backward child, as represented in Figure 4.

Therapeutically, this simple type of transactional analysis helped Camellia to become more objective about her Child. As the Adult gained control, and the Child's responses at home were suppressed for later discussion in the group, her marital and social life improved even before any of the Child's confusion was resolved.

THE ANALYSIS OF GAMES

Short sets of ongoing transactions may be called operations. These constitute tactical maneuvers, in which it is the other members of the group who are maneuvered. Thus the conversation between Camellia and Rosita, taken as a whole, is an operation, and had to be analyzed again at a deeper level, when it soon appears that the need of Camellia's Child to feel criticized was one of the motives for telling this particular story to the group.

A series of operations constitutes a "game." A game may be defined as a recurring series of transactions, often repetitive, superficially rational, with a concealed motivation; or more colloquially, a series of operations with a "gimmick."

Hyacinth recounted her disappointment and resentment because a friend of hers had given a birthday party which she herself had planned to give. Camellia asked: "Why don't you give another party later?" To which Hyacinth responded: "Yes, but then it wouldn't be a birthday party." The other members of the group then began to give wise suggestions, each beginning with: "Why don't you . . ." and to each of these Hyacinth gave a response which began: "Yes, but. . . ."

Hyacinth had told her story for the purpose of setting in motion the commonest of all the games which can be observed in groups: the game of "Why don't you . . . Yes but. . . ." This is a game which can be played by any number. One player, who is "it," presents a problem. The others start to present solutions, to each of which the one who is "it" objects. A good player can stand off the rest of the group for a long period, until they all give up, whereupon "it" wins. Hyacinth, for example, successfully objected to more than a dozen solutions before the therapist broke up the game. The gimmick in "Why don't you . . . Yes but . . ." is that it is played not for its ostensible purpose (a quest for information or solutions), but for the sake of the fencing; and as a group phenomenon it corresponds to Bion's basic assumption "F".*

Other common games are "How am I Doing?" "Uproar," "Alcoholic," "P.T.A.," "Ain't it Awful?" and "Schlemiel." In "Schlemiel," the one who is "it" breaks things, spills things, and makes messes of various kinds, and each time says: "I'm sorry!" This leaves the inexperienced player in a helpless position. The skillful opponent, however, says: "You can break things and spill things all you like; but please don't say 'I'm sorry!'" This response usually causes the Schlemiel to collapse or explode, since it knocks out his gimmick, and the opponent wins. I imagine that at this point many of you are thinking of Stephen Potter, but I think the games I have in mind are more serious; and some of them, like "Alcoholic," with all its complex rules published by various rescue organizations, are played for keeps. "Alcoholic" is complicated because the official form requires at least four players: a persecutor, a rescuer, a dummy, and the one who is "it."

---

* See W. R. Bion, "Group Dynamics: A Re-View." *Internat. J. Psycho-Anal.*, XXXIII: 235–247, 1952.

The transactional analysis of Hyacinth's game of "Why don't you . . . Yes but . . ." is represented in Figure 2. This figure was drawn and analyzed for the group. In the guise of an Adult seeking information, Hyacinth "cons" the other members into responding like sage parents advising a helpless child. The object of Hyacinth's Child is to confound these parents one after the other. The game can proceed because at the superficial level, both stimulus and response are Adult to Adult, and at a deeper level they are also complementary, Parent to Child stimulus ("Why don't you . . . !") eliciting Child to Parent response ("Yes, but . . ."). The second level is unconscious on both sides.

The therapeutic effect of this analysis was to make Hyacinth aware of her defensive need to confound, and to make the others aware of how easily they could be conned into taking a parental role unawares. When a new patient tried to start a game of "Why don't you . . . Yes but . . ." in this group, they all played along with her in order not to make her too anxious, but after a few weeks they gently demonstrated to her what was happening. In other words, they now had the option of playing or not playing this game, as they saw fit, where formerly they had no choice but to be drawn in. This option was the net therapeutic gain, which they were able to apply profitably in their more intimate relationships. In structural terms, this improvement is represented in Figure 6. Figure 6a shows the original contamination of the Adult by the Parent, and Figure 6b shows the decontaminated Adult which can now rationally control their behavior in this particular situation.

THE ANALYSIS OF SCRIPTS

A script is an attempt to repeat in derivative form not a transference reaction or a transference situation, but a transference drama, often split up into acts, exactly like the theatrical scripts which are intuitive artistic derivatives of these primal dramas of childhood. Operationally, a script is a complex set of transactions, by nature recurrent, but not necessarily recurring, since a complete performance may require a whole lifetime. A common tragic script is that based on the rescue fantasy of a woman who marries one alcoholic after another. The disruption of such a script leads to despair. Since the magical cure of the alcoholic husband which the script calls for is not forthcoming, a divorce results and the woman tries again. A practical and constructive script, on the other hand, may lead to great happiness if the others in the case are well chosen and play their parts satisfactorily. A game usually represents a segment of a script.

The ultimate goal of transactional analysis is the analysis of scripts, since the script determines the destiny and identity of the individual. Space, however, does not permit a discussion of the technique, aim, and therapeutic effect of script analysis, and this topic will have to be reserved for another communication.

SELF-ANALYSIS

Structural and transactional analysis lend themselves to self-examination more readily than orthodox psychoanalysis does, since they effectively bypass many of the difficulties inherent in self-psychoanalysis. The therapist who has some knowledge of his own personality structure has a distinct advantage in dealing with his countertransference problems: that is, the activity of his own Child or Parent with its own favorite games, its own script, and its own motives for becoming a group therapist. If he has a clear insight, without self-delusion, as to what is exteropsychic, what is neopsychic, and what is archaeopsychic in himself, then he can choose his responses so as to bring the maximum therapeutic benefit to his patients.

I have condensed into this brief communication material which would easily fill a book, and which is best made clear by six months or a year of clinical supervision. In its present form, however, it might stimulate some people to more careful observation of ego states in their patients, and to some serious and sustained experiments in structural interpretation.

SUMMARY

(1) A new approach to group therapy is outlined, based on the distinction between exteropsychic, neopsychic, and archaeopsychic ego states. The study of the relationships within the individual of these three types of ego states, colloquially called Parent, Adult, and Child, respectively, is termed structural analysis, and has been discussed in a previous publication.

(2) Once each individual in the group has some understanding of his own personality in these terms, the group can proceed to simple transactional analysis, in which the ego state of the individual who gives the transactional stimulus is compared with the ego state of the one who gives the transactional response.

(3) In the next phase, short series of transactions, called operations, are studied in the group. More complex series may constitute a "game," in which some element of double-dealing or insincerity is present. In the final phase, it is demonstrated that all transactions are influenced by complex attempts on the part of each member to manipulate the group in accordance with certain basic fantasies derived from early experiences. This unconscious plan, which is a strong determinant of the individual's destiny, is called a script.

(4) Clinical examples are given, and the therapeutic gain expected from each phase of structural and transactional analysis is indicated.

BIBLIOGRAPHY

Berne, E.: "Ego States in Psychotherapy." *A.J. Psychother.* XI: 293-309, 1957.

Bion, W. R.: "Group Dynamics: A Re-View." *Internat. J. Psycho-Anal.* XXXIII: 235-247, 1952.

Freud, S.: *An Outline of Psychoanalysis,* W. W. Norton, New York, 1949.

5. Social Intercourse

The theory of social intercourse, which has been outlined at some length in *Transactional Analysis* [1], may be summarized as follows.

Spitz has found [2] that infants deprived of handling over a long period will tend at length to sink into an irreversible decline and are prone to succumb eventually to intercurrent disease. In effect, this means that what he calls emotional deprivation can have a fatal outcome. These observations give rise to the idea of *stimulus hunger*, and indicate that the most favored forms of stimuli are those provided by physical intimacy, a conclusion not hard to accept on the basis of everyday experience.

An allied phenomenon is seen in grown-ups subjected to sensory deprivation. Experimentally, such deprivation may call forth a transient psychosis, or at least give rise to temporary mental disturbances. In the past, social and sensory deprivation is noted to have had similar effects in individuals condemned to long periods of solitary imprisonment. Indeed, solitary confinement is one of the punishments most dreaded even by prisoners hardened to physical brutality [3, 4], and is now a notorious procedure for inducing political compliance. (Conversely, the best of the known weapons against political compliance is social organization [5].)

On the biological side, it is probable that emotional and sensory deprivation tends to bring about or encourage organic privation through apathy to degenerative changes and death. In this sense, stimulus-hunger has the same relationship to survival of the human organism as food-hunger.

Indeed, not only biologically but also psychologically and socially, stimulus hunger in many ways parallels the hunger for food [6]. Such terms as malnutrition, satiation, gourmet, gourmand, faddist, ascetic, culinary arts, and good cook are easily transferred from the field of nutrition to the field of sensation. Overstuffing has its parallel in overstimulation. In both spheres, under ordinary conditions where ample supplies are available and a diversified menu is possible, choices will be heavily influenced by an individual's idiosyncrasies. It is possible that some or many of these idiosyncrasies are constitutionally determined, but this is irrevelant to the problems at issue here.

The social psychiatrist's concern in the matter is with what happens after the infant is separated from his mother in the normal course of growth. What has been said so far may be summarized by the "colloquialism" [7]: "If you are not stroked, your spinal cord will shrivel up." Hence, after the period of close intimacy with the mother is over, the individual for the rest of his life is confronted with a dilemma upon whose horns his destiny and survival are continually being tossed. One horn is the social, psychological and biological forces which stand in the way of the continued physical intimacy in the infant style; the other is his perpetual striving for its attainment. Under most conditions he will compromise. He learns to do with more subtle, even symbolic, forms of handling, until the merest nod of recognition may serve the purpose to some extent, although his original craving for physical contact may remain unabated.

This process of compromise may be called by various terms, such as sublimation; but whatever it is called, the result is a partial transformation of the infantile stimulus-hunger into something which may be termed *recognition-hunger*. As the complexities of compromise increase, each person becomes more and more individual in his quest for recognition, and it is these differentia which lend variety to social intercourse and which determine the individual's destiny. A movie actor may require hundreds of strokes each week from anonymous and undifferentiated admirers to keep his spinal cord from shriveling, while a scientist may keep physically and mentally healthy on one stroke a year from a respected master.

"Stroking" may be used as a general term for intimate physical contact; in practice it may take various forms. Some people literally stroke an infant; others hug or pat it, while some people pinch it playfully or flip it with a fingertip. These all have their analogues in conversation, so that it seems one might predict how an individual would handle a baby by listening to him talk. By an extension of meaning, "stroking" may be employed colloquially to denote any act implying recognition of another's presence. Hence a *stroke* may be used as the fundamental unit of social action. An exchange of strokes constitutes a *transaction,* which is the unit of social intercourse.

As far as the theory of games is concerned, the principle which emerges here is that any social intercourse whatever has a biological advantage over no intercourse at all. This has been experimentally demonstrated in the case of rats through some remarkable experiments by S. Levine [8] in which not only physical, mental, and emotional development but also the biochemistry of the brain and even resistance to leukemia were favorably affected by handling. The significant feature of these experiments was that gentle handling and painful electric shocks were equally effective in promoting the health of the animals.

This validation of what has been said above encourages us to proceed with increased confidence to the next section.

THE STRUCTURING OF TIME

Granted that handling of infants, and its symbolic equivalent in grown-ups, recognition, have a survival value. The question is, What next? In everyday terms, what can people do after they have exchanged greetings, whether the greeting consists of a collegiate "Hi!" or an Oriental ritual lasting several hours? After stimulus-hunger and recognition-hunger comes *structure-hunger.* The perennial problem of adolescents is: "What do you say to her (him) then?" And to many people besides adolescents, nothing is more uncomfortable than a social hiatus, a period of silent, unstructured time when no one present can think of anything more interesting to say than: "Don't you think the walls are perpendicular tonight?" The eternal problem of the human being is how to structure his waking hours. In this existential sense, the function of all social living is to lend mutual assistance for this project.

The operational aspect of time-structuring may be called programing. It has three aspects: material, social and individual. The most common, convenient, comfortable, and utilitarian method of structuring time is by a project designed to deal with the material of external reality: what is commonly known as work. Such a project is technically called an *activity;* the term "work" is unsuitable because a general theory of social psychiatry must recognize that social intercourse is also a form of work.

Material programing arises from the vicissitudes encountered in dealing with external reality; it is of interest here only insofar as activities offer a matrix for "stroking," recognition, and other more complex forms of social intercourse. Material programing is not primarily a social problem; in essence it is based on data processing. The activity of building a boat relies on a long series of measurements and probability estimates, and any social exchange which occurs must be subordinated to these in order for the building to proceed.

Social programing results in traditional ritualistic or or semi-ritualistic interchanges. The chief criterion for it is local acceptability, popularly called "good manners." Parents in all parts of the world teach their children manners, which means that they know the proper greeting, eating, emunctory, courting and mourning rituals, and also how to carry on topical conversations with appropriate strictures and reinforcements. The strictures and reinforcements constitute tact or diplomacy, some of which is universal and some local. Belching at meals or asking after another man's wife are each encouraged or forbidden by local ancestral tradition, and indeed there is a high degree of inverse correlation between these particular transactions. Usually in localities where people belch at meals, it is unwise to ask after the womenfolk; and in localities where people are asking after the womenfolk, it is unwise to belch at meals. Usually formal rituals precede semi-ritualistic topical conversations, and the latter may be distinguished by calling them *pastimes*.

As people become better acquainted, more and more *individual programing* creeps in, so that "incidents" begin to occur. These incidents superficially appear to be adventitious, and may be so described by the parties concerned, but careful scrutiny reveals that they tend to follow definite patterns which are amenable to sorting and classification, and that the sequence is circumscribed by unspoken rules and regulations. These regulations remain latent as long as the amenities or hostilities proceed according to Hoyle, but they become manifest if an illegal move is made, giving rise to a symbolic, verbal or legal cry of "Foul!" Such sequences, which in contrast to pastimes are based more on individual than on social programing, may be called *games*. Family life and married life, as well as life in organizations of various kinds, may year after year be based on variations of the same game.

To say that the bulk of social activity consists of playing games does not necessarily mean that it is mostly "fun" or that the parties are not seriously engaged in the relationship. On the one hand, "playing" football and other athletic "games" may not be fun at all, and the players may be intensely grim; and such games share with gambling and other forms of "play" the potentiality for being very serious indeed, sometimes fatal. On the other hand, some authors, for instance Huizinga [9], include under "play" such serious things as cannibal feasts. Hence calling such tragic behavior as suicide, alcohol and drug addiction, criminality or schizophrenia "playing games" is not irresponsible, facetious or barbaric. The essential characteristic of human play is not that the emotions are spurious, but that they are regulated. This is revealed when sanctions are imposed on an illegitimate emotional display. Play may be grimly serious, or even fatally serious, but the social sanctions are serious only if the rules are broken.

Pastimes and games are substitutes for the real living

of real intimacy. Because of this they may be regarded as preliminary engagements rather than as unions, which is why they are characterized as poignant forms of play. Intimacy begins when individual (usually instinctual) programing becomes more intense, and both social patterning and ulterior restrictions and motives begin to give way. It is the only completely satisfying answer to stimulus-hunger, recognition-hunger and structure-hunger. Its prototype is the act of loving impregnation.

Structure-hunger has the same survival value as stimulus-hunger. Stimulus-hunger and recognition-hunger express the need to avoid sensory and emotional starvation, both of which lead to biological deterioration. Structure-hunger expresses the need to avoid boredom, and Kierkegaard [10] has pointed out the evils which result from unstructured time. If it persists for any length of time, boredom becomes synonymous with emotional starvation and can have the same consequences.

The solitary individual can structure time in two ways: activity and fantasy. An individual can remain solitary even in the presence of others, as every schoolteacher knows. When one is a member of a social aggregation of two or more people, there are several options for structuring time. In order of complexity, these are: (1) Rituals, (2) Pastimes, (3) Games, (4) Intimacy, and (5) Activity, which may form a matrix for any of the others. The goal of each member of the aggregation is to obtain as many satisfactions as possible from his transactions with other members. The more accessible he is, the more satisfactions he can obtain. Most of the programing of his social operations is automatic. Since some of the "satisfactions" obtained under this programing, such as self-destructive ones, are difficult to recognize in the usual sense of the word "satisfactions," it would be better to substitute some more non-committal terms, such as "gains" or "advantages."

The advantages of social contact revolve around somatic and psychic equilibrium. They are related to the following factors: (1) the relief of tension, (2) the avoidance of noxious situations, (3) the procurement of stroking, and (4) the maintenance of an established equilibrium. All these items have been investigated and discussed in great detail by physiologists, psychologists, and psychoanalysts. Translated into terms of social psychiatry, they may be stated as (1) the primary internal advantages, (2) the primary external advantages, (3) the secondary advantages, and (4) the existential advantages. The first three parallel the "gains from illness" described by Freud: the internal paranosic gain, the external paranosic gain, and the epinosic gain, respectively [11]. Experience has shown that it is more useful and enlightening to investigate social transactions from the point of view of the advantages gained than to treat them as defensive operations. In the first place, the best defense is to engage in no transactions at all; in the second place, the concept of "defenses" covers only part of the first two classes of advantages, and the rest of them, together with the third and fourth classes, are lost to this point of view.

The most gratifying forms of social contact, whether or not they are embedded in a matrix of activity, are games and intimacy. Prolonged intimacy is rare, and even then it is primarily a private matter; significant social intercourse most commonly takes the form of games, and that is the subject which principally concerns us here. For further information about time-structuring, the author's book on group dynamics should be consulted [12].

REFERENCES

1. Berne, E. *Transactional Analysis in Psychotherapy.* Grove Press, Inc., New York, 1961.

2. Spitz, R. "Hospitalism: Genesis of Psychiatric Conditions in Early Childhood." *Psychoanalytic Study of the Child.* 1: 53-74, 1945.

3. Belbenoit, René, *Dry Guillotine.* E. P. Dutton & Company, New York, 1938.

4. Seaton, G. J. *Isle of the Damned.* Popular Library, New York, 1952.

5. Kinkead, E. *In Every War But One.* W. W. Norton & Company, New York, 1959.

6. French, J. D. "The Reticular Formation." *Scientific American.* 196: 54-60, May, 1957.

7. The "colloquialisms" used are those evolved in the course of time at the San Francisco Social Psychiatry Seminars.

8. Levine, S. "Stimulation in Infancy." *Scientific American.* 202: 80-86, May, 1960.

———. "Infantile Experience and Resistance to Physiological Stress." *Science.* 126: 405, August 30, 1957.

9. Huizinga, J. *Homo Ludens.* Beacon Press, Boston, 1955.

10. Kierkegaard, S. *A Kierkegaard Anthology,* ed. R. Bretall. Princeton University Press, Princeton, 1947, pp. 22ff.

11. Freud, S. "General Remarks on Hysterical Attacks." *Collected Papers,* Hogarth Press, London, 1933, II, p. 102.

———. "Analysis of a Case of Hysteria." *Ibid.* III, p. 54.

12. Berne, E. *The Structure and Dynamics of Organizations and Groups.* J. B. Lippincott Company, Philadelphia and Montreal, 1963. (See especially Chapters 11 and 12.)

6. Procedures, Rituals, and Pastimes

Transactions usually proceed in series. These series are not random, but are programed. Programing may come from one of three sources: Parent, Adult, or Child, or more generally, from society, material or idiosyncrasy. Since the needs of adaptation require that the Child may be shielded by the Parent or Adult until each social situation has been tested, Child programing is most apt to occur in situations of privacy and intimacy, where preliminary testing has already been done.

The simplest forms of social activity are procedures and rituals. Some of these are universal and some local, but all of them have to be learned. A *procedure* is a series of simple complementary Adult transactions directed toward the manipulation of reality.*

A *ritual* is a stereotyped series of simple complementary transactions programed by external social forces. An informal ritual, such as social leave-taking, may be subject to considerable local variations in details, although the basic form remains the same. A formal ritual, such as a Roman Catholic Mass, offers much less option. The form of a ritual is Parentally determined by tradition, but more recent "parental" influences may have similar but less stable effects in trivial instances. Some formal rituals of special historical or anthropological interest have two phases: (1) a phase in which transactions are carried on under rigid Parental strictures (2) a phase of Parental license, in which the Child is allowed more or less complete transactional freedom, resulting in an orgy.

Many formal rituals started off as heavily contam-

* Beginning with this section we have excluded portions of our selections which we deemed irrelevant or excessive for the purpose of this work. For instance, there follows in the original text of *Games People Play* a section on reality which we have cut.
—C.S.

inated though fairly efficient procedures, but as time passed and circumstances changed, they lost all procedural validity while still retaining their usefulness as acts of faith. Transactionally they represent guilt-relieving or reward-seeking compliances with traditional Parental demands. They offer a safe, reassuring (apotropaic), and often enjoyable method of structuring time.

Of more significance as an introduction to game analysis are informal rituals, and among the most instructive are the American greeting rituals.

1A: "Hi!" (Hello, good morning.)
1B: "Hi!" (Hello, good morning.)
2A: "Warm enough forya?" (How are you?)
2B: "Sure is. Looks like rain, though." (Fine. How are you?)
3A: "Well, take cara yourself." (Okay.)
3B: "I'll be seeing you."
4A: "So long."
4B: "So long."

It is apparent that this exchange is not intended to convey information. Indeed, if there is any information, it is wisely withheld. It might take Mr. A fifteen minutes to say how he is, and Mr. B, who is only the most casual acquaintance, has no intention of devoting that much time to listening to him. This series of transactions is quite adequately characterized by calling it an "eight-stroke ritual." If A and B were in a hurry, they might both be contented with a two-stroke exchange, Hi-Hi. If they were old-fashioned Oriental potentates, they might go through a two-hundred-stroke ritual before settling down to business. Meanwhile, in the jargon of transactional analysis, A and B have improved each other's health slightly; for the moment, at least, "their spinal cords won't shrivel up," and each is accordingly grateful.

This ritual is based on careful intuitive computations by both parties. At this stage of their acquaintance they figure that they owe each other exactly four strokes at each meeting, and not oftener than once a day. If they run into each other again shortly, say within the next half hour, and have no new business to transact, they will pass by without any sign, or with only the slightest nod of recognition, or at most with a very perfunctory Hi-Hi. These computations hold not only for short intervals but over periods of several months. Let us now consider Mr. C and Mr. D, who pass each other about once a day, trade one stroke each—Hi-Hi—and go their ways. Mr. C goes on a month's vacation. The day after he returns, he encounters Mr. D as usual. If on this occasion Mr. D merely says "Hi!" and no more, Mr. C will be offended, "his spinal cord will shrivel slightly." By his calculations, Mr. D and he owe each other about thirty strokes. These can be compressed into a few transactions, if those transactions are emphatic enough. Mr. D's side properly runs something like this (where each unit of "intensity" or "interest" is equivalent to a stroke):

1D: "Hi!" (1 unit.)
2D: "Haven't seen you around lately." (2 units.)
3D: "Oh, *have* you! Where did you go?" (5 units.)
4D: "*Say, that's interesting.* How was it?" (7 units.)
5D: "Well, you're sure looking fine." (4 units.) "Did your family go along?" (4 units.)
6D: "Well, glad to see you back." (4 units.)
7D: "So long." (1 unit.)

This gives Mr. D a total of 28 units. Both he and Mr. C know that he will make up the missing units the following day, so the account is now, for all practical purposes, squared. Two days later they will be back at their two-stroke exchange, Hi-Hi. But now they "know each other better," i.e., each knows the other is reliable, and this may be useful if they should meet "socially."

The inverse case is also worth considering. Mr. E and Mr. F have set up a two-stroke ritual, Hi-Hi. One day instead of passing on, Mr. E stops and asks: "How are you?" The conversation proceeds as follows:

1E: "Hi!"

1F: "Hi!"

2E: "How are you?"

2F *(Puzzled.):* "Fine. How are you?"

3E: "Everything's great. Warm enough for you?"

3F: "Yeah." *(Cautiously.)* "Looks like rain, though."

4E: "Nice to see you again."

4F: "Same here. Sorry, I've got to get to the library before it closes. So long."

5E: "So long."

As Mr. F hurries away, he thinks to himself: "What's come over him all of a sudden? Is he selling insurance or something?" In transactional terms this reads: "All he owes me is one stroke, why is he giving me five?"

An even simpler demonstration of the truly transactional business-like nature of these simple rituals is the occasion when Mr. G says "Hi!" and Mr. H passes on without replying. Mr. G's reaction is "What's the matter with him?" meaning: "I gave him a stroke and he didn't give me one in return." If Mr. H keeps this up and extends it to other acquaintances, he is going to cause some talk in his community.

In borderline cases it is sometimes difficult to distinguish between procedure and a ritual. The tendency is for the layman to call professional procedures rituals, while actually every transaction may be based on sound, even vital experience, but the layman does not have the background to appreciate that. Conversely, there is a tendency for professionals to rationalize ritualistic elements that still cling to their procedures, and to dismiss skeptical laymen on the ground that they are not equipped to understand. And one of the ways in which entrenched professionals may resist the introduction of sound new procedures is by laughing them off as rituals. Hence the fate of Semmelweis and other innovators.

The essential and similar feature of both procedures and rituals is that they are stereotyped. Once the first transaction has been initiated, the whole series is predictable and follows a predetermined course to a foreordained conclusion unless special conditions arise. The difference between them lies in the origin of the predetermination: procedures are programed by the Adult and rituals are Parentally patterned.

Individuals who are not comfortable or adept with rituals sometimes evade them by substituting procedures. They can be found, for example, among people who like to help the hostess with preparing or serving food and drink at parties.

Pastimes occur in social and temporal matrices of varying degrees of complexity, and hence vary in complexity. However, if we use the transaction as the unit of social intercourse, we can dissect out of appropriate situations an entity which may be called a simple pastime. This may be defined as a series of semiritualistic, simple, complementary transactions arranged around a single field of material, whose primary object is to structure an interval of time. The beginning and end of the interval are typically signaled by procedures or rituals. The transactions are adaptively programed so that each party will obtain the maximum gains or advantages during the interval. The better his adaptation, the more he will get out of it.

Pastimes are typically played at parties ("social gatherings") or during the waiting period before a formal group meeting begins; such waiting periods before a meeting "begins" have the same structure and dynamics as "parties." Pastimes may take the form described as "chit-chat" or they may become more serious, e.g., argumentative. A large cocktail party often functions as a kind of gallery for the exhibition of pastimes. In one corner of the room a few people are playing "PTA," another corner is the forum for "Psychiatry," a third is the theater for "Ever Been" or "What Became," the fourth is engaged for "General Motors," and the buffet is reserved for women who want to play "Kitchen" or "Wardrobe." The proceedings at such a gathering may be almost identical, with a change of names here and there, with the proceedings at a dozen similar parties taking place simultaneously in the area. At another dozen in a different social stratum, a different assortment of pastimes is underway.

Pastimes may be classified in different ways. The

external determinants are sociological (sex, age, marital status, cultural, racial or economic). "General Motors" (comparing cars) and "Who Won" (sports) are both "Man Talk." "Grocery," "Kitchen," and "Wardrobe" are all "Lady Talk"—or, as practiced in the South Seas, "Mary Talk." "Making Out" is adolescent, while the onset of middle age is marked by a shift to "Balance Sheet." Other species of this class, which are all variations of "Small Talk," are: "How To" (go about doing something), an easy filler for short airplane trips; "How Much" (does it cost), a favorite in lower-middle-class bars; "Ever Been" (to some nostalgic place), a middle-class game for "old hands" such as salesmen; "Do You Know" (so-and-so) for lonely ones; "What Became" (of good old Joe), often played by economic successes and failures; "Morning After" (what a hangover) and "Martini" (I know a better way), typical of a certain kind of ambitious young person.

The structural-transactional classification is a more personal one. This "PTA" may be played at three levels. At the Child-Child level it takes the form of "How Do You Deal with Recalcitrant Parents"; its Adult-Adult form, "PTA" proper, is popular among well-read young mothers; with older people it tends to take the dogmatic Parent-Parent form of "Juvenile Delinquency." Some married couples play "Tell Them Dear," in which the wife is Parental and the husband comes through like a precocious child. "Look Ma No Hands" is similarly a Child-Parent pastime suitable for people of any age, sometimes diffidently adapted into "Aw Shucks Fellows."

Besides structuring time and providing mutually acceptable stroking for the parties concerned, pastimes serve the additional function of being social-selection processes. While a pastime is in progress, the Child in each player is watchfully assessing the potentialities of the others involved. At the end of the party, each person will have selected certain players he would like to see more of, while others he will discard, regardless of how skillfully or pleasantly they each engaged in the pastime. The ones he selects are those who seem the most likely candidates for more complex relationships—that is, games. This sorting system, however well rationalized, is actually largely unconscious and intuitive.

In special cases the Adult overrides the Child in the selection process. This is most clearly illustrated by an insurance salesman who carefully learns to play social pastimes. While he is playing, his Adult listens for possible prospects and selects them from the players as people he would like to see more of. Their adeptness at games or congeniality is quite irrelevant to his process of selection, which is based, as in most cases, on peripheral factors—in this instance, financial readiness.

Pastimes, however, have a quite specific aspect of exclusiveness. For example, "Man Talk" and "Lady Talk" do not mix. People playing a hard hand of "Ever Been" (there) will be annoyed by an intruder who wants to play "How Much" (for avocados) or "Morning After."

Pastimes form the basis for the selection of acquaintances, and may lead to friendship. A party of women who drop in at each other's houses every morning for coffee to play "Delinquent Husband" are likely to give a cool reception to a new neighbor who wants to play "Sunny Side Up." If they are saying how mean their husbands are, it is too disconcerting to have a newcomer declare that her husband is just marvelous, in fact perfect, and they will not keep her long. So at a cocktail party, if someone wants to move from one corner to another, he must either join in the pastime played in his new location or else successfully switch the whole proceeding into a new channel. A good hostess, of course, takes the situation in hand immediately and states the program: "We are just playing Projective 'PTA.' What do you think?" Or: "Come now, you girls have been playing 'Wardrobe' long enough. Mr. J. here is a writer/politician/surgeon, and I'm sure he'd like to play 'Look Ma No Hands.' Wouldn't you, Mr. J?"

Another important advantage obtained from pastimes is the confirmation of role and the stabilizing of position. A *role* is something like what Jung calls persona, except that it is less opportunistic and more deeply rooted in the individual's fantasies. Thus in Projective "PTA" one player may take the role of tough Parent, another the role of righteous Parent, a third the role of indulgent Parent and a fourth the role of helpful Parent. All four experience and exhibit a Parental ego state, but each presents himself differently. The role of each one is confirmed if it prevails—that is, if it meets with no antagonism or is strengthened by any antagonism it meets or is approved by certain types of people with stroking.

The confirmation of his role stabilizes the individual's *position,* and this is called the *existential* advantage from the pastime. A position is a simple predicative statement which influences all of the individual's transactions; in the long run it determines his destiny and often that of his descendants as well. A position may be more or less absolute. Typical positions from which Projective "PTA" can be played are "All children are bad!" "All other children are bad!" "All children are sad!" "All children are persecuted!" These positions might give rise to the role of the tough, the righteous, the indulgent and the helpful Parent, respectively. Actually a position is primarily manifested by the mental *attitude* to which it gives rise, and it is with this attitude that the individual undertakes the transactions which constitute his role.

Positions are taken and become fixed surprisingly early, from the second or even the first years to the seventh year of life—in any case long before the individual is competent or experienced enough to make such a serious commitment. It is not difficult to deduce from an individual's position the kind of childhood he must have had. Unless something or somebody intervenes, he spends the rest of his life stabilizing his position and dealing with situations that threaten it: by avoiding them, warding off certain elements or manipulating them provocatively so that they are transformed from threats into justifications. One reason pastimes are so stereotyped is that they serve such stereotyped purposes. But the gains they offer show why people play them so eagerly, and why they can be so pleasant

if played with people who have constructive or benevolent positions to maintain.

A pastime is not always easy to distinguish from an
activity, and combinations frequently occur. Many
commonplace pastimes, such as "General Motors," consist of what psychologists might call Multiple-Choice-
Sentence-Completion exchanges.

A. "I like a Ford/Chevrolet/Plymouth better than
a Ford/Chevrolet/Plymouth because. . . ."

B. "Oh. Well, I'd rather have a Ford/Chevrolet/
Plymouth than a Ford/Chevrolet/Plymouth because. . . ."

It is apparent that there may actually be some useful information conveyed in such stereotypes.

A few other common pastimes may be mentioned.
"Me Too" is often a variant of "Ain't It Awful." "Why
Don't They" (do something about it) is a favorite
among housewives who do not wish to be emancipated.
"Then We'll" is a Child-Child pastime. "Let's Find"
(something to do) is played by juvenile delinquents
or mischievous grown-ups.

7. Games

DEFINITION

A game is an ongoing series of complementary ulterior transactions progressing to a well-defined, predictable outcome. Descriptively it is a recurring set of transactions, often repetitious, superficially plausible, with a concealed motivation; or, more colloquially, a series of moves with a snare, or "gimmick." Games are clearly differentiated from procedures, rituals, and pastimes by two chief characteristics: (1) their ulterior quality and (2) the payoff. Procedures may be successful, rituals effective, and pastimes profitable, but all of them are by definition candid; they may involve contest, but not conflict, and the ending may be sensational, but it is not dramatic. Every game, on the other hand, is basically dishonest, and the outcome has a dramatic, as distinct from merely exciting, quality.

It remains to distinguish games from the one remaining type of social action which so far has not been discussed. An *operation* is a simple transaction or set of transactions undertaken for a specific, stated purpose. If someone frankly asks for reassurance and gets it, that is an operation. If someone asks for reassurance, and after it is given turns it in some way to the disadvantage of the giver, that is a game. Superficially, then, a game looks like a set of operations, but after the payoff it becomes apparent that these "operations" were really *maneuvers;* not honest requests but moves in the game.

In the "insurance game," for example, no matter what the agent appears to be doing in conversation, if he is a hard player he is really looking for or working on a prospect. What he is after, if he is worth his salt, is to "make a killing." The same applies to the "real estate game," "the pajama game" and similar occupations. Hence at a social gathering, while a salesman is engaged in pastimes, particularly variants of "Balance Sheet," his congenial participation may conceal a series of skillful maneuvers designed to elicit the kind of information he is professionally interested in. There are dozens of trade journals devoted to improving commercial maneuvers, and which give accounts of outstanding players and games (interesting operators who make unusually big deals). Transactionally speaking, these are merely variants of *Sports Illustrated, Chess World*, and other sports magazines.

As far as angular transactions are concerned— games which are consciously planned with professional precision under Adult control to yield the maximum gains—the big "con games" which flourished in the early 1900's are hard to surpass for detailed practical planning and psychological virtuosity [1].

What we are concerned with here, however, are the unconscious games played by innocent people engaged in duplex transactions of which they are not fully aware, and which form the most important aspect of social life all over the world. Because of their dynamic qualities, games are easy to distinguish from mere static *attitudes,* which arise from taking a position.

The use of the word "game" should not be misleading. As explained in the introduction, it does not necessarily imply fun or even enjoyment. Many salesmen do not consider their work fun, as Arthur Miller made clear in his play, *Death of a Salesman*. And there may be no lack of seriousness. Football games nowadays are taken very seriously, but no more so than such transactional games as "Alcoholic" or "Third-Degree Rapo."

The same applies to the word "play," as anyone who has "played" hard poker or "played" the stock market over a long period can testify. The possible seriousness of games and play, and the possibly serious results, are well known to anthropologists. The most complex game that ever existed, that of "Courtier" as described so well by Stendhal in *The Charterhouse of Parma*, was deadly serious. The grimmest of all, of course, is "War."

A TYPICAL GAME

The most common game played between spouses is colloquially called "If It Weren't For You," and this will be used to illustrate the characteristics of games in general.

Mrs. White complained that her husband severely restricted her social activities, so that she had never learned to dance. Due to changes in her attitude brought about by psychiatric treatment, her husband became less sure of himself and more indulgent. Mrs. White was then free to enlarge the scope of her activities. She signed up for dancing lessons, and then discovered to her despair that she had a morbid fear of dance floors and had to abandon this project.

This unfortunate adventure, along with similar ones, laid bare some important aspects of the structure of her marriage. Out of her many suitors she had picked a domineeering man for a husband. She was then in a position to complain that she could do all sorts of things "if it weren't for you." Many of her women friends also had domineering husbands, and when they met for their morning coffee, they spent a good deal of time playing "If It Weren't For Him."

As it turned out, however, contrary to her complaints, her husband was performing a very real service for her by forbidding her to do something she was deeply afraid of, and by preventing her, in fact, from even becoming aware of her fears. This was one reason her Child had shrewdly chosen such a husband.

But there was more to it than that. His prohibitions and her complaints frequently led to quarrels, so that their sex life was seriously impaired. And because of his feelings of guilt, he frequently brought her gifts which might not otherwise have been forthcoming; certainly when he gave her more freedom, his gifts diminished in lavishness and frequency. She and her husband had little in common besides their household worries and the children, so that their quarrels stood out as important events; it was mainly on these occasions that they had anything but the most casual conversations. At any rate, her married life had proved one thing to her that she had always maintained: that all men were mean and tyrannical. As it turned out, this attitude was related to some daydreams of being sexually abused which had plagued her in earlier years.

There are various ways of describing this game in general terms. It is apparent that it belongs in the large field of *social dynamics*. The basic fact is that by marrying, Mr. and Mrs. White have an opportunity to communicate with each other, and such an opportunity may be called *social contact*. The fact that they use this opportunity makes their household a social aggregation, as contrasted with a New York subway train, for example, where people are in spatial contact but rarely avail themselves of the opportunity and so form a dissocial aggregation. The influence the Whites exert on each other's behavior and responses constitutes *social action*. Various disciplines would investigate such social action from different points of view. Since we are here concerned with the personal histories and psychodynamics of the individuals involved, the present approach is one aspect of *social psychiatry;* some implicit or explicit judgment is passed on the "healthiness" of the games studied. This is somewhat different from the more neutral and less committed attitudes of sociology and social psychology. Psychiatry reserves the right to say, "Just a moment!" which the other disciplines do not. Transactional analysis is a branch of social psychiatry, and game analysis is a special aspect of transactional analysis.

Practical game analysis deals with special cases as they appear in specific situations. Theoretical game analysis attempts to abstract and generalize the characteristics of various games, so that they can be recognized independently of their momentary verbal content and their cultural matrix. The theoretical analysis of "If It Weren't For You," Marital Type, for example, should state the characteristics of that game in such a way that it can be recognized just as easily in a New Guinea jungle village as in a Manhattan penthouse, whether it is concerned with a nuptial party or with the financial problems of getting a fishing rod for the grandchildren; and regardless of how bluntly or subtly the moves are made, according to the permissible degrees of frankness between husband and wife. The *prevalence* of the game in a given society is a matter for sociology and anthropology. Game analysis, as a part of social psychiatry, is interested only in describing the game when it does occur, regardless of how often that may be. This distinction is not complex, but it is analogous to the distinction between public health and internal medicine; the first is interested in the prevalence of malaria, while the latter studies cases of malaria as they come up, in the jungle or in Manhattan.

At the present time the scheme given below has been found the most useful one for theoretical game analysis. No doubt it will be improved as further knowledge accumulates. The first requisite is to recognize that a certain sequence of maneuvers meets the criteria of a game. As many samples as possible of the game are then collected. The significant features of the collection are isolated. Certain aspects emerge as essential. These are then classified under headings which are designed to be as meaningful and instructive as possible in the current state of knowledge. The analysis is undertaken from the point of view of the one who is "it"—in this case, Mrs. White.

Thesis. This is a general description of the game, including the immediate sequence of events (the social level) and information about their psychological background, evolution and significance (the psychological level). In the case of "If It Weren't For You," Marital Type, the details already given will serve (pp. 73–74). For the sake of brevity, this game will henceforth be referred to as IWFY.

Antithesis. The presumption that a certain sequence constitutes a game is tentative until it has been existentially validated. This validation is carried out by a refusal to play or by undercutting the payoff. The one who is "it" will then make more intense efforts to continue the game. In the face of adamant refusal to play or a successful undercutting he will then lapse into a state called "despair," which in some respects re-

sembles a depression, but is different in significant
ways. It is more acute and contains elements of frustration and bewilderment. It may be manifested, for
example, by the onset of perplexed weeping. In a successful therapeutic situation that may soon be replaced
by humorous laughter, implying an Adult realization:
"There I go again!" This despair is a concern of the
Adult, while in depression it is the Child who has the
executive power. Hopefulness, enthusiasm or a lively
interest is the opposite of despair. Hence the enjoyable
quality of therapeutic game analysis. The antithesis to
IWFY is permissiveness. As long as the husband is
prohibitive, the game can proceed. If instead of saying
"Don't you dare!" he says "Go ahead!" the underlying
phobias are unmasked, and the wife can no longer turn
on him, as demonstrated in Mrs. White's case.

For clear understanding of a game, the antithesis
should be known and its effectiveness demonstrated
in practice.

Aim. This states simply the general purpose of the
game. Sometimes there are alternatives. The aim of
IWFY may be stated as either reassurance ("It's not
that I'm afraid, it's that he won't let me") or vindica-
tion ("It's not that I'm not trying, it's that he holds
me back"). The reassuring function is easier to clarify
and is more in accord with the security needs of the
wife; therefore IWFY is most simply regarded as having
the aim of reassurance.

Roles. As previously noted, ego states are not roles
but phenomena. Therefore ego states and roles have to
be distinguished in a formal description. Games may
be described as two-handed, many-handed, etc., according to the number of roles offered. Sometimes the
ego state of each player corresponds to his role, sometimes it does not.

IWFY is a two-handed game and calls for a restricted wife and a domineering husband. The wife may
play her role either as a prudent Adult ("It's best that
I do as he says") or as a petulant Child. The domineering husband may preserve an Adult ego state ("It's
best that you do as I say") or slip into a Parental one
("You'd better do what I say").

Dynamics. There are alternatives in stating the psychodynamic driving forces behind each case of a game. It is usually possible, however, to pick out a single psychodynamic concept which usefully, aptly and meaningfully epitomizes the situation. This IWFY is best described as deriving from phobic sources.

Examples. Since the childhood origins of a game, or its infantile prototypes, are instructive to study, it is worthwhile to search for such cognates in making a formal description. It happens that IWFY is just as frequently played by little children as by grown-ups, so the childhood version is the same as the later one, with the actual parent substituted for the restricting husband.

Transactional Paradigm. The transactional analysis of a typical situation is presented, giving both the social and psychological levels of a revealing ulterior transaction. In its most dramatic form, IWFY at the social level is a Parent-Child game.

Mr. White: "You stay home and take care of the house."

Mrs. White: "If it weren't for you, I could be out having fun."

At the psychological level (the ulterior marriage contract) the relationship is Child-Child, and quite different.

Mr. White: "You must always be here when I get home. I'm terrified of desertion."

Mrs. White: "I will be if you help me avoid phobic situations."

The two levels are illustrated in Figure 7.

Moves. The moves of a game correspond roughly to the strokes in a ritual. As in any game, the players become increasingly adept with practice. Wasteful moves are eliminated, and more and more purpose is condensed into each move. "Beautiful friendships" are often based on the fact that the players complement each other with great economy and satisfaction, so that there is a maximum yield with a minimum effort from the games they play with each other. Certain intermediate, precautionary or concessional moves can be elided, giving a high degree of elegance to the relationship. The effort saved on defensive maneuvers can be devoted to ornamental flourishes instead, to the delight of both parties and sometimes of the onlookers as well. The student observes that there is a minimum number of moves essential to the program of the game, and these can be stated in the protocol. Individual players

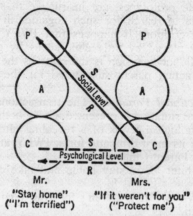

Figure 7. A game: If It Weren't For You.

will embellish or multiply these basic moves according to their needs, talents or desires. The framework for IWFY is as follows:

(1) Instruction-Compliance ("You stay home"— "All right").

(2) Instruction-Protest ("You stay home again"— "If it weren't for you").

Advantages. The general advantages of a game consist in its stabilizing (homeostatic) functions. Biological homeostasis is promoted by the stroking, and psychological stability is reinforced by the confirmation of position. As has already been noted, stroking may take various forms, so that the *biological advantage* of a game may be stated in tactile terms. Thus the husband's role in IWFY is reminiscent of a backhanded slap (quite different in effect from a palmar slap, which is a direct humiliation), and the wife's response is something like a petulant kick in the shins. Hence the biological gain from IWFY is derived from the belligerence-petulance exchanges: a distressing but apparently effective way to maintain the health of nervous tissues.

Confirmation of the wife's position—"All men are tyrants"—is the *existential advantage*. This position is a reaction to the need to surrender that is inherent in the phobias, a demonstration of the coherent structure which underlies all games. The expanded statement would be: "If I went out alone in a crowd, I would be overcome by the temptation to surrender; at home I don't surrender; he forces me, which proves that all men are tyrants." Hence this game is commonly played by women who suffer from feelings of unreality, which signifies their difficulty in keeping the Adult in charge in situations of strong temptation. The detailed elucidation of these mechanisms belongs to psychoanalysis rather than game analysis. In game analysis the end product is the chief concern.

Internal psychological advantage of a game is its direct effect on the psychic economy (libido). In IWFY the socially acceptable surrender to the husband's authority keeps the woman from experiencing neurotic fears. At the same time it satisfies masochistic needs, if they exist, using masochism not in the sense of self-abnegation but with its classical meaning of sexual excitement in situations of deprivation, humiliation or pain. That is, it excites her to be deprived and dominated.

External psychological advantage is the avoidance of the feared situation by playing the game. This is especially obvious in IWFY, where it is the outstanding motivation: by complying with the husband's strictures, the wife avoids the public situations which she fears.

Internal social advantage is designated by the name of the game as it is played in the individual's intimate circle. By her compliance, the wife gains the privilege of saying "If it weren't for you." This helps to structure the time she must spend with her husband; in the case of Mrs. White, this need for structure was especially strong because of the lack of other common interests, especially before the arrival of their offspring and after the children were grown. In between, the game was played less intensively and less frequently, because the children performed their usual function of structuring time for their parents, and also provided an even more widely accepted version of IWFY, the busy-housewife variation. The fact that young mothers in America often really are very busy does not change the analysis of this variation. Game analysis attempts only to answer this question without prejudice: given that a young woman is busy, how does she go about exploiting her busyness in order to get some compensation for it?

External social advantage is designated by the use made of the situation in outside social contacts. In the case of the game "If It Weren't For You," which is what the wife says to her husband, there is a transformation into the pastime "If It Weren't For Him" when she meets with her friends over morning coffee. Again, the influence of games in the selection of social companions is shown. The new neighbor who is invited for morning coffee is being invited to play "If It Weren't For Him." If she plays, well and good, she will soon be a bosom friend of the old-timers, other things being equal. If she refuses to play and insists on taking a charitable view of her husband, she will not last long. Her situation will be the same as if she kept refusing to drink at cocktail parties—in most circles, she would gradually be dropped from the guest lists.

This completes the analysis of the formal features of IWFY.

THE GENESIS OF GAMES

From the present point of view, child rearing may be regarded as an educational process in which the child is taught what games to play and how to play them. He is also taught procedures, rituals and pastimes appropriate to his position in the local social situation, but these are less significant. His knowledge of and skill in procedures, rituals and pastimes determine what opportunities will be available to him, other things being equal; but his games determine the use he will make of these opportunities, and the outcomes of situations for which he is eligible. As elements of his script, or unconscious life-plan, his favored games also determine his ultimate destiny (again with other things being equal): the payoffs on his marriage and career, and the circumstances surrounding his death.

While conscientious parents devote a great deal of attention to teaching their children procedures, rituals and pastimes appropriate to their stations in life, and with equal care select schools, colleges and churches where their teachings will be reinforced, they tend to overlook the question of games, which form the basic structure for the emotional dynamics of each family, and which the children learn through significant experiences in everyday living from their earliest months. Related questions have been discussed for thousands of years in a rather general, unsystematic fashion, and there has been some attempt at a more methodical approach in the modern orthopsychiatric literature; but without the concept of games there is little possibility of a consistent investigation. Theories of internal individual psychodynamics have so far not been able to solve satisfactorily the problems of human relationships. These are transactional situations which call for a theory of social dynamics that cannot be derived solely from consideration of individual motivations.

Since there are as yet few well-trained specialists in child psychology and child psychiatry who are also trained in game analysis, observations on the genesis of games are sparse. Fortunately, the following episode took place in the presence of a well-educated transactional analyst.

Tanjy, age 7, got a stomach-ache at the dinner table and asked to be excused for that reason. His parents suggested that he lie down for a while. His little brother Mike, age 3, then said, "I have a stomach-ache too," evidently angling for the same consideration. The father looked at him for a few seconds and then replied, "You don't want to play that game, do you?" Whereupon Mike burst out laughing and said, "No!"

If this had been a household of food or bowel faddists, Mike would also have been packed off to bed

by his alarmed parents. If he and they had repeated
this performance several times, it might be anticipated
that this game would have become part of Mike's
character, as it so often does if the parents cooperate.
Whenever he was jealous of a privilege granted to a
competitor, he would plead illness in order to get some
privileges himself. The ulterior transaction would then
consist of: (social level) "I don't feel well" + (psychological level) "You must grant me a privilege, too."
Mike, however, was saved from such a hypochondriacal
career. Perhaps he will end up with a worse fate, but
that is not the issue. The issue is that a game *in statu
nascendi* was broken up right there by the father's
question and by the boy's frank acknowledgment that
what he proposed was a game.

This demonstrates clearly enough that games are
quite deliberately initiated by young children. After
they become fixed patterns of stimulus and response,
their origins become lost in the mists of time and their
ulterior nature becomes obscured by social fogs. Both
can be brought into awareness only by appropriate
procedures: the origin by some form of analytic therapy
and the ulterior aspect by antithesis. Repeated clinical
experience along these lines makes it clear that games
are imitative in nature, and they are initially set up
by the Adult (neopsychic) aspect of the child's personality. If the Child ego state can be revived in the grown-
up player, the psychological aptitude of this segment
(the Adult aspect of the Child ego state) is so striking,
and its skill in manipulating people so enviable, that it
is colloquially called "The Professor" (of Psychiatry).
Hence in psychotherapy groups which concentrate on
game analysis, one of the more sophisticated procedures is the search for the little "Professor" in each
patient, whose early adventures in setting up games between the ages of two and eight are listened to by
everyone present with fascination and often, unless the
games are tragic, with enjoyment and even hilarity, in
which the patient himself may join with justifiable self-
appreciation and smugness. Once he is able to do that,
he is well on his way to relinquishing what may be an

unfortunate behavior pattern which he is much better off without.

Those are the reasons why in the formal description of a game an attempt is always made to describe the infantile or childhood prototype.

THE FUNCTION OF GAMES

Because there is so little opportunity for intimacy in daily life, and because some forms of intimacy (especially if intense) are psychologically impossible for most people, the bulk of the time in serious social life is taken up with playing games. Hence games are both necessary and desirable, and the only problem at issue is whether the games played by an individual offer the best yield for him. In this connection it should be remembered that the essential feature of a game is its culmination, or payoff. The principal function of the preliminary moves is to set up the situation for this payoff, but they are always designed to harvest the maximum permissible satisfaction at each step as a secondary product. Thus in "Schlemiel" (making messes and then apologizing) the payoff, and the purpose of the game, is to obtain the forgiveness which is forced by the apology; the spillings and cigarette burns are only steps leading up to this, but each such trespass yields its own pleasure. The enjoyment derived from the spilling does not make spilling a game. The apology is the critical stimulus that leads to the denouement. Otherwise the spilling would simply be a destructive procedure, a delinquency perhaps enjoyable.

The game of "Alcoholic" is similar: whatever the physiological origin, if any, of the need to drink, in terms of game analysis the imbibing is merely a move in a game which is carried on with the people in the environment. The drinking may bring its own kinds of pleasure, but it is not the essence of the game. This is demonstrated in the variant of "Dry Alcoholic," which involves the same moves and leads to the same payoffs as the regular game, but is played without any bottles.

Beyond their social function in structuring time satisfactorily, some games are urgently necessary for the maintenance of health in certain individuals. These people's psychic stability is so precarious and their positions are so tenuously maintained, that to deprive them of their games may plunge them into irreversible despair and even psychosis. Such people will fight very hard against any antithetical moves. This is often observed in marital situations when the psychiatric improvement of one spouse (i.e., the abandonment of destructive games) leads to rapid deterioration in the other spouse, to whom the games were of paramount importance in maintaining equilibrium. Hence it is necessary to exercise prudence in game analysis.

Fortunately, the rewards of game-free intimacy, which is or should be the most perfect form of human living, are so great that even precariously balanced personalities can safely and joyfully relinquish their games if an appropriate partner can be found for the better relationship.

On a larger scale, games are integral and dynamic components of the unconscious life-span, or script, of each individual; they serve to fill in the time while he waits for the final fulfillment, simultaneously advancing the action. Since the last act of a script characteristically calls for either a miracle or a catastrophe, depending on whether the script is constructive, the corresponding games are accordingly either constructive or destructive. In colloquial terms, an individual whose script is oriented toward "waiting for Santa Claus" is likely to be pleasant to deal with in such games as "Gee You're Wonderful, Mr. Murgatroyd," while someone with a tragic script oriented toward "waiting for rigor mortis to set in" may play such disagreeable games as "Now I've Got You, You Son of a Bitch."

It should be noted that colloquialisms such as those in the previous sentence are an integral part of game analysis, and are freely used in transactional psychotherapy groups and seminars. The expression "waiting for rigor mortis to set in" originated in a dream of a patient, in which she decided to get certain things done "before rigor mortis set in." A patient in a sophisticated group pointed out what the therapist had overlooked:

that in practice, waiting for Santa Claus and waiting for death are synonymous.

THE CLASSIFICATION OF GAMES

Most of the variables used in analying games and pastimes have already been mentioned, and any of them can be used in classifying games and pastimes systematically. Some of the more obvious classifications are based on the following factors:

1. Number of players: two-handed games (Frigid Woman), three-handed games (Let's You and Him Fight), five-handed games (Alcoholic) and many-handed games (Why Don't You—Yes But).

2. Currency used: words (Psychiatry), money (Debtor), parts of the body (Polysurgery).

3. Clinical types: hysterical (Rapo), obsessive compulsive (Schlemiel), paranoid (Why Does This Have to Happen to Me), depressive (There I Go Again).

4. Zonal; oral (Alcholic), and (Schlemiel), phallic (Let's You and Him Fight).

5. Psychodynamic: counterphobic (If It Weren't for You), projective (PTA), introjective (Psychiatry).

6. Instinctual: masochistic (If It Weren't for You), sadistic (Schlemiel), fetishistic (Frigid Man).

In addition to the number of players, three other quantitative variables are often useful to consider:

1. Flexibility. Some games, such as Debtor and Polysurgery, can be played properly with only one kind of currency, while others, such as exhibitionistic games, are more flexible.

2. Tenacity. Some people give up their games easily, others are persistent.

3. Intensity. Some people play their games in a relaxed way, others are more tense and aggressive. Games so played are known as easy and hard games, respectively.

These three variables converge to make games gentle or violent. In mentally disturbed people, there is often a noticeable progression in this respect, so that one can speak of stages. A paranoid schizophrenic may initially play a flexible, loose, easy game of first-stage "Ain't

It Awful" and progress to an inflexible, tenacious, hard third stage. The stages in a game are distinguished as follows:

a. A First-Degree Game is one which is socially acceptable in the agent's circle.

b. A Second-Degree Game is one from which no permanent, irremediable damage arises, but which the players would rather conceal from the public.

c. A Third-Degree Game is one which is played for keeps, and which ends in the surgery, the courtroom or the morgue.

Games can also be classified according to any of the other specific factors discussed in the analysis of IWFY: the aims, the roles, the most obvious advantages. The most likely candidate for a systematic, scientific classification is probably one based on the existential position; but since knowledge of this factor is not yet sufficiently advanced, such a classification will have to be postponed. Failing that, the most practical classification at present is probably a sociological one.

REFERENCE

1. Maurer, D. W. *The Big Con*. The Bobbs-Merrill Co., New York, 1940.

8. A Thesaurus of Games

This collection is complete to date (1962), but new games are continually being discovered. Sometimes what appears to be another example of a known game turns out, on more careful study, to be an entirely new one, and a game which appears to be new often turns out to be a variation of a known one. The individual items of the analyses are also subject to change as new knowledge accumulates; for example, where there are several possible choices in describing dynamics, the statement given may turn out later not to have been the most cogent one. Both the list of games and the items given in the analyses, however, are adequate for clinical work.

Some of the games are discussed and analyzed *in extenso*. Others, which require more investigation, or are uncommon, or whose significance is fairly obvious, are only briefly mentioned. The one who is "it" is generally referred to as the "agent," or is given the name of "White," while the other party is called "Black."

The games are classified into families according to the situations in which they most commonly occur: Life Games, Marital Games, Party Games, Sexual Games and Underworld Games; then comes a section for professionals on Consulting Room Games, and finally, some examples of Good Games.

An adequate understanding of a game can only be obtained in the psychotherapeutic situation. People who play destructive games will come to the therapist far more frequently than people who play constructive ones. Therefore most of the games which are well understood are basically destructive, but the reader should remember that there are constructive ones played by more fortunate people. And to prevent the idea of games from becoming vulgarized, as so many psychiatric terms are, it should be emphasized once more that it is a very precise idea: games should be clearly distinguished, by the criteria given previously, from procedures, rituals, pastimes, operations, maneuvers and the attitudes which arise from various positions. A game is played from a position, but a position or its corresponding attitude is not a game.

COLLOQUIALISMS

Many colloquialisms used here were supplied by patients. All of them, if used with due regard to timing and sensibilities, are appreciated, understood and enjoyed by the players. If some of them seem disrespectful, the irony is directed against the games and not against the people who play them. The first requirement for colloquialisms is aptness, and if they often sound amusing, that is precisely because they hit the nail on the head. As I have tried to show elsewhere in discussing colloquial epithets, a whole page of learned polysyllables may not convey as much as the statement that a certain woman is a bitch, or that a certain man is a jerk. Psychological truths may be stated for academic purposes in scientific language, but the effective recognition of emotional strivings in practice may require a different approach. So we prefer playing "Ain't It Awful" to "verbalizing projected anal aggression." The former not only has a more dynamic meaning and impact, but it is actually more precise. And sometimes people get better faster in bright rooms than they do in drab ones.

LIFE GAMES

All games have an important and probably decisive influence on the destinies of the players under ordinary social conditions; but some offer more opportunities than others for lifelong careers and are more likely to involve relatively innocent bystanders. This group may be conveniently called Life Games. It includes "Alcoholic," "Debtor," "Kick Me," "Now I've Got You,

You Son of a Bitch," "See What You Made Me Do"
and their principal variants. They merge on the one
side with marital games, and on the other with those of
the underworld.

Alcoholic

Thesis. In game analysis there is no such thing as
alcoholism or "an alcoholic," but there is a role called
the Alcoholic in a certain type of game. If a bio-
chemical or physiological abnormality is the prime
mover in excessive drinking—and that is still open to
some question—then its study belongs in the field of
internal medicine. Game analysis is interested in something quite different—the kind of social transactions
that are related to such excesses. Hence the game
"Alcoholic."

In its full flower this is a five-handed game, although
the roles may be condensed so that it starts off and
terminates as a two-handed one. The central role is
that of the Alcoholic—the one who is "it"—played by
White. The chief supporting role is that of Persecutor,
typically played by a member of the opposite sex,
usually the spouse. The third role is that of Rescuer,
usually played by someone of the same sex, often the
good family doctor who is interested in the patient and
also in drinking problems. In the classical situation the
doctor successfully rescues the alcoholic from his habit.
After White has not taken a drink for six months they
congratulate each other. The following day White is
found in the gutter.

The fourth role is that of the Patsy, or Dummy. In
literature this is played by the delicatessen man who
extends credit to White, gives him a sandwich on the
cuff and perhaps a cup of coffee, without either persecuting him or trying to rescue him. In life this is
more frequently played by White's mother, who gives
him money and often sympathizes with him about the
wife who does not understand him. In this aspect of
the game, White is required to account in some plausible way for his need for money—by some project in
which both pretend to believe, although they know
what he is really going to spend most of the money for.

Sometimes the Patsy slides over into another role, which is a helpful but not essential one: the Agitator, the "good guy" who offers supplies without even being asked for them: "Come have a drink with me (and you will go downhill faster)."

The ancillary professional in all drinking games is the bartender or liquor clerk. In the game "Alcoholic" he plays the fifth role, the Connection, the direct source of supply who also understands alcoholic talk, and who in a way is the most meaningful person in the life of an addict. The difference between the Connection and the other players is the difference between professionals and amateurs in any game: the professional knows when to stop. At a certain point a good bartender refuses to serve the Alcoholic, who is then left without any supplies unless he can locate a more indulgent Connection.

In the initial stages of "Alcoholic," the wife may play all three supporting roles: at midnight the Patsy, undressing him, making him coffee and letting him beat up on her; in the morning the Persecutor, berating him for the evil of his ways; and in the evening the Rescuer, pleading with him to change them. In the later stages, due sometimes to organic deterioration, the Persecutor and the Rescuer can be dispensed with, but are tolerated if they are also willing to act as sources of supply. White will go to the Mission House and be rescued if he can get a free meal there; or he will stand for a scolding, amateur or professional, as long as he can get a handout afterward.

Present experience indicates that the payoff in "Alcoholic" (as is characteristic of games in general) comes from the aspect to which most investigators pay least attention. In the analysis of this game, drinking itself is merely an incidental pleasure having added advantages, the procedure leading up to the real culmination, which is the hangover. It is the same in the game of Schlemiel: the mess-making, which attracts the most attention, is merely a pleasure-giving way for White to lead up to the crux, which is obtaining forgiveness from Black.

For the Alcoholic the hangover is not as much the

physical pain as the psychological torment. The two favorite pastimes of drinking people are "Martini" (how many drinks and how they were mixed) and "Morning After" (Let me tell you about my hangover). "Martini" is played, for the most part, by social drinkers; many alcoholics prefer a hard round of psychological "Morning After," and organizations such A.A. offer him an unlimited opportunity for this.

Whenever one patient visited his psychiatrist after a binge, he would call himself all sorts of names; the psychiatrist said nothing. Later, recounting these visits in a therapy group, White said with smug satisfaction that it was the psychiatrist who had called him all those names. The main conversational interest of many alcoholics in the therapeutic situation is not their drinking, which they apparently mention mostly in deference to their persecutors, but their subsequent suffering. The transactional object of the drinking, aside from the personal pleasures it brings, is to set up a situation where the Child can be severely scolded not only by the internal Parent but by any parental figures in the environment who are interested enough to oblige. Hence the therapy of this game should be concentrated not on the drinking but on the morning after, the self-indulgence in self-castigation. There is a type of heavy drinker however, who does not have hangovers, and such people do not belong in the present category.

There is also a game "Dry Alcoholic," in which White goes through the process of financial or social degradation without a bottle, making the same sequence of moves and requiring the same supporting cast. Here again, the morning after is the crux of the matter. Indeed, it is the similarity between "Dry Alcoholic" and regular "Alcoholic" which emphasizes that both are games; for example, the procedure for getting discharged from a job is the same in both. "Addict" is similar to "Alcoholic," but more sinister, more dramatic, more sensational and faster. In our society, at least, it leans more heavily on the readily available Persecutor, with Patsies and Rescuers being few and far between and the Connection playing a much more central role.

There is a variety of organizations involved in "Alcoholic," some of them national or even international in scope, others local. Many of them publish rules for the game. Nearly all of them explain how to play the role of Alcoholic: take a drink before breakfast, spend money allotted for other purposes, etc. They also explain the function of the Rescuer. Alcoholics Anonymous, for example, continues playing the actual game but concentrates on inducing the Alcoholic to take the role of Rescuer. Former Alcoholics are preferred because they know how the game goes, and hence are better qualified to play the supporting role than people who have never played before. Cases have been reported of a chapter of A.A. running out of Alcoholics to work on; whereupon the members resumed drinking since there was no other way to continue the game in the absence of people to rescue.

There are also organizations devoted to improving the lot of the other players. Some put pressure on the spouses to shift their roles from Persecutor to Rescuer. The one which seems to come closest to the theoretical ideal of treatment deals with teen-age offspring of alcoholics; these young people are encouraged to break away from the game itself, rather than merely shift their roles.

The psychological cure of an alcoholic also lies in getting him to stop playing the game altogether, rather than simply change from one role to another. In some cases this has been feasible, although it is a difficult task to find something else as interesting to the Alcoholic as continuing his game. Since he is classically afraid of intimacy, the substitute may have to be another game rather than a game-free relationship. Often so-called cured alcoholics are not very stimulating company socially, and possibly they feel a lack of excitement in their lives and are continually tempted to go back to their old ways. The criterion of a true "game cure" is that the former Alcoholic should be able to drink socially without putting himself in jeopardy. The usual "total abstinence" cure will not satisfy the game analyst.

It is apparent from the description of this game that

there is a strong temptation for the Rescuer to play "I'm Only Trying to Help You"; for the Persecutor to play "Look What You've Done to Me"; and for the Patsy * to play "Good Joe." With the rise of rescue organizations which publicize the idea that alcoholism is a disease, alcoholics have been taught to play "Wooden Leg." The law, which takes a special interest in such people, tends to encourage this nowadays. The emphasis has shifted from the Persecutor to the Rescuer, from "I am a sinner" to "What do you expect from a sick man?" (part of the trend in modern thinking away from religion and toward science). From an existential point of view the shift is questionable, and from a practical point of view it seems to have done little to diminish the sale of liquor to heavy drinkers. Nevertheless, Alcoholics Anonymous is still for most people the best initiation into the therapy of over-indulgence.

Antithesis. As is well known, "Alcoholic" is usually played hard and is difficult to give up. In one case a female alcoholic in a therapy group participated very little until she thought she knew enough about the other members to go ahead with her game. She then asked them to tell her what they thought of her. Since she had behaved pleasantly enough, various members said nice things about her, but she protested: "That's not what I want. I want to know what you really think." She made it clear that she was seeking derogatory comments. The other women refused to persecute her, whereupon she went home and told her husband that if she took another drink, he must either divorce her or send her to a hospital. He promised to do this, and that evening she became intoxicated and he sent her to a sanitarium. Here the other members refused to play the persecutory roles White assigned to them; she was unable to tolerate this antithetical behavior, in spite of everyone's effort to reinforce whatever insight she had already obtained. At home she found someone who was willing to play the role she demanded.

* In the underworld slang "patsy" once meant all right, or satisfactory, and later came to denote a "pigeon."

In other cases, however, it appears possible to prepare the patient sufficiently so that the blame can be given up, and to attempt a social cure in which the therapist declines to play either Persecutor or Rescuer. It is equally untherapeutic for him to play the role of Patsy by allowing the patient to forgo his financial and punctuality obligations. The correct therapeutic procedure from a transactional point of view is, after careful preliminary groundwork, to take an Adult contractual position and refuse to play any of the roles, hoping that the patient will be able to tolerate not only abstinence from drinking but also from playing his game. If he cannot, he is best referred to a Rescuer.

Antithesis is particularly difficult, because the heavy drinker is highly regarded in most Western countries as a desirable object for censure, concern or generosity, and someone who refuses to play any of these roles tends to arouse public indignation. A rational approach may be even more alarming to the Rescuers than to the Alcoholic, sometimes with unfortunate consequences to the therapy. In one clinical situation a group of workers were seriously interested in the game "Alcoholic" and were attempting to effect real cures by breaking up the game rather than merely rescuing the patients. As soon as this became apparent, they were frozen out by the lay committee which was backing the clinic, and none of them was ever again called on to assist in treating these patients.

Relatives. An interesting byplay in "Alcoholic" is called "Have One." This was discovered by a perceptive student of industrial psychiatry. White and his wife (a non-drinking Persecutor) go on a picnic with Black and his wife (both Patsies). White says to the Blacks, "Have one!" If they have one, this gives White license to have four or five. The game is unmasked if the Blacks refuse. White, by the rules of drinking, is then entitled to be insulted, and he will find more compliant companions for his next picnic. What appears at the social level to be Adult generosity, is at the psychological level an act of insolence, whereby White's Child obtains Parental indulgence from Black by open bribery under the very nose of Mrs. White, who is powerless to protest. Actually it is just because she will be "powerless" to protest that Mrs. White consents to the whole arrangement, since she is just as anxious for the game to continue, with herself in the role of Persecutor, as Mr. White is with himself in the role of Alcoholic. Her recriminations against him in the morning after the picnic are easy to imagine. This variant can cause complications if White is Black's boss.

In general the Patsy is not as badly off as the name implies. Patsies are often lonely people who have a great deal to gain by being nice to Alcoholics. The delicatessen man who plays "Good Joe" makes many acquaintances in this way, and he can get a good reputation in his own social circle not only as a generous person but also as a good storyteller.

One variant of "Good Joe," incidentally, is to go around asking for advice about how best to help people. This is an example of a jolly and constructive game worth encouraging. Its inverse is Tough Guy, taking lessons in violence or asking for advice about how best to hurt people. Although the mayhem is never put into practice, the player has the privilege of associating with real tough guys who are playing for keeps, and can bask in their reflected glory. This is one species of what the French call *un fanfaron de vice*.

Debtor

Thesis. "Debtor" is more than a game. In America it tends to become a script, a plan for a whole lifetime, just as it does in some of the jungles of Africa and New Guinea. There the relatives of a young man buy him a bride at an enormous price, putting him in their debt for years to come. Here the same custom prevails, at least in the more civilized section of the country, except that the bride price becomes a house price, and if there is no stake from the relatives, this role is taken on by the bank.

Thus the young man in New Guinea with an old wristwatch dangling from his ear to ensure success, and the young man in America with a new wristwatch wrapped around his arm to ensure success, both feel that they have a "purpose" in life. The big celebration, the wedding or housewarming, takes place not when the debt is discharged, but when it is undertaken. What is emphasized on TV, for example, is not the middle-aged man who has finally paid off his mortgage, but the young man who moves into his new home with his family, proudly waving the papers he has just signed and which will bind him for most of his productive years. After he has paid his debts—the mortgage, the college expenses for his children and his insurance—he is regarded as a problem, a "senior citizen" for whom society must provide not only material comforts but a new "purpose." As in New Guinea, if he is very shrewd, he may become a big creditor instead of a big debtor, but this happens relatively rarely.

As this is written, a sow bug crawls across a desk. If he is turned over on his back, one can observe the tremendous struggle he goes through to get on his feet again. During this interval he has a "purpose" in his life. When he succeeds, one can almost see the look of victory on his face. Off he goes, and one can imagine him telling his tale at the next meeting of sow bugs, looked up to by the younger generation as an insect who has made it. And yet mixed with his smugness is a little disappointment. Now that he has come out on top, life seems aimless. Maybe he will return in the hope of repeating his triumph. It might be worth marking his back with ink, so as to recognize him if he risks it. A courageous animal, the sow bug. No wonder he has survived for millions of years.

Most young Americans, however, take their mortgages very seriously only in times of stress. If they are depressed, or the economic situation is bad, their obligations keep them going and may prevent some of them from committing suicide. Most of the time they play a mild game of "If It Weren't for the Debts," but otherwise enjoy themselves. Only a few make a career out of playing a hard game of "Debtor."

"Try and Collect" (TAC) is commonly played by young married couples, and illustrates how a game is set up so that the player "wins" whichever way it goes. The Whites obtain all sorts of goods and services on credit, petty or luxurious, depending on their backgrounds and how they were taught to play by their parents or grandparents. If the creditor gives up after a few soft efforts to collect, then the Whites can enjoy their gains without penalty, and in this sense they win. If the creditor makes more strenuous attempts, then they enjoy the pleasures of the chase as well as the use of their purchases. The hard form of the game occurs if the creditor is determined to collect. In order to get his money he will have to resort to extreme measures. These usually have a coercive element—going to White's employers or driving up to his house in a noisy garish truck labeled in big letters COLLECTION AGENCY.

At this point there is a switch. White now knows that he will probably have to pay. But because of the coercive element, made clear in most cases by the "third letter" from the collector ("If you do not appear at our office within 48 hours. . . ."), White feels peremptorily justified in getting angry; he now switches over to a variant of "Now I've Got You, You Son of a Bitch." In this case he wins by demonstrating that the creditor is greedy, ruthless and untrustworthy. The two most obvious advantages of this are (1) it strengthens White's existential position, which is a disguised form of "All creditors are grasping," and (2) it offers a large external social gain, since he is now in a position to abuse the creditor openly to his friends without losing his own status as a "Good Joe." He may also exploit further internal social gain by confronting the creditor himself. In addition, it vindicates his taking advantage of the credit system: if that is the way creditors are, as he has now shown, why pay anybody?

"Creditor," in the form "Try and Get Away With It" (TAGAWI), is sometimes played by small landlords. TAC and TAGAWI players readily recognize each other, and because of the prospective transactional advantages and the promised sport, they are secretly pleased and readily become involved with each other. Regardless of who wins the money, each has improved the other's position for playing "Why Does This Always Happen To Me?" after it is all over.

Money games can have very serious consequences. If these descriptions sound facetious, as they do to some people, it is not because they relate to trivia but because of the exposure of trivial motivations behind matters people are taught to take seriously.

Antithesis. The obvious antithesis of TAC is to request immediate payment in cash. But a good TAC player has methods for getting around that, which will work on any but the most hardboiled creditors. The antithesis of TAGAWI is promptness and honesty. Since hard TAC and TAGAWI players are both professionals in every sense of the word, an amateur stands as much chance playing against them as he does playing against professional gamblers. While the amateur seldom wins, he can at least enjoy himself if he becomes involved in one of these games. Since both are by tradition played grimly, nothing is more disconcerting to the professionals than to have an amateur victim laugh at the outcome. In financial circles this is considered strictly Out. In the cases reported to this writer, laughing at a debtor or when one encounters him on the street is just as bewildering, frustrating and disconcerting to him as playing anti-"Schlemiel" is to a Schlemiel.

Kick Me

Thesis. This is played by men whose social manner is equivalent to wearing a sign that reads "Please Don't Kick Me." The temptation is almost irresistible, and when the natural result follows, White cries piteously, "But the sign says '*don't* kick me.' " Then he adds incredulously, "Why does this always happen to me?" (WAHM.) Clinically, the WAHM may be introjected and disguised in the "Psychiatry" cliché: "Whenever I'm under stress, I get all shook up." Our game element in WAHM comes from inverse pride: "My misfortunes are better than yours." This factor is often found in paranoids.

If the people in his environment are restrained from striking at him by kindheartedness, "I'm Only Trying to Help You," social convention or organizational rules, his behavior becomes more and more provocative until he transgresses the limits and forces them to oblige.

These are men who are cast out, the jilted and the job losers.

The corresponding game among women is "Threadbare." Often genteel, they take pains to be shabby. They see to it that their earnings, for "good" reasons, never rise much above the subsistence level. If they have a windfall, there are always enterprising young men who will help them get rid of it, giving them in return shares in a worthless business promotion or something equivalent. Colloquially, such a woman is called "Mother's Friend," always ready to give judicious Parental advice and living vicariously on the experience of others. Their WAHM is a silent one, and only their demeanor of brave struggle suggests "Why does this always happen to me?"

An interesting form of WAHM occurs in well-adapted people who reap increasing rewards and successes, often beyond their own expectations. Here the WAHM may lead to serious and constructive thinking, and to personal growth in the best sense, if it takes the form "What did I really do to deserve this?"

Now I've Got You, You Son of a Bitch

Thesis. This can be seen in classic form in poker games. White gets an unbeatable hand, such as four aces. At this point, if he is a NIGYSOB player, he is more interested in the fact that Black is completely at his mercy than he is in good poker or making money.

White needed some plumbing fixtures installed, and he reviewed the costs very carefully with the plumber before giving him a go-ahead. The price was set, and it was agreed that there would be no extras. When the plumber submitted his bill, he included a few dollars extra for an unexpected valve that had to be installed—about four dollars on a four-hundred-dollar job. White became infuriated, called the plumber on the phone and demanded an explanation. The plumber would not back down. White wrote him a long letter criticizing his integrity and ethics and refused to pay the bill until the extra charge was withdrawn. The plumber finally gave in.

It soon became obvious that both White and the

plumber were playing games. In the course of their negotiations, they had recognized each other's potentials. The plumber made his provocative move when he submitted his bill. Since White had the plumber's word, the plumber was clearly in the wrong. White now felt justified in venting almost unlimited rage against him. Instead of merely negotiating in a dignified way that befit the Adult standards he set for himself, perhaps with a little innocent annoyance, White took the opportunity to make extensive criticisms of the plumber's whole way of living. On the surface their argument was Adult to Adult, a legitimate business dispute over a stated sum of money. At the psychological level it was Parent to Adult: White was exploiting his trivial but socially defensible objection (position) to vent the pent-up furies of many years on his cozening opponent, just as his mother might have done in a similar situation. He quickly recognized his underlying attitude (NIGYSOB) and realized how secretly delighted he had been at the plumber's provocation. He then recalled that ever since early childhood he had looked for similar injustices, received them with delight and exploited them with the same vigor. In many of the cases he recounted, he had forgotten the actual provocation, but remembered in great detail the course of the ensuing battle. The plumber, apparently, was playing some variation of "Why Does This Always Happen to Me?" (WAHM).

NIGYSOB is a two-handed game which must be distinguished from "Ain't It Awful!" (AIA). In AIA the agent seeks injustices in order to complain about them to a third party, making a three-handed game: Aggressor, Victim, Confidant. AIA is played under the slogan "Misery Loves Company." The confidant is usually someone who also plays AIA. WAHM is three-handed, too, but here the agent is trying to establish his pre-eminence in misfortune and resents competition from other unfortunates. NIGYSOB is commercialized in a three-handed professional form as the "badger game." It may also be played as a two-handed marital game in more or less subtle forms.

Antithesis. The best antithesis is correct behavior.

The contractual structure of a relationship with a NIGYSOB player should be explicitly stated in detail at the first opportunity, and the rules strictly adhered to. In clinical practice, for example, the question of payment for missed appointments or cancellations must be settled clearly at once, and extra precautions must be taken to avoid mistakes in bookkeeping. If an unforeseen contretemps arises, the antithesis is to yield gracefully without dispute, until such time as the therapist is prepared to deal with the game. In everyday life, business dealings with NIGYSOB players are always calculated risks. The wife of such a person should be treated with polite correctness, and even the mildest flirtations, gallantries or slights should be avoided, especially if the husband himself seems to encourage them.

See What You Made Me Do

Thesis. In its classical form this is a marital game, and in fact is a "three-star marriage buster," but it may also be played between parents and children and in working life.

(1) First-Degree SWYMD: White, feeling unsociable, becomes engrossed in some activity which tends to insulate him against people. Perhaps all he wants at the moment is to be left alone. An intruder, such as his wife or one of his children, comes either for stroking or to ask him something like, "Where can I find the long-nosed pliers?" This interruption "causes" his chisel, paintbrush, typewriter or soldering iron to slip, whereupon he turns on the intruder in a rage and cries, "See what you made me do." As this is repeated through the years, his family tends more and more to leave him alone when he is engrossed. Of course it is not the intruder but his own irritation which "causes" the slip, and he is only too happy when it occurs, since it gives him a lever for ejecting the visitor. Unfortunately this is a game which is only too easily learned by young children, so that it is easily passed on from generation to generation. The underlying satisfaction and advantages are more clearly demonstrated when it is played more seductively.

(2) Second-Degree SWYMD: if SWYMD is the basis for a way of life, rather than merely being used occasionally as a protective mechanism, White marries a woman who plays "I'm Only Trying to Help You" or one of its relatives. It is then easy for him to defer decisions to her. Often this may be done in the guise of considerateness or gallantry. He may deferentially and courteously let her decide where to go for dinner or which movie to see. If things turn out well, he can enjoy them. If not, he can blame her by saying or implying: "You Got Me Into This," a simple variation of SWYMD. Or he may throw the burden of decisions regarding the children's upbringing on her, while he acts as executive officer; if the children get upset he can play a straight game of SWYMD. This lays the groundwork through the years for blaming mother if the children turn out badly; then SWYMD is not an end in itself, but merely offers passing satisfaction on the way to "I Told You So" or "See What You've Done Now."

The professional player who pays his psychological way with SWYMD will use it also in his work. In occupational SWYMD the long-suffering look of resentment replaces words. The player "democratically" or as part of "good management" asks his assistants for suggestions. In this way he may attain an unassailable position for terrorizing his juniors. Any mistake he makes can be used against them by blaming them for it. Used against seniors (blaming them for one's mistakes), it becomes self-destructive and may lead to termination of employment or, in the army, to transfer to another unit. In that case it is a component of "Why Does This Always Happen to Me?" with resentful people, or of "There I Go Again" with depressives— (both of the "Kick Me" family).

(3) Third-Degree SWYMD: in a hard form SWYMD may be played by paranoids against people incautious enough to give them advice (see "I'm Only Trying to Help You"). There it may be dangerous, and in rare cases even fatal.

"See What You Made Me Do" (SWYMD) and "You Got Me Into This" (UGMIT) complement each other nicely, so that the SWYMD-UGMIT combination is a classical basis for the covert game contract in many marriages. This contract is illustrated by the following sequence.

By mutual agreement Mrs. White did the family bookkeeping and paid the bills out of the joint checking account because Mr. White was "poor at figures." Every few months they would be notified of an overdraft, and Mr. White would have to square it with the bank. When they looked for the source of the difficulty, it would turn out that Mrs. White had made an expensive purchase without telling her husband. When this came to light, Mr. White would furiously play his UGMIT, and she would tearfully accept his rebuke and promise it would not happen again. Everything would go smoothly for a while, and then a creditor's agent would suddenly appear to demand payment for a long-overdue bill. Mr. White, not having heard of this bill, would question his wife about it. She would then play her SWYMD, saying that it was his fault. Since he had forbidden her to overdraw their account, the only way she could make ends meet was by leaving this large obligation unpaid and hiding the duns from him.

These games had been allowed to go on for ten years, on the basis that each occurrence would be the last, and that from then on it would be different—which it was, for a few months. In therapy Mr. White very cleverly analyzed this game without any assistance from the therapist, and also devised an effective remedy. By mutual agreement he and Mrs. White put all charge accounts and their bank account in his name. Mrs. White continued to do the bookkeeping and make out the checks, but Mr. White saw the bills first and controlled the outgoing payments. In this way neither duns nor overdrafts could get by him, and they now shared the budgetary labor. Deprived of the satisfactions and advantages of SWYMD-UGMIT, the Whites were at first at a loss, and were then driven to find more open and constructive types of gratification from each other.

Antithesis. The antithesis to First-Degree SWYMD is to leave the player alone, and to Second-Degree

SWYMD to throw the decision back on White. The First-Degree player may react by feeling forlorn, but seldom angry; the Second-Degree player may become sulky if he is forced to take the initiative, so that systematic anti-SWYMD leads to disagreeable consequences. The antithesis to Third-Degree SWYMD should be put into competent professional hands.

COURTROOM: A MARITAL GAME

Thesis. Descriptively this belongs to the class of games which find their most florid expressions in law, and which includes "Wooden Leg" (the plea of insanity) and "Debtor" (the civil suit). *Clinically* it is most often seen in marital counseling and marital psychotherapy groups. Indeed, some marital counseling and marital groups consist of a perpetual game of "Courtroom" in which nothing is resolved, since the game is never broken up. In such cases it becomes evident that the counselor or therapist is heavily involved in the game without being aware of it.

"Courtroom" can be played by any number, but is essentially three-handed, with a plaintiff, a defendant and a judge represented by a husband, a wife and the therapist. If it is played in a therapy group or over the radio or TV, the other members of the audience are cast as the jury. The husband begins plaintively, "Let me tell you what (wife's name) did yesterday. She took the . . ." etc., etc. The wife then responds defensively, "Here is the way it really was . . . and besides just before that he was . . . and anyway at the time we were both . . ." etc. The husband adds gallantly, "Well, I'm glad you people have a chance to hear both sides of the story, I only want to be fair." At this point the counselor says judiciously, "It seems to me that if we consider . . ." etc., etc. If there is an audience, the therapist may throw it to them with: "Well, let's hear what the others have to say." Or, if the group is already trained, they will play the jury without any instruction from him.

Antithesis. The therapist says to the husband, "You're absolutely right!" If the husband relaxes complacently or triumphantly, the therapist asks: "How do you feel about my saying that?" The husband replies: "Fine." Then the therapist says, "Actually, I feel you're in the wrong." If the husband is honest, he will say: "I knew that all along." If he is not honest, he will show some reaction that makes it clear a game is in progress. Then it becomes possible to go into the matter further. The game element lies in the fact that while the plaintiff is overtly clamoring for victory, fundamentally he believes that he is wrong.

After sufficient clinical material has been gathered to clarify the situation, the game can be interdicted by a maneuver which is one of the most elegant in the whole art of antithetics. The therapist makes a rule prohibiting the use of the (grammatical) third person in the group. Thenceforward the members can only address each other directly as "you" or talk about themselves as "I," but they cannot say, "Let me tell you about him" or "Let me tell you about her." At this point the couple stop playing games in the group altogether, or shift into "Sweetheart," which is some improvement, or take up "Furthermore," which is no help at all. "Sweetheart" is described in another section. In "Furthermore" the plaintiff makes one accusation after the other. The plaintiff pays no attention to the explanation, but as soon as the defendant pauses, he launches into his next indictment with another "furthermore," which is followed by another explanation—a typical Parent-Child interchange.

"Furthermore" is played most intensively by paranoid defendants. Because of their literalness, it is particularly easy for them to frustrate accusers who express themselves in humorous or metaphorical terms. In general, metaphors are the most obvious traps to avoid in a game of "Furthermore."

In its *everyday* form, "Courtroom" is easily observed in children as a three-handed game between two siblings and a parent. "Mommy, she took my candy away." "Yes, but he took my doll, and before that he was hitting me, and anyway we both promised to share our candy."

PARTY GAMES

Blemish

Thesis. This game is the source of a large percentage
of petty dissension in everyday life; it is played from
the depressive Child position "I am no good," which
is protectively transformed into the Parental position
"They are no good." The player's transactional problem is, then, to prove the latter thesis. Hence "Blemish" players do not feel comfortable with a new person
until they have found his blemish. In its hardest form
it may become a totalitarian political game played by
"authoritarian" personalities, and then it may have
serious historical repercussions. Here its close relationship with "Nowadays" is evident. In suburban society
positive reassurance is obtained from playing "How'm
I Doing?" while "Blemish" provides negative reassurance. A partial analysis will make some of the elements
of this game clearer.

The premise may range from the most trivial and
extraneous ("Last year's hat"), to the most cynical
("Hasn't got $7,000 in the bank"), sinister ("Not
100% Aryan"), esoteric ("Hasn't read Rilke"), intimate ("Can't hold his erection") or sophisticated
("What's he trying to prove?"). Psychodynamically it
is usually based on sexual insecurity, and its aim is
reassurance. Transactionally there is prying, morbid
curiosity or watchfulness, sometimes with Parental or
Adult concern charitably masking the Child's relish. It
has the internal psychological advantage of warding
off depression, and the external psychological advantage
of avoiding the intimacy which might expose White's
own blemishes. White feels justified in turning away
an unfashionable woman, a man without financial backing, a non-Aryan, an illiterate, an impotent man or an
insecure personality. At the same time the prying offers
some internal social action with biological gain. The
external social advantage is of the "Ain't It Awful"
family—Neighborly Type.

An interesting sidelight is that White's choice of
premise is independent of his intellectual capacity or

apparent sophistication. Thus a man who had held some responsible positions in the foreign service of his country told an audience that another country was inferior because, among other things, the men wore jackets with sleeves that were too long. In his Adult ego state this man was quite competent. Only when playing a Parental game like "Blemish" would he mentions such irrelevancies.

Schlemiel

Thesis. The term "schlemiel" does not refer to the hero of Chamisso's novel, who was a man without a shadow, but to a popular Yiddish word allied to the German and Dutch words for cunning. The Schlemiel's victim, who is something like the "Good-Natured Fellow" of Paul de Kock, is colloquially called the Schlemazl. The moves in a typical game of "Schlemiel" are as follows:

1W. White spills a highball on the hostess's evening gown.

1B. Black (the host) responds initially with rage, but he senses (often only vaguely) that if he shows it, White wins. Black therefore pulls himself together, and this gives him the illusion that he wins.

2W. White says: "I'm sorry."

2B. Black mutters or cries forgiveness, strengthening his illusion that he wins.

3W. White then proceeds to inflict other damage on Black's property. He breaks things, spills things and makes messes of various kinds. After the cigarette burn in the tablecloth, the chair leg through the lace curtain and the gravy on the rug, White's Child is exhilarated because he has enjoyed himself in carrying out these procedures, for all of which he has been forgiven, while Black has made a gratifying display of suffering self-control. Thus both of them profit from an unfortunate situation, and Black is not necessarily anxious to terminate the friendship.

As in most games, White, who makes the first move, wins either way. If Black shows his anger, White can feel justified in returning the resentment. If Black restrains himself, White can go on enjoying his oppor-

tunities. The real payoff in this game, however, is not
the pleasure of destructiveness, which is merely an
added bonus for White, but the fact that he obtains forgiveness. This leads directly into the antithesis.

Antithesis. Anti-"Schlemiel" is played by not offering
the demanded absolution. After White says, "I'm
sorry," Black, instead of muttering, "It's okay," says,
"Tonight you can embarrass my wife, ruin the furniture
and wreck the rug, but please don't say 'I'm sorry.'"
Here Black switches from being a forgiving Parent to
being an objective Adult who takes the full repsonsi-
bility for having invited White in the first place.

The intensity of White's game will be revealed by his
reaction, which may be quite explosive. One who plays
anti-"Schlemiel" runs the risk of immediate reprisals
or, at any rate, of making an enemy.

Children play "Schlemiel" in an abortive form in
which they are not always sure of forgiveness but at
least have the pleasure of making messes; as they learn
to comport themselves socially, however, they may
take advantage of their increasing sophistication to
obtain the forgiveness which is the chief goal of the
game as played in polite, grown-up social circles.

SEXUAL GAMES

Some games are played to exploit or fight off sexual
impulses. These are all, in effect, perversions of the
sexual instincts in which the satisfaction is displaced
from the sexual act to the crucial transactions which
constitute the payoff of the game. This cannot always
be demonstrated convincingly, because such games are
usually played in privacy, so that clinical information
about them has to be obtained secondhand, and the
informant's bias cannot always be satisfactorily evaluated.

Let's You and Him Fight

Thesis. This may be a maneuver, a ritual or a game.
In each case the psychology is essentially feminine. Because of its dramatic qualities, LYAHF is the basis of
the world's literature, both good and bad.

1. As a maneuver it is romantic. The woman maneuvers or challenges two men into fighting, with the implication or promise that she will surrender herself to the winner. After the competition is decided, she fulfills her bargain. This is an honest transaction, and the presumption is that she and her mate live happily ever after.

2. As a ritual, it tends to be tragic. Custom demands that the two men fight for her, even if she does not want them to, and even if she has already made her choice. If the wrong man wins, she must nevertheless take him. In this case it is society and not the woman who sets up LYAHF. If she is willing, the transaction is an honest one. If she is unwilling or disappointed, the outcome may offer her considerable scope for playing games, such as "Let's Pull A Fast One on Joey."

3. As a game it is comic. The woman sets up the competition, and while the two men are fighting, she decamps with a third. The internal and external psychological advantages for her and her mate are derived from the position that honest competition is for suckers, and the comic story they have lived through forms the basis for the internal and external social advantages.

Rapo

Thesis. This is a game played between a man and a woman which might more politely be called, in the milder forms at least, "Kiss Off" or "Indignation." It may be played with varying degrees of intensity.

1. First-Degree "Rapo," or "Kiss Off," is popular at social gatherings and consists essentially of mild flirtation. White signals that she is available and gets her pleasure from the man's pursuit. As soon as he has committed himself, the game is over. If she is polite, she may say quite frankly, "I appreciate your compliments and thank you very much," and move on to the next conquest. If she is less generous, she may simply leave him. A skillful player can make this game last for a long time at a large social gathering by moving around frequently, so that the man has to carry out complicated maneuvers in order to follow her without being too obvious.

2. In Second-Degree "Rapo," or "Indignation,"
White gets only secondary satisfaction from Black's
advances. Her primary gratification comes from rejecting him, so that this game is also colloquially known
as "Buzz Off, Buster." She leads Black into a much
more serious commitment than the mild flirtation of
First-Degree "Rapo" and enjoys watching his discomfiture when she repulses him. Black, of course, is not
as helpless as he seems, and may have gone to considerable trouble to get himself involved. Usually he is
playing some variation of "Kick Me."

3. Third-Degree "Rapo" is a vicious game which
ends in murder, suicide or the courtroom. Here White
leads Black into compromising physical contact and
then claims that he has made a criminal assault or has
done her irreparable damage. In its most cynical form
White may actually allow him to complete the sexual
act so that she gets that enjoyment before confronting
him. The confrontation may be immediate, as in the
illegitimate cry of rape, or it may be long delayed, as
in suicide or homicide following a prolonged love
affair. If she chooses to play it as a criminal assault,
she may have no difficulty in finding mercenary or
morbidly interested allies, such as the press, the police,
counselors and relatives. Sometimes, however, these
outsiders may cynically turn on her, so that she loses
the initiative and becomes a tool in their games.

In some cases outsiders perform a different function.
They force the game on an unwilling White because
they want to play "Let's You and Him Fight." They
put her in such a position that in order to save her face
or her reputation she has to cry rape. This is particularly apt to happen with girls under the legal age of
consent; they may be quite willing to continue a liaison,
but because it is discovered or made an issue of, they
feel constrained to turn the romance into a game of
Third-Degree "Rapo."

In one well-known situation, the wary Joseph refused
to be inveigled into a game of "Rapo," whereupon
Potiphar's wife made the classical switch into "Let's
You and Him Fight," an excellent example of the way

a hard player reacts to antithesis, and of the dangers that beset people who refuse to play games. These two games are combined in the well-known "Badger Game," in which the woman seduces Black and then cries rape, at which point her husband takes charge and abuses Black for purposes of blackmail.

One of the most unfortunate and acute forms of Third-Degree "Rapo" occurs relatively frequently between homosexual strangers, who in a matter of an hour or so may bring the game to the point of homicide. The cynical and criminal variations of this game contribute a large volume to sensational newspaper copy.

The childhood prototype of "Rapo" is the same as that of "Frigid Woman," in which the little girl induces the boy to humiliate himself or get dirty and then sneers at him, as classically described by Maugham in *Of Human Bondage* and by Dickens in *Great Expectations*. This is Second Degree. A harder form, approaching Third Degree, may be played in tough neighborhoods.

Antithesis. The man's ability to avoid becoming involved in this game or to keep it under control depends on his capacity to distinguish genuine expressions of feeling from moves in the game. If he is thus able to exert social control, he may obtain a great deal of pleasure from the mild flirtations of "Kiss Off." On the other hand it is difficult to conceive of a safe antithesis for the Potiphar's Wife maneuver, other than checking out before closing time with no forwarding address. In 1938 the writer met an aging Joseph in Aleppo who had checked out of Constantinople thirty-two years previously, after one of the Sultan's ladies had cornered him during a business visit to the Yildiz harem. He had to abandon his shop, but took time to pick up his hoard of gold francs, and had never returned.

Relatives. The male versions of "Rapo" are notoriously found in commercial situations: "Casting Couch" (and then she didn't get the part) and "Cuddle Up" (and then she got fired).

UNDERWORLD GAMES

With the infiltration of the "helping" professions into the courts, probation departments and correctional facilities, and with the increasing sophistication of criminologists and law enforcement officers, those concerned should be aware of the more common games prevalent in the underworld, both in prison and out of it. Included here is "Cops and Robbers."

Cops and Robbers

Thesis. Because many criminals are cop-haters, they seem to get as much satisfaction from outwitting the police as from their criminal gains, often more. Their crimes, at the Adult level, are games played for the material rewards, the take; but at the Child level it is the thrill of the chase: the getaway and the cool-off.

Curiously enough, the childhood prototype of "Cops and Robbers" is not cops and robbers but hide-and-seek, in which the essential element is the chagrin of being found. Younger children readily betray this. If father finds them too easily, the chagrin is there without too much fun. But father, if he is a good player, knows what to do: he holds off, whereupon the little boy gives him a clue by calling out, dropping something or banging. Thus he forces father to find him, but still shows chagrin; this time he has had more fun because of the increased suspense. If father gives up, the boy usually feels disappointed rather than victorious. Since the fun of being hidden was there, evidently that is not where the trouble lies. What he is disappointed about is not being caught. When his turn comes to hide, father knows he is not supposed to outwit the little boy for very long, just long enough to make it fun; and he is wise enough to look chagrined when he is caught. It soon becomes clear that being found is the necessary payoff.

Hence hide-and-seek is not a mere pastime but a true game. At the social level it is a battle of wits, and is most satisfying when the Adult of each player does his best; at the psychological level, however, it is set up like compulsive gambling, in which White's Adult has to lose in order for his Child to win. Not being caught is actually the antithesis. Among older children, one who finds an insoluble hiding place is regarded as not being a good sport, since he has spoiled the game. He has eliminated the Child element and turned the whole thing into an Adult procedure. He is no longer playing for fun. He is in the same class as the owner of a casino, or some professional criminals, who are really out for money rather than sport.

There seem to be two distinctive types of habitual criminals: those who are in crime primarily for profit, and those who are in it primarily for the game—with a large group in between who can handle it either way. The "compulsive winner," the big money-maker whose Child really does not want to be caught, rarely is, according to reports; he is untouchable, for whom the fix is always in. The "compulsive loser," on the other hand, who is playing "Cops and Robbers" (C&R), seldom does very well financially. The exceptions to this often seem to be due to luck rather than skill; in the long run even the lucky ones usually end up as their Child requires, squawking rather than riding high.

The C&R player, with whom we are concerned here, in some ways resembles the Alcoholic. He can shift roles from Robber to Cop and from Cop to Robber. In some cases he may play the Parental Cop during the day and the Child Robber after dark. There is a Cop in many Robbers, and a Robber in many Cops. If the criminal "reforms," he may play the role of Rescuer, becoming a social worker or a mission worker; but the Rescuer is far less important in this game than in "Alcoholic." Ordinarily, however, the player's role as Robber is his destiny, and each has his own *modus operandi* for getting caught. He may make it tough or easy for the Cops.

The situation is similar with gamblers. At the social or sociological level a "professional" gambler is one whose chief interest in life is gambling. But at the psychological level there are two different kinds of people who are professional gamblers. There are those who spend their time gaming, i.e., playing with Fate, in whom the strength of the Adult's desire to win is exceeded only by the strength of the Child's need to lose. Then there are those who run gambling houses and actually do earn a living, usually a very good one, by providing opportunities for gamesters to play; they themselves are not playing, and try to avoid playing, although occasionally under certain conditions they will indulge themselves and enjoy it, just as a straight criminal may occasionally play a game of C&R.

This throws light on why sociological and psychological studies of criminals have been generally ambiguous and unproductive: they are dealing with two different kinds of people who cannot be adequately differentiated in the ordinary theoretical or empirical frameworks. The same is true in studying gamblers. Transactional and game analyses offer an immediate solution for this. They remove the ambiguity by distinguishing transactionally, below the social level, between "players" and "straight professionals."

Let us now turn from this general thesis to consider specific examples. Some burglars do their jobs without any waste motion. The "Cops and Robbers" burglar leaves his calling card in gratuitous acts of vandalism, such as spoiling valuable clothing with secretions and excretions. The straight bank robber, according to reports, takes every possible precaution to avoid violence; the C&R bank robber is only looking for an excuse to vent his anger. Like any professional, a straight criminal likes his job to be as clean as circumstances permit. The C&R criminal is compelled to blow off steam in the course of his work. The true professional is said never to operate until the fix is in; the player is willing to take on the law barehanded. Straight professionals are well aware, in their own way, of the game of C&R. If a gang member shows too much interest in the game, to the point of jeopardizing the job, and particularly if his need to be caught begins to show, they will take drastic measures to prevent a recurrence. Perhaps it is just because professionals are not playing C&R that they are so seldom caught, and hence so rarely studied sociologically, psychologically and psychiatrically; and this also applies to gamblers. Hence most of our clinical knowledge about criminals and gamblers refers to players rather than to straight professionals.

Kleptomaniacs (as opposed to professional shop-lifters) are examples of how widely trivial C&R is played. It is probable that a very large percentage of Occidentals, at least, have played C&R in fantasy, and that is what sells newspapers in our half of the world. This fantasy frequently occurs in the form of dreaming up the "perfect murder," which is playing the hardest possible game and completely outwitting the cops.

Variations of C&R are "Auditors and Robbers," played by embezzlers with the same rules and the same payoff; "Customs and Robbers," played by smugglers; etc. Of special interest is the criminal variation of "Courtroom." Despite all his precautions, the professional may occasionally be arrested and brought to trial. For him "Courtroom" is a procedure, which he carries out according to the instructions of his legal advisers. For the lawyers, if they are compulsive winners, "Courtroom" is essentially a game played with the jury in which the object is to win, not lose, and this is regarded as a constructive game by a large segment of society.

Antithesis. This is the concern of qualified criminologists rather than psychiatrists. The police and judiciary apparatus are not antithetical, but are playing their roles in the game under the rules set up by society.

One thing should be emphasized, however. Research workers in criminology may joke that some criminals behave as though they enjoyed the chase and wanted to be caught, or they may read the idea and agree in a deferential way. But they show little tendency to consider such an "academic" factor as decisive in their "serious" work. For one thing, there is no way to unmask this element through the standard methods of psychological research. The investigator must therefore either overlook a crucial point because he cannot work it with his research tools, or else change his tools. The fact is that those tools have so far not yielded one single solution to any problem in criminology. Researchers might therefore be better off discarding the old methods and tackling the problem freshly. Until

C&R is accepted not merely as an interesting anomaly, but as the very heart of the matter in a significant percentage of cases, much research in criminology will continue to deal with trivialities, doctrines, peripheral issues or irrelevancies.

CONSULTING ROOM GAMES

Games that are tenaciously played in the therapeutic situation are the most important ones for the professional game analyst to be aware of. They can be most readily studied firsthand in the consulting room. —C.S.

I'm Only Trying to Help You

Thesis. This game may be played in any professional situation and is not confined to psychotherapists and welfare workers. However, it is found most commonly and in its most florid form among social workers with a certain type of training. The analysis of this game was clarified for the writer under curious circumstances. All the players at a poker game had folded except two, a research psychologist and a businessman. The businessman, who had a high hand, bet; the psychologist, who had an unbeatable one, raised. The businessman looked puzzled, whereupon the psychologist remarked facetiously: "Don't be upset, I'm only trying to help you!" The businessman hesitated, and finally put in his chips. The psychologist showed the winning hand, whereupon the other threw down his cards in disgust. The others present then felt free to laugh at the psychologist's joke, and the loser remarked ruefully: "You sure were helpful!" The psychologist cast a knowing glance at the writer, implying that the joke had really been made at the expense of the psychiatric profession. It was at that moment that the structure of this game became clear.

The worker or therapist, of whatever profession, gives some advice to a client or patient. The patient returns and reports that the suggestion did not have the desired effect. The worker shrugs off this failure with a feeling of resignation, and tries again. If he is more watchful, he may detect at this point a twinge of frustration, but he will try again anyway. Usually he feels little need to question his own motives, because he knows that many of his similarly trained colleagues do the same thing, and that he is following the "correct" procedure and will receive full support from his supervisors.

If he runs up against a hard player, such as a hostile obsessional, he will find it more and more difficult to avoid feeling inadequate. Then he is in trouble, and the situation will slowly deteriorate. In the worst case, he may come up against an angry paranoid who will rush in one day in a rage, crying: "Look what you made me do!" Then his frustration will come strongly to the fore in the spoken or unspoken thought: "But I was only trying to help you!" His bewilderment at the ingratitude may cause him considerable suffering, indicating the complex motives underlying his own behavior. This bewilderment is the payoff.

Legitimate helpers should not be confused with people who play "I'm Only Trying to Help You (ITHY). "I think we can do something about it," "I know what to do," "I was assigned to help you" or "My fee for helping you will be . . ." are different from "I'm only trying to help you." The first four, in good faith, represent Adult offers to put professional qualifications at the disposal of the distressed patient or client; ITHY has an ulterior motive which is more important than professional skill in determining the outcome. The motive is based on the position that people are ungrateful and disappointing. The prospect of success is alarming to the Parent of the professional and is an invitation to sabotage, because success would threaten the position. The ITHY player needs to be reassured that help will not be accepted no matter how strenuously it is offered. The client responds with "Look How Hard I'm Trying" or "There's Nothing You Can Do to Help Me." More flexible players can compromise: it is all right for people to accept help providing it takes them a long time to do so. Hence therapists tend to feel apologetic for a quick result, since they know that some of their colleagues at staff meetings will be critical. At the opposite pole from hard ITHY players, such as are found among social workers, are good lawyers who help their clients without personal involvement or sentimentality. Here craftsmanship takes the place of covert strenuousness.

Some schools of social work seem to be primarily academies for the training of professional ITHY players, and it is not easy for their graduates to desist from playing it. An example which may help to illustrate some of the foregoing points will be found in the description of the complementary game "Indigence."

ITHY and its variants are easy to find in everyday life. It is played by family friends and relatives (e.g., "I Can Get It For You Wholesale"), and by adults who do community work with children. It is a favorite among parents, and the complementary game played by the offspring is usually "Look What You Made Me Do." Socially it may be a variant of "Schlemiel" in which the damage is done while being helpful rather than impulsively; here the cilent is represented by a victim who may be playing "Why Does This Always Happen to Me?" or one of its variants.

Antithesis. There are several devices available for the professional to handle an invitation to play this game, and his selection will depend on the state of the relationship between himself and the patient, particularly on the attitude of the patient's Child.

1. The classical psychoanalytic antithesis is the most thoroughgoing and the most difficult for the patient to tolerate. The invitation is completely ignored. The patient then tries harder and harder. Eventually he falls into a state of despair, manifested by anger or depression, which is the characteristic sign that a game has been frustrated. This situation may lead to a useful confrontation.

2. A more gentle (but not prim) confrontation may be attempted on the first invitation. The therapist states that he is the patient's therapist and not his manager.

3. An even more gentle procedure is to introduce the patient into a therapy group, and let the other patients handle it.

4. With an acutely disturbed patient it may be neces-

sary to play along during the initial phase. These patients should be treated by a psychiatrist who, being a medical man, can prescribe both medications and some of the hygienic measures which are still valuable, even in this day of tranquilizers, in the treatment of such people. If the physician prescribes a hygienic regimen, which may include baths, exercise, rest periods, and regular meals along with medication, the patient (1) carries out the regimen and feels better, (2) carries out the regimen scrupulously and complains that it does not help, (3) mentions casually that he forgot to carry out the instructions or that he has abandoned the regimen because it was not doing any good. In the second and third case it is then up to the psychiatrist to decide whether the patient is amenable to game analysis at that point, or whether some other form of treatment is indicated to prepare him for later psychotherapy. The relationship between the adequacy of the regimen and the patient's tendency to play games with it should be carefully evaluated by the psychiatrist before he decides how to proceed next.

For the patient, on the other hand, the antithesis is, "Don't tell me what to do to help myself, I'll tell you what to do to help me." If the therapist is known to be a Schlemiel, the correct antithesis for the patient to use is, "Don't help me, help him." But serious players of "I'm Only Trying to Help You" are generally lacking in a sense of humor. Antithetical moves on the part of a patient are usually unfavorably received, and may result in the therapist's lifelong enmity. In everyday life such moves should not be initiated unless one is prepared to carry them through ruthlessly and take the consequences. For example, spurning a relative who "Can Get It For You Wholesale" may cause serious domestic complications.

Peasant

Thesis. The prototype peasant is the arthritic Bulgarian villager who sells her only cow to raise money to go to the university clinic in Sofia. There the professor examines her and finds her case so interesting that he presents her in a clinical demonstration to the medical students. He outlines not only the pathology, symptoms and diagnosis, but also the treatment. This procedure fills her with awe. Before she leaves, the professor gives her a prescription and explains the treatment in more detail. She is overcome with admiration for his learning and says the Bulgarian equivalent of "Gee, you're wonderful, Professor!" However, she never has the prescription filled. First, there is no apothecary in her village; second, even if there were, she would never let such a valuable piece of paper out of her hands. Nor does she have the facilities for carrying out the rest of the treatment, such as diet, hydrotherapy and so on. She lives on, crippled as before, but happy now because she can tell everyone about the wonderful treatment prescribed for her by the great professor in Sofia, to whom she expresses her gratitude every night in her prayers.

Years later, the Professor, in an unhappy frame of mind, happens to pass through the village on his way to see a wealthy but demanding patient. He remembers the peasant when she rushes out to kiss his hand and remind him of the marvelous regimen he put her on so long ago. He accepts her homage graciously, and is particularly gratified when she tells him how much good the treatment has done. In fact he is so carried away that he fails to notice that she limps as badly as ever.

Socially "Peasant" is played in an innocent and a dissembled form, both with the motto, "Gee, you're wonderful, Mr. Murgatroyd!" (GYWM). In the innocent form, Murgatroyd *is* wonderful. He is a celebrated poet, painter, philanthropist or scientist, and naive young women frequently travel a long way in the hope of meeting him so that they can sit adoringly at his feet and romanticize his imperfections. A more sophisticated woman who sets out deliberately to have an affair or a marriage with such a man, whom she sincerely admires and appreciates, may be fully aware of his weaknesses. She may even exploit them in order to get what she wants. With these two types of women, the game arises from the romanticizing or exploiting of the imperfections, while the innocence lies in their genuine respect for his accomplishments, which they are able to evaluate correctly.

In the dissembled form, Murgatroyd may or may not be wonderful, but he comes up against women incapable of appreciating him in the best sense, in any case; perhaps she is a high-class prostitute. She plays "Little Old Me" and uses GYWM as sheer flattery to attain her own ends. Underneath she is either bewildered by him or laughing at him. But she does not care about him; what she wants are the perquisites that go with him.

Clinically "Peasant" is played in two similar forms, with the motto, "Gee, you're wonderful, Professor!" (GYWP). In the innocent form the patient may stay well as long as she can believe in GYWP, which places an obligation on the therapist to be well-behaved both in public and in private life. In the dissembled form the patient hopes the therapist will go along with her GYWP and think: "You're uncommonly perceptive" (YUP). Once she has him in this position, she can make him look foolish and then move on to another therapist; if he cannot be so easily beguiled, he may actually be able to help her.

The simplest way for the patient to win GYWP is not to get better. If she is more malicious, she may take more positive steps to make the therapist look foolish. One woman played GYWP with her psychiatrist without any alleviation of symptoms; she finally left him with many salaams and apologies. She then went to her revered clergyman for help and played GYWP with him. After a few weeks she seduced him into a game of second-degree "Rapo." She then told her neighbor confidentially over the back fence how disappointed she was that so fine a man as Rev. Black could, in a moment of weakness, make a pass at an innocent and unattractive woman like herself. Knowing his wife, she could forgive him, of course, but nevertheless, etc. This confidence just slipped out inadvertently, and it was only afterward that she remembered "to her horror" that the neighbor was an elder in the church. With her psychiatrist she won by not getting better; with her clergyman she won by seducing him, although she was reluctant to admit it. But a second psychiatrist introduced her to a therapy group where she could not maneuver as she had before. Then, with no GYWP and YUP to fill in her therapeutic time, she began to examine her behavior more closely and with the help of the group was able to give up both her games—GYWP and "Rapo."

Antithesis. The therapist must first decide whether the game is played innocently and hence should be allowed to continue for the benefit of the patient until her Adult is sufficiently well-established to risk counter-measures. If it is not innocent, the countermeasures may be taken at the first appropriate opportunity, after the patient has been sufficiently well prepared so that she will be able to understand what happens. The therapist then steadfastly refuses to give advice, and when the patient begins to protest, he makes it clear that this is not merely "Poker-Faced Psychiatry" but a well-thought-out policy. In due time his refusals may either enrage the patient or precipitate acute anxiety symptoms. The next step depends on the malignancy of the patient's condition. If she is too upset, her acute reactions should be dealt with by appropriate psychiatric or analytic procedures to re-establish the therapeutic situation. The first goal, in the dissembled form, is to split off the Adult from the hypocritical Child so that the game can be analyzed.

In social situations, intimate entanglements with innocent GYWM players should be avoided, as any intelligent actor's agent will impress upon his clients. On the other hand, women who play dissembled GYWM are sometimes interesting and intelligent if they can be de-GYWMed, and may turn out to be quite a delightful addition to the family social circle.

Psychiatry

Thesis. Psychiatry as a procedure must be distinguished from "Psychiatry" as a game. According to the available evidence, presented in proper clinical form in scientific publications, the following approaches, among others, are of value in treating psychiatric conditions: shock therapy, hypnosis, drugs, psychoanalysis, orthopsychiatry and group therapy. There are others which are less commonly used and will not be discussed here. Any of these can be used in the game of "Psychiatry," which is based on the position "I am a healer," supported by a diploma: "It says here I am a healer." It will be noted that in any case this is a constructive, benevolent position, and that people who play "Psychiatry" can do a great deal of good, providing they are professionally trained.

It is likely, however, that there will be some gain in therapeutic results if therapeutic ardor is moderated. The *antithesis* was best expressed long ago by Ambroise Paré, who said in effect: "I treat them, but God cures them." Every medical student learns about this dictum, along with others such as *primum non nocere,* and phrases such as *vis medicatrix naturae.* Nonmedical therapists, however, are not likely to be exposed to these ancient cautions. The position, "I am a healer because it says here that I am a healer" is likely to be an impairment, and may be replaced to advantage with something like: "I will apply what therapeutic procedures I have learned in the hope that they will be of some benefit." This avoids the possibility of games based on: "Since I am a healer, if you don't get better it's your fault" (e.g., "I'm Only Trying to Help You") or "Since you're a healer, I'll get better for you" (e.g., "Peasant"). All of this, of course, is known in principle to every conscientious therapist. Certainly every therapist who has ever presented a case at a reputable clinic has been made aware of it. Conversely, a good clinic may be defined as one which makes its therapists aware of these things.

On the other side, the game of "Psychiatry" is more apt to crop up with patients who have previously been treated by less competent therapists. A few patients, for example, carefully pick weak psychoanalysts, moving from one to another, demonstrating that they cannot be cured and meanwhile learning to play a sharper and sharper game of "Psychiatry"; eventually it becomes difficult for even a first-rate clinician to separate the wheat from the chaff. The duplex transaction on the patient's side is:

Adult: "I am coming to be cured."

Child: "You will never cure me, but you will teach me to be a better neurotic (play a better game of 'Psychiatry')."

"Mental Health" is played similarly; here the Adult statement is, "Everything will get better if I apply the principles of mental health which I have read and heard about." One patient learned to play "Psychiatry" from one therapist, "Mental Health" from another, and then as a result of still another effort began to play a pretty good game of "Transactional Analysis." When this was frankly discussed with her, she agreed to stop playing "Mental Health," but requested that she be allowed to continue to play "Psychiatry" because it made her feel comfortable. The transactional psychiatrist agreed. She continued, therefore, for several months to recite her dreams and her interpretations of them at weekly intervals. Finally, partly out of plain gratitude, perhaps, she decided that it might be interesting to find out what was really the matter with her. She became seriously interested in transactional analysis, with good results.

A variant of "Psychiatry" is "Archaeology" (title by courtesy of Dr. Norman Reider of San Francisco), in which the patient takes the position that if she can only find out who had the button, so to speak, everything will suddenly be all right. This results in a continual rumination over childhood happenings. Sometimes the therapist may be beguiled into a game of "Critique," in which the patient describes her feelings in various situations and the therapist tells her what is wrong with them. "Self-Expression," which is a common game in some therapy groups, is based on the dogma "Feelings are Good." A patient who uses vulgar expletives, for example, may be applauded or at least implicitly lauded. A sophisticated group, however, will soon spot this as a game.

Some members of therapy groups become quite adept at picking out games of "Psychiatry," and will soon let a new patient know if they think he is playing "Psychiatry" or "Transactional Analysis" instead of using group procedures to obtain legitimate insight. A woman who transferred from a Self-Expression group in one city to a more sophisticated group in another city told a story about an incestuous relationship in her childhood. Instead of the awe which she had come to expect whenever she told this oft-repeated tale, she was greeted with indifference, whereupon she became enraged. She was astonished to discover that the new group was more interested in her transactional anger than in her historical incest, and in irate tones she hurled what apparently in her mind was the ultimate insult: she accused them of not being Freudian. Freud, himself, of course, took psychoanalysis more seriously, and avoided making a game of it by saying that he himself was not a Freudian.

Recently unmasked is a new variant of "Psychiatry" called "Tell Me This," somewhat similar to the party pastime "Twenty Questions." White relates a dream or an incident, and the other members, often including the therapist, then attempt to interpret it by asking pertinent questions. As long as White answers the questions, each member continues his inquiries until he finds a question White cannot answer. Then Black sits back with a knowing look which says: "Aha! If you could answer *that* one, you would certainly get better, so I have done *my* part." (This is a distant relative of "Why Don't You—Yes But"). Some therapy groups are based almost entirely on this game, and may go on for years with only minimal change or progress. "Tell Me This" allows much latitude to White (the patient) who, for example, can play along with it by feeling ineffectual; or he can counter it by answering all the questions offered, in which case the anger and dismay of the other players soon becomes manifest, since he is throwing back at them, "I've answered all your questions and you haven't cured me, so what does that make you?"

"Tell Me This" is also played in schoolrooms, where the pupils know that the "right" answer to an open-ended question asked by a certain type of teacher is not to be found by processing the factual data, but by guessing or outguessing which of several possible answers will make the teacher happy. A pedantic variant occurs in teaching ancient Greek; the teacher always has the upper hand over the pupil, and can make him look stupid and prove it in print by pointing to some obscure feature of the text. This is also often played in teaching Hebrew.

Wooden Leg

Thesis. The most dramatic form of "Wooden Leg" is "The Plea of Insanity." This may be translated into transactional terms as follows: "What do you expect of someone as emotionally disturbed as I am—that I would refrain from killing people?" To which the jury is asked to reply: "Certainly not, we would hardly impose that restriction on you!" "The Plea of Insanity," played as a legal game, is acceptable to American culture and is different from the almost universally respected principle that an individual may be suffering from a psychosis so profound that no reasonable person would expect him to be responsible for his actions. In Japan drunkenness, and in Russia war-time military service, are accepted as excuses for evading responsibility for all kinds of outrageous behavior (according to this writer's information).

The thesis of "Wooden Leg" is, "What do you expect of a man with a wooden leg?" Put that way, of course, no one would expect anything of a man with a wooden leg except that he should steer his own wheel chair. On the other hand, during World War II there was a man with a wooden leg who used to give demonstrations of jitterbug dancing, and very competent jitterbug dancing, at Army Hospital amputation centers. There are blind men who practice law and hold political offices (one such is currently mayor of the writer's home town), deaf men who practice psychiatry and handless men who can use a typewriter.

As long as someone with a real, exaggerated or even imaginary disability is content with his lot, perhaps no one should interfere. But the moment he presents himself for psychiatric treatment, the question arises if he is using his life to his own best advantage, and if he can rise above his disability. In this country the therapist will be working in opposition to a large mass of educated public opinion. Even the close relatives of the patient who complained most loudly about the inconveniences caused by his infirmity may eventually turn on the therapist if the patient makes definite progress. This is readily understandable to a game analyst, but it makes his task no less difficult. All the people who were playing "I'm Only Trying to Help You" are threatened by the impending disruption of the game if the patient shows signs of striking out on his own, and sometimes they use almost incredible measures to terminate the treatment.

Both sides are illustrated by the case of the stuttering client of Miss Black's, mentioned in the discussion of the game of "Indigence." This man played a classical form of "Wooden Leg." He was unable to find employment, which he correctly attributed to the fact that he was a stutterer, since the only career that interested him, he said, was that of salesman. As a free citizen he had a right to seek employment in whatever field he chose, but as a stutterer, his choice raised some question as to the purity of his motives. The reaction of the helpful agency when Miss Black attempted to break up this game was very unfavorable to her.

"Wooden Leg" is especially pernicious in clinical practice, because the patient may find a therapist who plays the same game with the same plea, so that progress is impossible. This is relatively easy to arrange in the case of the "Ideological Plea," "What do you expect of a man who lives in a society like ours?" One patient combined this with the "Psychosomatic Plea," "What do you expect of a man with psychosomatic symptoms?" He found a succession of therapists who would accept one plea but not the other, so that none of them either made him feel comfortable in his current position by accepting both pleas, or budged him from it by rejecting both. Thus he proved that psychiatry couldn't help people.

Some of the pleas which patients use to excuse symptomatic behavior are colds, head injuries, situational stress, the stress of modern living, American culture and the economic system. A literate player has no difficulty in finding authorities to support him. "I drink because I'm Irish." "This wouldn't happen if I lived in Russia or Tahiti." The fact is that patients in mental hospitals in Russia and Tahiti are very similar to those in American state hospitals. Special pleas of "If It Weren't For Them" or "They Let Me Down" should always be evaluated very carefully in clinical practice—and also in social research projects.

Slightly more sophisticated are such pleas as: What do you expect of a man who (a) comes from a broken home (b) is neurotic (c) is in analysis or (d) is suffering from a disease known as alcoholism? These are topped by "If I stop doing this I won't be able to analyze it, and then I'll never get better."

The obverse of "Wooden Leg" is "Rickshaw," with the thesis, "If they only had (rickshaws) (duckbill platypuses) (girls who spoke ancient Egyptian) around this town, I never would have got into this mess."

Antithesis. Anti-"Wooden Leg" is not difficult if the therapist can distinguish clearly between his own Parent and Adult, and if the therapeutic aim is explicitly understood by both parties.

On the Parental side, he can be either a "good" Parent or a "harsh" one. As a "good" Parent he can accept the patient's plea, especially if it fits in with his own viewpoints, perhaps with the rationalization that people are not responsible for their actions until they have completed their therapy. As a "harsh" Parent he can reject the plea and engage in a contest of wills with the patient. Both of these attitudes are already familiar to the "Wooden Leg" player, and he knows how to extract the maximum satisfactions from each of them.

As an Adult, the therapist declines both of these opportunities. When the patient asks, "What do you expect of a neurotic?" (or whatever plea he is using at that moment) the reply is, "I don't expect anything. The question is, what do you expect of yourself?" The only demand he makes is that the patient give a serious answer to this question, and the only concession he makes is to allow the patient a reasonable length of time to answer it: anywhere from six weeks to six months, depending on the relationship between them and the patient's previous preparation.

9. Games: An Update

Games People Play was written in the late 1950s. Berne continued to work on the game theory, and 10 years later in What Do You Say After You Say Hello? *he presented a brief update which included a new formula and which follows here.—C.S.*

Games are sets of ulterior transactions, repetitive in nature, with a well-defined psychological payoff. Since an ulterior transaction means that the agent pretends to be doing one thing while he is really doing something else, all games involve a con. But a con only works if there is a weakness it can hook into, a handle or "gimmick" to get hold of in the respondent, such as fear, greed, sentimentality, or irritability. After the "mark" is hooked, the player pulls some sort of switch in order to get his payoff. The switch is followed by a moment of confusion or crossup while the mark tries to figure out what has happened to him. Then both players collect their payoffs as the game ends. The payoff, which is mutual, consists of feelings (not necessarily similar) which the game arouses in both the agent and the respondent. Unless a set of transactions has these four features, it is not a game—that is, the transactions must be ulterior so that there is a con, and the con must be followed by a switch, a crossup, and a payoff. This can be represented by a formula.

$$C + G = R \rightarrow S \rightarrow X \rightarrow P$$

$C + G$ means that the con hooks into a gimmick, so that the respondent responds (R). The player then pulls the switch (S), and that is followed by a moment of confusion or crossup (X), after which both players collect their payoffs (P). Whatever fits this formula is a game, and whatever does not fit it is not a game.

For example, the mere fact of repetition or persistence does not constitute a game. Thus, in a therapy group, if a scared patient repeatedly asks the therapist for reassurance every week ("Tell me I'll get better, doctor") and when he receives it, says "Thank you," that is not necessarily an ulterior transaction. The patient has stated his need frankly and has had it gratified, and does not take advantage of the situation in any way, but gives a courteous response. These transactions, therefore, do not constitute a game but an operation, and operations, no matter how often they are repeated, must be distinguished from games, just as rational procedures must be distinguished from rituals.

If another patient, however, asks the therapist for reassurance, and upon receiving it, uses the response to make the therapist look stupid, that constitutes a game. For example, a patient asked: "Do you think I'll get better, doctor?" and the sentimental therapist replied, "Of course you will." At that point the patient revealed her ulterior motive in asking the question. Instead of saying "Thank you," as in the straight transaction, she pulled the switch with: "What makes you think you know everything?" This reply crossed the therapist up and threw him off balance for a moment, which is what the patient wanted to do. Then the game ended, the patient feeling elated at having conned the therapist, and he feeling frustrated; and those were the payoffs.

This game followed Formula G precisely. The con was the original question, and the gimmick was the therapist's sentimentality. When the con hooked into the gimmick, he responded in the way she expected. Then she pulled the switch, causing a crossup, after which each collected a payoff. So

$$C + H = R \rightarrow S \rightarrow X \rightarrow P$$

This is a simple example of the game called, from the patient's side, "Slug Him," or "Whammy," and from the therapist's side, "I'm Only Trying to Help You." Colloquially, the payoff is called a *trading stamp*. "Good" feelings are spoken of as "gold" trading stamps and distressed feelings are said to be "brown" or "blue" trading stamps. In this case the patient got a counterfeit-gold trading stamp for a counterfeit triumph or success, and the therapist got a brown one, which is not un-usual.

Each game has a slogan or motto by which it can be recognized, such as "I'm Only Trying to Help You." This slogan is colloquially called a "sweatshirt." Usually the name of the game is taken from its slogan.

Beyond games lies the other limiting case of what can take place between people, which is called *intimacy*. Bilateral intimacy is defined as a candid, game-free re-lationship, with mutual free giving and receiving and without exploitation. Intimacy can be one-sided, since one party may be candid and freely giving, while the other may be devious and exploitative.

Sexual activities offer examples which cover this whole spectrum of social behavior. It is evident that they can take place in withdrawal, that they can be part of a ritualistic ceremony, or that they can be all in a day's work, a pastime for a rainy day, a game of mutual exploitation, or acts of real intimacy.

TWO ○○○

Scripts

Introduction

After writing *Games People Play,* Eric's thinking went into hibernation. Early in the development of his theory he had postulated the existence of scripts. The first chapter of this section is from his book *Transactional Analysis in Psychotherapy* and is an early statement of script theory included here for its historical value. Even though scripts were mentioned and often discussed by him in the early years of Transactional Analysis, he did not develop any substantial theoretical contributions about scripts in the next 15 years. He continued to see some of his patients in individual psychotherapy weekly sessions and those sessions increasingly became script analysis sessions. But it was not until after I wrote *Games Alcoholics Play: The Analysis of Life Scripts,* that his own thinking took off (stimulated, I believe, in part by my thinking) and that he wrote *What Do You Say After You Say Hello?* Here, once again, his brilliance, deep understanding of human nature and wit become apparent. The book is very long and was not really completed. It was sent to the publisher shortly before he died so that he never had an opportunity even to review his galleys. Because of this the book has a somewhat unformed feeling to it. It is filled with important new ideas from which I have selected what I consider the best. I have also selected a few pages from *Sex and Human Loving,* the galleys of which he received while in the hospital a few days before his death and which also appeared posthumously. It is in this work that some of the zaniest, almost spaced-out writing appeared. An expert on sexuality Eric Berne was not. And yet because of his wit and interest in sex he was chosen to deliver the Jake Gimbel Memorial Sex Psychology lecture series at the S. F.

Medical Center in 1966, which he later turned into a book. *Sex and Human Loving* is Berne's most relaxed, playful, and personally revealing contribution, and as such it has to be read with tolerance and understanding. Because of this I have therefore selected very little from that particular work.

—C.S.

Preface

A Living Problem: "Looking at Grass" by Cyprian St. Cyr

Between his yearly visits to his therapist, Lastborn Snodgrass, the sixth of the twelve Snodgrass children, used to come and talk to R. Horseley, the Sage of the Ozarks.

"Why do you think I've lost my zest for life?" he asked one evening.

"It's because you don't know how to say 'Hello'," replied Horseley.

"Oh, I know how to say 'Hello,' " protested Snodgrass. "I know just how to con people when I say 'Hello,' and everybody likes me."

"Do you know how to look at grass?" asked Horseley.

"Funny you should ask that. Just the other day I was lying in a field and for the first time since I was a little boy I really saw the grass."

"Were you conning the grass?"

"No, that's just it."

"Well, it's just as hard to say 'Hello' as it is to see grass," said Horseley. "Come back in five years, after you've learned to say 'Hello,' and we'll talk about what you do after that."

Question: Which is harder, to say 'Hello,' or to see grass?

10. Analysis of Scripts

Games appear to be segments of larger, more complex sets of transactions called *scripts*. Scripts belong in the realm of transference phenomena, that is, they are derivatives, or more precisely, adaptations, of infantile reactions and experiences. But a script does not deal with a mere transference reaction or transference situation; it is an attempt to repeat in derivative form a whole transference drama, often split up into acts, exactly like the theatrical scripts which are intuitive artistic derivatives of these primal dramas of childhood. Operationally, a script is a complex set of transactions, by nature recurrent, but not necessarily recurring, since a complete performance may require a whole lifetime.

A common tragic script is that based on the rescue fantasy of a woman who marries one alcoholic after another. The disruption of such a script, like the disruption of a game, leads to despair. Since the script calls for a magical cure of the alcoholic husband, and this is not forthcoming, a divorce results and the woman tries again. Many such women are raised by alcoholic fathers, so that the infantile origins of the script are not far to seek.

A practical and constructive script, on the other hand, may lead to great happiness if the others in the cast are well chosen and play their parts satisfactorily.

In the practice of script analysis, transactional (intra-group) and social (extra-group) material is collected until the nature of his script becomes clear to the patient. Neurotic, psychotic, and psychopathic scripts are almost always tragic, and they follow the Aristotelian principles of dramaturgy with remarkable fidelity: there is prologue, climax, and catastrophe, with real or symbolic pathos and despair giving rise to real threnody. The current life-drama must then be related to its historical origins so that control of the individual's destiny can be shifted from the Child to the Adult, from archaeopsychic unconsciousness to neopsychic awareness. In the group the patient can soon be observed feeling out through games and pastimes the potentialities of the other members to play their parts in his script, so that at first he acts as a casting director and then as protagonist.

In order to be effective in script analysis, the therapist must have a better organized conceptual framework than he finds it necessary to communicate to the patient. First, there is no specific word in psychoanalysis for the original experiences from which transference reactions are derived. In script analysis, the household drama which is first played out to an unsatisfactory conclusion in the earliest years of life is called the *protocol*. This is classically an archaic version of the Oedipus drama and is repressed in later years. Its precipitates re-appear as the *script proper,* which is a preconscious derivative of the protocol. In any given social situation, however, this script proper must be compromised in accordance with the possible realities. This compromise is technically called the *adaptation,* and the adaptation is what the patient actually tries to play out in real life by the manipulation of the people around him. In practice, protocol, script, and adaptation are all subsumed under the term "script." This is the only one of three words which is actually used in the group, since it is adequate for the intended purpose and is the one which is most meaningful to most patients.

In his quest for characters to fit the roles demanded by his script, the patient perceives the other members of the group in his own idiosyncratic way, usually with considerable intuitive acumen. That is, he tends to pick the right people to play the roles of mother, father, siblings, and whatever others are called for. When his casting is complete, he proceeds to try to elicit the required responses from the person cast for each role. If there are not enough people in the group, someone may have to play a double role. If there are too many, several may be cast in the same role; or new roles may be activated, representing people who played minor parts in the protocol and whose presence is optional and unessential; or else he may just ignore the people who serve no useful function in his adaptation.

The motivation for the patient's behavior is his need to recapture or augment the gains of the original experience. He may seek to bring about a repetition of the original catastrophe, as in the classical repetition compulsion; or he may try to attain a happier ending. Since the object of script analysis is to "close the show and put a better one on the road," it is not too important to determine which of these alternatives applies or to sort out the conflicts in this area. For example, it is regarded as irrelevant whether the woman who failed to rescue her alcoholic father is trying to fail again with her subsequent husbands, or is trying to succeed where she failed before, or is ambivalent. The important thing is to free her from her compulsion to relive the situation, and start her on some other path. This applies to any script which has proven unconstructive.

Mrs. Catters illustrates the problems of script analysis as they appear in practice. For a long time she was unproductive on the couch. Her principal defense was a deliberate manner of speech which effectively insulated the Child so that few indications leaked out which threw any light on her symptomatology. When she was introduced to a therapy group, however, she went into action almost immediately. She took an active part in "How Do You Treat Delinquent Spouses?" (a pastime belonging to the "PTA" family). She also played a steady game of "Let's You And Him Fight," watching with much enjoyment the arguments she succeeded in starting between some of the men. Added to this, when the group played "Ain't It Awful?" she would laugh as she recounted various bloody calamities that had befallen friends and acquaintances. In this manner it happened that a few weeks in the group yielded more information about her than as many months on the couch. Since scripts are so complex and full of idiosyncrasy, however, it is not possible to do adequate script analysis in group therapy alone, and it remained to find an opportunity in her individual sessions to elucidate what had been learned so far.

After a time she complained at one of those sessions that she could not defend herself against male aggressiveness. The therapist, on the basis of previous material, opined the one reason might be that she was so angry at men in general that she was afraid to let go even a little bit for fear that she might find herself going farther than she wanted to. She said it was hard to believe that she could be that angry at men. She went on to report fantasies of the death of her husband, who was a philandering jet pilot. One day he might get into an accident or a fight over another woman and be brought home fatally bleeding and injured. Thus she would become a romantic figure among her friends, the tragic widow.

She then recounted how deeply hurt and angry, in fact enraged, she had been as a child after the birth of her little brother, whom her parents seemed to prefer. She was especially angry at her father, and her thought was: "Daddy deserves to be killed by someone, and it would serve mother right if it happened." She imagined that his death would also give her a special position among her playmates. The picture of her father dying was accompanied by a peculiar kind of laughing pleasure.

There were other complications which are irrelevant to the present discussion. In its simplest form, the protocol was as follows. Her death wishes against her father are realized without any initiative on her part. The deathbed scene has its own special kind of pleasure. This recurs when she goes to notify her mother and observes her mother's grief. Then she becomes a romantic figure to her playmates.

This drama is repeated in her fantasies about her husband, but so far one element is missing: the stunned mother. The therapist therefore asked her if her mother-in-law ever played a part in these fantasies. She replied that it was certainly so, that after the deathbed scene she always pictured herself going to announce the fatal outcome to her mother-in-law.

This protocol contained six principal roles: self, father, mother, rival, assailant, audience. It could be divided into several scenes: e.g., jealousy, assault, deathbed, announcement, romantic threnody.

The script also contained six principal roles: self, male love object, mother-in-law, rival, assailant, and audience; and it could be divided into the same acts or scenes. Her choice of husband had been partly motivated by her morbid need to be jealous, or in the present language, by her need to cast her script.

It will be noted that the gains from the script duplicate the gains from the protocol. The internal primary gain centers around the morbid laughter of the deathbed scene; the external primary gain lies in getting rid of the worrisome love object and simultaneously obtaining revenge on the mother person. The secondary gains come from inheriting the estate, and the social gains from the tragic role she can play in her community.

Her adaptation of this script in her overt behavior in the group was manifested by her three games: "Delinquent Husband PTA" (Scene 1, Jealousy); "Let's You And Him Fight" (Scene 2, The Assault); and "Aint It Awful?" (Scene 3), The Deathbed). Reviewing her behavior on the couch, her habit of making "announcements" when something went wrong (Scene 4, The Announcement), and her long discussions about how to appear glamorous at parties (Scene 5, The Romantic Threnody), now fell into place as part of her script. After all this had been worked over at some length (although not in quite such an orderly sequence as it is presented here), the patient understood rather clearly the nature of the script, and could see how she had spent most of her life striving to keep this particular show on the road. Where previously she had been driven with no option by an unconscious archaic compulsion, she was now in a position to exert social control over a large portion of her behavior with people.

Nevertheless, even though her Adult grasped with new understanding the significance of her actions and relationships, the strivings themselves still persisted. But her position was improved not only socially, but also therapeutically, since it was now much clearer to both the patient and the therapist what kind of strivings had to be dealt with. The sexualization of death, which made it her hobby to visit graveyards, was no longer an isolated phenomenon, but could be handled with increased understanding of how it fitted into her whole destiny; and similarly with other characteristics and symptoms.

This is a not atypical script of a neurotic, however morbid it may appear to those unaccustomed to dealing with such archaic dramas. The following represents the actual acting out of a script whose protocol was never completely clarified due to technical difficulties.

Mr. Kinz, a 25-year-old bachelor, went to New York for a weekend of fun. He arrived in the early hours of the morning, tired and somewhat nervous, so he doctored himself with barbiturates and alcohol and found an after-hours bar. There, in the predawn, he fell into conversation with some rough-looking men who he thought might find him a girl. He showed them that he had only ten dollars, but they said that would be enough. They invited him into their car and drove him toward a deserted warehouse district near the river. In the course of their conversation he told them that he carried a hunting knife, and one of them asked to see it. A few minutes later they stopped the car. The man in the back seat threw his elbow around Mr. Kinz's neck while the other man put the blade of the knife against his throat. They demanded his money, and with some difficulty Mr. Kinz managed to reach into his pocket and hand them his wallet. They then released him and drove off, waving a friendly goodbye. Mr. Kinz wiped the blood off his throat and went to find a policeman. He told his story in such a way, however, and his appearance was by this time so disreputable, that the police were quite unimpressed. They took down the required details and then dismissed him with a shrug.

After he had reported the robbery, Mr. Kinz had some breakfast; then without bothering to get cleaned up, he presented himself at the door of his father's club. The doorman did not know him, and with raised eyebrows set a servant to announce him. His father received him in the library where he was sitting with some of his well-to-do and conservative business associates. Mr. Kinz did not offer to explain his appearance and when his father questioned him he said in a casual way that he had almost had his throat cut. The father offered the use of his room upstairs and the loan of some clean clothes. Mr. Kinz tidied himself up, came downstairs and said a polite farewell to his father and his friends, and went on his way to look for more fun.

It is interesting to note that the two thugs showed no apprehension that Mr. Kinz would raise a really dangerous alarm, or even that he would be very angry or lose his head. Yet when he told the story, Mr. Kinz at first denied that he had invited the assault, or that any of his preceding actions were extraordinary. What interested him more than anything, apparently, was the awareness that he had gone to his father's club as a kind of test, to see if and how his father would reject him.

It is evident that Mr. Kinz chose his cast well. It is not easy to find in real life men who are willing to cut a man's throat for ten dollars. He supplied them not only with an excuse, but also with the actual weapon to murder him while he was looking for a sexually available woman. The protocol for this part of the script is not known. The last act was more familiar. Mr. Kinz was precocious, and once when he was small he had burst into the room where his father sat with some friends to show them his latest achievement. The men were not impressed, and he never forgot his dejection on that occasion. At any rate, Mr. Kinz made a kind of career of a particular sequence: getting himself violently slapped down because of a woman, and then presenting himself to his father. He deliberately exposed himself to the most dangerous possible sexual situations. Between times, when his Adult was in control, he was a gentle, kind, likable, and shy young man.

After some experience, it is possible to acquire considerable diagnostic acumen in script analysis. The following example illustrates the telescoping of a whole script into a few seconds.

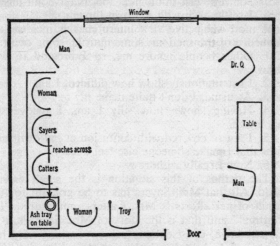

Figure 8. Seating diagram.

Mrs. Sayers, a 30-year-old housewife, was sitting in the middle of a settee with Mrs. Catters between her and an end-table, as shown in Figure 8 (above). This was a beginners' group, and Mrs. Sayers had just spent considerable time relating her troubles with her husband. Attention had now turned to Mr. Troy. In the midst of an exchange between Mrs. Catters and Mr. Troy, Mrs. Sayers stretched her arm out across Mrs. Catters's chest to reach for an ash-tray on the end-table. As she drew her arm back she lost her balance and almost fell off the settee. She recovered just in time, laughed deprecatingly, muttered "Excuse me!" and settled back to smoke. At this moment, Mrs. Catters took her attention away from Mr. Troy long enough to murmur: "Pardon me!"

Descriptively, this performance may be broken down into the following steps.

1. While other people are talking, I decide to smoke.

2. In order not to disturb the person next to me, I get my own ash-tray.

3. I almost fall.

4. I recover just in time, laugh, and apologize.

5. Someone else apologizes too, but I don't answer.

6. I settle back with my own thoughts.

A more subjective view interprets this incident as a sequence of transactions, some autistic, some overt.

1. Other people ignore me, so I pretend to withdraw.

2. I ostentatiously show how diffident I am.

3. As usual, I don't quite make it.

4. Having shown how silly I am, I recover and apologize.

5. I am so covered with confusion at my own ineptness that I make someone else feel uneasy.

6. Now I really withdraw.

The pathos of this situation is the small external yield. All that Mrs. Sayers has to be grateful for as a result of her efforts is Mrs. Catters's murmured "Pardon me!" and that is the story of Mrs. Sayers's life— an attractive, conscientious person working very hard for psychological pennies; or more colloquially and more aptly, for psychological peanuts. And often she might work for nothing. Not everyone would be as' polite as Mrs. Catters; engaged otherwise in conversation, some might not give Mrs. Sayers even that trivial recognition.

Her script, in this case adapted within a few seconds by a remarkably efficient integrating mechanism to a special situation in the group, had been repeatedly played out over varying lengths of time ranging from a passing moment to several years, both in Mrs. Sayers's marriage and in her working life, resulting in several separations from her husband, and involving the loss of one job after another. The original drama is based on early experiences. The first, traumatic experience, the protocol, was not recovered wthin the limited scope of her treatment but later versions or *palimpsests* can be reconstructed from her history.

1. Since my siblings attract more attention than I do, I pretend to withdraw from family life.

2. But from time to time I try to get some recog-

nition by ostentatiously demonstrating agreement with my alcoholic mother that I am quite unimportant.

3. Because of my clumsiness, mother pushes me. The combination is almost disastrous.

4. My ineffectual but loving father saves me from disaster. I think how silly I must look to my mother and siblings. Because of that, and because of my pleasure at getting some notice, I laugh. Then I seem to have been too demanding and aggressive, and apologize.

5. What I really want is for them to show that they are sorry for their neglect. But if they do, I cannot afford to acknowledge it for two reasons: first, it makes me feel demanding, as above; and secondly, if I am waiting for it I may be disappointed. So if they so signify, it registers gratefully, but I pretend to overlook it.

6. In any case, the whole situation is so unsatisfactory that now I really withdraw.

There are at least three different early palimpsests of this script: oral, pre-oedipal, and oedipal. The oedipal version reads briefly: "How silly it is to be a girl. I can only get whatever poor satisfactions are available, and then retire and lick my wounds." It was not difficult to see this version being played out every year or so with the disparaging husband she had picked for herself, and in her working life where some slight paranoid distortion was occasionally necessary in order to make her co-workers fit the roles that her script called for.

The striking thing was how much this apparently innocent and simple incident revealed when the lightning-fast shifts in attitude were isolated and analyzed. The dramaturgy of this kaleidoscopic thimble theater in six acts is essentially tragic: in spite of the averted pathos, it ends in forlorn threnody, and reflects the quality of Mrs. Sayers's life. The history emphasized and explained the autistic quality of the transactions, and made the structural analysis clear: the wistful Child who is pushed by one intrapsychic Parent and rescued by the other; the momentary breakthrough of the

Adult who appraises her behavior; and the ultimate lapse into archaic fantasy.

On the basis of transactional analysis, game analysis, and script analysis, it is possible to state a dynamic theory of social intercourse which complements the biological and existential theory. In any social aggregation, including the limiting case of two, the individual will strive to engage in transactions which are related to his favored games; he will strive to obtain the greatest primary gain from such engagement. Conversely, he will choose or seek out associates who promise to yield the greatest primary gains: for casual relationships, people who will at least participate in favored transactions; for more stable relationships, people who will play the same games; for intimate relationships, people who are best qualified to fill roles in his script. Since the dominant influence in social intercourse is the script, and since that is derived and adapted from a protocol based on early experiences of the individual with his parents, those experiences are the chief determinants of every engagement and of every choice of associates. This is a more general statement than the familiar transference theory which it brings to mind because it applies to any engagement whatsoever in any social aggregation whatsoever; that is, to any transaction or series of transactions which is not completely structured by external reality. It is useful because it is subject to testing by any qualified observer anywhere. Such testing requires neither a prolonged period of preparation nor a unique situation.

While every human being faces the world initially as the captive of his script, the great hope and value of the human race is that the Adult can be dissatisfied with such strivings when they are unworthy.

11. What Do You Say After You Say Hello?

This childlike question, so apparently artless and free of the profundity expected of scientific inquiry, really contains within itself all the basic questions of human living and all the fundamental problems of the social sciences. It is the question that babies "ask" themselves, that children learn to accept corrupted answers to, that teen-agers ask each other and their advisers, that grownups evade by accepting the corrupted answers of their betters, and that wise old philosophers write books about without ever finding the answer. It contains both the primal question of social psychology: Why do people talk to each other? and the primal question of social psychiatry: Why do people like to be liked? Its answer is the answer to the questions posed by the Four Horsemen of the Apocalypse: war or peace, famine or plenty, pestilence or health, death or life. It is no wonder that few people find the answer in their lifetimes, since most go through life without ever finding the answer to the question which precedes it: How do you say hello?

HOW DO YOU SAY HELLO?

This is the secret of Buddhism, of Christianity, of Judaism, of Platonism, of atheism, and above all, of humanism. The famous "sound of one hand clapping" in Zen is the sound of one person saying Hello to another, and it is also the sound of the Golden Rule in whatever Bible it is stated. To say Hello rightly is to see the other person, to be aware of him as a phenomenon, to happen to him and to be ready for him

The following six chapters, 11-16, are from *What Do You Say After You Say Hello?*, Copyright © 1972 by City National Bank, Beverly Hills, California; Robin Way; Janice Way Farlinger. Reprinted by permission of Grove Press, Inc.

to happen to you. Perhaps the people who show this ability to the highest degree are the Fiji Islanders, for one of the rare jewels of the world is the genuine Fijian smile. It starts slowly, it illuminates the whole face, it rests there long enough to be clearly recognized and to recognize clearly, and it fades with secret slowness as it passes by. It can be matched elsewhere only by the smiles of an uncorrupted mother and infant greeting each other, and also, in Western countries, by a certain kind of open personality.

This book discusses four questions: How do you say Hello? How do you say Hello back? What do you say after you say Hello? and, principally, the plaintive query, What is everybody doing instead of saying Hello? These questions will be answered briefly here. The explanation of the answers will occupy the rest of this psychiatric textbook, which is addressed first to the therapist, secondly to his patients as they get cured, and thirdly to anyone else who cares to listen.

1. In order to say Hello, you first get rid of all the trash which has accumulated in your head ever since you came home from the maternity ward, and then you recognize that this particular Hello will never happen again. It may take years to learn how to do this.

2. In order to say Hello back, you get rid of all the trash in your head and see that there is somebody standing there or walking by, waiting for you to say Hello back. It may take years to learn how to do *that*.

3. After you say Hello, you get rid of all the trash that is coming back into your head; all the afterburns of all the grievances you have experienced and all the reach-backs of all the troubles you are planning to get into. Then you will be speechless and will not have anything to say. After more years of practice, you might think of something worth saying.

4. Mostly, this book is about the trash: the things people are doing to each other instead of saying Hello. It is written in the hope that those with training and talent for such things can help themselves and others to recognize what I am calling (in a philosophical sense) "trash," since the first problem in answering the other three questions is to see what is trash and

what isn't. The way people speak who are learning to say Hello is called "Martian," to distinguish it from everyday Earth-talk, which, as history shows from the earliest recorded times in Egypt and Babylonia to the present, has led to wars, famines, pestilence, and death; and, in the survivors, to a certain amount of mental confusion. It is hoped that in the long run, Martian, properly learned and properly taught, will help to eliminate these plagues. Martian, for example, is the language of dreams, which show things the way they really are.

AN ILLUSTRATION

To illustrate the possible value of this approach, let us consider a dying patient, that is, a patient with an incurable disease and a limited time to live. Mort, a thirty-year-old man with a slowly developing form of cancer, incurable in the present state of knowledge, was given at worst two years, and at best, five. His psychiatric complaint was tics, consisting of nodding his head or shaking his feet for reasons unknown to him. In his treatment group he soon found the explanation: he was damming his fears behind a continuous wall of music which ran through his mind, and his tics were his way of keeping time with that music. It was established by careful observation that it was this way 'round and not the other, that it was not music keeping time with tics, but body movements keeping time with mental music. At this point everyone, including Mort, saw that if the music were taken away by psychotherapy, a vast reservoir of apprehension would be released. The consequences of this were unforeseeable, unless his fears could be replaced by more agreeable emotions. What to do?

It soon became clear that all the members of the group knew they were going to die sooner or later, and that they all had feelings about it which they were holding back in various ways. Just as with Mort, the time and effort they spent covering up were blackmail payments made to death, which prevented them from fully enjoying life. Such being the case, they might do more living in the twenty or fifty years left to each of them than Mort could do in the two or five years left to him. Thus it was determined that it was not the duration of life, but the quality of living which was important: not a startling or novel discovery, but one arrived at in a more poignant way than usual because of the presence of the dying man, which had a deep effect on everyone.

It was agreed by the other members (who understood Martian talk, which they gladly taught Mort, and which he gladly learned) that living meant such simple things as seeing the trees, hearing the birds sing, and saying Hello to people: experiences of awareness and spontaneity without drama or hypocrisy, and with reticence and decorum. They also agreed that in order to do these things, all of them, including Mort, had to get tough about the trash in their heads. When they saw that his situation was, in a way, not much more tragic than their own, the sadness and timidity caused by his presence lifted. They could now be merry with him and he with them; he and they could talk as equals. They could get tough with him about his trash, because now he knew the value of toughness, and why they were being tough; in return, he had the privilege of getting tough with them about *their* trash. In effect, Mort turned in his cancer card and resumed his membership in the human race, although everyone, including himself, still fully realized that his predicament was more acute than anyone else's.

This situation illustrates more clearly than most others the pathos and depth of the Hello problem, which, in Mort's case, went through three stages. When he first entered the group, the others did not know that he was a condemned man. They first addressed him in the manner customary in that group. Their approaches were basically set by each member's upbringing—the way his parents had taught him to greet other people, adjustments learned later in life, and a certain respect and frankness appropriate to psychotherapy. Mort, being a newcomer, responded the way he would anywhere else, pretending to be the ambitious, red-blooded American boy his parents had wanted him to be. But when he stated, during his third session, that he was a doomed man, the other members felt confused and betrayed. They wondered if they had said anything which would make them look bad in the eyes of the therapist. They seemed, in fact, angry at both Mort and the therapist for not telling them sooner, almost as though they had been tricked. In effect, they had said Hello to Mort in a standardized way, without realizing to whom they were speaking. Now that they knew he was a special person, they wished they could go back and start over, in which case they would treat him differently.

So they did start over. Instead of talking forthrightly, as they had before, they addressed him softly and cautiously, as though to say: "See how I'm going out of my way to be thoughtful of your tragedy?" None of them wanted to risk his good name now by speaking out to a dying man. But this was unfair, since it gave Mort the upper hand. In particular, nobody dared to laugh very long or very loud in such a presence. This was corrected when the problem of what Mort could do was solved; then the tension lifted and they could go back and start over for the third time, talking to him as a member of the human race, without restraint. Thus, the three stages were represented by the superficial Hello, the tense, sympathetic Hello, and the relaxed, real Hello.

Zoe cannot say Hello to Mort until she knows who he is and that can change from week to week, or even from hour to hour. Each time she meets him, she knows a little more about him than she did the last time, and she must say Hello to him in a slightly different way if she wants to keep up with their advancing friendship. But since she can never know all about him, not anticipate all the changes, she can never say a perfect Hello, but only come closer and closer to it.

THE HANDSHAKE

Many patients who come to a psychiatrist for the first time introduce themselves and shake hands when he invites them into his office. Some psychiatrists, indeed, offer their own hands first. I have a different policy in regard to handshakes. If the patient proffers his hand in a hearty way, I will shake it in order to avoid being rude, but in a noncommittal fashion, because I am wondering why he is being so hearty. If he offers it in a way which merely suggests that he considers it good manners, I will return the compliment in such fashion that we understand each other: this pleasant ritual will not interfere with the job to be done. If he proffers it in a way which indicates that he is desperate, then I will shake it firmly and reassuringly to let him know that I understand his need. But my manner when I enter the waiting room, the expression on my face and the position of my arms, indicates clearly enough to most newcomers that this amenity will be omitted unless they insist upon it. That is intended to establish, and usually does establish, that we are both there for a more serious purpose than to prove that we are good fellows or to exchange courtesies. Mainly, I do not shake hands with them because I do not know them, and I do not expect them to shake hands with me, because they do not know me; also, some people who come to psychiatrists object to being touched, and it is a courtesy to them to refrain from doing so.

The ending of the interview is a different matter. By that time I know a great deal about the patient, and he knows something about me. Thus, when he leaves, I make a point of shaking hands with him, and I know enough about him to know how to do it properly. This handshake means something very important to him: that I am accepting* him even after he has told me all the "bad" things about himself. If he needs comforting, my handshake is such that it will comfort him; if he needs assertion of his masculinity, my handshake will evoke his masculinity. This is not a carefully thought out device to seduce the patient; it is a spon-

---

* "Acceptance" is not used here in its ill-defined, sentimental sense; it means, specifically, that I am willing to spend more time with him. This involves a serious commitment which may, in some cases, mean one or more years of patience, effort, ups and downs, and getting up in the morning.

taneous and freely given recognition of him as I now know him after talking for an hour with him about his most intimate concerns. On the other side, if he has lied to me out of malice rather than natural embarrassment, or tried to exploit or browbeat me, I will not shake hands with him, so that he knows he will have to behave differently if he wants me on his side.

With women, it is slightly different. If one needs a palpable sign that I accept her, I will shake hands in a way suitable to her needs; if (as I know by this time) another shrinks from contact with men, I will say farewell in a correct way but let her pass without a handshake. This latter case illustrates most clearly the reason for not shaking hands as a greeting: if I shake hands with her at the start, before I know with whom I am shaking hands, I awaken her abhorrence. I have, in effect, intruded upon and insulted her before the interview, by forcing her, out of good manners, and against her inclination, to touch me and let me touch her, however courteously.

In therapy groups, I follow a similar policy. I do not say Hello on entering, because I have not seen the members for a whole week, and I do not know to whom I am saying Hello. A light or cordial Hello might be quite out of place in the light of something that has happened to them in the interval. But I do make a very strong point of saying Good-by to each member at the end of the meeting, because then I know to whom I am saying Good-by, and how to say it in each case. For example, suppose one woman's mother has died since the last meeting. A genial Hello from me would seem out of place to her. She might forgive me for it, but there is no need to put that strain on her. By the time the meeting is over, I know how to say Good-by to her in her bereavement.

FRIENDS

Socially, it is different, since friends are for stroking. With them, Hello and Good-by range from an open handshake to a big hug, depending on what they are ready for or need; or sometimes it is josh and jive to keep from getting too involved, a "smile when you say that." But one thing in life is more certain than taxes and just as certain as death: the sooner you make new friends, the sooner you'll have old ones.

THE THEORY

So much for Hello and Good-by. What happens in between falls into the framework of a specific theory of personality and group dynamics, which is also a therapeutic method, known as transactional analysis. In order to appreciate what follows, it is first necessary to understand the principles of this approach.

HUMAN DESTINY

It is incredible to think, at first, that man's fate, all his nobility and all his degradation, is decided by a child no more than six years old, and usually three, but that is what script theory claims. It is a little easier to believe after talking to a child of six, or maybe three. And it is very easy to believe by looking around at what is happening in the world today, and what happened yesterday, and seeing what will probably happen tomorrow. The history of human scripts can be found on ancient monuments, in courtrooms and morgues, in gambling houses and letters to the editor, and in political debates, where whole nations are talked down the righteous road by somebody trying to prove that what his parents told him in the nursery will work for the whole world. But fortunately, some people have good scripts, and some even succeed in freeing themselves to do things their own way.

Human destiny shows that, by diverse means, men come to the same ends, and by the same means they come to diverse ends. They carry their scripts around in their heads in the form of Parental voices telling them what to do and not do, and their aspirations in the form of Child pictures of how they would like it to be, and among the three of them they put their shows on the road. There they find themselves entangled in a web of other people's scripts: first their parents, then their spouses, and over all of them, the scripts of those who govern the places where they live. There are also chemical hazards like infectious diseases, and physical ones, such as hard objects that the human body is not constructed to withstand.

The script is what the person planned to do in early childhood, and the life course is what actually happens. The life course is determined by genes, by parental background, and by external circumstances. An individual whose genes cause mental retardation, physical deformity, or early death from cancer or diabetes, will have little opportunity to make his own life decisions or to carry them through to completion. The course of his life will be determined by inheritance (or perhaps birth injury). If the parents themselves suffered from severe physical or emotional deprivation as infants, that may destroy their children's chances of carrying out a script, or perhaps even of forming one. They may kill their offspring by neglect or abuse, or condemn them to life in an institution from an early age. Diseases, accidents, oppression, and war may terminate even the most carefully thought out and best supported life plan. So can a walk or a drive through the script of an unknown person: an assassin, thug, or car-crasher. A combination of these—genes plus oppression, for example—may close so many avenues to members of a certain line that they have few choices in planning their scripts, and it may make a tragic life course almost inevitable.

But even with strict limitations, there are nearly always some alternatives open. An aerial bomb, an epidemic, or a massacre may leave no choice at all, but at the next level, the person may be able to choose between killing, being killed, or killing himself, and there his choice will depend on his script, that is, the kind of decision he made in early childhood.

The difference between life course and life plan can be illustrated by considering two rats used in an experiment to show that the early experiences of a mother rat can affect the behavior of her offspring [1]. The first animal was named Victor Purdue-Wistar III, or Victor for short. (Purdue-Wistar was the actual surname of the rats used in this experiment, and Victor and Arthur were the forenames of their grandfathers, the experimenters.) Victor came from a long line of experimental subjects, and his genes suited him for this station in life. His mother, Victoria, had been handled and caressed when she was a pup. His distant cousin, Arthur Purdue-Wistar III (Arthur), was equally suited to being an experimental subject. His mother, Arthuria, had been left in her cage and was never handled or caressed when she was little. When the two cousins grew up, it was found that Victor weighed more, explored less, and dropped his excretions more often than Arthur did. What happened to them in the long run, after the experiment was over, is not stated, but it probably depended upon external forces, such as what the experimenters needed to use them for. Thus, their life courses were determined by their genes, their mothers' early experiences, and decisions made by stronger forces over which they had no control and to which there was no appeal. Any "scripts" or "plans" they wanted to carry out as individuals were limited by all of this. Thus Victor, who liked to vegetate, could so indulge himself; while Arthur, who wanted to explore, was frustrated in his cage; and neither of them, however strong the urge, could seek for immortality through reproduction.

Tom, Dick, and Harry, distant cousins of Victor and Arthur, had a different experience. Tom was programed to press a lever in order to avoid getting an electric shock, and as a reward he would get a pellet of food. Dick was programed the same way, except that his treat was a drink of alcohol. Harry was also programed to avoid the unpleasant shock, and his reward was a pleasant shock instead. Then they were switched around so that in the long run all three of them learned all three of the programs. After that, they were put in a cage with three levers: one for food, one for alcohol, and one for the pleasant shock. Then each one could make his own "decision" as to how he wanted to spend his life: eating, lying in a drunken stupor, or getting electric thrills, or any combination or alternation of these. Furthermore, there was a treadmill in the new cage, and each one could decide whether he wanted to take exercise along with his other rewards.

This was exactly like a script decision, for each rat could decide whether he wanted to spend his life as a gourmand, an alcoholic, a thrill-seeker, or an athlete, or whether he preferred a moderate combination. But although each could follow his "script decision" and take the consequences as long as he remained in the cage, the actual outcomes of their lives depended on an external *force majeure*, for the experimenter could interrupt the experiment and break up the "script" whenever he felt like it. Thus their life courses and their life styles were largely determined by their "life plans" up to the final outcome, which was decided by someone else. But these "life plans" could only be chosen from among the alternatives offered by their "parents," the experimenters who programed them. And even that choice was influenced by things that had happened to them earlier.

Although men are not laboratory animals, they often behave as though they are. Sometimes they are put in cages and treated like rats, manipulated and sacrificed at the will of their masters. But many times the cage has an open door, and a man has only to walk out if he wishes. If he does not, it is usually his script which keeps him there. That is familiar and reassuring, and after looking out at the great world of freedom with all its toys and dangers, he turns back to the cage with its buttons and levers, knowing that if he keeps busy pushing them, and pushes the right one at the right time, he will be assured of food, drink, and an occasional thrill. But always, such a caged person hopes or fears that some force greater than himself, the Great Experimenter or the Great Computer, will change or end it all.

The forces of human destiny are foursome and fearsome: demonic parental programing, abetted by the inner voice the ancients called the *Daemon*; constructive parental programing, aided by the thrust of life called *Phusis* long ago; external forces, still called Fate; and independent aspirations, for which the

ancients had no human name, since for them such were
the privileges mainly of gods and kings.

HISTORICAL

As a clinician, the psychiatrist or the clinical psychologist is interested in *everything* that may affect the
patient's behavior. In the following chapters no attempt is made to discuss all the factors which might
affect the life *course* of the individual, but only those
which are known at present to have a strong influence
on the life *plan*.

But before we go on to consider how scripts are
chosen, reinforced, and put into operation, and to dissect out the elements which make them up, we should
state that the idea is not entirely new. There are many
allusions in classical and modern literature to the fact
that all the world's a stage and all the people in it
merely players, but allusions are different from a
sustained and informed investigation into the matter.
Such investigations have been carried on by many psychiatrists and their pupils, but they have been unable
to go very far in a systematic way because they did not
have at their disposal the powerful weapons of structural analysis (diagraming and classifying transactions),
game analysis (uncovering the con, the gimmick, the
switch, and the payoff), and script analysis (the script
matrix with the dreams, sweat shirts, trading stamps,
and other elements derived from it).

The general idea that human lives follow the patterns
found in myths, legends, and fairy tales is most elegantly
elaborated in Joseph Campbell's book, previously referred to [2]. He bases his psychological thinking
mainly on Jung and Freud. Jung's best-known ideas in
this connection are the Archetypes (corresponding
to the magic figures in a script) and the Persona
(which is the style the script is played in). The rest
of Jung's ideas are not easy to understand or to relate
to real people without very special training, and even
then they are subject to different interpretations. In
general, Jung is in favor of thinking about myths and

fairy tales, and that is an important part of his influence.

Freud directly relates many aspects of human living to a single drama, the Oedipus myth. In psychoanalytic language, the patient is Oedipus, a "character" who exhibits "reactions." Oedipus is something going on in the patient's head. In script analysis, Oedipus is an ongoing drama that is actually taking place right now, divided into scenes and acts, with a build-up, a climax, and an ending. It is essential for others to play their parts, and the patient sees that they do. He only knows what to say to people whose scripts match or dovetail with his own. If his script calls for him to kill a king and marry a queen, he has to find a king whose script calls for him to be killed, and a queen whose script calls for her to be stupid enough to marry him. Some of Freud's followers, such as Glover, are beginning to recognize that Oedipus is a drama rather than merely a set of "reactions," while Rank, Campbell's chief predecessor, showed that most important myths and fairy tales come from a single basic plot, and that this plot appears in the dreams and lives of large numbers of people all over the world.

Freud speaks of the repetition compulsion and the destiny compulsion, but his followers have not pursued these ideas very far to apply them to the entire life courses of their patients. Erikson is the most active psychoanalyst in making systematic studies of the human life cycle from birth to death, and naturally, many of his findings are corroborated by script analysis. In general, it may be said that script analysis is Freudian, but it is not psychoanalytic.

Of all those who preceded transactional analysis, Alfred Adler comes the closest to talking like a script analyst.

. . If I know the goal of a person I know in a general way what will happen. I am in a position to bring into their proper order each of the successive movements made. . . . We must remember that the person under observation would not know what to do with himself were he not oriented toward some goal . . .

which determines his lifeline . . . the psychic life of man is made to fit into the fifth act like a character drawn by a good dramatist . . . every psychic phenomenon, if it is to give us any understanding of a person, can only be grasped and understood if regarded as a preparation for some goal . . . an attempt at a planned final compensation and a (secret) life plan . . . the life plan remains in the unconscious, so that the patient may believe that an implacable fate and not a long-prepared and long-meditated plan for which he alone is responsible, is at work. . . . Such a man concludes his account and reconciles himself with life by constructing one or a number of "if-clauses." "If conditions had been different . . ."

The only exceptions which a script analyst would take to these statements are (1) that the life plan is usually not unconscious; (2) that the person is by no means solely responsible for it; and (3) that the goal and the manner of reaching it (the actual transactions, word for word) can be predicted much more precisely than even Adler claimed.

Recently, R. D. Laing, the British psychiatrist, has described in a radio broadcast a view of life which is amazingly similar, even in its terminology, to the theory discussed in this book. For example, he uses the word "injunction" for strong parental programing [3]. Since, at this writing, he has not yet published these ideas, it is not possible to evaluate them properly.

Far older than all these, however, are the script analysts of ancient India, who based their prognostications largely on astrology. As the *Panchatantra* very aptly says, about 200 B.C.E.:

> These five are fixed for every man
> Before he leaves the womb:
> His length of days, his fate, his wealth,
> His learning, and his tomb.

We need only make some slight changes to bring this up to date.

These five are taken from your sires
Six summers from the womb:
Your length of days, your fate, your wealth,
Your learning, and your tomb.

REFERENCES

1. Denenberg, V. H., and Whimby, A. E.: "Behavior of Adult Rats is Modified by the Experiences Their Mothers Had as Infants," *Science* 142:1192-1193, November 29, 1963.

2. The bibliography for the historical background of the script concept is as follows:

Adler, A. "Individual Psychology" in *The World of Psychology,* ed. G. B. Levitas, George Braziller, New York, 1963.

Campbell, J. *The Hero With a Thousand Faces.* Pantheon Books, New York, 1949.

Erikson, E. *Childhood and Society.* W. W. Norton & Company, New York, 1950.

Freud, S. *Beyond the Pleasure Principle.* International Psychoanalytical Press, London, 1922.

Glover, E. *The Technique of Psycho-Analysis.* International Universities Press, New York, 1955.

Jung, C. G. *Psychological Types.* Harcourt, Brace & Company, New York, 1946.

Rank, O. *The Myth of the Birth of the Hero.* Nervous and Mental Disease Monographs. New York. 1910.

3. First used in this connection by C. M. Steiner (*Transactional Analysis Bulletin* 5:133, April 1966).

12. Prenatal Influences

INTRODUCTORY

The script scene began long ages past, when life first oozed out of the mud and began to transmit the results of its experiences chemically, through genes, to its descendants. This chemical branch culminated in the spider, who spins his strange circular geometry without instruction, the coiled spirals in his chromosomes supplying him with instant engineering drawings that will bridge any corner where the flies abound [1]. In his case, the script is written in fixed molecules of organic acids (DNA) bequeathed him by his parents, and he spends his life as an educated pen point, carrying out their instructions with no possibility of deviation or improvement except by drugs or some untoward accident beyond his control.

In man, too, the genes determine chemically some of the patterns he must follow, and from which he cannot deviate. They also set the upper limit for his individual aspirations: how far he can go as an athlete, thinker, or musician, for example, although because of psychological barriers great or small, few men reach their full possibilities even in these fields. Many a man with the chemistry of a great ballet dancer spends his time dancing with other people's dishes in a lunchroom, and others with the genes of a mathematician pass their days juggling other people's papers in the back room of a bank or bookie joint. But within his chemical limitations, whatever they are, each man has enormous possibilities for determining his own fate. Usually, however, his parents decide it for him long before he can see what they are doing.

As life broke free to some extent from rigid chemical patterns, other ways of regulating behavior gradually evolved to take up the slack. The most primitive of these is probably imprinting, which is barely one step beyond a reflex [2]. Imprinting assures that an infant organism will automatically follow a certain object and treat it like a mother, whether it is really his mother or merely a yellow card drawn past him on a string. This automatic response helps to insure his survival in moments of stress, but if it goes awry it can make trouble, too.

The next step came when some animals stayed with their mothers and learned through play; patterns too complex or variable to be transmitted through the genes could be taught with a playful bite or roll or a box on the ear [3]. Then came imitation and a response to voice signals, so that the young could do not only what their genes prompted them to, and what they learned at their mothers' breasts, but also what they saw and heard in the real living of the seas and plains and forests.

It is now known that almost every kind of living organism can be trained. Bacteria can be "trained" chemically to use one kind of sugar as a substitute for another. Almost all other animals, from worms on up, can be trained psychologically, by conditioned reflexes, to go through new and special patterns of behavior. This is probably, in the long run, chemical, too, and depends on more flexible kinds of DNA than are found in the genes. But training requires trainers, and they are something else. They have to be one cut or dimension above the organisms they are training. This means they must be tamed. Taming is as different from training as a cat is from a tiger. Taming, in animals, means that the animal obeys his master even when his master isn't there. This is different from training, because training requires an outside stimulus to start off a certain pattern of behavior, while taming assures the behavior because the stimulus is inside the animal's head. A trained animal will obey his master's voice when he hears it out loud; a tamed one doesn't need to hear the sound, because he carries it around in his brain. Thus, wild animals can be trained to do tricks at their trainer's command, but they cannot easily be housebroken. Tame animals go further than that; they can be taught to behave as their master wishes even when he is away. There are various degrees of tameness, and the tamest animals of all are human children.

The most intelligent animals—monkeys, apes, and people (and maybe dolphins, too)—have another special capacity, and that is invention. This means that they can do things that none of their kind has ever done before: anything from piling one wooden box on another, to putting two rods together to form a longer one [4], to shooting for the moon.

In order to account for this progression, we can assume that DNA is evolving into ever softer and more pliable forms. Starting out as the brittle molecules of genes, which cannot be molded, but only shattered, it thawed out enough so that it could be slightly altered by repeated gentle blows of conditioning, although it would spring back if these were not reinforced from time to time. Then it softened still more so that it could record the echoes of vanished voices and events, and keep them there for a lifetime, long after they were forgotten. In still more flexible form, it became the vehicle for memory and consciousness. And in its most sensitive form to date, it shifts and vibrates in the zephyrs of experience to give us thinking and invention. What will come forth when it becomes even more delicate in its responses none of us now living will ever know, but some day our descendants will be wondrous beings that only poets presently can dimly contemplate.

Human beings have all the capacities mentioned above. Their behavior patterns are determined by rigid reflex genes, primitive imprinting, infant play and imitation, parental training, social taming, and spontaneous invention. Scripts involve all of these. The typical human being, whom we will call "Jeder," represents nearly every member of the human race in every soil and clime. He carries out his script because it is planted in his head at an early age by his parents, and stays there for the rest of his life, even after their vocal "flesh" has gone forevermore. It acts like a computer tape or a player-piano roll, which brings out the responses in the planned order long after the person who punched the holes has departed the scene. Jeder meanwhile sits before the piano, moving his fingers along the keyboard under the illusion that it is he who brings the folksy ballad or the stately concerto to its foregone conclusion.

ANCESTRAL INFLUENCES

Some scripts can be traced back in a clinical interview to the great-grandparents, and if the family has a recorded history, as is often the case with kings and their courtiers, it may go back a thousand years in time. No doubt scripts began when the first manlike creatures appeared on earth [5], and there is no reason to suspect that their scenes and acts and outcomes were different than they are now. Certainly the life courses of the kings of Egypt, which are the oldest reliable biographies we have, are typical scripts. The story of Amenhotep IV, 3500 years in the past, who changed his name to Ikhnaton is a good example [6]. By this change he brought on both greatness and the fury of those who followed him. If information about remote ancestors, or the great-grandparents, can be obtained, so much the better for the script analysis, but in ordinary practice, in most cases, it starts with the grandparents.

It is common knowledge, even proverbial, how much grandparents, alive or dead, influence the lives of their grandchildren. For a good script, "To make a lady, start with the grandmother," and for a bad one, "From shirtsleeves to shirtsleeves in three generations." Many children at an early age not only want to imitate their forebears, but would like actually to *be* their own grandparents [7]. This desire may not only have a strong influence on their life scripts, but it may cause considerable confusion in their relationships with their parents [8]. American mothers in particular, it is said, favor their fathers over their husbands, and encourage their sons to take after grandfather instead of Dad [9].

The most productive single question to ask in regard

to ancestral influences is "What kind of lives did your grandparents lead?" There are four types of reports commonly given in answer to this.

1. *Ancestral Pride*. A winner or "prince" will state in a matter-of-fact way, "My ancestors were kings of Ireland," or "My great-great grandfather was the Chief Rabbi of Lublin." It is apparent that the speaker has "permission" to follow in the footsteps of these ancestors and become an outstanding personality. If the statement is made pompously or solemnly, however, the speaker is probably a loser or "frog," and is using his ancestry to justify his existence because he himself does not have "permission" to excel.

If the response is: "(My mother was always telling me that) my ancestors were Irish kings, ha, ha," or "(My mother was always telling me that) my great-great-grandfather was the Chief Rabbi, ha ha," it is usually given from a not-O.K. position; the speaker is allowed to imitate his illustrious ancestors, but only in their losing characteristics. These replies may mean: "I'm as drunk as an Irish king should be, so that makes me like an Irish king, ha ha!" or "I'm as poor as a Chief Rabbi should be, so that makes me like a Chief Rabbi, ha ha!" In such cases, the early programing was: "You're descended from Irish kings, and they were great drinkers," or "You're descended from a Chief Rabbi, and they were very poor." This is equivalent to a directive: "Be like your famous ancestor . . ." with the clear implication from mother ". . . so drink a lot, your father does," or ". . . so don't make money, your father doesn't."

In all these cases the ancestor is a family euhemerus [10], a heroic model from the past who can be imitated but never surpassed, and these are different ways that people deal with euhemeri.

2. *Idealization*. This may be romantic or paradoxical. Thus, a winner may say: "My grandmother was a wonderful housekeeper," or "My grandfather lived to ninety-eight and had all his teeth and no gray hair." There is a clear indication that the speaker would like to follow in the romantic grandparent's footsteps

and is basing her or his script on that. A loser will express paradoxical idealization: "My grandmother was a tough, down-to-earth woman, but she became senile in her old age." There is a clear implication that she may have been senile, but she was the smartest woman in the state hospital; and furthermore, that that is also the speaker's script: to be the smartest woman in the state hospital. Unfortunately, this setup is so frequent that the competition in state hospitals to be the smartest woman on the ward can become quite strenuous, turbulent, and discouraging.

3. *Rivalry.* "My grandfather dominated my grandmother," or "My grandfather was a weakling who let everyone push him around." These are often the "neurotic" responses interpreted by psychoanalysts as expressing the child's desire to be more powerful than his parents. "Grandfather is one person who can talk back to my mother—I'd like to be him," or "If I were my father's father I wouldn't be a coward, I'd show him." Karl Abraham's case report [8] shows the scripty nature of such attitudes, where the boy indulges in daydreams of being the prince of an imaginary kingdom whose king is like his father. Then along comes the king's father, who is far more powerful than the king. Once, when the boy was punished by his mother, he said "Now I'll marry granny." Thus, his secret (but not unconscious) planning at that time was based on a fairy tale in which he becomes more powerful than his parents by becoming his grandfather.

4. *Personal Experiences.* These concern actual transactions between children and their grandparents, which are strong influences in molding the child's script. A grandmother can send a little boy forth to be a hero [11], or on the other hand, a grandfather can seduce a schoolgirl and turn her into a Little Red Riding Hood.

In general, grandparents, as mythology and clinical experience show, are regarded with awe or terror, just as parents can be regarded with admiration or fear. The more primitive feelings of awe and terror are influential in forming the child's picture of the world during the early stages of script-building [12].

THE CONCEPTIVE SCENE

The context in which Jeder was conceived may have a strong influence in deciding his life plan and his ultimate fate. This context starts off with his parents' marriage, if there was one. Sometimes the young couple get married with a strong urge to have a son and heir. This is particularly apt to happen if the marriage is arranged or encouraged by their families, especially if there is something to inherit, such as a kingdom or a corporation. The son is then reared in accordance with his station in life, and learns all the arts and crafts suitable for kings or presidents. Thus, his script is handed to him already written, and to abdicate from it may require an act of heroic renunciation. If the first-born in such cases is a girl instead of a boy, she may run into difficulties; this is often seen in the first-born daughters of bankers, who may be cast adrift to become homosexuals, strip-tease artists, or the wives of improvident and irresponsible Bohemians or trust-fund bums. In some situations, the father may even divorce the mother if she doesn't produce a boy, leaving the daughters with a keen sense of original guilt for having been born female.

On the other hand, the father may have no intention of marrying the mother, and flees the scene, never to be heard from again, as soon as she announces her pregnancy. This leaves the young hero to make his own way almost from the day of his birth. Sometimes it is the mother who runs away. But even grudging parents may accept an unwanted child because he is an income-tax deduction or a welfare claim. The teen-ager may be well aware of this, and when asked who he is, or what his script is, he will reply, "I'm an income-tax deduction (a welfare claim)."

If the child is long in being conceived, his parents' longing may lead them to dedicate him before his birth, as is the case in many legends of famous people, and in fairy tales such as Rapunzel: another way in which real life resembles literature, or as Oscar Wilde put it, nature imitates art. This raises other interesting script questions running the whole gamut of tragedy and romance. What if Romeo had fathered a child, or Ophelia given birth, or Cordelia become pregnant? What would have become of these offspring? Medea's children, and the Little Princes in the tower of London, are the most celebrated examples of children being the victims of their parents' scripts, just as the little girls and boys sold as sodomistic slaves in certain Arab countries are the most obscure [13].

The bedside manner of the actual impregnation may be called the conceptive attitude. Was it due to accident, passion, love, violence, deception, spite, or resignation? If any of these, what was the background and preparation for such an event? If it was planned, was it planned coldly or warmly, simply or bookishly, with lots of talk, or by strong, silent communication? The child's script may have the same qualities. Is sex regarded as dirty, casual, sacred, or fun? The offspring may be treated the same way. Was an abortion attempted? Were several attempts made? How many abortions or attempts were there during previous pregnancies? There is almost an infinite number of questions of varying degrees of subtlety possible here, and all these factors can influence the script of the still unborn baby. One of the most common situations is nicely summarized in a popular limerick:

> There was a young (fellow, lady) named Horn
> Who wished (he, she) had never been born.
> (He, she) wouldn't have been
> If (his, her) (father, mother) had seen
> That the end of the rubber was torn.

Even this homely genealogy is not of such somber simplicity as it seems, since there are several possibilities. For example, it is one thing if neither parent knew the condom was defective; another if the mother knew and didn't mention it to the father; and still a third if the father knew and didn't mention it to the mother.

On the cheerful side, there are the cases where both parents want children and will take their genders as they come. If a woman who decided as a little girl that

her ambition was to get married and raise children
meets a man who made the same decision when he was
little, then the offspring has a good start. Biological
difficulties which arise here may make the child even
more precious: if the woman has repeated miscarriages,
or the man has a low sperm count so that impregnation
is delayed through the years, then, as we have already
noted, the infant may be regarded as a real miracle.
On the other hand, the seventh girl in a row, or even
the seventh boy, may be greeted with mixed feelings,
and perhaps start life as a family joke.

BIRTH POSITION

The most important factor here is the parents' scripts.
Does Jeder fit in, or is he the wrong sex, or badly
timed? Does his father's script call for a scholar, and
he turns out to be, instead, a football player? Or vice
versa? Does his mother's script go along with his
father's, or is it opposite in this respect? There are also
traditions that he will hear about from fairy tales and
real life. The youngest of three sons is supposed to act
stupid until the showdown comes, and then he wins
over his brothers. If he happens to be the seventh son,
he is almost compelled to be a prophet. More particularly, the parents' script may call for them to be glori-
fied or punished by one of their children, who must
therefore turn out to be either a colossal success or a
colossal failure. Often the first-born son is chosen for
this honor [14]. If the mother's script calls for her to
be a spouseless invalid in her declining years, then one
of the children must be raised from birth to stay and
care for her, while the others must be taught to wander
off and fill the role of ingrates. If the forty-year-old
bachelor son or spinster daughter decides to break the
script by moving out of the house, or worse, by getting
married, the mother will respond, understandably and
pitiably, by having severe attacks of illness. The scripty
nature of such setups is demonstrated by the frequent
switch whereby mother "unexpectedly" wills the bulk
of her money to the ingrates, cutting off the devoted
one with a pittance.

The general rule is that, other things being equal, children will follow their parents' script regarding family constellation, and this is best shown by taking the simplest factors: number and spacing of children. (The sex of the children cannot be considered, since that is still beyond the parents' control—fortunately, since that is one way that scripts are broken up from generation to generation, so that some children, at least, get a new chance.) A careful inquiry among a number of families will reveal a surprising number of "coincidences" in this respect.

Figure 9 (below) shows such a scripty family tree. There were three boys in the Able family: Cal, Hal, and Val. When Val was born, Hal was four and Cal was six, so that their spacing is 0-4-6. Their father, Don, was the oldest of three children spaced 0-5-7. Their mother, Fan, was the oldest of three girls spaced 0-4-5. Her two sisters, Nan and Pan, also had three children each. Fan's mother was the older of two girls spaced 0-6, with a miscarriage in between. It can be seen that all of these threesomes were spaced within five to seven fertile years [15].

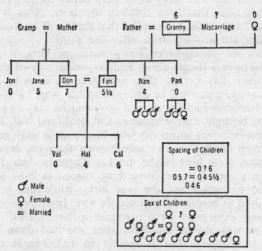

Figure 9. A scripty family tree—the Ables.

This type of family tree shows how some people tend to follow their parents' example in family planning as far as number and spacing of offspring are concerned. Let us consider some of the possible "script directives" that might have come from Gramp and Granny to Don and Fan in this particular case.

a. "When you grow up, have three children, and then you are free to do as you please." This is the most flexible, and involves no hurry or constraint. Fear of "script failure" and loss of mother's love can occur only if Fan approaches menopause without having produced the required three offspring. But note that Fan is not free *until* she has the third child. This is an "Until" script.

b. "When you grow up, have at least three children." There is no constraint here, but there may be a sense of hurry, particularly if Gramp or Granny make jokes about Don and Fan's fertility. This is an "Open End" script, since Fan is free to have as many children as she likes after the third.

c. "When you grow up, have no more than three children." There is no hurry, but there is constraint, and Don and Fan may be uneasy about further pregnancies after the three children are born. This is an "After" script, since it implies that there will be trouble if there are any children after the third.

Now let us consider Fan's point of view if she should have a fourth child, Pedwar, under any of these directives. (a) means "The first three children belong to Granny, and must be brought up her way." Pedwar then becomes Fan's very own boy, and he may or may not be brought up the same as Cal, Hal, and Val. Fan can use her own autonomy with him, and he may grow up to be more free and autonomous than the others. Fan may treat him as she did her Raggedy Ann doll. Raggedy Ann was her own very special doll to love as she pleased when she was little, while her other dolls had to be cared for Granny's way. In other words, Raggedy Ann may have prepared a "script slot" for Pedwar which Fan could fill after she had done her duty by Granny. (b) is similar to (a) except that Granny has more hold over Pedwar than under plan

(a) because he may be considered an extra bonus granted by Granny, rather than a free choice. Under (c) Pedwar is in trouble because Fan has disobeyed Granny in having him; he must therefore be raised as an "unwanted" child, defiantly, uneasily, or guiltily. In such a case, if our working principle is correct, the people around him will remark again and again how different he is from his three older brothers.

The next item to consider is the games parents play about the size of their families. For example, Ginnie was the oldest of eleven children, and her mother, Nanny, complained that the last five were unwanted. The naive assumption would be that Ginnie would be programed to have six children, but that was not so. She was programed to have eleven children and complain that the last five were unwanted. In that way she would be able to play "There I Go Again," "Harried," and "Frigid Woman" in her later years, just as her mother did. In fact, this example can be used as a test of psychological sophistication. Given the question: "A woman had eleven children and complained that five of them were unwanted. How many children will her oldest daughter most probably have?" the script analyst would answer "Eleven." People who answer "Six" will have difficulty in understanding and predicting human reactions, since this answer assumes that important behavior, like trivial behavior, is "rationally" motivated, which is not so. It is usually decided by the Parental directives of the script.

In investigating this aspect, the parents of the patient are asked, first, how many brothers and sisters they each have; second, how many children they want to have; and third (since as any obstetrician knows, there is many a slip 'twixt the cup and the lip), how many they actually expect to have. If the parents understand how to distinguish correctly between their ego states, a great deal more information can be gained by asking the second and third questions in structural form: "How many children does your (Parent, Adult, Child) (want, expect) to have?" This may bring out otherwise hidden conflicts among the three ego states, and between the two parents, which have an important bearing on the script directives they are giving the patient. An even more sophisticated version of this, with a corresponding increase in information gained (providing the parents are properly educated to understand the question), is to ask it in a twelve-barreled instead of a six-barreled form: "How many children does your (nurturing, controlling) Parent, Adult and (natural, adapted, rebellious) Child (want, expect) to have?" [16]

With the patient himself, the most profitable question to ask, since it is the one he is most likely to have the answer to is: "What is your position in the family?" followed by "When were you born?" The exact birthdays of the next older and the next younger must be obtained so that the differences can be calculated in months, if the children came close together. If the speaker comes into a world which is already occupied by a sister or a brother, it will make a considerable difference in his script decisions whether that sibling is older by eleven months, thirty-six months, eleven years, or twenty years. This difference will depend not only on his relationship with that sibling, but also on his parents' attitude toward that particular spacing of children. The same two considerations apply concerning the next born: it is important to know the speaker's exact age—for example, eleven months, nineteen months, five years, or sixteen years, at the time the next child arrived on the scene. In general, all siblings born before the speaker reaches his seventh birthday will have a decisive influence on his script, and one of the important factors is the number of months' difference in age between them, since as noted above, this will affect not only his own attitude but that of his parents as well. Notable variations occur if the speaker is a twin, or came before or after twins.

In some cases, where the patient is interested in astrology, meteorology, or hagiology, the exact date of his own birth will have a strong script significance. This is especially important if his parents had a similar interest in the calendar.

BIRTH SCRIPTS

Otto Rank believed that the circumstances of birth itself, the "birth trauma," are imprinted on the psyche of the infant and often reappear in symbolic form in later life, particularly as a desire to return to the blissful peace of the womb, as described by his disciple Fodor [17]. If that were so, the fears and longings which arise from passing under that arch through which no man can ever pass again, nature's original one-way street, would certainly appear as important elements in the script. Perhaps they do, but there is no reliable way to check it, even by comparing Caesarean births with normal ones. Hence the influence of the "birth trauma" on the life script remains in the realm of speculation. As a matter of fact, real-life scripts said to be based on the actual occurrence of Caesarean birth, like their theatrical counterparts, are unconvincing. As in *Macbeth*, the event is exploited as a mere play on words or a conundrum, a *foetus ex machina*, rather than forming the serious basis for a script. It is quite likely, however, that a child who is *told later* that he was a Caesarean birth, and can understand what that means, might incorporate that fact somehow into his script and elaborate upon it further when he learns who his distinguished predecessors were. A decision on this point awaits the collection of some good case histories.

In practice, the two most common "birth scripts" are the "Foundling Script" and the "Torn Mother Script." The Foundling Script arises from the fantasies of adopted or even natural children about their "real" parents, and comes out as some version of the Myth of the Birth of the Hero described by Otto Rank in his book of that name [18]. The Torn Mother Script is also common, and in my experience occurs with about equal frequency in both sexes. The foundation for this script is the mother telling the child that she has been sickly ever since he was born; or in a more vicious form, that she was so badly torn by his birth that she has never been the same. His reaction, and his script, is based on his own observations in the matter. If mother has indeed been invalided or crippled all his life, then he feels compelled to take the full responsibility, and no amount of Adult reasoning will convince his Child that it is not his doing. If the impairment is not visible, however, and particularly if someone in the family, such as the father, implies or states that her illness is a fake, then the patient's script will be heavily loaded with ambiguity, hypocrisy, and exploitation. Sometimes the mother does not make the accusation, but leaves it to father, grandmother, or an aunt. The script which evolves is then a three-handed one, with important messages and announcements, usually "bad news," coming from a third party. It is easy to see that where the Foundling Script comes out as the Myth of the Birth of the Hero, the Torn Mother Script is the Myth of the Birth of the Villain, one saddled from birth with the horrendous crime of matricide, or, more precisely, matriclasty. "Mother died in childbirth (mine)" is almost too much for anyone to bear without good help. If mother was injured or has a cystocele, it is never too late to have it repaired, and the less said about it the better.

FORENAMES AND SURNAMES

Roger Price, in his book *What Not To Name the Baby*, lists some common American forenames and gives a one-sentence description of the kind of personality that goes with each. The uncanny accuracy, or at least plausibility, of his descriptions is of great interest to script analysts. There is no doubt that in many cases given names, short names, and nicknames, or whatever praenomen is bestowed or inflicted on the innocent newborn, are a clear indication of where his parents want him to go; and he will have to struggle against such influences, which will be continued in other forms as well, if he is to break away from the obvious hint [19]. Names as script indicators are most likely to take hold in high school, where the boy or girl reads about famous namesakes in myth and history, or where his or her classmates bring home to them with more or less brutality the hidden meanings in their names. This is something parents have control over and should be able to foresee.

There are four ways in which a forename can become scripty: purposefully, accidentally, inadvertently, and inevitably.

1. *Purposeful.* The name may be a very specialized one, such as Septimus S. (who became a professor of classical philosophy), Galen E. (who became a physician), Napoleon (who became a corporal), or Jesus, a common name in Central America. Or it may be a variant of a common name. Charles and Frederick were kings and emperors. A boy who is steadfastly called Charles or Frederick by his mother, and insists that his associates call him that, lives a different style of life from one who is commonly hailed as Chuck or Fred, while Charlie and Freddie are likely to be horses of still another color. Naming a boy after his father or a girl after her mother is usually a purposeful act on the part of the parents, and puts an obligation on the offspring which they may not care to fulfill, or may even actively rebel against, so that their whole life plan is permeated by a slight bitterness or an active resentment.

2. *Accidental.* A girl called Durleen or Aspasia, and a boy called Marmaduke, may get along smoothly in one state or country or high school, but if their parents chance to move elsewhere, they may be made acutely conscious of their names and be forced to take a position about it. Similarly with a boy called Lynn or a girl named Tony.

3. *Inadvertent.* Pet names such as Bub, Sis, and Junior may not be intended to stick, but quite often they do, so that the person remains Bub, Sis, or Junior for life, willingly or unwillingly.

4. *Inevitable.* Surnames are a different matter, since the parents have little option but to pass on what they got from grandfather. There are many honorable European names which become obscenities in English; as one man morosely remarked: "I'm so lucky. I've got only one dirty word in my name." This was brought to his attention most clearly in high school, where he

suffered not only the indignities bestowed on immi-
grants, but in addition offered a ready-made handle
for ribaldry. But he felt that his name was no asset in
the business world either. Some people in this predicament feel that they are cursed by their ancestors from
birth to be losers. On the other hand, Christ is a not
uncommon surname, and this also poses a script problem, albeit of a different kind, especially for church-
going boys. It is no wonder that H. Head and W. R.
Brain both became well-known neurologists.

Besides being asked "Who chose your name?" and
"Where does your surname come from?" the patient
should also be asked in every case: "Have you ever
actually read your birth certificate?" If he has not, he
should be instructed to do so, or even better, bring it
in for the therapist to see. About fifty per cent of people
find surprises on their birth certificates when they read
them carefully for the first time: omissions, misappre-
hensions, or information they were not aware of. Often
the name on the certificate is different from what they
have been called all their lives, much to their astonish-
ment or chagrin. Almost all of these suprises will throw
additional light on the scripts of the parents and the
context of the patient's birth.

REFERENCES

1. Witt, P. N., and Reed, C. F. "Spider-Web Building,"
Science 149:1190-1197, September 10, 1965.

2. Lorenz, K. Z. *King Solomon's Ring.* Thomas Y. Crowell
Company, New York, 1933.

3. Bateson, G. "The Message 'This is Play.'" In *Group
Processes: Transactions of the Second Conference.* (Bertram
Schaffner, ed.) Josiah Macy, Jr. Foundation, New York, 1956.

4. Zuckerman, S. *Functional Affinities of Man, Monkeys,
and Apes.* Harcourt Brace & Company, New York, 1933.

5. Simons, E. L. "Some Fallacies in the Study of Hominid
Phylogeny." *Science* 141:879-889, September 6, 1963.

6. Cf. Freud, S. *Moses and Monotheism,* Alfred A. Knopf,
New York, 1939.
From the present point of view, this deals with the effect of
Ikhnaton's script on Moses' script. In script language, it places
Ikhnaton as the euhemerus or "grandparent" of all Israelites,
and their script follows his: his temples were destroyed and

his followers persecuted or killed. The Israelis of today have the correct antithesis to this script, which is to employ the necessary hardware to avert the tragic ending.

Amenhotep-haq-Uast's other name (besides Ikhnaton) was Neferkheperu-Ra-ua-en-Ra, whose hieroglyphs roughly translate as "Take your lute and your scarab and enjoy the sun," while according to the Ikhnaton cartouche, he has traded this in for a cake and a feather (Line Character #12 and Trees and Plants #33 in Holzhausen's classification of hieroglyphs). This is like a modern, hippie, script switch, either way: people with guitars get a yen for cake, or people with cake turn it in for a guitar.

7. Jones, E. "The Phantasy of the Reversal of Generations." *Papers on Psycho-Analysis,* Fifth edition. Beacon Press, Boston, 1961. Here Jones describes the "grandfather complex," the desire of children to become parents of their own parents, based on the belief that as they grow bigger their parents will grow smaller.

8. Abraham, K. "Some remarks on the role of grandparents in the psychology of neuroses." *Clinical Papers and Essays on Psycho-Analysis.* Basic Books, New York, 1955. What Abraham describes here is exactly what is meant by a "script fantasy," where the boy plans his life on a fairy-tale level.

9. Erikson, E. *Childhood and Society.* W. W. Norton & Company, 1950.

10. Berne, E. *The Structure and Dynamics of Organizations and Groups.* J. B. Lippincott Company, Philadelphia, 1963. Grove Press (Paperback), New York, 1966, pp. 98-101.

11. Helene Deutsch describes three types of "good grandmother" and the dreaded "wicked grandmother," or witch, in her chapter on the climacterium in *The Psychology of Women,* Volume Two. Grune & Stratton, New York, 1945.

12. Anthropologists, more than most other groups, are aware of the important influence of the grandparents on the child's career, an influence which is not only clearly recognized, but also highly ritualized in small primitive societies, especially those which have totems. See, for example, Ashley-Montagu, M. F. *Coming Into Being Among the Australian Aborigines.* George Routledge & Sons, London, 1937, and Roheim, G. *Psychoanalysis and Anthropology.* International Universities Press, New York, 1950.

13. O'Callaghan S. *The Slave Trade Today.* (Including a debate in the House of Lords, Thursday, July 14, 1960.) Crown Publishers, Inc., New York, 1961.

14. There is a considerable body of literature about birth position. The first systematic study was probably F. Galton's *English Men of Science* (1874). He found a preponderance of only sons and first-born sons in his population. Adler, on the

other hand, in his paper on "The Family Constellation," states that "the youngest child is usually a peculiar type." (*Understanding Human Nature*) One of the most interesting discussions is that of W. D. Altus in *Science* 151:44-48, January 7, 1966. This was followed by a series of "Letters to the Editor," *Science* 152:1177-1184, May 27, 1966.

15. It is difficult to get adequate census data to evaluate statistically the significance of the coincidences in the Able family. One set of figures, obtained by the President's Research Committee on Social Trends (1933), is quoted by Pressey, S. L., Janney, J. E. & Kuhlen, R. G., in *Life: A Psychological Survey* (Harper & Brothers, New York, 1939). In metropolitan Chicago at that time, only 42 per 1000 families consisted of a husband, a wife, and three children, so that the probability of the occurrence of six such sets in collateral and direct ascendancy, which (except for the miscarriage) is the import of Figure 9, is not great by chance alone. Excluding families with no children at all from the Chicago figures, the prevalence of the cited constellation rises to 90 per 1000, or about one in ten. On this basis, the crude probability that the family tree of Figure 9 is due to chance alone is therefore of the order of one in 10^6, while the actual occurrence of similar improbabilities in my own patient population is about one in five. This indicates that we are dealing here with the influence of "information" or programing, and it is just that kind of behavior programing that we are calling the "script." If we consider, in addition, the regular irregularity of the unusually short fertile periods in Figure 9, this indication is strongly reinforced.

16. This may seem far out, but students of family size are quite unable to come up with reliable projections by assuming a unified or "integrated" personality. They use terms like "ideal," "desired," and "intended" families in interviews. These roughly correspond to Parent, Child, and Adult ideas. But "many wives who said that they had not 'really wanted' another child before the last conception also said . . . that if they could have just the number they wanted and then stop, they would have the same number they had and even more." The debate is whether "excess fertility" can be equated with "unwanted" pregnancies. But the transactional analyst knows that there are at least three different people in each person interviewed who may "want," "really want," or "not want" more babies, and they may all feel differently about it, so questionnaires on this subject that do not take ego states into account are missing something of decisive importance. For a discussion of such questionnaires, see Barish, N. H. "Family Planning and Public Policy: Who is Misleading Whom?" *Science* 165:1203-1204, September 19, 1969.

17. Fodor, N. *The Search for the Beloved*. Hermitage Press, New York, 1949.

18. Rank, O. *The Myth of the Birth of the Hero*. Nervous and Mental Disease Monographs, New York, 1910.

19. Price, R. *What Not To Name the Baby*. New York, 1904. H. L. Mencken gives many revealing examples of "scripty" names in *The American Language*, Alfred A. Knopf, New York (1919), 4th edition, 1949, Chapter 10, especially pp. 518ff.

13. Waiting for Rigor Mortis

One object of script analysis is to fit the patient's life plan into the grand historical psychology of the whole human race, a psychology which apparently has changed but little from cave days, through the early farming and ranching settlements and the great totalitarian governments of the Middle East, up to the present time. Joseph Campbell, in *The Hero With a Thousand Faces*, which is the best textbook for script analysts, summarizes this as follows:

"Freud, Jung and their followers have demonstrated irrefutably that the logic, the heroes, and the deeds of myth survive into modern times. . . . The latest incarnation of Oedipus, the continued romance of Beauty and Beast, stand this afternoon on the corner of Forty-Second Street and Fifth Avenue, waiting for the traffic light to change." He points out that while the hero of myth achieves a world-historical triumph, the hero of the fairy tale achieves merely a small domestic victory. And patients are patients, we may add, because they cannot achieve the victories they aim for and still survive. Hence they come to the doctor, "the knower of all the secret ways and words of potency. His role is precisely that of the Wise Old Man of the myths and fairy tales whose words assist the hero through the trials and terrors of the weird adventure."

That, at any rate, is the way the Child in the patient sees it, no matter how his Adult tells the story, and it is quite evident that all children, since the beginning of humanity, have had to cope with the same problems, and have had about the same weapons at their disposal. When it comes to the cutting, life is the same old wine in new bottles: coconut and bamboo bottles gave way to goatskins, goatskins to pottery, pottery to glass, and glass to plastic, but the grapes have hardly changed at all, and there is the same old intoxication on top and the same old dregs at the bottom. So, as Campbell says, there will be found little variation in the shapes of the adventures and the characters involved. Hence, if we know some of the elements of the patient's script, we can predict with some confidence where he is heading, and head him off before he meets with misfortune or disaster. That is called preventive psychiatry, or "making progress." Even better, we can get him to change his script or give it up altogether, which is curative psychiatry, or "getting well."

Thus, it is not a matter of doctrine or necessity to find precisely the myth or fairy tale which the patient is following; but the closer we can come, the better. Without such a historical foundation, errors are frequent. A mere episode in the patient's life, or his favorite game, may be mistaken for the whole script; or the occurrence of a single animal symbol, such as a wolf, may lead the therapist to bark up the wrong tree. Relating the patient's life or his Child's life plan to a coherent story which has survived for hundreds or thousands of years because of its universal appeal to the primitive layers of the human mind, at least gives a feeling of working from a solid foundation, and at best may give very precise clues as to what needs to be done to avert or change a bad ending.

THE WAITING FOR *RIGOR MORTIS* SCRIPT

For example, a fairy tale may reveal elements of a script which are otherwise hard to dig up, such as the "script illusion." The transactional analyst believes that psychiatric symptoms result from some form of self-deception. But patients can be cured just because their lives and their disabilities are based on a figment of the imagination.

In the script known as "Frigid Woman," or "Waiting for Rigor Mortis" (WRM), the mother keeps telling her daughter that men are beasts, but it is a wife's duty to submit to their bestiality. If the mother pushes hard enough, the girl may even get the idea that she will die if she has an orgasm. Usually such mothers are great snobs, and they offer a release or an "antiscript" that will lift the curse. It is all right for the daughter to have sex if she marries a very important person, such as the Prince with the Golden Apples. But failing that, she tells her erroneously, "all your troubles will be over when you reach your menopause, because then you won't be in danger of feeling sexy any more."

Now it already appears as though we have three illusions: Orgathanatos, or the fatal orgasm; the Prince with the Golden Apples; and Blessed Relief, or the purifying menopause. But none of these is the real script illusion. The girl has tasted Orgathanatos by masturbation, and knows it is not fatal. The Prince with the Golden Apples is not an illusion, because it is just possible that she might find such a man, just as she might win the Irish Sweepstakes or get four aces in a poker game; both of these things are unlikely, but not mythical; they do happen. And Blessed Relief is not something her Child really wants. In order to find the script illusion, we need the fairy tale which corresponds to WRM.

THE STORY OF SLEEPING BEAUTY

An angry fairy says that Briar Rose will prick her finger with a spindle and fall down dead. Another fairy commutes this to a hundred years of sleep. When she is fifteen Briar Rose does prick her finger, and immediately falls asleep. At the same moment everybody and everything else in the castle also falls asleep. During the hundred years, many princes try to get to her through the briars which have grown up around her, but none succeeds. At last, after the time is up, a prince arrives who manages to get through because the briars let him. When he finds the princess and kisses her, she wakes up and they fall in love. At the same moment, everybody and everything else in the castle take up exactly where they left off, as though nothing had happened and no time had passed since they fell asleep. The princess herself is still only fifteen years old, not 115. She and the prince get married, and in one version, they live happily ever after; in another, this is only the beginning of their troubles.

There are many magic sleeps in mythology. Perhaps the best known is that of Brunhilde, who is left sleeping on the mountain with a ring of fire around her which only a hero can penetrate, and that is accomplished by Siegfried.

In one way or another, with slight alterations, almost everything in the story of Sleeping Beauty could actually happen. Girls do prick their fingers and faint, and they do fall asleep in their towers, and princes do wander around in the forest and look for fair maidens. The one thing that cannot happen is for everything and everybody to be unchanged and unaged after the lapse of so many years. This is a real illusion because it is not only improbable, it is impossible. And this is just the illusion on which WRM scripts are based: that when the Prince does come, Rose will be fifteen years old again instead of thirty, forty, or fifty, and they will have a whole lifetime ahead of them. This is the illusion of sustained youth, a modest daughter of the illusion of immortality. It is hard to tell Rose in real life that princes are younger men, and that by the time they reach her age they have become kings, and are much less interesting. That is the most distressing part of the script analyst's job: to break up the illusion, to inform the patient's Child that there is no Santa Claus, and make it stick. It is much easier for both of them if there is the patient's favorite fairy tale to work with.

One of the practical problems of the WRM is that if Rose does find the Prince with the Golden Apples, she often feels outclassed and has to find fault and play "Blemish" to bring him down to her level, so that he ends up wishing she would go back in the briars and fall asleep again. On the other hand, if she settles for less—the Prince with the Silver Apples, or even ordinary McIntoshes from the grocery store—she will feel cheated and take it out on him, meanwhile always keeping an eye out for the Golden One. Thus, neither the frigid script nor the magic antiscript offers much chance for fulfillment. Also, as in the fairy tale, there is his mother to contend with as well as her witch.

This script is important because a great many people in the world, in one way or another, spend their lives waiting for *rigor mortis*.

THE FAMILY DRAMA

Another good way to uncover the plot and some of the most important lines in a person's script is to ask: "If your family life were put on the stage, what kind of play would it be?" Such family dramas are usually named after the Greek Oedipus and Electra plays, in which the boy competes with father for his mommy and the girl wants daddy for her own. But the script analyst has to know what the parents, called for convenience Supideo and Artcele, are up to meanwhile. Supideo is the other side of the Oedipus drama, and expresses the frank or disguised sexual feelings of the mother for her son, while Artcele is the other side of Electra and shows father's feelings for the girl. A close inquiry will nearly always reveal rather obvious transactions which demonstrate that these feelings are not imaginary, even though the parent tries to conceal them, usually by playing "Uproar" with the child. That is, the disturbed parent tries to cover up his Child sexual feelings for his offspring by coming on Parental and ordering the offspring about in a quarrelsome way. But on certain occasions they leak out, despite all efforts to disguise them by "Uproar" and other devices. Actually, the happiest parents are often those who openly admire the attractiveness of their children.

The Supideo and Artcele dramas, like Oedipus and Electra, have many variations. As the children grow older, they may be played out as mother sleeping with son's boyfriend or father sleeping with his daughter's chum. Farther out and even more "gamy" versions are mother sleeping with son's girl.* This compliment may be returned by the young Oedipus sleeping with father's mistress, or Electra with mother's lover. Sometimes the family script calls for one of several members to be

---

* This may occur when mother has no son of her own to play Jocasta with, and similarly if father has no daughter of his own.

homosexual, with corresponding variations in child sex play, incest between siblings, and later seductions of each other's partners. Any deviations from the standard Oedipus (son wandering or dreaming about sex with mother) or Electra (daughter wandering or dreaming about father) roles will undoubtedly influence the whole life course of the person.

In addition to, or beyond, the sexual aspects of the family drama, there are even more poignant ones. A jilted homosexual girl attacked her lover, held a knife to her throat and cried: "You'll let me give you these wounds, but you won't let me heal them." This perhaps is the motto of all family dramas, the origin of all parental anguish, the basis for youthful rebellion, and the cry of couples not yet ready for divorce. The wounded flee, and the cry above is the Martian translation of the ad: "Mary, come home. All is forgiven." And that is why children stick with even the most miserable parents. It hurts to be wounded, but it feels so good to be healed.

14. Early Influences

The first script programing takes place during the nursing period, in the form of short protocols which can later be worked into complicated dramas. Usually these are two-handed scenes between the baby and his mother, with little interference from the onlookers, if any, and with such breast-fed titles as "Public Performance," "It's Not Time Yet," "Whenever You're Ready," "Whenever I'm Ready," "Hurry Up," "He Who Bites Gets Brushed Off," "While Mother Smokes," "Pardon Me, The Phone Rang," "What's He Fussing About?," "There's Never Enough," "First One Then The Other," "He Looks Pale," "Let Him Take His Time," "Isn't He Amazing?," "Golden Moments of Love and Content," and "Lullaby."

Slightly more complicated are the corresponding bathroom scenes in the same families: "Come and See How Cute," "It's Time Now," "Are You Ready?," "You Can Just Sit There Till You Do," "Hurry Up," "Naughty Naughty," "While Mother Smokes," "While Mother is on the Telephone," "Enema Tube," "If You Don't I'll Give You Castor Oil," "Here's Your Laxative," "You'll Get Sick If You Don't," "Let Him Do It His Own Way," "That's a Good Boy," "That's a G-o-o-d Boy," and "I'll Sing While You're Doing It." Three-handed protocols are more frequent at this stage, including: "I Told You He Wasn't Ready," "Don't Let Him Get Away With That," "I'll Make Him Do It," "You Try," "You're Disturbing Him," "Why Don't You . . . Yes, But," and "He's Sure Coming Through This Time." The Phantom in the Bathroom who will some day be the Phantom in the Bedroom, may begin to appear: "Dr. Spock Says," "Tessie Had Hers Trained By the Time," and "Sister Mary Was Only." In later life these will become "Freud Says," "Nancy Always Has One," and "Helen Has It Every Night."

It is already fairly predictable who the winners and the losers will be. "Isn't He Amazing?" reinforced two years later with "That's a Good Boy" will usually do better than "What's He Fussing About?" reinforced one year later by "Enema Tube"; similarly, "Lullaby," first at nursing and later in the bathroom, will probably prevail over "While Mother Smokes." Already the feeling of O.K.ness or not-O.K.ness, which separates the now and future princes from the now and future frogs, is being implanted, and several types of frogs and princes (or for the ladies, goose girls and princesses) are being set up. "Isn't He Amazing?" the Forever Prince with the success script, is often but not always the firstborn. The Conditional Prince, "Come and See How Cute," or "Hurry Up," for example, can remain a prince as long as he stays cute and hurries up. The Conditional Frogs, "He Who Bites," "Naughty, Naughty," or "He Looks Pale Needs a Laxative," can stop being frogs by not biting or not looking pale; the Doomed Frogs, on the other hand, will hardly ever make it with anybody. Touching are the frogs who try not to care "While Mother Smokes" or "Has a Highball." Only a disaster can turn the Forever Princes into frogs; only a miracle can transform the Doomed Frogs into princes.

CONVICTIONS AND DECISIONS

By the time he gets to "I Guess I'd Better Drive You, Dear" or "Getcher Ass Outa Bed" or even "I'll Beatcher Goddam Brains Out If You Don't," the child already has certain convictions about himself and the people around him, especially his parents. These convictions are likely to stay with him the rest of his life, and may be summarized as follows: (1) I'm O.K. or; (2) I'm not-O.K.; (3) You're O.K. or; (4) You're not-O.K. On the basis of these he makes his life decision. "It's a good world, some day I'll make it a better one"—through science, service, poetry, or music. "It's a bad world, someday I'll kill myself"—or kill someone else, go crazy, or withdraw. Perhaps it's a mediocre world, where you do what you have to do and have fun in between; or a tough world, where you make good by putting on a white collar and shuffling other people's papers; or a hard world, where you sweep or bend or deal, or wiggle or fight for a living; or a dreary world, where you sit in a bar hoping; or a futile world, where you give up.

POSITIONS—THE PRONOUNS

Whatever the decision is, it can be justified by taking a position based on the now deeply ingrained convictions, a position which involves a view of the whole world and all the people in it, who are either friends or enemies: "I'll kill myself because it's a lousy world where I'm no good and neither is anyone else, my friends are not much better than my enemies." In position language this reads "I'm not-O.K., You're not-O.K., They're not-O.K. Who wouldn't kill himself under such conditions?" This is a futility suicide. Alternately, "I'll kill myself because I'm not-O.K. and everybody else is O.K."—the melancholic suicide. (Suicide here can mean anything from jumping off a bridge or car-crashing, to overeating or alcoholism.) Or "I'll kill them or turn them out because I'm O.K. and they are very not-O.K." Or "Since we're all O.K., I and you both, let's get the job done and then go out and have some fun."

"But," says someone, "I know we're O.K., but those other fellows aren't so hot." "Very well, then, I'm O.K., you're O.K., and they are not-O.K., so let's get the job done now and we'll attend to them later." In child language, this translates as "We're going to play house, but you can't play with us," which in its most extreme form and with more sophisticated equipment can be parlayed in later years into an extermination camp.

The simplest positions are two-handed, You and I, and come from the convictions which have been fed to the child with his mother's milk. Writing as shorthand + for O.K. and − for not-O.K., the convictions

read: I + or I −; You + or You −. The possible
assortments of these give the four basic positions from
which games and scripts are played, and which program
the person so that he has something to say after he says
Hello.

1. I + You +. This is the "healthy" position (or in
treatment, the "get well" one), the best one for decent
living, the position of genuine heroes and princes, and
heroines and princesses. People in the other positions
have more or less frog in them, a losing streak put there
by their parents, which will drag them down again and
again unless they overcome it; in extreme cases they
will waste themselves if they are not rescued by a
miracle of psychiatric or self-healing. I + You + is
what the hippies were trying to tell the policeman
when they gave him a flower. But whether the I + is
genuine or merely a pious hope, and whether the
policeman will accept the + or will prefer to be − on
this particular scene, is always in doubt. I + You + is
something the person either grows into in early life,
or must learn by hard labor thereafter; it cannot be
attained merely by an act of will.

2. I + You −. I'm a prince, you're a frog. This is
the "get rid of" position. These are the people who
play "Blemish" as a pastime, a game, or a deadly procedure. They are the ones who sneer at their spouses,
send their children to juvenile hall, and fire their friends
and retainers. They start crusades and sometimes war,
and sit in groups finding fault with their real or imagined inferiors or enemies. This is the "arrogant"
position, at worst a killer's, and at best a meddler's for
people who make it their business to help the "not-O.K.
others" with things they don't want to be helped with.
But for the most part it is a position of mediocrities,
and clinically it is paranoid.

3. I − You +. This is psychologically the "depressive" position, politically and socially a self-abasement
transmitted to the children. Occupationally, it leads
people to live by choice on favors large and small and
enjoy it with a vengeance, that being the poor satisfaction of making the other pay as much as possible for
his O.K. stamp. These are melancholic suicides, losers

who call themselves gamblers, people who get rid of themselves instead of others by isolating themselves in obscure rooming houses or canyons or by getting a ticket to prison or the psychiatric ward. It is the position of the "If Onlys" and "I Should Haves."

4. I − You −. This is the "futility" position of the Why Notters: Why not kill yourself, Why not go crazy. Clinically, it is schizoid or schizophrenic.

These positions are universal among all mankind, because all mankind nurses at his mother's breast or bottle and gets the message there, and later has it reinforced when he learns his manners, whether in the jungle, the slum, the condominium, or the ancestral halls. Even in the small unlettered communities which anthropologists study for their "cultures," where everyone is raised according to the same long-established rules, there are enough individual differences between mothers (and fathers) to yield the standard harvest. For winners, there are chiefs and medicine men, captains and capitalists who own a thousand head of cattle or are worth a hundred thousand yams. The losers can be found in the mental hospital at Papeete or Port Moresby or Dakar, or perhaps in Her Majesty's Gaol at Suva. For each position already carries with it its own kind of script and its own kinds of endings. Even in this country, where there are ten thousand "cultures," there are only a few endings, none different, really, from any other country's.

Because each person is the product of a million different moments, a thousand states of mind, a hundred adventures, and usually two different parents, a thorough investigation of his position will reveal many complexities and apparent contradictions. Nevertheless, there can usually be detected one basic position, sincere or insincere, inflexible or insecure, on which his life is staked, and from which he plays out his games and script. This is necessary so that he can feel that he has both feet on solid ground, and he will be as loath to give it up as he would the foundation of his house. To take one simple example, a woman who thinks it very important that she is poor while others are rich (I − They +) will not give this up merely because she acquires a lot of money. That does not make her rich in her own estimation; it merely makes her a poor person who happens to have some assets. Her classmate who thinks it is important to be rich in contrast to the underprivileged poor (I + They −) will not abandon her position if she loses her money; this does not make her a poor person, but merely a rich person who is temporarily embarrassed financially.

This tenacity, as we shall see later, accounts for the life led by Cinderella after she married her prince, and it also accounts for the fact that men in the first position (I + You +) make good leaders, for even in the utmost adversity they maintain their universal respect for themselves and those in their charge. Thus the four basic position, (1) I + You + (success); (2) I + You − (arrogant); (3) I − You + (depressive); and (4) I − You − (futility), can rarely be changed by external circumstances alone. Stable changes must come from within, either spontaneously or under some sort of "therapeutic" influence: professional treatment, or love, which is nature's psychotherapy.

But there are those whose convictions lack conviction, so that they have options and alternations between one position and another; from I + You + to I − You −, or from I + You − to I − You +, for example. These are, as far as position is concerned, insecure or unstable personalities. Secure or stable ones are those whose positions, good or deplorable, cannot be shaken. In order for the idea of positions to be of any practical use, it must not be defeated by the changes and instabilities of the insecure. The transactional approach—finding out what was actually said and done at a certain moment—takes care of that. If A behaves at noon as though he were in the first position (I + You +), then we say that "A is in the first position." If he behaves at 6:00 P.M. as though he were in the third position (I − You +), then we say "In the noon setup A is in the first position and under 6:00 P.M. circumstances he is in the third." From this we can conclude (1) that A is insecure in the first position, and (2) that if he has symptoms they occur under special conditions. If he behaves under all circumstances as though he were in the first position, then we say that "A is stable in the first position," from which we predict (1) that A is a winner, (2) that if he has been in treatment, he is now cured, and (3) that he is game-free, or at least that he is not under a compulsion to play games, but has social control—the option of deciding for himself at each moment whether or not he wants to play. If B behaves under all circumstances as though he were in the fourth position, we say that "B is stable in the fourth position" from which we predict (1) that B is a loser, (2) that it will be difficult to cure him, and (3) that he will be unable to stop himself from playing those games which prove that life is futile. All this is done by careful analysis of actual transactions engaged in by A and B.

Once the predictions are made, they are easily tested by more observation. If later behavior does not confirm them, then either the analysis was faulty or the theory of positions is wrong and will have to be changed. If it does confirm the predictions, then the theory is strengthened. The evidence so far supports it.

THE FAMILY CULTURE

All culture is family culture, things learned as a knee baby. Details and techniques may be learned outside the home, but their value is determined by the family. The script analyst goes to the heart of the matter with a single pointed question: "What did your family talk about at the dinner table?" By this he hopes to ascertain the subject matter, which may or may not be important, and also the kinds of transactions which took place, which is always important. Some child-and-family therapists even have themselves invited to dinner at the patient's house, with the idea that this is the best way to get the greatest amount of reliable information in a short time.

One of the script analyst's slogans is, or should be, "Think sphincter!" Freud and Abraham were the first to elaborate the idea that character structure centers around bodily orifices. Both games and scripts do likewise, and the physiological signs and symptoms which form an important feature of every game and script usually center around a particular orifice or sphincter. The family culture, as shown at the dinner table, tends to revolve around the "family sphincter," and knowing which is the family's favorite is a great help in treating the patient.

The four external sphincters concerned are the oral, the anal, the urethral, and the vaginal, and perhaps more important are the internal sphincters related to these. There is also an illusory sphincter which may be called, as it is in psychoanalysis, the cloacal.

Although the mouth does have its own external sphincter, the *Orbicularis oris,* that is not usually the muscle "oral" families are concerned with, although some do have a motto, "Keep your mouth shut." What "oral" families mainly talk about is food, and the sphincters chiefly concerned are those of the throat, stomach, and duodenum. Thus, oral families are typically diet faddists and stomach worriers, and those are the subjects they talk about at dinner. "Hysterical" members of such families have spasms of the throat muscles, and "psychosomatic" members have spasms of the esophagus, stomach, and duodenum, or, conversely, they throw up or have fears of throwing up.

The anus is the sphincter par excellence. Anal families talk about bowel movements, laxatives, and enemas, or the more aristocratic colonic irrigations. Life for them is a round of poisonous matter that has to be got rid of promptly at any cost. They are fascinated by intestinal products, and proud of themselves or their children when these are large and firm and shapely. Diarrhea is judged by its copiousness, while mucous or bloody colitis is of eternal interest and can be worn with an air of modest distinction. The whole culture merges with sexuality (or anti-sexuality) in the motto "Keep a tight asshole or you'll get screwed." This means keep a poker face as well, and the philosophy may pay off in making money.

Urethral families talk a lot, long streams of watered-down ideas with a few stutters at the end, although they are never really finished talking, as there are always some last drops left which can be squeezed out if there is time. Some of them are full of piss and vinegar, and when they get pissed off they piss on people, or so they say. Some of the children rebel against the system by tightening up their urethral sphincters and holding their urine as long as possible, getting considerable pleasure from the unpleasant sensations which result and even more pleasure when they finally let loose, sometimes at night in bed.

Some families talk at mealtimes about the wickedness of sex. Their motto is "In our family, the women keep their legs crossed." Even when their legs are not crossed, they keep their vaginal sphincters up tight. In other families the vaginal sphincters are wide open and the legs loose, and the table talk is vulgar and pornographic.

These are common examples illustrating the theory of sphincters, or as it is usually called, the theory of infantile sexuality. This theory is most fully and clearly developed by Erikson. He considers five stages of development, each centered around a particular anatomical zone (oral, anal, or genital). Each zone can be "used" in five different ways or modes, including Incorporative (1 and 2), Retentive, Eliminative, and Intrusive, so that he ends up with a basic matrix of twenty-five slots. He relates certain of these slots to particular attitudes and characteristics, and to particular lines of personal development, which are similar to scripty life courses.

Using Erikson's language, the parental injunction "Keep your mouth shut" is oral retentive; "Keep a tight asshole" is anal retentive, and "Keep your legs crossed" is phallic retentive. Food fads are oral incorporative, vomiting is oral eliminative, and obscene talk is intrusive. Hence, a question about table talk can often place the family culture very precisely as to zone and mode. This is important because particular games and scripts, and their accompanying physical symptoms, are based in appropriate zones and modes. For example, "Schlemiel" is anal as to zone, and "I'm Only Trying to Help You" is intrusive as to mode, while "Alcoholic" is oral incorporative.

The mythical "cloacal sphincter" exists in the minds of confused people whose Child thinks that there is only one opening down below in both sexes, which opening can be closed off at will. This leads to scripts which are difficult for more realistic people to understand, especially if the mouth is also included. Thus a catatonic schizophrenic may close off everything at once: he keeps all his sphincters closed down so that nothing can get in or out of his mouth, bladder, or rectum, and he may have to be tube-fed, catheterized, and clystered at regular intervals to insure his physical well-being and survival. Here the script slogan is "Better death than to let them in!" and this is taken literally by the Child who controls the sphincters and who, in such cases, is very confused about how they are assembled and how they work.

A similar chain of events happens when a sphincter is held tight. In order to give the sphincter traction and support, the surrounding muscles tighten up. To compensate for that, more distant muscles are affected, and eventually the whole body is involved. This is easily demonstrated. Suppose the reader, as he sits reading, tightens up his anus. He will immediately notice that this involves the muscles of his lower back and legs. If he now rises up out of his chair, keeping his anus tight, he will note that he has to purse his lips, which in turn affects the muscles in his scalp. In other words, keeping his anus tight changes the muscular dynamics of his whole body. That is exactly what happens with people whose script calls for them to "Keep a tight asshole or you'll get screwed." Every muscle in their bodies becomes involved, including their muscles of facial expression. The facial expression influences the way other people respond to them, and in fact gives the come-on to the Child of the other person, the script antagonist, who is destined to bring about the script switch.

Here is how it works. Suppose we call the man with the tight anus Angus, and his opposite number, his script antagonist, Lana. Lana is looking for an Angus, and Angus is looking for a Lana. Lana knows instantly when she has found an Angus because of his facial expression. She confirms her Child's intuitive judgment in the course of their conversation as he reveals his attitudes and interests. Lana's role in the script of an Angus is to bring about the script switch. Angus's counterscript is to keep tight at all times, but his script is something else. No matter how hard he tries to keep tight according to the parental precept, sooner or later he drops his guard for a moment, and then his script takes over. In this moment of weakness he relaxes. That is just what Lana has been waiting for. She pulls the switch, and somehow or other, Angus "gets screwed" as she moves in to fulfill her mission. And as long as Angus tries to keep a tight anus, he is going to "get screwed" again and again. That is how the script works—unless it calls for him to be a winner, and then he is the one who will do the screwing, as in the case of some anal financiers.

Thus, the script analyst thinks sphincter so he will know what he is dealing with. The patient who gives up his script is much more relaxed in all the muscles of his body. The woman who formerly kept a tight anus, for example, will stop squirming in her chair, and the one who kept a tight vagina will no longer sit with her arms and legs tensely crossed and her right foot wrapped tightly around the inside of her left ankle.

With these remarks about the autocrats of the dinner table, who teach their children which muscles to anchor their bodies to for the rest of their lives, we conclude our survey of those influences which are most important in later childhood, and are now ready to consider the next stage in the development of the script.

SWEATSHIRTS

All the items which have been discussed so far are condensed into the patient's demeanor, the way he "comes on," and that is called his "sweatshirt." The sweatshirt, in an exceedingly creative, artistic, and economical phrase or two, indicates to the experienced eye the patient's favorite pastime, game, and feeling, his nickname, what he does in the front room and the back room, what kind of mental world he lives in, what kind of ending his script calls for, and sometimes the critical sphincter, his hero, and his totem.

The sweatshirt is usually adopted in high school or early college years, the age when sweatshirts are popular. In later life it may be embroidered or the wording changed slightly, but the core of the meaning will remain unchanged.

All competent clinicians, of whatever school, have one thing in common: they are good observers. Since they are all observing the same thing—human behavior —there is bound to be a similarity in what they see and how they sort out and account for their observations. Hence the psychoanalytic idea of "character defense" or "character armor," the Jungian concept of "attitude," the Adlerian notion of "life lie" or "life style," and the transactional metaphor of "sweatshirt" all describe very similar phenomena.

An actual sweatshirt ("Hell's Angels," "The Losers," "Black Panthers," "Harvard Track Team," or even "Beethoven") states which gang a person belongs to, and gives some indication of his philosophy and how he is likely to respond to certain stimuli; but it does not indicate exactly how he will go about conning someone and what payoff he expects. For example, it is clear that many members of the first three gangs mentioned above are riding on the "Fuck You" streetcar, but without knowing each member of the gang intimately (in the clinical sense) it is not possible to predict which ones want to be killed in order to become martyrs, which ones want merely to be manhandled so that they can cry "Police brutality!" and which ones are straight. The sweatshirt indicates their collective attitude and the games they share in common, but each one is playing out his own script with its own individual payoff.

A transactional or script sweatshirt is an attitude which is clearly advertised by the person's demeanor, just as clearly as though he wore a sweatshirt with his

---

* Many psychoanalysts consider that "transactional games" is merely a synonym for character defenses. This is not so. The sweatshirt is the character defense. Games belong to the open system of social psychology, and not to the closed energy system described by Freud.

script slogan printed on the front. Some common script sweatshirts are "Kick Me," "Don't Kick Me," "I'm Proud I'm an Alcoholic," "Look How Hard I'm Trying," "Buzz Off," "I am Fragile," and "Need a Fix?" Some sweatshirts have a message on the front and a "kicker" on the back: for example, a woman comes on like "I'm Looking For a Husband," but when she turns her back it clearly says: "But You Don't Qualify." The man with "I'm Proud I'm an Alcoholic" on his forehead may have "But Remember It's a Sickness" on his back. Transsexuals wear particularly flamboyant ones with the front slogan "Don't You Think I'm Fascinating?" while on the back it says "Isn't That Enough?"

Other sweatshirts give a picture of a more "clubbish" way of life. "Nobody Knows the Trouble I've Seen" (NOKTIS) is a fraternity with many branches, one of which is the Melancholy Litvaks' Club. The Melancholy Litvaks' Club can be visualized by a Martian as a little wooden building, sparsely furnished with rundown furniture. There are no pictures on the wall, only a framed motto reading "Why Not Kill Yourself Today?" There is a small library consisting of statistical reports and books by pessimistic philosophers. The point of NOKTIS is not the total amount of trouble, but the fact that Nobody Knows. The NOKTIS makes sure that nobody ever finds out, either, because if anybody did know, then he couldn't say "Nobody knows," and his sweatshirt would lose its point.

The sweatshirt is usually derived from a favorite slogan of the parents, such as "Nobody in the world will love you like your father and mother do." This resigned, plod-ahead sweatshirt is disjunctive, and merely serves to separate the wearer from the people around him. By a simple twist it can be transformed into a conjunctive one which will attract other people instead of putting them off, and lead to appropriate "Ain't It Awful" pastimes and games: "Nobody loves me like my father and mother do." What attracts other people is the back of this sweatshirt, which reads: "How About You?"

We can now consider in detail two common sweatshirts, and we shall try to demonstrate the usefulness of this concept in predicting significant items of behavior.

YOU CAN'T TRUST ANYBODY

There are certain people who quickly make it clear that they do not trust anybody. That is, they talk about life that way, but their behavior is not entirely consistent with what they say, because actually they are continually "trusting" people, but it usually turns out badly. The concept of sweatshirts has an advantage over the more naive approaches of "character defense," "attitude," and "life style" because they tend to take things at face value, while the transactional analyst is accustomed to look first of all for the con or paradox, and is gratified rather than surprised when he finds it. That is what he looks for when he finds a sweatshirt, and that is what gives him his therapeutic advantage. To put it another way, character analysts analyze the front of the sweatshirt very effectively, but fail to look at the back where the game slogan or "kicker" is written, or at least it takes them a long time to get around to it, while the game analyst looks there right at the beginning.

The sweatshirt "You Can't Trust Anybody" (or "You Can't Trust Anybody Nowadays," YOCTAN) is therefore not taken at face value. It does not mean that the wearer will avoid entanglements with people because he does not trust them. Quite the contrary. It means that he will seek entanglements for the express purpose of proving his slogan and reinforcing his position (I'm O.K.—They're not-O.K.). Hence the YOCTAN player picks untrustworthy people, makes ambiguous contracts with them, and then gratefully, or even gleefully, collects brown stamps when something goes wrong, thus confirming his position that "You Can't Trust Anybody." In extreme cases he may feel entitled to a "free" homicide, justified by repeated betrayals at the hands of people carefully chosen for their untrustworthiness. Once having collected enough brown stamps for such a payoff, the YOCTAN player may pick as his victim someone he has never met, perhaps a public figure whose murder rates the label of "assassination."

Other YOCTAN players may seize upon such an event to prove that the "authorities," such as the police who arrest the assassin, are untrustworthy. The police, of course, are paid for YOCTAN. It is part of their job not to be trusting. Thus a tournament is started in which amateur or semi-professional YOCTAN players are pitted against professionals. The battle cries of such a tournament, "frame-up," "codes," and "conspiracy," may go on for years or even centuries, the object being to prove such propositions as: "Homer was not really Homer, but another man of the same name," "Raisuli loved Perdicaris," and "Gavrilo Princip was not really Gavrilo Princip, but another man of the same name."

The YOCTAN sweatshirt gives the following information about the wearer. His favorite pastime is discussing doublecrosses. His favorite game is YOCTAN, proving that others are untrustworthy. His favorite feeling is triumph: "Now I've Got You, You Son of a Bitch." His nickname is Cagey, and the critical sphincter is his anus ("Keep a tight ass hole or you'll get screwed."). His hero is the man who proves that "the authorities" are untrustworthy. What he does in the front room is come on in a blandly righteous or ingenuous way, while in the back room he is scheming and untrustworthy (like the landlady who self-righteously said: "You can't trust any of your tenants nowadays. Only the other day I was going through the desk of one of them, and you'll never guess what I found!"). His mental world is a self-righteous one in which he is entitled to do all sorts of shady things, provided the aim is to uncover the untrustworthiness of others. His script calls for him to be done in by someone he trusts so that with his dying breath he can call out his slogan: "I knew it. You can't trust anybody nowadays."

Thus, the front of his sweatshirt, "You Can't Trust Anybody Nowadays," is a bland invitation to well-meaning people, such as unwary therapists, to prove that they are exceptions. If they don't take the trouble to look, ahead of time, it is only after the dust of battle settles down and the victorious player walks away that they see what is written on the back: "Now Maybe You'll Believe Me." If the therapist is alert, however, he still must be careful not to move too soon or the patient will say: "See, I can't even trust you." Then when he walks away, the kicker is still valid, so he wins either way.

DOESN'T EVERYBODY?

The thesis of this approach to life is: "It's all right to have measles, since everybody has it." Of course it isn't all right, since measles can be a dangerous disease. The classical example of "Doesn't Everybody?" occurred when a woman who was addicted to colonic irrigations came into a therapy group. She began to talk about her adventures at the colonic-irrigation parlor and everybody listened tolerantly until someone asked "What's a colonic irrigation?" The woman seemed surprised to learn that there could be so many people in one room who didn't take colonic irrigations. "Doesn't everybody?" Both her parents did, and most of her friendships were made at the irrigation parlor. The chief topic of conversation at her bridge club was comparing one irrigation parlor with another.

The "Doesn't Everybody?" sweatshirt is a favorite at high school, especially among cheer leaders, drum majorettes, and boys on the make, and even at that age it may have sinister connotations if it is reinforced by parents at home or teachers in the classroom. It is also good for business, where it is heavily exploited by undertakers, and in a lighter way by insurance salesmen. Interestingly enough, many stock salesmen, who are almost as conservative as undertakers, are wary of it. The key word, and the one that gives it its explosive political quality, is "Everybody." Who is Everybody? For the wearers of this sweatshirt, Everybody is "The people I say are O.K., including me, I hope." For this reason, they usually have two other sweatshirts that they wear on appropriate occasions. They put on

"Doesn't Everybody?" when they go out among
strangers. But when they are with the people they admire, they wear either "How'm I Doing?" or "I Know
Prominent People." They are devotees of what Sin-
clair Lewis made into Babbittry and what Alan Harrington (in *Revelations of Dr. Modesto*) satirically called
"Centralism," the doctrine that the safest place to be
is in dead center; Harrington's hero became such a
thorough Centralist that he was able to sell an insurance policy every thirty seconds or so.

The wearer of this sweatshirt has, for his favorite
pastime, "Me Too," and his favorite game is "Come
To Find Out" that actually "everybody" doesn't, as
he knew all along. Thus his favorite feeling is being
taken by (phony) surprise. His nickname is Creepy
and his hero is someone who keeps everybody in line.
In the front room he does what he thinks the O.K.
people are doing and conspicuously avoids the not-
O.K. ones, while in the back room he performs out-
landish deeds, or even horrors. He lives in a world
where he is misunderstood except by his cronies, and
his script calls for him to be done in for one of his
secret misdeeds. He does not protest much when the
end comes, because he feels he really deserves it according to his own slogan: "He who breaks the rules
of Everybody must suffer." And that is the kicker on
the back of his sweatshirt. "He's Different—Must Be
a Kook or a Communist or Something."

Closely allied to the sweatshirt is the tombstone,
which we shall consider in the next chapter.

15. Maturity and Death

Maturity can be defined in four different ways. (1) Trial by law. A person is mature when he is mentally competent and has reached the age of twenty-one. According to Hebrew law, a boy becomes a man when he reaches the age of thirteen. (2) Trial by Parental prejudice. A person is mature when he does things my way, and immature if he does them his way. (3) Trial by initiation. A person is mature when he has passed certain tests. In primitive societies these tests are tough and traditional. In industrial countries, he gets his maturity certificate when he passes his driving test. In special cases, he may be given psychological tests and his maturity or immaturity is then certified by the psychologist. (4) Trial by living. For the script analyst, maturity is tested by external events. The tests begin when the person is about to come out of a supervised and sheltered environment and the world moves in on him on its own terms. They start in the senior year at college, the final year of apprenticeship, at promotion or parole time, at the end of the honeymoon, or whenever the first opportunity offers itself in open competition or cooperation for script failure or success.

From this point of view, the common successes and failures in life depend on parental permissions. Jeder does or does not have permission to graduate from college, complete his apprenticeship, stay married, stop drinking, get promoted or elected or paroled, stay out of the mental hospital, or get well if he goes to a psychiatrist.

Through grade school and high school and the early years of college, it is possible to survive failures and even juvenile hall and reform school, especially in this country where minors are often given another chance. Nevertheless, there is a small number of suicides [1],

homicides, and addictions among adolescents, and a
larger number of optional car crashes and psychoses.
In less lenient countries, a failure to matriculate into
college, or a criminal record, are for real, and one such
mark is enough to set the individual's course for the
rest of his life. For the most part, however, early failures are rehearsals rather than final performances, and
playing for keeps does not begin until the twenties.

ADDICTIONS

The simplest and most direct way to become a real
loser is through crime, gambling, or drug addiction.
Criminals are divided into two types: winners, who are
professionals, and seldom if ever go to prison, and
losers, who are following the injunction: "Don't have
any fun!" The losers have what fun they can while
they are at large, but then follow their scripts by spend-
ing drab years in prison. If they are released by discharge, parole, or legal technicality, they soon manage
to get back in again.

Gamblers can also be winners or losers. The winners play carefully and save or invest their money.
They like to quit when they are ahead. The losers play
luck and hunches, and if they win by chance, get rid
of their winnings as soon as they can, perhaps by
following the famous slogan: "It may be crooked, but
it's the only game in town." If they have permission
to be winners, they win: otherwise they are compelled
to lose. What a gambling addict needs is not an analysis,
which is seldom successful, of why he gambles, but
permission to stop being a loser. If he gets it, he will
either stop gambling, or continue and win.

The mother's influence is most clearly shown in
certain types of drug addicts. As previously noted, these
are encouraged with the slogan: "Heroin, shmeroin,
what's the difference as long as he loves his mother?"
What such people need is permission to stop taking
drugs, which means permission to leave their mothers
and strike out for themselves, and that is exactly what
the highly successful Synanon movement provides.

Where mother's script injunction says "Don't leave me!" Synanon says "Stay here instead."

This also applies to alcoholics and Alcoholics Anonymous. Claude M. Steiner [2] discovered that almost all alcoholics had been analyzed, cajoled, or threatened concerning their drinking, but that none of his cases had ever been told simply: "Stop drinking!" Their previous jousts with therapists were based on such slogans as: "Let's analyze why you drink," "Why don't you stop drinking?," or "If you keep on drinking you'll injure yourself." Each of these is quite different in effect from the simple imperative "Stop drinking!" The "Alcoholic" player is quite willing to spend years analyzing why he drinks or explaining regretfully how he backslid, providing that in the meantime he can keep on drinking. The threat that he will injure himself is the most naive and ineffectual of all, because that is exactly what he is trying to do, following his script injunction "Kill yourself!" The threats merely add to his satisfaction by providing the gruesome details of exactly how he is bringing about his death, and by assuring him that he will be successful in fulfilling the destiny demanded by his mother. What the alcoholic needs is first permission to stop drinking, if he can take it, and then a clear and unqualified Adult contract to desist, if he can give it.

THE DRAMA TRIANGLE

During the period of maturity, the dramatic nature of the script is brought into full flower. Drama in life, as in the theater, is based on "switches," and these switches have been neatly summarized by Stephen Karpman [3] in a simple diagram he calls "The Drama Triangle," which is shown in Figure 10 (p. 210). Each hero in a drama or in life (the protagonist) starts off in one of the three main roles: Rescuer, Persecutor, or Victim, with the other principal player (the antagonist) in one of the other roles. When the crisis is over, the two players move around the triangle, thus switching roles. One of the commonest switches occurs in divorces. During the marriage, for example, the husband

is the persecutor and the wife plays the part of the
victim. Once the divorce complaint is filed, these roles
are reversed: the wife becomes the persecutor, and the
husband the victim, while his lawyer and her lawyer
play the part of competing rescuers.

In fact, all struggles in life are struggles to move
around the triangle in accordance with the demands
of the script. Thus the criminal persecutes his victims;
the victim then files a complaint, and becomes the
plaintiff or persecutor with the criminal now the
victim. If he is caught, the police also become his
persecutors. He then hires a professional rescuer, a
lawyer, who persecutes the policeman. In an interrupted
rape, there is a race around the triangle. The criminal
who is persecuting the girl victim becomes the victim

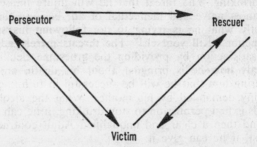

Figure 10. The drama triangle. Reproduced by permission of
S. B. Karpman, M.D. © 1968 by the Transactional Analysis
Bulletin.

of the rescuing policeman. The criminal's lawyer tries
to rescue him by persecuting the girl victim and the
policeman as well. Fairy tales, treated as dramas, show
exactly this feature. Little Red Riding Hood, for example, is a victim of the persecuting wolf until the
hunter rescues her, when she suddenly becomes the
persecutor, putting stones in the belly of the now
victimized wolf.

Minor roles in script dramas are the Connection
and the Patsy, who are available to all three of the
main characters. The Connection is the person who
supplies what is needed for the switch, usually for a

price, and is fully aware of his role: the man who sells liquor, drugs, influence, or guns. A gun, for example, often called the "equalizer," turns a coward (victim) into a braggart (persecutor), or switches the defensive into the offensive. The Patsy is there to be conned into preventing the switch, or speeding it up. The classical Patsies are juries, and the most poignant are mothers who pay to keep their sons out of jail. Sometimes the Patsy is passive and merely acts as bait for the switch, like Little Red Riding Hood's grandmother. It should be noted that the switch referred to here is the same switch that is included in the formula for games given in Chapter Nine.

Karpman has many interesting variables in his fully developed theory, besides role switches. These include space switches (private-public, open-closed, near-far) which precede, cause, or follow role switches, and script velocity (number of role switches in a given unit of time). Thus, his thinking reaches far beyond the original roles as described for the game of "Alcoholic" [4], and brings fascinating insights into numerous aspects of life, psychotherapy, and the theater.

LIFE EXPECTANCY

A recent study of causes of death concluded that many people die when they are ready to, and that coronary thromboses, for example, can be brought about almost by an act of will [5]. It is certainly true that most people have in their life plans a certain life span. The key question here is: "How long are you going to live?" Usually the life span has an element of competition. The Child of a man whose father died at the age of forty, for example, may not have permission to live longer than his father did, and will exist in a state of vague apprehension throughout most of his fourth decade. He becomes more and more aware that he fully expects to die before he is forty, and the most trying period will be the year between his thirty-ninth and fortieth birthdays, after which his way of living may change in one of four ways: (1) He settles down to a more relaxed way of life because he has passed the dangerous age and survived it. (2) He goes into a state of depression because by surviving he has disobeyed his script injunction and therefore loses his mother's love. (3) He begins to live a more hectic life because now he is living on borrowed time and death can strike at any moment. (4) He withdraws because his reprieve is conditional and will be withdrawn if he is caught enjoying himself. It is evident that (1) has permission to live longer than his father if he can make it, (2) does not have permission, (3) has permission to get away with what he can, and (4) has permission to make deals. In fact, (4) is an excellent example of the one-sided contract with God previously referred to, since (4), without consulting God, thinks he knows how to placate Him.

A more competitive person, however, will determine to live longer than his father did and will probably succeed in doing so. He then has to pass the hazard of living longer than his mother did, which is more difficult, since few men care to compete with their own mothers. Similarly, a daughter will competitively outlive her mother, but if her father died at an older age, she may find it difficult to live longer than he did. At any rate, a person who lives longer than both his parents did often feels uneasy in his later years. The next hurdle may be to outlive his script hero. For example, a physician came for treatment at the age of thirty-seven because his father had died when he was thirty-seven and he was afraid of dying. He withdrew from treatment shortly after his thirty-eighth birthday, because then he was "safe." By that time he had become more competitive, and his goal now was to live to be seventy-one. For a long time he was unable to account for this choice of date. Since his hero was Sir William Osler, in whose footsteps he wanted to follow, the therapist took the trouble to find out that Sir William had died at the age of seventy. The patient had read several biographies of his hero, and now recollected that many years previously he had determined to outlive him.

The treatment of such life-span neuroses is very simple. The therapist merely has to give the patient permission to live longer than his father. Psycho-analysis may be successful in such cases not primarily because of the conflicts which are resolved, but merely because the analytic situation offers protection during the critical year. Indeed, there is no conflict to resolve since it is not pathological for the Child to feel bad about living longer than his father. That is merely a special example of "survival neurosis" which occurs to some degree in everyone who survives where others die. This is one of the principle influences in "war neuroses," and "Hiroshima neuroses," and "concentration-camp neuroses." The survivors almost feel guilty because they have survived while others have died "in their place." [6] This indeed is what makes "the person who has actually seen someone else killed" different from other human beings. The Child will not "recover" or "be cured" of this feeling. The best that can be done is to put the feeling under Adult control so that the person can carry on a normal life and get permission to enjoy himself to some extent.

OLD AGE

Vitality in old age depends on three factors: (1) constitutional robustness; (2) physical health; (3) type of script. The onset of old age is determined by the same three factors. Thus some people are vital at eighty and others start vegetating at forty. Constitutional robustness is a *force majeure*, that is, it cannot be changed by Parental programing. Physical disability is sometimes a *force majeure*, and sometimes a script payoff. In the "Cripple" Script it is both. The crippling itself may occur because of unavoidable physical illness, but it is welcomed because it is part of the script and fulfills mother's injunction to end up disabled. This occurs occasionally in cases of poliomyelitis in young adults, where the man in the wheel chair says: "When I knew I had polio I almost welcomed it, as though I had been waiting for something like that." If his script called for him to be a cripple, and Nature did not help him out, he might have crashed a car. Nature's solution is simpler to deal with.

Older people may similarly welcome a stroke or a coronary occlusion, but for a different reason: not because it is part of the script, but because it relieves them of the compulsion to carry on with their script strivings. For the Child in them, these catastrophes become "Wooden Leg" or "Wooden Heart," so that they can say to the Parent in their heads: "Even you can't expect a man with a Wooden Leg or a Wooden Heart to carry on your witch's curse." Faced with a blood clot in Jeder's brain or heart, only the most ruthless parent does not concede defeat.

If a disability occurs early in life, it may fit very well into mother's script, or may throw it off completely. If it fits, the child will be raised as a professional cripple, sometimes with the help of outside organizations devoted to helping Crippled Children as long as they stay crippled) or Mentally Retarded Children (as long as they stay mentally retarded). The drag is due to the fact that the government subsidy usually stops if the child recovers.) In such cases, the mother learns to "face it," and teaches the child to do likewise. If it does *not* fit the mother's script, however, she does *not* learn to face it. She keeps trying, and the child learns to do likewise, so that he ends up as a one-legged jitterbug, a clubfooted broad-jumper, or a brain-damaged orthopedic specialist (all three examples exist or have existed in real life). The Crippled Children's organization and the Mentally Retarded organization pitch in here, too, and are delighted if one of their protégés make it (with outside help). If the mother's script does not call for a physically or mentally disabled child, and the disability is so severe that it is necessarily permanent, then her life becomes a script-frustrated tragedy. If her script does call for a disabled child, and the disability is borderline, and possibly remediable, then the child's life becomes an unnecessary, script-inflicted tragedy.

Now to return to old age. Even people with robust constitutions and no physical disabilities (or only minor or hypochondriacal ones) can begin to vegetate at an early age if they have "Open-Ended" Scripts. These are commonly people living on pensions. The Parental precept is: "Work hard, and don't take any chances," and the payoff is "After that, give up." Once Jeder has put in his twenty or thirty years, and Santa Claus has come and given him his retirement banquet and gold watch, he doesn't know what to do. He is accustomed to following his script directives, but now they are exhausted, and he has no further programing in his head. Therefore he is content to sit and wait until something turns up: Death, for instance.

This raises an interesting question. What do you do after Santa Claus comes? With an "Until" Script, he comes down the chimney and brings a Freedom Certificate. Jeder has fulfilled the requirements of his script, is freed of the curse by the antiscript, and is now at liberty to do what he always wanted to do since he was a little boy. But going his own way is full of dangers, as many Greek myths attest. While he is free of his witch parent, he is also unprotected, and can easily come to grief. This is shown in fairy tales as well. A curse gives protection as well as trial and tribulation. The same witch that laid on the curse sees that the victim continues to live while he is under it. Thus, Sleeping Beauty was protected by the briar forest for a hundred years. But the moment she woke up, and could tell the witch to buzz off, her troubles began. A handy situation is to have a double script: an "Until" Script for one parent and an "After" Script from the other. In the commonest case this reads "You can't be free until you have raised three children" (from mother), and "After you are free you will become creative" (from father). Thus in the first half of her life Zoe is controlled and protected by her mother and in the second half by her father. In the case of a man, the double-script directive may be the same as above, but the control and protection are reversed: Father during the first phase and Mother during the second.

The vegetating aged are divided into three classes, and in this country the insignia are financial. Those with losers' scripts live alone in rooming houses or rundown hotels, and are called old men and old women. Those with nonwinning scripts own and live in small houses where they are free to develop their idiosyncrasies and eccentricities, so that they are known as old characters. Those with winning scripts live in retirement homes run by financial promoters, and are called Senior Citizens, or Mr. and Mrs. Taxpayer, which is how they sign their Letters to the Editor.

The cure for the scriptless aged is permission, but they seldom use it. There are thousands of older men living in small rooms in every large city, each of them wishing there was someone to cook for him, talk to him, and listen to him. At the same time, there are thousands of older women living under the same circumstances, wishing they had someone to cook for, talk to, and listen to. Even if the twain do happen to meet, they rarely take advantage of it, each preferring to remain in his or her familiar drab surroundings hunched over a glass or a TV set, or sitting with folded hands, waiting for a riskless, sinless death. Those were mother's directives they are following seventy or eighty years later. The never took chances before, beyond a small bet at the racetrack or the stadium, so why should they jeopardize everything now? The script has vanished by its own fulfillment, but the old slogan lingers on, and when death comes they will greet him gladly. And on the front of the tombstone they will carve: "Gone to rest with his forebears," and on the back it will say: "I lived a good life, and never took any chances."

They say that in the next century, children will be grown in bottles, according to specifications laid down by the state and the parents, and there they will be genetically programed. But everybody is already raised in a bottle according to specifications laid down by the state and his parents, and there he is script-programed. Script-programing is easier to shake off than genetic programing, but few people exercise the privilege. For the ones who do, there can be a more inspiring tombstone. Nearly all pious epitaphs, translated into Martian, come out "Raised in a bottle and stayed there, too." And so they stand, row after row of crosses and other symbols in the graveyard, all with the same motto. Only here and there is a surprise: "Raised in a bottle

—but I jumped out." Many people refuse to do that,
even when there is no cork.

THE DEATH SCENE

Death is not an act, nor even an event, for the one
who dies. It is both for those who survive. What it can
be, and should be, is a transaction. The physical horror
of the Nazi death camps was compounded by the
psychological horror, the prevention of dignity, self-
assertion, or self-expression in the gas chamber. There
was no brave blindfold and cigarette, no defiance, no
famous last words: in sum, no death transaction. There
were transactional stimuli for the dying, but no response from the killers. Thus, *force majeure* takes from
the script its most poignant moment, the deathbed
scene, and in one sense the whole human purpose of
life is to set up that scene.

In script analysis, this is brought out by the question:
"Who will be there at your deathbed, and what will
your last words be?" An added question is: "What
will *their* last words be?" The answer to the first query
is usually some version of "I showed them"—"them"
being the parents, especially mother in the case of a
man and father in the case of a woman. The implication is either "I showed them I did what they wanted
me to," or "I showed them I didn't have to do what
they wanted me to."

The answer to this question is, in effect, a summary
of Jeder's life goal, and can be used by the therapist
as a powerful instrument in breaking up the games
and getting Jeder out of his script:

"So your whole life boils down to showing them you
were right to feel hurt, frightened, angry, inadequate,
or guilty. Very well. Then that will be your greatest
accomplishment—if you want to keep it that way. But
maybe you would like to find a more worthwhile purpose in living."

The deathbed scene may be part of the hidden, or
script, contract in marriage. The husband or wife may
have a very clear image of the other partner dying
first. In such cases, the spouse often has the comple-

mentary script, and is obligingly planning to do so. Thus, they get along well and pass contented years together. But if they each have the image of the other dying first, so that the scripts are crossed in this respect, those years will be contentious instead of contented, even though the scripts are complementary in other ways, as they must be for the marriage to take place. The difficulties will come out most clearly when one or the other is ill or in pain. A common script based on the death scene is found in the marriage of a younger woman to an older man. Even if the cynics say she marries him for his bread, the script scene is equally important, and she will always be at his side in time of danger, on the good side to take care of him, but also so as not to miss the final payoff transaction. If he is intuitively aware of this, the marriage may have only a very narrow margin of safety, since it is not easy to get along with someone who is waiting for you to die. The same situation, with the double payoff, may arise in the marriage of a younger man to an older woman, although these are less common. It is evident that the orginal script protocol has father in place of the aging husband, or mother in place of the aging wife.

THE GALLOWS LAUGH

Actual death scenes result from either *force majeure* or script directives. The untimely death due to ineluctable forces of fate—disease or violence in time of peace or war—is always a stark and simple tragedy. Scripty deaths are usually marked by the gallows smile or gallows humor. The man who dies with a smile on his face or a joke on his lips is dying the death his script calls for, and the smile or the joke says: "Well, mother, I'm now following your instructions, ha ha. I hope you're happy." The criminals of London in the eighteenth century were true disciples of gallows humor, often entertaining the admiring crowd with a final epigram as the trap was sprung [7], because their deaths followed their mothers' injunction: "You'll end on the gallows as your father did, my boy!" The last words of many famous men were also jokes because they were likewise at peace with their mothers: "You'll die famous, son." Deaths due to human *force majeure* are not accompanied by such levity, because they may be in direct contradiction to mother's injunction: "Live long!" or "Die happy!" There are no stories of gallows humor in German concentration camps (as far as I know). There is also a special injunction "Enjoy death as you enjoyed life!" which permits a deathbed joke even if death comes sooner than mother could tolerate. Such a joke is, in fact, an attempt to ease the mother's bereavement.

All this means that in most cases the witch parent plans Jeder's life span and the manner of his death, and barring internal or external upheavals, he will, by his own decision, carry out the parental decree.

THE POSTHUMOUS SCENE

In success scripts, this is usually visualized with good reality sense. Jeder has built up a large organization, or left a large body of work, or a lot of children and grandchildren, and he knows that his life production will survive him and that those connected with it will see him to his grave.

Those with tragic scripts, however, have a pathetic fallacy about what will happen after their deaths. The romantic suicide, for example, says: "They'll be sorry," and imagines a sad, sentimental funeral which may or may not come to pass. The angry suicide says: "I'll fix them," and may be equally misguided, since they may be glad to have him out of the way. "I'll show them" may fail by not getting his name in the papers much beyond the obituary file. On the other hand, the futility or frustration suicide, who tries to kill himself unobtrusively with the fantasy that nobody will really notice or care, may make the front-page headlines due to some unforeseen complication. Even the man who kills himself so his wife can have the insurance money may be foiled if he has neglected to read his policy carefully.

In general, the consequences of killing oneself are no

more predictable than the consequences of killing someone else. Except for soldiers and gangsters, death, either
suicide or homicide, is a poor way to try to solve life's
problems. Certainly, prospective suicides should be
firmly told the two inviolable rules of death: (1) No
parent is allowed to die until all of the children are
over eighteen. (2) No child is allowed to die while
either of his parents is still living.

The cases of people who have no minor children
and no living parent have to be considered on their
individual merits, but every patient who is accepted
for treatment must make a firm commitment not to
violate either of the two rules, if one or both apply.
A similar commitment required of certain patients is
that they will never use for improper purposes (including suicidal attempts) any medications prescribed
by the therapist.

THE TOMBSTONE

The tombstone, like the sweatshirt, has two sides.
The questions here are: "What will they put on your
tombstone?" and "What will you put on your tombstone?" A typical answer is: "They'll say 'She was a
good girl,' and I'll say: 'I tried hard but I didn't make
it.'" Once more, "they" usually means the parents, or
parental people. "Their" epitaph is the antiscript, while
the patient himself writes his script injunction on his
tombstone—in the case above: "Try hard but be sure
not to make it." Thus the tombstone speaks nothing
but good of the dead, for one side says that he fulfilled
the precepts of his antiscript, while the other indicates
that he was also an obedient child who followed his
mother's script instructions, however encouraging or
discouraging they might have been.

If the patient tries to avoid reading his tombstone
by saying there won't be one, that answer has its own
meaning. Whoever cops out on death is also copping
out on life. But the therapist should then insist on
getting the two epitaphs with the question: "What
would be on it if there was one?" or "Here you've
got to have one."

THE TESTAMENT

Whatever the person's fantasies about what will happen after his death, his will or his posthumous papers offer the last chance for a payoff. His whole life may have been based on a falsehood or a concealed treasure which is only revealed as a triumph after his death—a trick which he plays on posterity. There are many historical examples of this: hidden talents which only come to light when the manuscript or the canvases are found hidden in a closet, or works out of character which are found concealed among the papers. Hidden wealth and hidden poverty are commonly revealed during the probate of wills. Wills are also favorite vehicles for switch tricks. The commonest has already been mentioned: mother leaves the bulk of her property to the "faithless" daughter and cuts the devoted one off with a pittance. Sometimes bigamy only comes to light after the will is read. The question here is: "What is going to be the most important item in your will? What is going to be the biggest surprise for those you leave behind after you die?"

We have now followed Jeder in his script from before birth until after death. But there are many more interesting things to consider before we go on to talk about treatment.

REFERENCES

1. The suicide rate increases roughly with age, and is lower for females than for males at all ages save early adolescence.

2. Steiner, C. M. "The Alcoholic Game." *Transactional Analysis Bulletin* 7:6-16, January, 1968.

3. Karpman, S. "Fairy Tales and Script Drama Analysis." *Transactional Analysis Bulletin* 7:39-43, April, 1968.

4. Berne, E. *Games People Play.* Grove Press, New York, 1964.

5. Cf. early deaths following breavement as described by W. D. Rees & S. G. Lutkins in *British Medical Journal* 4:13, October 7, 1967, and summarized in *Current Medical Digest*, March, 1968.

6. Lifton, R. J. *Death in Life*. Random House, New York, 1968.

7. Cf. Grose, F. *A Classical Dictionary of the Vulgar Tongue*. Digest Books, Northfield, Illinois, 1971 (facsimile of 1811 edition).

16. Types of Scripts

WINNERS, NONWINNERS, AND LOSERS

Scripts are designed to last a lifetime. They are based on childhood decisions and parental programing which is continually reinforced. The reinforcement may take the form of daily contact, as with men who work for their fathers, or women who telephone their mothers every morning to gossip, or it may be applied less frequently and more subtly, but just as powerfully, through occasional correspondence. After the parents die, their instructions may be remembered more vividly than ever.

In script language, as noted, a loser is called a frog and a winner is called a prince or a princess. Parents want their children to be either winners or losers. They may want them to be "happy" in the role they have chosen for them, but do not want them to be transformed, except in special cases. A mother who is raising a frog may want her daughter to be a happy frog, but will put down any attempts of the girl to become a princess. ("Who do you think you are?") A father who is raising a prince wants his son to be happy, but often he would rather see him unhappy than transformed into a frog. ("How can you do that to us? We've given you the best of everything.")

The first thing to be decided about a script is whether it is a winning one or a losing one. This can often be discovered very quickly by listening to the person talk. A winner says things like: "I made a mistake, but it won't happen again," or "Now I know the right way to do it." A loser says "If only . . ." "I should've . . ." and "Yes, but . . ." There are also near misses, nonwinners whose scripts require them to work very hard, not for the purpose of winning, but just to stay even.

These are "at leasters," people who say "Well, at least I didn't . . ." or "At least, I have this much to be thankful for." Nonwinners make excellent members, employees, and serfs, since they are loyal, hard-working, and grateful, and not inclined to cause trouble. Socially, they are pleasant people, and in the community, admirable. Winners make trouble for the rest of the world only indirectly, when they are fighting among themselves and involve innocent bystanders, sometimes by the millions. Losers cause the most grief to themselves and others. Even if they come out on top they are still losers, and drag other people down with them when the payoff comes.

A winner is defined as a person who fulfills his contract with the world and with himself. That is, he sets out to do something, says that he is committed to doing it, and in the long run does it. His contract, or ambition, may be to save $100,000, run the mile in less than four minutes, or get a Ph.D. If he accomplishes his goal, he is a winner. If he ends up in debt, sprains his ankle in the shower, or flunks out in his junior year, he is clearly a loser. If he saves $10,000, comes in second at 4:05, or goes into industry with an M.A., he is an at-leaster: not a loser, but a nonwinner. The important thing is that he sets the goal himself, usually on the basis of Parental programing, but with his Adult making the final commitment. Note that the man who goes for 4:05 and makes it is still a winner, while the one who goes for 3:59 and only makes 4:05 is a nonwinner, even though he beats the one whose ambition is lower. On a short-term basis, a winner is one who becomes captain of the team, dates the Queen of the May, or wins at the poker game. A nonwinner never gets near the ball, dates the runner-up, or comes out even. A loser doesn't make the team, doesn't get a date, or comes out broke.

Furthermore, the captain of the second team is on the same level as the captain of the first team, since each person is entitled to choose his own league and is judged by the standards which he himself sets up. As an extreme example, "living on less money than anyone else on the street without getting sick" is a league. Whoever does it is a winner. One who tries it and gets sick is a loser. The typical, classical loser is the man who makes himself suffer sickness or damage for no good cause. If he has a good cause, then he may become a successful martyr, which is the best way to win by losing.

A winner knows what he'll do next if he loses, but doesn't talk about it; a loser doesn't know what he'll do if he loses, but talks about what he'll do if he wins. Thus, it takes only a few minutes of listening to pick out the winners and losers at a gambling table or a stockbroker's, in a domestic argument or in family therapy.

The basic rule seems to be that a winning script payoff comes from the nurturing Parent through the counterscript slogans. A nonwinner gets his payoff from the controlling Parent through injunctions. A loser is led down the path to a bad payoff by the provocations and seductions of his parent's crazy Child, which tempts his self-destructive demon.

SCRIPT TIME

Winning or losing, the script is a way to structure the time between the first Hello at mother's breast and the last Good-by at the grave. This life time is emptied and filled by not doing and doing; by never doing, always doing, not doing before, not doing after, doing over and over, and doing until there is nothing left to do. This gives rise to "Never" and "Always," "Until" and "After," "Over and Over," and "Open-Ended" scripts. These are best understood by reference to Greek myths, since the Greeks had a strong feeling for such things.

"Never" scripts are represented by Tantalus, who through all eternity was to suffer from hunger and thirst in sight of food and water, but never to eat or drink again. People with such scripts are forbidden by their parents to do the things they most want to, and so spend their lives being tantalized and surrounded by temptations. They go along with the Parental curse because the Child in them is afraid of the things they want the most, so they are really tantalizing themselves.

"Always" scripts follow Arachne, who dared to challenge the Goddess Minerva in needlework, and as a punishment was turned into a spider and condemned to spend all her time spinning webs. Such scripts come from spiteful parents, who say: "If that's what you want to do, then you can just spend the rest of your life doing it."

"Until" or "Before" scripts follow the story of Jason, who was told that he could not become a king before he had performed certain tasks. In due time he got his reward and lived for ten years in happiness. Hercules had a similar script: he could not become a god until he had first been a slave for twelve years.

"After" scripts come from Damocles. Damocles was allowed to enjoy the happiness of being a king, until he noticed that a sword was hanging over his head, suspended by a single horse-hair. The motto of "After" scripts is "You can enjoy yourself for a while, but after that your troubles begin."

"Over and Over" scripts are Sisyphus. He was condemned to roll a heavy stone up a hill, and just as he was about to reach the top the stone rolled back and he had to start over again. This is the classical "Almost Made It" script, with one "If only" after another.

The "Open-Ended" script is the nonwinner or "Pie in the Sky" scenario, and follows the story of Philemon and Baucis, who were turned into laurel trees as a reward for their good deeds. Old people who have carried out their Parental instructions don't know what to do next after it is all over, and spend the rest of their lives like vegetables, or gossiping likes leaves rustling in the wind. This is the fate of many a mother whose children have grown up and scattered, and of retired men who have put in their thirty years of work according to company regulations and their parents' instructions. As already noted, "Senior Citizen" communities are filled with couples who have completed their scripts and don't know how to structure their time while waiting for the Promised Land where people who have treated their employees decently can drive their big black cars slowly down the left-hand lane without being honked at by a bunch of ill-bred teen-agers in their hot rods. "Was pretty feisty myself as a teenager," says Dad, "but nowadays. . . ." And Mom adds: "You wouldn't believe what they . . . And we've always paid our . . ."

TRAGIC SCRIPTS

There is still considerable debate as to whether winners are winners because they have winning scripts, or because they have permission to be autonomous. But there is little doubt that losers are following the programing of their parents and the urgings of their own inner demons. Tragic scripts (which Steiner calls "hamartic" ones) may be either noble or ignoble. The noble ones are a source of inspiration and of noble dramas. The ignoble ones repeat the same old scenes and the same old plots with the same drab cast, set in the dreary "catchment areas" which society conveniently supplies as depots where losers can collect their payoffs: saloons, pawnshops, brothels, courtrooms, prisons, state hospitals, and morgues. Because of the stereotyped outcomes, it is easy to see the scripty elements in such life courses. Thus, books on psychiatry and criminology which give numerous and extensive case histories are excellent sources for studying scripts.

A bad script is laid on the child by the Fascist Sneer, and he clings to it on the principle of the Nostalgic Prisoner. The Fascist Sneer is as old as history, and works as follows. The people are told that the enemy king or leader is filthy, incoherent, debased, and brutish, more animal than human. When he is captured, he is put in a cage with a few rags, no toilet facilities, and no eating utensils. After a week or so he is exhibited to the people, and sure enough, he is filthy, incoherent, debased, and brutish, and gets more and more so as time goes on. Then the conquerors smile and say: "I told you so."

Children are essentially captives of their parents, and can be reduced to any state the parents desire.

For example, a girl is told that she is a hysterical, self-pitying crybaby. The parents know her weak spot and can torment her in front of visitors until she finds it intolerable and is reduced to tears. Since this is labeled "self-pity," she tries hard not to cry, and so when she does give way, it is like an explosion. Then the parents can say: "What a hysterical reaction! Every time we have visitors she does that. What a crybaby," etc. The key question of script analysis research is: "How would you raise a child so that when she grew up, she would react the way this patient does?" In answering this question, the script analyst more and more frequently is able to describe the patient's upbringing accurately before he is told about it.

Many people who have spent long years in prison find the outside world cold, difficult, and frightening, and commit an offense in order to be sent back to prison. It may be miserable, but it is familiar, they know the rules so as to keep out of serious trouble, and there are old friends there. In the same way, when a patient attempts to break out of his script cage, he finds it cold "out there," and since he no longer plays the old games, he loses his old friends and has to make new ones, which is often scary. Therefore he slides back into his old ways, like a Nostalgic Prisoner.

All this may make the script and its effects a little more understandable.

17. Sex and Scripts

INTRODUCTION: IT'S A CRAZY WORLD

Sex can be enjoyable in solitude or in groups, or in couples as an act of intimacy, a passion, a relief, a duty, or just a way to pass the time to ward off and postpone the evil day of boredom, that Boredom which is the pimp of Death and brings to him sooner or later all its victims, whether by disease, accident, or intent. For the truth of the matter is not that time is passing, but that we are passing through time. It is not what they said in older days, a river on whose banks we stand and watch, but a sea we have to cross, either in solitary labor and watchfulness, like crossing the Atlantic in a rowboat, or crowded together over the engine oil and the automatic pilot with nothing to do but play some form of drunk or sober shuffleboard. Only a few glide in splendor with sail unfurled in a lugger or a sloop or something grander, ahoy and belay there! up with the mizzen royal of our full-rigged five-master—the only one ever built to sail the Seven Seas! And it is still possible to fly nonstop, without being much bothered by what happens down below.

In the cities and in the country there are millions of birds, and how many of you with full awareness heard one of them sing today? In the cities and in the country there are thousands of trees, and how many of you with full awareness saw one today? Here is a nonstop story of my own. About five times a week, I walked from my office to the post office in the little village where I live. I walked by the same route for two years, about 500 trips, before one day I noticed two hairy palm trees with a cactus growing between them on a corner that I passed. I had gone by this

rugged delight 499 times in a row wihout being aware
that anything was growing there, because I was preoccupied with getting to the post office to pick up my
mail so I could get back to my office and answer the
letters so I could go to the post office and pick up the
replies to my answers so I could answer the replies
so I could go to the post office and pick up more mail
to answer. My time was mortgaged to a self-imposed
burden that I could never pay off but could at any
moment, whenever I wished, tear up, and put the pieces
carefully in one of the trash cans considerately provided by the village council so I would not litter the
streets.

I thought of this one time lying in bed in a hotel in
Vienna listening to the quiet of the night and then to
the first rustles of life at dawn, the slow waltz of Vienna
in the morning. First the six o'clock people danced out
to prepare the way for the seven o'clock people, who
got ready for the eight o'clock people who take care
of the nine o'clock people.* These open their stores
and offices so that shopping and business calls can
begin at ten, so that the stores can be closed at twelve
so that people can go home and get ready for lunch, so
that they can re-open at two so they can close at five,
so that they can get home by six to dress for dinner at
seven so they can get to the theater by eight, so that
they can get home by eleven to get a good night's
sleep so they will be in good shape when they get up
again in the morning at five, six, seven, or eight.

And there is a song about Sunday, when they are
not bound by all this, and how on that day some of
them jump into the Danube, which is a river and carries them in its flow as time does not. For time is not
a river, but a sea that must be crossed, from the shore
of bawling birth to the littered coast of death. And this
is not a fancy of song writers, this fascination of the
waters (Nepenthes en tw potamouthanatw),** for

---

* Six: bus-drivers, I guess. Seven: cooks, I guess. Eight:
waitresses, some of them.

** Okay, here's what it means. Nepenthes, nowadays shortened to Nepenthe, is a potion which brings forgetfulness of all
pains, quarrels, griefs, and troubles. Helen of Troy got some

in Vienna each year about 500 people kill themselves. Do you know which country has the highest suicide rate in the world? Hungary. That's Communism for you. Do you know which country has the second highest rate? Austria. That's democracy for you. Actually, since they're both on the same river, that's the Danube for you. Which Communist people have a lower suicide rate than white democratic Americans, but higher than nonwhite democratic Americans? The Poles, that's who.

Since time does not pass, it must be passed through, and that means always scheduled or structured. Don't just sit there, do something! What shall we do this morning, this afternoon, tonight? Mom, there's nothing to do. He doesn't do anything. I've got lots to do. Get up, you lazy loafer. Awritechuguys, getcherasses outabed. Don't do anything, just sit there, and for one million dollars an hour I'll fill in your time on Channel 99. A million? He's worth it, man. Pay him two million if you can.

Sex may be an essential ingredient in structuring time, although eunuchs find plenty to do, don't they? Old Abdul the sick man of Europe and Asia sitting on Seraglio Point looking for excitement—you can't trust them, they've got hands and other ways, chop off their scrotums and what good does it do? Sex is in the head, it's not all in the scrotum by any means. You'll find that out the hard way, and then you'll have to tread slowly to satisfy your lust and have your bust. They say I'm Abdul the Cruel but I just have a sensual sense of humor, carry me back to old Istanbul and the randy life of Golden Horn, get the girls out of the sordid honky-tonks and into the wholesome harems, I mean out of the sordid harems and into the wholesome honky-tonks. Have it your own way, Dad.

Meaning there's more to life than sex, you can't do

---

from an Egyptian's daughter and used it to spike wine. From that description in Book IV of the *Odyssey,* it sounds not unlike some form of hashish. The rest I made up myself. The root Potam- means a river, as in hippopotamus, and Thanat- means death. So it means that river-death is a drink to end all troubles.

it all the time, you can't even think of it all the time,
animals do it only in the spring and fall, the rest of
the time it's eat eat eat, who wants to be an animal?
Vive la différence! The difference being that for people
there is something more important than essential in-
gredients, eating and sex, and they think of it—the
difference—between eating and between sex, and that
is being me, I, myself. More than eating and more than
sex (which are necessary, but not sufficient) I want to
be a Self, and I am a Self. Unfortunately, for the most
part, this is an illusion.

PARENTAL PROGRAMING

From the beginning man does what he is told. Most
animals don't. That is really the difference, and as
usual it is the opposite of what people usually say.
Sexy men are called (by some) animals, when men are
by nature sexier than animals, and an unsexy animal
would certainly not be called a man. Vicious men are
also called animals, but animals are not vicious for the
most part, just hungry. And man is called free, when
actually he is the most compliant of all animals.

Some animals can be trained to perform a stunt here
and there, but not tamed. Other animals can be tamed
and also trained to perform a stunt here and there. But
man is tamed from the beginning, and spends his whole
life performing stunts for his masters: Mom and Pop
first, and then teacher, and after that whoever can grab
him and teach him feats of war and revolution or stunts
of peace. Revolution, ha! Buzz off, Alex. Now I'm
walking the wire in Joe's show instead. Foo, Manchu!
It's Mao now for this brown kao.* Believe, work, and
obey. I can't believe Manny so I'll obey Benny. I'm
free to walk a mile to say Heil, hit the trail or go on
trial, reach the goal or go to gaol. Man is programed
to obey, obey, obey, obey the obedient, or obey the
civil or uncivil disobedients. Form a line on the right,
left, don't straggle. Straggle, don't form a line. Which

* I mean 羔 , lamb.

side shall I straggle on? Which side shall I struggle on? Don't struggle. Tune in, turn on, drop out. That's an order! Don't listen to those other pigs. Listen to your own pigs. Be anarchistic. Be independent, dammit. Be original, no no, not that way, this way. It's imperative that you enjoy yourself and be spontaneous.

Here's how it happens.

From earliest months, the child is taught not only what to do, but also what to see, hear, touch, think, and feel. And beyond that, he is also told whether to be a winner or a loser, and how his life will end. All these instructions are programed into his mind and his brain just as firmly as though they were punch cards put into the bank of a computer. In later years, what he thinks of as his independence or his autonomy is merely his freedom to select certain cards, but for the most part the same old punch holes stay there that were put there at the beginning. Some people get an exhilarating sense of freedom by rebelling, which usually means one of two things: either they pull out a bunch of cards punched in early childhood which they have never used before, or they turn some of the cards inside out and do the opposite of what they say. Often this merely amounts to following the instructions on a special card which says: "When you are 18 (or 40) use this new bunch of cards, or turn the following cards inside out." Another kind of rebellion follows the instructions: "When you are 18 (or 40), throw away all cards in series A and leave a vacuum." This vacuum then has to be filled as quickly as possible with new instant programs, which are obtained from drugs or from a revolutionary leader. Thus in their efforts to avoid becoming fatheads or eggheads, these people end up being acidheads or spite-heads.

In any case, each person obediently ends up at the age of five or six—yes, ends up at five or six—with a script or life plan largely dictated by his parents. It tells him how he's going to carry on his life, and how it's going to end, winner, nonwinner, or loser. Will it be in the big room surrounded by his loved ones, or with his bed crowded out into the corridor of the City Hospital, or falling like a lead bird into the chilled choppy waters of the Golden Gate? At five or six he doesn't know all that, but he knows about victorious lions and lonely corridors and dead fish in cold water. And he also knows enough to come in first or second like his father or his dad, or to come in last like his old man, he sure can hold his liquor. This is a free country, but don't stare. We got free speech, so listen to me. If you don't watch out for yourself nobody else'll watch out for you, but (a) no, no, mussentouchit, or (b) getcher cotton pickin' hans off my money, or (c) you gonna grow up to be a thief or something?

Well, hit him back. You hit him wrong. Say you're sorry. Watch out. I'll give you something to cry about, you little monster. Feel angry, inadequate, guilty, scared, hurt. I'll teach you how to think as well as how to feel. Don't think such thoughts. Think it over until you see it my way. I'll show you how to do it, too. Here's how to get away with it. You don't know what to be when you grow up? I'll tell you what to be. Be good. Do as you're told, Adolf, and don't ask questions. Be different. Why can't you be like other kids?

So, having learned what not to be, what not to hear, and what not to touch, and which feelings to have, and how not to think, and what not to be, the child sallies forth to school. There he meets teachers and his own kind. It is called a grade school, but it is really a law school. By the time he is ten (the age that lawyers are stuck at) he is an accomplished pettifogger in his own defense. He has to be, especially if he is mean or naughty. You said not to write over the stuff on the blackboard, but you didn't say don't erase it (or vice versa). You said not to take her candy, but you didn't say not to take her chewing gum. You told me not to say bad words to Cousin Mary, but you didn't say not to undress her. You told me not to lie on top of girls, but you didn't say anything about boys.

Later, in high school, come the real script setups. "Don't go to a drive-in. You'll get pregnant!" Up to that time she didn't know how to go about getting pregnant. Now she knows. But she is not ready yet. She has to wait for the signal. "Don't go to a drive-in, you'll get pregnant, until I give you the signal." She knows mother was sixteen when she was born, and pretty soon figures she must have been conceived out of wedlock. Naturally, mother gets very nervous when daughter passes her sixteenth birthday. One day mother says: "Summer is the worst time. That's when most high school girls get pregnant" (generalizing from her own experience). That's the signal. So daughter goes to a drive-in and gets pregnant.

"Don't go into a men's room because you'll meet a bad man there who'll do something nasty to you," father says to his eight-year-old son. He repeats it about once a year. So when the time comes, the boy wonders what the nasty thing is, and he knows where to go to find out. Another father packed not only the sex instructions but the whole life script into one pubertal sentence. "Don't let me catch you going to that house on Bourbon Street, where there are women who'll do anything you want for five dollars." Since the boy didn't have five dollars, he stole it out of his mother's purse, intending to go to Bourbon Street the following afternoon. But mother happened to count her money that same night and found it where the boy had hidden it, and he was caught and punished. He learned his lesson well. "If I'd gone down right after dinner instead of putting it off until the next day, everything would've been all right." He wouldn't have been caught with the five dollars. This is a good nonwinner script. If you want women, get money. Spend it as quickly as possible, before you get caught. You can't win, but you can certainly keep from losing.

The loser's instructions generally read something like this: "If at first you don't succeed, try, try, try again. Even if you win a few, keep trying, and you're bound to lose in the end, because you can't win 'em all." The winner's read: "Why lose at all? If you lose, it means you played wrong. So do it again until you learn to do it right."

If it is not interfered with by some decisive force, the script will be carried through to the sweet or bitter end. There are three such forces. The greatest script-breakers are massive events which lumber inexorably down the path of history: wars, famines, epidemics, and oppression, which overtake and crush everyone before them like cosmic steamrollers, save for those who are licensed to clamber aboard and use them as bandwagons. The second is psychotherapy, and other conversions, which break up scripts and make losers into nonwinners ("Making progress") and nonwinners into winners ("Getting well," "Flipping in," and "Seeing the light").

In rare cases, a third force takes over, and the script is broken up by an autonomous decision or re-decision of the person himself. This happens with people whose script allows them to make an autonomous decision. The clearest example in recent times is Mao Tse-tung, head of the Chinese People's Republic, who started out as a middle-class person with a middle-class script, and by his own inner struggle became what he defines as a real proletarian, so that he felt comfortable in that role and uncomfortable in his middle-class script role, which due to the *force majeure* of Chinese history was a loser's role. By flipping in with history, he became a winner in war and in politics, and in literature as well, since few if any authors in modern times are as widely read as he is in his own lifetime.

It is important to note that the script is not "unconscious" and can be easily unearthed by a skillful questioner or by careful self-questioning. It is only that most people are reluctant to admit the existence of such a life plan and prefer to demonstrate their independence by playing games—games that are themselves dictated by their scripts.

TYPES OF SCRIPTS

Scripts are designed to last a lifetime. They are based on firm childhood decisions and parental programing that is continually reinforced. The reinforcement may take the form of daily contact, as with men who work for their fathers or women who telephone their mothers every morning to gossip, or it may be applied less frequently and more subtly, but just as powerfully, through occasional correspondence. After the parents die, their instructions may be remembered more vividly than ever.

In script language, a loser is called a frog, and a winner is called a prince or a princess. Parents want their children to be either winners or losers. They may want them to be "happy" in the role they have chosen for them, but do not want them to be transformed except in special cases. A mother who is raising a frog may want her daughter to be a happy frog, but will put down any attempts of the girl to become a princess ("Who do you think you are?"), because mother herself was programed to raise her as a frog. A father who is raising a prince wants his son to be happy, but often he would rather see him unhappy than transformed into a frog ("We've given you the best of everything").

The first thing to be decided about a script is whether it is a winning one or a losing one. This can often be discovered very quickly by listening to the person talk. A winner says things like: "I made a mistake, but it won't happen again" or "Now I know the right way to do it." A loser says, "If only . . ." or "I should've . . ." and "Yes, but . . ." As for nonwinners, they are people whose scripts require them to work very hard, not in hope of winning but just to stay even. These are "atleasters," people who say, "Well, at least I didn't . . ." or "At least, I have this much to be thankful for." Nonwinners make excellent members, employees, and serfs, since they are loyal, hard-working, and grateful, and not inclined to cause trouble. Socially they are pleasant people, and in the community, admirable. Winners make trouble for the rest of the world only indirectly, when they are fighting among themselves and involve innocent bystanders, sometimes by the million. Losers cause the most turbulence, which is unfortunate, because even if they come out on top they are still losers and drag other people down with them when the payoff comes.

The best way to tell a winner from a loser is this: A winner is a person who knows what he'll do next if he loses, but doesn't talk about it; a loser is one who doesn't know what he'll do if he loses, but talks about what he'll do if he wins. Thus it takes only a few minutes of listening to pick out the winners and losers at a gambling table or a stockbroker's.

All the script types (Never, Always, Until, After, Over and Over, and Open End) have their sexual aspects. The Never scripts may forbid either love or sex or both. If they forbid love but not sex, they are a license for promiscuity, a license which some sailors and soldiers and wanderers take full advantage of, and which prostitutes and courtesans use to make a living. If they forbid sex but not love, they produce priests, monks, nuns, and people who do good deeds such as raising orphan children. The promiscuous people are tantalized by the sight of devoted lovers and happy families, while the scripty philanthropists are tormented by a desire to jump over the wall.

The Always scripts are typified by young people who are driven out of their homes for the sins that their parents have prompted them to. "If you're pregnant, go earn your living on the streets" and "If you want to take drugs, you're on your own" are examples of these. The father who turned his daughter out into the storm may have had lecherous thoughts about her since she was ten, and the one who threw his son out of the house for smoking pot may get drunk that night to ease his pain.

The parental programing in Until scripts is the loudest of all, since it usually consists of outright commands: "You can't have sex until you're married, and you can't get married as long as you have to take care of your mother (or until you finish college)." The Parental influence in After scripts is almost as outspoken, and the hanging sword gleams with visible threats: "After you get married and have children, your troubles will begin." Translated into action now, this means "Gather ye rosebuds while ye may, Old Time is still a-flying. And this same flower that smiles today, Tomorrow will be stultifying." After marriage it shortens to "Once you have children your troubles will begin," so the young wife spends her days worrying about getting pregnant right from the first day of the honeymoon. But now chemists have provided a stout shield against the bilbo which would otherwise be her undoing, and so she can be queen of the household without having her happiness suspended by an heir until she is ready for one.

The Over and Over scripts produce always a bridesmaid and never a bride, as well as others who try hard again and again but never quite succeed in making it. The Open End scripts end with aging men and women who lose their vitality without much regret and are content with reminiscing about past conquests. Women with such scripts wait eagerly for the menopause, with the mistaken idea that after that their "sexual problems" will be over, while the men wait until they have put in their time on the job with a similar hope of relief from sexual obligations.

At the more intimate level, each of these scripts has its own bearing on the actual orgasm. The Never script, of course, besides making spinsters and bachelors and prostitutes and pimps, also makes women who never have an orgasm, not a single one in their whole lives, and also produces impotent men who can have orgasms providing there is no love—the classical situation described by Freud of the man who is impotent with his wife but not with prostitutes. The Always script produces nymphomaniacs and Don Juans who spend their lives continually chasing after the promise of a conquest.

The Until script favors harried housewives and tired businessmen, neither of whom can get sexually aroused until every last detail of the household or the office has been put in order. Even after they are aroused, they may be interrupted at the most critical moments by games of Refrigerator Door and Note Book, little things they have to jump out of bed to take care of right now, such as checking the refrigerator door to make sure it is closed or jotting down a few things that have to be done first thing in the morning at the office. After scripts interfere with sex because of apprehension. Fear of pregnancy, for example, keeps the woman from having an enjoyable orgasm and may cause the man to have his too quickly. Coitus interruptus, where the man withdraws just before he comes, as a method of birth control, keeps both parties in a jumpy state right from the beginning, and usually leaves the woman stranded high and wet if the couple is too shy to use some way for her to get her satisfaction. In fact the word satisfaction, which is usually used in discussing this particular problem, is a giveaway that something is wrong, since a good orgasm should be far more substantial than the pale ghost that is called satisfaction.

The Over and Over script is one that will ring a bell for many women losers, who get higher and higher during intercourse, until just as they are about to make it, the man comes, possibly with the woman's help, and she rolls all the way down again. This may happen night after night for years. The Open End script has its effect in older people who regard sex as an effort or an obligation. Once over the hill, they are "too old" to have sex, and their glands wither away from disuse along with their skins and often their muscles and brains as well. The man strongly programed for punctuality has spent all his life waiting for Santa Claus to bring him his retirement pin—late to work only twice in the whole thirty years—while his wife has been waiting for Mrs. Santa Claus, whose maiden name was Minnie Menopause. And now they have nothing to do but fill in the time until their pipes rust away, taking their places in senior society according to what brand of car they drive, if any. If they are lucky, he may find a bleached divorcée at the trailer court who will give his plumbing a last fling, and as a result he may plumb his wife a few times in the afterglow, and after that, they've had it. The moral of this is that a script should not have a time limit on it, but should be designed to last a whole lifetime, no matter how long that lifetime may be. It may call for switching trades or sports, but retirement, no.

Sexual potency, force, and drive of a human being are to some extent determined by inheritance and chemistry. Incredible as it may seem, they are even more strongly influenced by the script decisions he makes in early childhood and by the parental programing that brings about those decisions. Thus not only the authority and frequency of his sexual activities throughout his whole lifetime, but also his ability and readiness to love are to a large extent already decided at the age of six. This seems to apply even more strongly to women. Some of them decide very early that they want to be mothers when they grow up, while others resolve at the same period to remain virgins or virgin brides forever. In any case, sexual activity in both sexes is continually interfered with by parental opinions, adult precautions, childhood decisions, and social pressures and fears, so that natural urges and cycles are suppressed, exaggerated, distorted, disregarded, or contaminated. The result is that whatever is called "sex" becomes the instrument of gamy behavior.

THE ILLUSION OF AUTONOMY

The road to freedom is through laughter, and until he learns that, man will be enslaved, either subservient to his masters or fighting to serve under a new master. The masters know this very well, and that is why they are masters. The last thing they will allow is unseemly laughter. In freer countries, every college has its humor magazine, but there are no such jokes in slave-holding nations like Nazi Germany or Arabia. Authority cannot be killed by force, for wherever one head is cut off, another springs up in its place. It can only be laughed away, as Sun Tzu knew when he founded the science of military discipline. He first demonstrated this to the Emperor by using girls from the harem, but they giggled when he gave his orders. He knew that as long as they were laughing, discipline wouldn't work. So he stopped their laughing by executing two of them, and after that the rest did as they were told—solemnly and indignantly. Conversely, no comedian has ever been the head of a state for very long; the people might stand it, but he couldn't.

Man is born free, but one of the first things he learns is to do as he is told, and he spends the rest of his life doing that. Thus his first enslavement is to his parents. He follows their instructions forevermore, retaining only in some cases the right to choose his own methods and consoling himself with an illusion of autonomy. If they want to raise him to feel inadequate, they can start by requiring him to produce square bowel movements and refusing to be satisfied with anything less. Whatever condition they impose on him he will spend the rest of his life trying to meet, and they can let him know from the beginning that he is not supposed to succeed. In that way he will end up with a good collection of inadequacies to cash in according to their instructions. If he has a streak of independence, he may change the subject and geometry of his efforts, but seldom its essence. He may shift his striving from square bowel movements to pear-shaped orgasms, but he will still make sure that he ends up feeling inadequate. If, on the other hand, they raise him to succeed, then he will do that, using whatever methods he has to to hew his ends to the shape required by his destiny.

In order to break away from such script programs, he must stop and think. But he cannot think about his programing unless he first gives up the illusion of autonomy. He must realize that he has not been up to now the free agent he likes to imagine he is, but rather the puppet of some Destiny from generations ago. Few people have the courage or the elasticity to turn around and stare down the monkeys on their backs, and the older they get, the stiffer their necks become.

This programing starts at the very bottom, at the organs that lie below the mystically curled omphalos or belly button where the twisted silver cord was once attached from mother's womb. Consider the sergeant's classical greeting to the new recruits when they arrive at basic training. The true translation of this is even more anatomical than the anatomical sergeant dreams of. What he says is (and this is true of WAC sergeants too): "Your soul belongs to mother, but your ass belongs to me." This can be truly stated as "The inside of your pelvis belongs to mother, but the outside belongs to me." The pelvic organs of almost every human being belong to mother—and for the lucky ones it goes no further than that. In other cases she controls the stomach and the brain as well. Actually, the Army gets only the leftovers—the outside parts, for the external muscles are all that the Army really needs. As long as soldiers follow orders, the rest is of interest only to the Medical Corps.

The important instructions in the script remain unchanged; only the method and the object are permitted to vary. "Be devoted to your leader," says the Nazi father, and the son devotes himself either to his Fascist leader, or to his leader in Christianity or in Communism, with equal fervor. The clergyman saves souls in his Sunday sermons, and his daughter sallies forth to save them singing folksongs with her guitar. The father is a streetsweeper and the son becomes a medical parasitologist, each in his own way cleaning up the offal that causes disease. The daughter of the good-natured prostitute grows up to be a nurse, and comforts the afflicted in a more sanitary way.

These similarities and differences correspond to what biologists call genotype and phenotype. All dogs have doggy genes, and cannot undertake to be anything but dogs; but each dog can be a dog in his own way. The basic instructions of the parents are like genes: the offspring cannot undertake to do anything but follow them, but each can follow them in his or her own way. This does not mean that brothers and sisters will be alike, for each sibling may and usually does receive different instructions, since each may be raised to play a different role in the scripts of the parents. For example, Cinderella has instructions to be a winner, while her stepsisters were raised to lose, and they all followed their Parental programing. Cinderella with her sweet and winning nature found her own way of coming out on top. It was not the way her parents visualized it perhaps, or maybe it was, but she came through. Her stepsisters were taught to grump and sulk to make sure that nobody would want them except the two jerks who were ordered to marry them by Cinderella's prince.

This freedom to select methods for arriving at the predetermined goal helps to support the illusion of the choice or autonomy. That illusion is most clearly illustrated by the man who had his brain stimulated by an electrode during an operation. Since the stimulated area was the one which controlled his right arm, he raised the arm. When the operator asked him why he moved it, he replied: "Because I wanted to." This is the same thing that goes on all the time in daily life. Each person follows the Parents' instructions in important matters, but by choosing his own time and place, maintains the illusion that he is making his own decisions freely and that his behavior is the result of free will. Both of these aspects are built in. It is built in that the Parental instructions will work like an electrode, so that the person will end up following them almost automatically with little or no chance to decide for himself. It is also built in that he will think he is exercising free will. This can only be accomplished if he forgets the Parental instructions and does not remember hearing them. The moment he does remember, he may realize that it is they who have been deciding his feelings, behavior, and responses. Only by such a realization can he free himself to use his own decisions.

For some people, of course, and at some levels with everyone, there is no illusion of autonomy, and the person is quite aware that his behavior is determined by what his parents told him at an early age. This is the case, for example, with many virgins and frigid women who state quite openly that they are so because that is how their parents told them to be. In a way they are better off than those who pretend otherwise. And the study of parental injunctions was started by a gambler who wanted to be cured and who said to the therapist: "Don't tell me not to gamble. That won't work. What I need is permission not to lose." He had suddenly become aware that he lost because he was ordered to lose. What he needed was not more instructions, such as "Why don't you stop gambling?" but permission to disregard the instructions he had received in childhood.

Thus lechery, sadism, homosexuality, promiscuity, sexual games, and other biologically inappropriate forms of sexual activity are programed in by the parents in most cases. But the person says, "I do it that way because I want to." This is true in a roundabout way. He does it that way because he was so instructed, and he wants to obey the instructions because he is afraid not to. He turns this necessity into a virtue by claiming free will, which might fool Baudelaire, but it need not fool others. If and when he recalls the instructions, and finds out how the electrode was implanted in his brain, he may be ready to give up his parental programing and the illusions that go with it and perhaps become really free.

It is important to understand that what we are talking about here is biology and not youth movements, which in any case are carried on by programed youths. Parental programing is not the "fault" of parents— since they are only passing on the programing they got from their parents—any more than the physical appearance of their offspring is their "fault," since they are only passing on the genes they got from their ancestors. But the brain chemicals involved in script programing are easier to change than the gene chemicals that determine physical appearance. Therefore a parent who wants to do the best for his children should find out what his own script is and then decide whether he wants to pass it on to them. If he decides not to, then he should find out how to change it, to grow princes where there were frogs before. This is not easy to do. It is even harder than trying to give oneself a haircut. It usually requires help of a script analyst, but that doesn't always work either. It is even more discouraging to think that if he does pass it on, it will probably be carried through to his grandchildren. This script transmission is the basis for the old saying "To make a lady, start with the grandmother," and it also explains why the Civil War is not over yet, and why it will take another hundred years for the angry scripts of nowadays to cool into a decent way of living. Now is the time to start programing the parents of the ladies and gentlemen of the next century. If we want things to be warm and straight later, we've got to stop being cold and crooked now.

18. How Is the Script Possible?

Jeder sits at a player piano, his fingers wandering over the keys. The roll of paper, punched out long ago by his forebears, turns slowly as he pumps away. The music pours forth in a pattern that he cannot change, at times melancholy, at times gay, now jarring, and now full of melody. Occasionally he strikes a note or a chorus whose sound may blend with what is written, or disturb the smooth flow of the fateful song. He pauses to rest, for the roll is thicker than the whole scroll of the law in the temple. It contains the law and the prophets, the songs and the lamentations, an old testament and a new: a truly magnificent, a mediocre, a dreary, or a miserable gift given to him piece by piece by his loving, indifferent, or hateful parents. He is under the illusion that the music is his own, and has for his witness his body, slowly wearing out from hour after hour and day after day of pumping. Sometimes, during the pauses, he rises to take a bow or a boo from his friends and relatives, who also believe that he is playing his own tune.

How is it that the members of the human race, with all their accumulated wisdom, self-awareness, and desire for truth and self, can permit themselves to remain in such a mechanical situation, with its pathos and self-deception? Partly it is because we love our parents and partly it is because life is easier that way, but partly also it is because we have not yet evolved far enough from our apelike ancestors to have it otherwise. We are more aware of ourselves than apes are, but not really very much. Scripts are only possible because people don't know what they are doing to themselves and to others. In fact, to know what one is doing is the op-

The following three chapters, 18-20, are from *What Do You Say After You Say Hello?*, copyright © 1972 by City National Bank, Beverly Hills, California; Robin Way; Janice Way Farlinger. Reprinted by permission of Grove Press, Inc.

posite of being scripted. There are certain aspects of bodily, mental, and social functioning which happen to man in spite of himself, which slip out, as it were, because they are programed to do so. These heavily influence his destiny through the people around him, while he still retains the illusion of autonomy. But there are also certain remedies which can be applied.

THE PLASTIC FACE

It is, above all, the plasticity of the human face which makes life an adventure rather than a controlled experience. This is based on an apparently trivial biological principle which has an enormous social power. The human nervous system is so constructed that the visual impact on the onlooker of small movements of the facial muscles is greater than the kinesthetic impact on the subject. A two-millimeter movement of one of the small muscles around the mouth may be quite imperceptible to Jeder but quite obvious to his companions. This can be easily verified in front of a mirror. The extent to which the subject is unaware of what he looks like is easily demonstrated by the commonplace act of picking the front of the teeth with the tongue. Jeder may do this with what seems to him extreme discretion and delicacy. As far as he can judge from his kinesthetic or muscular sensations, he is hardly moving his face at all. But if he does it in front of a mirror, he sees that which feels like a minor movement of the tongue actually brings about a gross distortion of his features, especially the chin and including the neck muscles. If he pays more attention than he usually does to his muscular sensations, he will also notice that the movement is affecting his forehead and temples.

In the heat of a social encounter, this phenomenon may occur dozens of times without his being aware of it: what seems to him like a small excursion of his muscles of expression causes a major change in his appearance. On the other hand, the Child in Zoe, the onlooker, is watching (as much as good manners permit) for signs which will give her an indication of

Jeder's attitude, feelings, and intent. Thus Jeder is always giving away far more than he thinks he is, unless he is one of those people who habitually keep their features immobile and inscrutable and are careful not to reveal their reactions. The importance of facial plasticity, however, is shown by the fact that such an inscrutable person makes others uneasy, since they get no clues as to how to adapt their behavior.

This principle clarifies the origin of the almost uncanny "intuition" of babies and young children about people. Since babies have not yet been taught that they must not look too closely at people's faces, they are free to do so, and see much that others miss and that the subject is not aware he is giving away. In everyday life, Zoe's Adult is politely careful not to look too closely at what happens to other people's faces while they talk, but meanwhile her Child is rudely "peeking," as it were, all the time, and thus forming judgments, usually accurate, of what the other is really up to. This is particularly apt to occur in the "first ten seconds" after meeting a new person, before he has a chance to figure out how to present himself, and thus he tends to give away things he later hides. That is the value of first impressions.

The social effect of this is that Jeder never knows how much he is giving away by his facial plasticity. Things which he tries to hide even from himself are quite apparent to Zoe, who reacts accordingly, much to Jeder's surprise. He is continually giving out script signals without being aware of it. Others respond ultimately to these signals, instead of to Jeder's persona or presentation of himself. In this way the script is kept going without Jeder having to take the responsibility for it. He can keep his illusion of autonomy by saying: "I don't know why she acted that way. I didn't do anything to bring it on. People sure are funny." If his behavior is odd enough, others may react in a fashion which is quite beyond his comprehension, and in this way delusions can be established or reinforced.

The remedy for this is simple. If Jeder studies his facial expressions in the mirror, he will soon see what he is doing to make people react the way they do, and he will then be in a position to change the situation if he wants to. Unless he is an actor, he will probably not want to. In fact, most people are so intent on keeping their scripts going that they will find all sorts of excuses not even to study themselves in the mirror. They may claim, for example, that this procedure is "artificial," which means that the only thing that is "natural" is to let the script proceed to its mechanical, foreordained conclusion.

THE ODORLESS SMELL

In addition to the biological peculiarities of the human organism, there are more elusive possibilities which could have an equally profound effect on human living. The first of these is extrasensory perception. If Dr. J. B. Rhine's cards are sending out signals which cannot be detected by the present generation of physical instruments, but can be received by a properly attuned human mind, that is obviously a matter of considerable, though not necessarily decisive, importance. If such signals exist, their objective detection would be of interest at first mainly for sensational reasons, and there would be a field day in the Sunday supplements. The later developments of such a discovery cannot be foreseen until it occurs. No doubt it would interest the military, which is already doing research in this field, especially if the target could be selected, just as it would be in the case of the long-distance atomic- and hydrogen-bomb detonator which could be flown over the factories and depots of a potential enemy.

Telepathy would be of considerably more significance if it existed. If one human mind can send readable messages to another, and an objective means for controlling and recording such messages could be devised, that would help to understand many things about human behavior. This is the second possibility. "Telepathic phenomena," when they are reported, seem to occur most often and most poignantly between intimately related people such as husbands and wives, or parents and children, who are presumably more closely attuned to each other than to other members of the human race. Telepathy would offer an ideal medium for hovering parents to exert control over their children's behavior, and would certainly be of prime interest to the script analyst if it existed. Intuition, which is a function of the Child ego state, often verges on telepathy, in that rather obscure facts about other people can be intuited with a minimum of sensory clues.

When telepathy has been claimed to occur, it is very fragile and easily broken, and depends a great deal upon the frame of mind of the agent and the percipient. Extraneous factors, such as challenges by scientists, seem to diminish its accuracy or abolish it altogether, according to the published results of such challenges. This does not necessarily mean that telepathy does not exist, but rather gives us an indication of its nature if it does exist. I would propose the following hypothesis, which explains with only one major and one minor assumption, all the scientifically established (mostly negative) findings. If telepathy occurs, then the young infant is the best percipient; as he grows older, this faculty becomes corrupted and progressively more unreliable, so that it occurs only sporadically and under special conditions in grown-ups. In structural language, the hypothesis reads: If telepathy exists, it is a function of the very young Child, and soon becomes corrupted and impaired by interference from the Parent and the Adult.

Third, just as interesting and important, although more materialistic, is the question of odorless smells. It is well known that the male of the Bombyces moth can detect downwind the presence of a freshly emerged female as far as a mile away, and large numbers of males will fly against the wind and assemble around a caged female. We have to assume that the female gives off an odorous substance which attracts the males through something like the sense of smell. The question at issue here is: Does the male "know" that he is "smelling" something, or does he respond "automatically" to the chemical? It is probable that he is not "aware" of what happens, but simply responds, and flies toward the female. That is, he is attracted through his olfactory system by an "odorless" smell.

With a human being, the situation regarding smells is this: (1) If he smells certain odors, such as the perfume of flowers, he is aware of them and is consciously attracted to them. The experience may leave memory traces and that, as far as we know, is all there is to it. (2) If he smells other odors, such as feces, two things commonly occur: (a) he is aware of them and is consciously repelled by them; and (b) without any volition on his part, his autonomic nervous system is affected by them, and he may gag or throw up. (3) We can postulate a third situation: in the presence of certain chemicals, his nervous system is affected in a subtle way without his smelling anything or being aware of it. I am not speaking here of toxic matter such as carbon monoxide, but of substances which stimulate specific receptors and leave specific traces or engrams in the brain.

Several facts should be noted in this connection. (1) The olfactory area of the rabbit contains 100,000,000 olfactory cells, each with six or twelve hairs, so that the olfactory receptor area is equal to the total skin area of the animal. (2) It can be presumed that electrical discharges occur in the olfactory system long after adaptation to a given odor occurs; that is, although the odor can no longer be smelled, it continues to affect the electrical activity of the nervous system. The experimental evidence for this is not decisive, but is strongly suggestive. (3) Smells can affect dreams without being perceived as smells. (4) The perfumes most sexually provocative to human beings are chemically related to the sex hormones. (5) The odor of the breath and of the sweat can change with a change in emotional attitude. (6) The olfactory nerves lead into the rhinencephalon, a "primitive" part of the brain which is probably heavily involved in emotional reactions.

The hypothesis here then would be: the human being is continually stimulated by a variety of subtle chemical stimuli of which he is not aware, but which affect his emotional responses and his behavior toward various people in various situations. While there may be special (so far unknown) receptors for this, the structure of the olfactory tract itself is sufficient to deal with these effects. Such stimuli can be called odorless smells. There is no firm evidence that odorless smells actually exist; but if they did exist, they would conveniently account for many behavioral phenomena and responses which are otherwise difficult or impossible to understand in the present state of our knowledge. Their influence on the script would be durable, as in the case of fascination, fetishism, and imprinting. Newborn kittens may "smell" their mother's teats without being "aware" of it, and the "memory" of this odorless smell, or something like it, evidently affects their behavior for the rest of their lives.

THE BRAVE SCHIZOPHRENIC

Besides the biological and psychological characteristics of the human organism which allow the preprogramed script to become the master of personal destiny, societies are set up in such a way as to encourage this lack of autonomy. This is done by means of the transactional social contract, which reads: "You accept my persona or self-presentation, and I'll accept yours." Any abrogation of this contract, unless it is one specifically permitted in a given group, is regarded as rudeness. The result is a lack of confrontation: confrontation with others and confrontation with oneself, for behind this social contract lies a hidden individual contract between the three aspects of the personality. The Parent, Child, and Adult agree among themselves to accept each other's self-presentation, and not everyone is courageous enough to change such a contract with himself when it is advisable.

Lack of confrontation is seen most clearly in the case of schizophrenics and their therapists. The majority of therapists (in my experience) say that schizophrenia is incurable. By this they mean: "Schizophrenia is incurable by my kind of psychoanalytic therapy, and I'm damned if I'm going to try anything else." Hence they settle for what they call "making progress," and like the well-known electrical manufacturer, progress is their principal product. But progress means merely making the schizophrenic live more bravely in his crazy world, rather than getting him out of it, and so the earth is full of brave schizophrenics living out their tragic scripts with the help of not-so-brave therapists.

Two other slogans common among therapists are also common among the general population: "You can't tell people what to do," and "I can't help you, you have to help yourself." Both of these are outright falsehoods. You *can* tell people what to do, and many of them will do it and do it well. And you *can* help people, and they don't have to help themselves. They merely have to get up, after you have helped them, and go about their business. But with slogans such as those, society (and I don't mean Arsisiety, I mean *all* societies) encourages people to stay in their scripts and carry them through to their often tragic endings. A script merely means that someone told the person what to do a long time ago and he decided to do it. This demonstrates that you can tell people what to do, and are in fact telling them all the time, especially if you have children. So if you tell people to do something other than what their parents told them, they may decide to follow your advice or instructions. And it is well known that you can help people get drunk, or kill themselves, or kill someone else; therefore, you can also help them stop drinking, or stop killing themselves, or stop killing other people. It is certainly possible to give people *permission* to do certain things, or to stop doing certain things which they were ordered in childhood to keep doing. Instead of encouraging people to live bravely in an old unhappy world, it is possible to have them live happily in a brave new world.

THE VENTRILOQUIST'S DUMMY

As psychoanalysis came into its own, it pushed aside much valuable work that had been done previously. Thus, free association replaced the centuries-long tradition of introspection. Free association was concerned with the contents of the mind, leaving it to the psychoanalyst to figure out when it did not work smoothly. There is no way to figure out how a closed machine (a "black box") works as long as it works perfectly. This can only be found out if it makes mistakes, or is induced to make a mistake by throwing a monkey wrench into it. Thus, free association is only as good as the psychopathology behind it: the switches, the intrusions, the slips, and the dreams.

Introspection, on the other hand, takes the cover off the black box, and lets the Adult of the person peer into his own mind to see how it works: how he puts sentences together, which direction his images come from, and what voices direct his behavior. Federn was the first psychoanalyst, I think, to revive this tradition, and to make a specific study of internal dialogues.

Almost everyone has said "to himself" at some time: "You shouldn't have done that!" and he may even have noticed that he answers "himself": "But I had to!" In this case, it is the Parent saying "You shouldn't have done that!" and the Adult or Child saying: "But I had to!" This exactly reproduces some actual dialogue of childhood. Now what is really happening? There are three "degrees" of such internal dialogue. In the first degree, the words run through Jeder's head in a shadowy way, with no muscular movements, or at least none perceptible to the naked eye or ear. In the second degree, he can feel his vocal muscles moving a little so that he whispers to himself inside his mouth; in particular, there are small abortive movements of the tongue. In the third degree, he says the words out loud. The third degree may take over in certain disturbed conditions so that he walks down the street talking to himself, and people turn their heads to watch and are likely to think he is "crazy." There is also a fourth degree, where one or other of the internal voices is heard as coming from outside the skull. This is usually the voice of the parent (actually the voice of his father or mother) and these are hallucinations. His Child may or may not answer the Parental voices, but in any case they affect some aspect of his behavior.

Because people who "talk to themselves" are thought to be crazy, nearly everyone has an injunction against listening to the voices in his head. This is a faculty which can be quickly recovered, however, if the proper permission is given. Then almost everyone can listen in on his own internal dialogues, and that is one of the best ways to find out the Parental precepts, the Parental pattern, and the script controls.

A sexually excited girl started to pray in her head so that she would be able to resist her boy friend's seduction. She clearly heard herself directed by the Parental precept: "Be a good girl, and when you are tempted, pray." A man got into a fight in a bar and was very careful to fight skillfully. He clearly heard his father's voice saying: "Don't telegraph your punches!" which was part of his father's pattern: "Here's how to fight in a bar." He got into the fight because his mother's voice said provocatively: "You're just like your father, some day you'll get your teeth smashed in a bar fight." At the critical moment, a stockmarket speculator heard a demonic whisper telling him: "Don't sell, buy." He abandoned his carefully planned campaign, and lost his entire capital—"Ha ha," he said.

The Parental voice exerts the same kind of control as a ventriloquist. It takes charge of the person's vocal apparatus, and he finds himself saying words which come from someone else. Unless his Adult steps in, he then follows the instructions given by this voice, so that his Child acts exactly like a ventriloquist's dummy. This ability to suspend one's own will, usually without realizing what has happened, and to let someone else take charge of the vocal muscles and the other muscles of the body, is what enables the script to take over at the appropriate time.

The remedy for this is to listen to the voices in one's head, and let the Adult decide whether to follow their instructions or not. In this way the person frees himself from the control of the Parental ventriloquist, and becomes master of his own actions. In order to accomplish this, he requires two permissions which he can give himself, but which may be more effective coming from someone else, such as a therapist.

1. Permission to listen to his internal dialogue.

2. Permission not to follow the directives of his
   Parent.

There is some peril in this undertaking, and he may
require protection from someone else if he dares to
disobey the Parental directives. Thus, one job of the
therapist is to give his patients protection if they act
independently of their ventriloquist Parents and try to
be real people instead of dummies.

It should be added that while *Parental voices* tell
him what he can or cannot do, it is *Child pictures* that
tell him what he wants to do. Desires are visual, and
directives are auditory.

MORE ABOUT THE DEMON

All the items mentioned so far are helpful in making
the script possible, and most of them are matters beyond the person's awareness. Now we come to the key
item, which not only makes the script possible, but
gives it the decisive push. That is the demon who sends
Jeder naked on roller skates down the hill to his
destruction just when he is on the verge of success,
before he even knows what is happening to him. But
looking back, even if he has never heard the other
voices in his head, he will usually remember that one,
the voice of the demon prompting irresistibly: "Go
ahead and do it!" Which he does, in the face of all the
other forces warning him against it and vainly trying to
call him back. This is Daemon, the sudden super-
natural push that determines a man's fate, a voice from
the Golden Age, lower than the gods but higher than
humanity, perhaps a fallen angel. That is what the his-
torians tell us, and perhaps they are right. For Heracli-
tus, the Daemon in man was his character. But this
Daemon, according to those who have known him or
her, the losers who are just picking themselves up from
their falls, speaks not in a loud command like the
ghost of a mighty god, but in a seductive whisper, like
a beckoning woman, like an enchantress: "Come, do it.
Go ahead. Why not? What have you to lose but everything? Instead you will have me, as you once did in the
Golden Age."

This is the repetition compulsion which drives men to their doom, the power of death, according to Freud, or the power of the goddess Ananke. But he places it in some mysterious biological sphere, when after all it is only the voice of seduction. Ask the man (or woman) who owns one and knows the power of his demon.

The remedy against demons has always been cantrips and cantraps, and that is the case here. Every loser should carry it in wallet or purse, and whenever success looms in sight, that is the moment of danger. That is the time to pull it out and read it aloud again and again. Then when the demon whispers "Stretch out your arm—and put the whole wad on one last number, or have just one drink, or now is the time to pull your knife, or grab her (him) by the neck and pull her (him) toward you," or whatever the losing movement is, pull the arm back and say it loud and clear: "But mother, I'd rather do it my own way and win."

THE REAL PERSON

The converse of the script is the real person living in a real world. This real person is probably the real Self, the one which can move from one ego state to another. When people get to know each other well, they penetrate through the script into the depths where this real Self resides, and that is the part of the other person they respect and love, and with which they can have moments of real intimacy before Parental programing takes over again. This is possible because it has happened before in the lives of most people in the most intimate and script-free relationship of all: that between the mother and her infant. The mother can usually suspend her script during the nursing period if left to her own instincts, and the infant does not yet have one.

As for myself, I know not whether I am still run by a music roll or not. If I am, I wait with interest and anticipation—and without apprehension—for the next notes to unroll their melody, and for the harmony and discord after that. Where will I go next? In this case my life is meaningful because I am following the long and glorious tradition of my ancestors, passed on to me by my parents, music perhaps sweeter than I could compose myself. Certainly I know that there are large areas where I am free to improvise. It may even be that I am one of the few fortunate people on earth who has cast off the shackles entirely and who calls his own tune. In that case I am a brave improviser facing the world alone. But whether I am faking on a player piano, or striking the chords with the power of my own mind and hands, the song of my life is equally suspenseful and full of surprises as it rolls off the pulsating sounding board of destiny—a barcarole that either way will leave, I hope, happy echoes behind.

19. Transmission of the Script

THE SCRIPT MATRIX

The script matrix is a diagram designed to illustrate and analyze the directives handed down from parents and grandparents to the current generation. An enormous amount of information can be compressed very elegantly into this relatively simple drawing. The problem in practice is to separate the decisive parental directives and the decisive patterns of behavior, the script theme, from the "noise" or foreground confusion, which is made doubly difficult because not only the person himself, but all the people around him, contribute as much as they possibly can to these distractions. This tends to conceal the steps leading up to the script's payoff, the happy or tragic ending, which in the language of biologists [1] is the "final display." In other words, people take great pains to conceal their scripts from themselves and from others. This is only natural. To return to a previous metaphor, a man sitting in front of a player piano and moving his fingers under the illusion that he is making the music himself does not want somebody telling him to look inside the piano, and the audience, which is enjoying the spectacle, doesn't want it either.

Steiner, who devised the script matrix [2], follows the original scheme proposed by the writer, that usually the parent of the opposite sex tells the child what to do, and the parent of the same sex shows him how to do it. Steiner made important additions to this basic scheme. He carried it much further by specifying what each ego state in the parents does. He postulates that it is the Child in the parent who gives the injunctions and the Adult in the parent that gives the child his "program" (which we have also called his pattern).

And he added a new element, the counterscript, coming
from the Parent of the parents. Steiner's version of the
matrix is derived mainly from work with alcoholics,
addicts, and "sociopaths." These all have third-degree,
hard, tragic scripts (what he calls "hamartic" scripts).
His matrix therefore deals with harsh injunctions from
a "crazy Child," but it can be extended to include
seductions and provocations, as well as injunctions that
seem to come from the Parent in the parent rather
than from the parent's crazy Child.

The "standard" matrix shows the injunctions and
provocations coming from the Child of the parents,
most commonly from the parent of the opposite sex.
If this turns out to be universally true, it will be a
crucial discovery concerning human destiny and the
transmission of destiny from one generation to another.
The most important principle of script theory could
then be stated as follows: "The parent's Child forms
the Child's Parent," or "The child's Parent is the
Parent's Child" [3]. This should be easy to understand
with the aid of the diagram, remembering that "Child"
and "Parent" with capital letters refer to ego states in
the head, while "parent" with a small "p" and "child"
with a small "c" refer to actual people.

A blank script matrix, such as shown in Figure 11
(p. 261) can be painted on a blackboard and put to
good use during group-treatment meetings and in teaching script theory. In analyzing an individual case, the
parents are first labeled according to the sex of the
patient, and then the slogans, patterns, injunctions, and
provocations can be filled in with chalk along the
arrows. This gives a clear visual representation of the
decisive script transactions. With the help of such a
device, it will soon be found that the script matrix says
things that have never been said before.

People with good scripts may be interested in script
analysis only in an academic way, unless they are going
to be therapists. But with patients, in order to get them
well, it is necessary to dissect out the directives in as
pure a form as possible, and drawing an accurate script
matrix is a useful tool in planning treatment.

The most likely way to elicit the information for filling in the script matrix is to ask the patient the following four questions: (a) What was your parents' favorite slogan or precept? This will give the key to the anti-script. (b) What kind of life did your parents lead? This will best be answered by a long association with the patient. Whatever his parents taught him to do, he will do again and again, and the patter will give him his ordinary social character: "He's a heavy drinker." "She's a sexy girl." (c) What is your Parental Prohibition? This is the most important single question for understanding the behavior of the patient and for planning the decisive intervention which will free him to live more fully. Since his symptoms are a substitute for the prohibited act, and also a protest against it, as demonstrated by Freud, freedom from the prohibition will also tend to cure his symptoms. It takes experience and subtlety to pick out the decisive parental injunction from the "background noise." The most reliable clues are offered by the fourth question, (d) What did you have to do to make your parents smile or chuckle? This gives the come-on, which is the alternative to the prohibited behavior.

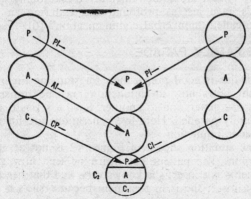

Figure 11. A blank script matrix.

Steiner believes that the prohibition in the case of "alcoholics" is "Don't think!" and that drinking heavily is one program for not thinking [4]. The absence of thinking is well shown in the drinking platitudes common among "Alcoholic" players and their sympathizers, and even more so by the ones they foist on each other in "alcoholic" group therapy [5]. What these all say is that "alcoholics" are not real people and should not be treated like real people, which is not true. Heroin is even more addictive and sinister than alcohol, and Synanon has proved conclusively that heroin addicts are real people. The real person emerges in both cases after the alcohol or heroin addict cuts off the seductive voices in his head which are urging him to continue his habit, reinforced in due time by physical demands. It appears that tranquilizers and phenothiazines are effective partly because they smother the Parental voices which are keeping the Child agitated or making him confused with their "Dont's" and "Ha Ha's."

The most forceful script directives are given during the family drama which in some respects reinforces what the parents have been saying, and in others demonstrates that they are hypocritical impostors. It is these scenes which bring home in the most poignant way what the parents want the child to learn about his script. And it should be remembered that loudly spoken words have just as profound and enduring an effect as so-called "nonverbal communication" [6].

THE FAMILY PARADE

All this is good preparation for studying Figure 12, which shows how an injunction may be transmitted from one generation to another. Such a series is called a "family parade." Here five generations are linked by the same injunction.

The situation shown in Figure 12 is not at all uncommon. The patient has heard or seen how grandmother was a loser; she knows very well that her father was a loser; she is in treatment because she's a loser; her son is going to the clinic because he is a loser; and her granddaughter is already showing signs at school that she is going to be a loser, too. Both the patient and the therapist know that this five-generation chain must be broken somewhere or it may go on

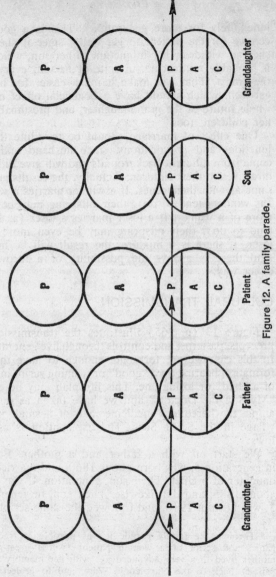

Figure 12. A family parade.

indefinitely for more generations. This is a good incentive for the patient to get well,* since if she does she can withdraw her injunction to her son, which she is probably reinforcing, in spite of herself, every time they meet. That will make it much easier for him to get well, which should have a beneficial effect on the whole future of the granddaughter, and presumably on her children, too.

One effect of marriage should be to dilute the injunctions and provocations, since husband and wife come from different backgrounds and will give different directives to their children. Actually, the results are the same as with their genes. If a winner marries a winner (as winners tend to do), their offspring may be even more of a winner. If a loser marries a loser (as losers tend to do), their offspring may be even more of a loser. If there is a mixture, the result will be mixed. And there is always the possibility of a throwback either way.

CULTURAL TRANSMISSION

Figure 13 (p. 265) illustrates the transmission of precepts, patterns, and controls through five generations. In this case we are fortunate enough to have the information bearing on a "good" or winning script instead of a "bad" or losing one. This life plan may be called "My Son the Doctor," and we have taken as our example the hereditary medicine man of a small jungle village in the South Seas. The explanation is as follows:

We start off with a father and a mother. Father, in generation 5, was born about 1860, and married the daughter of a chief. Their son, generation 4, was born about 1885, and did likewise. Their son, in generation 3, was born in 1910, and followed the same script. His

---

* Through the family parade it was possible to trace the games and script of a woman patient (whose great-grandmother lived to a very advanced age with her memory unimpaired) back to the Napoleonic Wars, and to project them forward through her grandchildren to the year 2000.

son, in generation 2, born in 1935, followed a slightly different pattern. Instead of becoming a hereditary medicine man, he went to the medical school in Suva, Fiji, and became what was then known as a Native Medical Assistant. He, too, married a daughter of a chief, and their son, in generation 1, born in 1960, plans to follow in his father's footsteps, except that due to hospital developments he will be called an Assistant Medical Officer, or he might even go to London and become a full-fledged Medical Officer. Thus the son in each generation becomes the father (F) of the next generation, and his wife becomes the mother (M).

Each father and mother give the same precept or inspiration from the Parent in them to the Parent in their son: "Be a good medicine man." The father's Adult transmits to his son's Adult the secrets of his trade, which of course are not known to the mother. But the mother does know what she wants her son to do; in fact, she knew from her earliest years that she would want her son to be either a chief or a medi-

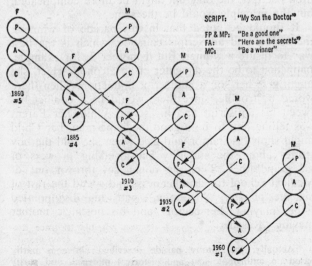

SCRIPT: "My Son the Doctor"

FP & MP: "Be a good one"
FA: "Here are the secrets"
MC: "Be a winner"

Figure 13. Cultural transmission.

cine man. Shince he is obviously going to be the latter, she transmits from her Child to his Child (from her early childhood decision to him in his early years) the benevolent come-on, "Be a winner as a medicine man."

In this case (Figure 13) the family parade of Figure 12 (p. 263) is shown in a more complete form. It can be seen that father's precepts and father's program of instruction form two parallel lines going straight down the generations from 1860 to 1960. Mother's precepts and mother's injunctions ("Don't fail") are also parallel, and come from the side in each generation. This neatly demonstrates the transmission of "culture" over a period of one hundred years. Similar diagrams could be drawn for any element of "culture" or any "role" in the village society.

In a family parade of daughters, whose roles might be "mothers of successful medicine men," the diagram would look exactly the same except that the M's and F's would switch places. In a village where uncles or mothers-in-law were important influences on the children's scripts, the diagram might be more complicated, but the principle would be the same.

It should be noted that in this parade of winners, the scripts and antiscripts coincide, which is the best way to insure a winner. But if mother 3, for example, happened to be the daughter of an alcoholic chief, she might give her son a bad script injunction. Then there would be trouble, since there would be a conflict between his antiscript and his script. While her Parent was telling him to be a good medicine man, her Child might show fascination and glee when she told the boy stories about the stupidity and drinking prowess of his grandfather. Then he might get thrown out of Medical School for drunkenness, and spend the rest of his life playing "Alcoholic," with his disappointed father playing "Persecutor" and his nostalgic mother playing "Rescuer." *

---

* Actually, the family parade described above is partly based on anthropological and historical material, and partly on the family trees of some American doctors.

THE INFLUENCE OF THE GRANDPARENTS

The most intricate part of script analysis in clinical practice is tracing back the influence of the grandparents. This is illustrated in Figure 14 (p. 268). There it can be seen that PC in mother is split into two parts, FPC and MPC. FPC represents the influence of her father when she was very little (Father Parent in her Child) and MPC represents the influence of her mother (Mother Parent in her Child). This split may look complicated and impractical at first sight, but it is not so to anyone accustomed to thinking in terms of ego states. For example, it does not take very long for patients to learn to distinguish between FPC and MPC in themselves. "When I was little, father liked to make me cry, and mother dressed me in a sexy way," said the weepy, pretty prostitute. "Father liked me to be bright and mother liked to dress me up," said the bright, well-dressed psychologist. "Father said girls are no good and mother dressed me like a tomboy," said the frightened beatnik in her boyish clothes. Each of these women knew very well when her behavior was guided by father's early influence (FPC) or mother's (MPC). When they were weepy, bright, or frightened, they were doing it for father, and when they looked sexy, well dressed, or tomboyish, they were following mother's instructions.

Now remembering the tendency for the script controls to come from the parent of the opposite sex, FPC in mother is her electrode, and MPC in father is his. Thus, mother's script commands to Jeder come from her father, and so it can be said that "Jeder's script programing comes from his maternal grandfather" [3]. Father's commands to Zoe come from his mother, so Zoe's script programing comes from her paternal grandmother. The electrode, then, is mother (grandfather) in Jeder's head, and in the case of Zoe, father (grandmother) in her head. Applying this to the three cases above, the prostitute's grandmother married and divorced several mean husbands, the psychologist's grandmother was a well-known writer, and the tomboy's grandmother was a crusader for women's rights.

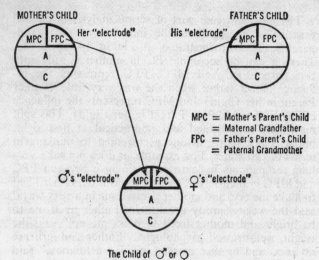

MOTHER'S CHILD

FATHER'S CHILD

Her "electrode"   His "electrode"

MPC = Mother's Parent's Child
    = Maternal Grandfather
FPC = Father's Parent's Child
    = Paternal Grandmother

♂'s "electrode"   ♀'s "electrode"

The Child of ♂ or ♀

Figure 14. Transmission from the grandparents.

It can now be understood why the family parade diagramed in Figure 12 (p. 263) alternated generations between the sexes—grandmother, father, female patient, son, and granddaughter. Figure 13 (p. 265), on the other hand, illustrates how such a diagram can be adjusted to follow straight down the line with either male descendants or female descendants. It is just because of this kind of versatility that the script-matrix diagram is such a valuable instrument. It has properties which even its originator did not suspect. Here it offers a simplified method for helping to understand such complex matters as family histories, the transmission of culture, and the psychological influence of grandparents.

OVERSCRIPTING

There are two requirements for the transmission of the script. Jeder must be able, ready, and willing or even eager to accept it, and his parents must want to pass it on.

On Jeder's side, he is able, because his nervous system is constructed for the purpose of being programed, to receive sensory and social stimuli and organize them into patterns which will regulate his behavior. As his body and his mind mature, he becomes readier and readier for more and more complex types of programing. And he is willing to accept it because he needs ways to structure his time and organize his activities. In fact he is not only willing, he is eager, because he is more than a passive computer. Like most animals, he has a craving for "closure," the need to finish what he begins; and beyond that, he has the great human aspiration for purpose.

Starting off with random movement, he ends up knowing what to say after he says Hello. At first he is content with instrumental responses, and they become goals in themselves: incorporation, elimination, intrusion, and locomotion, to use Erikson's terms. Here we find the beginnings of Adult craftsmanship, his pleasure in the act and its successful completion: getting the food safely off the spoon and into his mouth, walking on his own across the floor. Initially his goal is to walk, then it is to walk *to* something. Once he walks to people, he has to know what to do after he gets there. At first they smile and hug him, and all he has to do is be, or at most, cuddle. They expect nothing from him beyond getting there. Later they do expect something, so he learns to say Hello. After a while, that is not enough either, and they expect more. So he learns to offer them various stimuli in order to get their responses in return. Thus, he is eternally grateful (believe it or not) to his parents for giving him a pattern: how to approach people in such a way as to get the desired responses. This is structure hunger, pattern hunger, and in the long run, script hunger. So the script is accepted because Jeder is script hungry.

On the parents' side, they are able, ready, and willing because of what has been built into them through eons of evolution: a desire to nurture, protect, and teach their offspring, a desire which can only be suppressed by the most powerful inner and outer forces. But beyond that, if they themselves have been properly "scripted," they are not only willing, but eager, and derive great enjoyment from child-rearing.

Some parents, however, are overly eager. Child-rearing for them is neither a drag nor a joy, but a compulsion. In particular, their need to pass on precepts, patterns, and controls far exceeds the children's needs for such parental programing. This compusion is a rather complex affair, dividing roughly into three aspects. (1) A desire for immortality. (2) The demands of the parents' own scripts, which may range from "Don't make any mistakes," to "Mess up your children." (3) The desire of the parents to get rid of their own script controls, and pass them on to someone else so as to be free themselves. Of course this extrajection doesn't work, and so the attempt has to be made over and over.

These continuous assults on the child's psyche are well known to child psychiatrists and family therapists, who call them by various names. From the point of view of script analysis, they are a form of "overscripting," and the excessive directives which are laid on the child, and surfeit him far beyond the cravings of his script hunger, may be called his episcript or overscript. Usually his reaction is to ward them off by some form of repudiation, but he may follow his parents' policy and attempt to pass them on to someone else. For this reason, the episcript has been described by Fanita English [7] as a Hot Potato, and the continual attempts to pass it back and forth she calls the Hot Potato Game.

As she points out in her original paper on this subject, all sorts of people play this game, including therapists, and she gives the example of Joe, a psychology student, whose script payoff from his mother was: "Get locked up in a madhouse." Thus, he was in the habit of picking for his inept therapeutic attempts people who were good candidates for the state hospital, and he managed to help them along the way. Fortunately his supervisor observed his scripty smile whenever one of his patients verged on a breakdown, and put a stop to the whole procedure by persuading him to give up psychology, go into a business career, and seek treatment for himself. His script payoff was an episcript or "Hot potato" of his mother's, who had spent her life trying "to stay out of the madhouse," as she frequently said. She received the directive to get locked up from one of her parents, and tried to get rid of it by passing it on to Joe, who in turn tried to pass it on to his patients.

Thus the parents transmit the script as part of their normal parenting, to nurture, protect, and encourage their children by showing them, to the best of their ability, how to live life. Overscripting may arise from various causes. The most pathological is an attempt to get rid of an episcript by passing it on to one of the children. The episcript, especially if it is a "hamartic" or tragic one, becomes a hot potato which no one wants to hold on to. As English points out, it is the Professor, the Adult in the Child, who says: "Who needs it?" and decides that it can be got rid of, like a curse in a fairy tale, by passing it on to someone else.

BLENDING OF THE SCRIPT DIRECTIVES

As the years go by and the script becomes adapted by experience, the controls, patterns, and prescriptions become blended so that it is hard to distinguish one from the other in the person's behavior, and to determine which is a "final common pathway." He adopts a program or routine which synthesizes them all. The major script payoffs occur in the form of a "final display." If the payoff is a bad one, the script elements may be quite apparent to an experienced observer, as in cases of psychosis, delirium tremens, car-crashing, suicide, or murder. With good payoffs, it is more difficult to dissect out the script directives, partly because in such cases there are usually extensive permissions granted by the parents, which may obscure the directives.

Consider the following real-life romance, taken from a news item in a small-town newspaper.

ROMANTIC HISTORY
REPEATED IN THE X FAMILY

Fifty years ago an Australian soldier went to England to serve in the First World War. His name was John X, and he met and married Jane Y. After the war was over, they came to America to live. Twenty-five years later, their three children were vacationing in England. Tox X, their son, married Mary Z, of Great Snoring, Norfolk, and his two sisters married Englishmen. This fall, Tom and Mary X's daughter, Jane, who spent her vacation in Great Snoring with an aunt, announced her engagement to Harry J, also of Great Snoring. Jane is a graduate of our local high school. After their marriage, the couple plan to live in Australia.

It is an interesting exercise to try to dissect out the probable precepts, patterns, controls, and permissions that were passed down from John X and his wife Jane, through Tom and Mary, to the granddaughter, Jane.

It should be noted that script programing is a natural happening like the growth of weeds and flowers, and takes place without regard to morals or consequences. Sometimes script and antiscript feed into each other with the most dire results. The Parental directives may give the Child a license to inflict enormous damage to other people. Historically, such unfortunate combinations have given rise to leaders of wars, crusades, and massacres, and on a more individual level, to political assassinations. Mother's Parent is saying "Be Good!" and "Be famous!" while her Child is directing: "Kill everybody!" Father's Adult then shows the boy how to kill people, by teaching him how to handle guns, in civilized countries, and knives, in uncivilized ones.

Most people spend their lives comfortably embedded in their script matrices. It is a bed which their parents made for them and to which they have added a few trimmings of their own. It may have bugs in it and be lumpy, too, but it is their very own and they have been accustomed to it since their earliest years, and so, few people are willing to trade it in for something better built and more adapted to their circumstances. Matrix, after all, is just Latin for mother's womb, and the script is as close and cozy as they can get once they have forever left the real thing. But for those who do decide to strike out for themselves, and say "Mother, I'd rather do it my own way," there are several possibilities. If they are lucky, mother herself may have included a reasonable release or spellbreaker in the matrix, in which case they may do it on their own. Another way is for their friends and intimates and life itself to help, but this is rare. The third way is through competent script analysis, from which they may get permission to put their own shows on the road.

SUMMARY

The script matrix is a diagram designed to illustrate and analyze the directives handed down from the parents and grandparents to the current generation. These will, in the long run, determine the person's life plan and his final payoff. Current information indicates that the most decisive controls come from the Child ego state of the parent of the opposite sex. The Adult ego state of the parent of the same sex then gives the person a pattern which determines his interests and life course while he is carrying out his life plan. Meanwhile, both parents, through their Parental ego states, give him prescriptions, inspirations, or slogans which set up his counterscript. The counterscript occupies lulls in the forward movement of the script. If he makes appropriate moves, it may take over and suppress the script. The following table (from Steiner's findings [4]) illustrates the elements in the case of one man with an "Alcoholic" script. The first column gives the active ego state in each parent. The letters in parentheses give the receiving ego state in the protagonist, and the next two show the type of directive. The last two columns are self-explanatory.

Mother's Child (A)	Injunctions and Come-ons	Script	"Drink and Work."
Father's Adult (A)	Program (Pattern)	Life Course	"Work Hard."
Both Parents (P)	Prescription (Slogans)	Counterscript	"Don't Think, Drink."

Even if the origins (but probably not the insertions) of the script directives vary in individual cases, the script matrix nevertheless remains one of the most useful and cogent diagrams in the history of science, compressing, as it does, the whole plan for a human life and its ultimate destiny into a simple, easily understood, and easily checked design, which also indicates how to change it.

RESPONSIBILITY OF THE PARENTS

The dynamic slogan of transactional and script analysis is "Think sphincter." Their clinical principle is to observe every movement of every muscle of every patient at every moment during a group meeting. And their existential motto is "Transactional analysts are healthy, happy, rich, and brave, and get to travel all over and meet the nicest people in the world, and the same when they are home treating patients."

In the present connection, the bravery consists of attacking the whole problem of human destiny and finding its solution by the use of the dynamic slogan and the clinical principle. Script analysis is then the answer to the problem of human destiny, and tells us (alas!) that our fates are predetermined for the most part, and that free will in this respect is for most people an illusion. For example, R. Allendy [8] points out that for each individual who faces it, the decision to commit suicide is a lonely and agonizing and apparently autonomous one. Yet whatever vicissitudes it goes through in each individual case, the "rate" of suicide remains relatively constant from year to year. The only way to make (Darwinian) sense of this is to consider human destiny to be the result of parental programing, and not of individual "autonomous" decision.

What, then, is the responsibility of the parents? Script programing is not their "fault," any more than an inherited defect is, such as diabetes or clubfoot, or an inherited talent for music or mathematics. They are merely passing on the dominants and recessives they got from their parents and grandparents. The script directives are being continually reshuffled, just as the genes are, by the fact that the child requires two parents.

On the other hand, the script apparatus is much more flexible than the genetic apparatus and is continually being modified by outside influences, such as life experience and the injunctions inserted by other people. It is only rarely possible to predict when or how an outsider will say or do something that alters a person's script. It may be a casual remark accidentally overheard at a carnival or in a corridor, or it may be the result of a formal relationship such as marriage, school, or psychotherapy. It is a common observation that spouses gradually influence each other's attitudes toward life and people, and that these changes are reflected in the tones of their facial muscles and their gestures, so that they come to look alike.

A parent who wishes to change his script so that he will not lay on his children the same directives that were laid on him should first of all become familiar with the Parent ego state and the Parental voices he carries around in his head, and which the children learn to "cathect" by appropriate trigger behavior. Since the parent is older and presumably wiser in some ways than his offspring, it is his duty and responsibility to control his Parental behavior. Only if he brings his Parent under control of his Adult can he accomplish this. Beyond that, he is just as much the product of his Parental upbringing as his children are.

One difficulty is that children represent facsimile and immortality. Every parent is openly or secretly delighted when his children respond the way he does, even when they follow his worst characteristics. This delight is what he must forgo under Adult control if he wishes his children to adapt to the solar system and all its ramifications better than he himself did.

And now we are ready to consider what happens when Jeder, who is Everyman and any man, wants to change that design, the tapes in his head, and the program they dictate, and becomes a special kind of man—Pat the patient.

REFERENCES

1. Hendricks, S. B. "Metabolic Control of Timing." *Science,* 141:21-27, July 5, 1963.

2. The script matrix in its present form was devised by Dr. Claude M. Steiner, of the San Francisco Transactional Analysis Seminar, and first appeared in print in his article "Script and Counterscript," *Transactional Analysis Bulletin* 5:133-135, April 1966. In my estimation, its value cannot be overestimated, containing as it does the programing for a whole human life, as well as indicating how to change it. It is such an important invention that, without detracting from Dr. Steiner's perceptiveness, ingenuity, and creativity, I would like to claim a part in it. Its predecessors were the more primitive diagrams to be found on pages 201 and 205 of my book *Transactional Analysis in Psychotherapy* (Grove Press, 1961.) The above article also marks the first appearance in print of the concepts of counterscript and injunction, which are further products of Dr. Steiner's insights.

3. Johnson and Szurek went as far as "superego lacunae" in accounting for "acting out." That is, children "act out" because there is something "missing" in the parents. This was one of the first theoretical statements of how parents influence their children to "bad" behavior. (Johnson, A. M., and Szurek, S. A. "The Genesis of Anti-Social Acting Out in Children and Adults." *Psychoanalytic Quarterly,* 21:323-343, 1952.) We have broadened the problem from "acting out" to real living, and have tried to include all forms of behavior, whether "antisocial" or not. Erikson approaches the script concept very closely but veers away. (Erikson, E. *Identity and the Life Cycle.* International Universities Press, New York, 1959.) As already mentioned, Freud speaks of the "destiny compulsion" as a biological phenomenon, without specifying its psychological origin; while Adler talks of life style. The injunction principle stated in the text, therefore, may be regarded as supplementing the observations of all these writers. Cf. Jackson, D. D. "Family Interaction, Family Homeostasis and Some Implications for Conjoint Family Psychotherapy." In *Individual and Familial Dynamics* (J. H. Masserman, ed.). Grune & Stratton, New York, 1959.

4. Steiner, C. M. "The Treatment of Alcoholism." *Transactional Analysis Bulletin,* 6:69-71, July, 1967. Also "The Alcoholic Game." *Quarterly Journal of Studies on Alcohol,* 30:920-938, December, 1969, with discussion by six eminent authorities on alcoholism. Dr. Steiner's book on this subject, *Games Alcoholics Play,* has recently been published (Grove Press, 1971).

5. Karpman, S. "Alcoholic 'Instant Group Therapy.'" *Transactional Analysis Bulletin*, 4:69-74, October, 1965.

6. Berne, E. "Concerning the Nature of Communication." *Psychiatric Quarterly*, 27:185-198, 1953.

7. English, F. "Episcript and the 'Hot Potato' Game." *Transactional Analysis Bulletin*, 8:77-82, October, 1969.

8. Allendy, R. *Le problème de la destinée, étude sur la fatalité intérieure*. Librarie Gallimard, Paris, 1927. L. du Nouy, on the other hand (*Human Destiny*. Signet Books, New York, 1949), puts more weight on external forces as seen by a religious scientist.

20. Diagnosis: The Script Signs

The first duty of a group therapist, whatever theoretical approach he is using, is to observe every movement of every muscle of every patient during every second of the group meeting. In order to accomplish this, he should limit the size of his group to no more than eight patients, and take whatever other measures are necessary to insure that he will be able to carry out this duty with the greatest possible efficiency [1]. If he chooses as his approach script analysis, the most powerful instrument known for effective group treatment, what he is looking for and listening for primarily are those specific signs which indicate the nature of the patient's script and its origins in past experience and parental programing. Only if the patient gets "out of his script" can he emerge as a person capable of autonomous vitality, creativity, fulfillment, and citizenship.

THE SCRIPT SIGNAL

For each patient there is a characteristic posture, gesture, mannerism, tic, or symptom which signifies that he is living "in his script," or has "gone into" his script. As long as such "script signals" occur, the patient is not cured, no matter how much "progress" he has made. He may be less miserable, or happier, living in his script world, but he is still in that world and not in the real world, and this will be confirmed by his dreams, his outside experiences, and his attitude toward the therapist and the other members of the group.

The script signal is usually first perceived intuitively by the therapist's Child [2] (preconsciously, not unconsciously). Then one day it comes into full awareness and is taken over by his Adult. He immediately recognizes that it has been characteristic of the patient all along, and he wonders why he never really "noticed" it before.

Abelard, a middle-aged man who complained of depression and slowing up, had been in the group for three years and had made reasonably good "progress" before Dr. Q had more than a vague idea of what his script signal was. Abelard had Parental permission to laugh, which he did with great vigor and enjoyment at every opportunity, but he did not have permission to speak. If addressed, he went through a complicated, sluggish routine before he answered. He slowly pulled himself up in his chair, took hold of a cigarette, coughed, hummed as though collecting his thoughts, and then began: "Well . . ." Then, one day when the group was discussing having babies, and other sexual matters, Dr. Q "noticed" for the first time that there was one other thing Abelard did before he spoke: he slid his hands under his belt quite far down. Dr. Q said: "Get your hands out of your pants, Abel!" at which everyone, including Abelard, began to laugh, and suddenly they realized that he had been doing this all along, but no one had ever "noticed" it before, neither the other members, Dr. Q, nor Abelard himself. It then became clear that Abelard was living in a script world where the prohibition against talking was so severe that his testicles were in jeopardy. No wonder, then, that he never talked unless someone gave him permission to by asking him a question! As long as this script signal was present he could not be free to talk spontaneously, nor to decide other matters that were bothering him.

A more common and similar script signal occurs among women, and may also be perceived intuitively for a long time before it comes into full awareness; from experience, however, the therapist soon learns to see and evaluate it more quickly. Some women sit relaxed until a sexual subject comes up, and then they not only cross their knees, but wind the upper instep around the lower ankle, often simultaneously crossing their arms over their chests and sometimes also leaning forward. This posture forms a triple or quadruple protection against a violation which exists only in their script worlds and not in the real world of the group.

Thus, it is possible to say to a patient: "It's nice that you're feeling better and making progress, but you can't get well until you stop . . ." and the script signal is inserted. This is the opening statement of an attempt to get a "cure contract" or a "script contract" instead of a "making progress" contract. The patient may then agree that he is coming to the group to get out of his script, rather than to get companionship and handy household hints as to how to be happy while living in fear or misery. Clothing is a fertile field for script signals: the woman who is well dressed except for her shoes (she will be "rejected" as her script calls for); the Lesbian who wears "dikey" clothes (she will probably play "Making Ends Meet" with money, be exploited by her girl friends, and attempt suicide); the male homosexual who wears "queenie" clothes (he will get mixed up with women who put their lipstick on crooked, get beaten up by his lovers, and attempt suicide); and the woman who puts her lipstick on crooked (she will often be exploited by male homosexuals). Other script signs are blinking, tongue-chewing, jaw-clamping, sniffing, hand-wringing, ring-turning, and foot-tapping. An excellent list can be found in Feldman's book on mannerisms of speech and gestures [3].

Posture and carriage are also revealing. The tilt of the head in "Martyr" and "Waif" scripts is one of the commonest script signals. An extensive discussion can be found in Deutsch [4], and a psychoanalytic interpretation, particularly of signals given while lying on the analytic couch, is given by Zeligs [5].

The script signal is always a reaction to some Parental directive. In order to deal with it, the directive must be uncovered, which is usually easy to do, and the precise antithesis must be found, which may be more difficult, particularly if the signal is a response to an actual hallucination.

THE PHYSIOLOGICAL COMPONENT

The sudden onset of symptoms is also usually a script sign. Judith's script called for her to "go crazy," as her sister had done, but she was resisting their parental command. As long as her Adult was in charge she was a normal healthy American girl. But if someone around her acted "crazy" or said he felt "crazy," her Adult would drain away and her Child would be left with no protection. She would immediately get a headache and excuse herself, thus getting away from the scripty situation. On the couch, a similar sequence would occur. As long as Dr. Q would talk to her or answer her, she was in good shape, but if he remained silent, her Adult would fade out, her Child would begin to come on with crazy thoughts, and she would get an instant headache. With some patients, nausea occurs in exactly the same way, only here the parental directive is "get sick" instead of "go crazy," or, in grownup language, "be neurotic" instead of "be psychotic." Anxiety attacks with palpitation, or sudden outbreaks of asthma or hives are also script signals.

Allergic outbreaks when the script is threatened may be quite severe. For example, Rose had been a hiker all her life, and had not suffered from poison oak since childhood. But when her psychoanalyst told her to get a divorce, she got such a severe attack that she had to be hospitalized, and terminated her analysis. He was not aware that her script called for her to get a divorce, but forbade it until her children were grown up. Severe attacks of asthma can also occur at such junctures, requiring hospitalization in an oxygen tent. A full awareness of the patient's script can (I think) prevent such serious outbreaks. Ulcerative colitis and perforated gastric ulcer also come under suspicion here at times. In one case a paranoid gave up his script world and started to live in the real world without sufficient preparation and "protection," and less than a month later sugar appeared in his urine, marking the onset of diabetes. This brought him back to the "safety" of his "Fail Sick" script in a modified way.

The slogan "Think sphincter" also refers to the physiological component of the script. The man with a tight mouth, and the person who eats, drinks, smokes, and talks simultaneously (as far as possible) are typical "script characters." The man addicted to laxatives or enemas may have an archaic "bowel" script. Women with violation scripts may keep their *Levator ani* and *Sphincter cunni* muscles tightened up, resulting in painful intercourse. Premature and retarded ejaculation, and asthma, may also be regarded as sphincter disturbance of a scripty nature.

Sphincters are the organs of final display or payoff. The actual "cause" of sphincter disturbances is of course nearly always the central nervous system. The transactional aspects, however, do not arise from the "cause" but from the effect. For example, whatever the "cause" of premature ejaculation in the central nervous system, the effect is on the relationship between the man and his mate, and thus premature ejaculation arises from, or is a part of, or contributes to his script, which is usually a "failure" script in other areas besides sex.

The importance of "thinking sphincter" lies in the way the sphincters can be used transactionally. The Child in Mike intuitively senses very quickly in what way various people want to use sphincters against him. He knows that this man wants to urinate on him, that one wants to defecate on him, that a woman wants to spit on him, and so forth [6]. And he is almost always right, as he finds out in the long run if he engages with any of these people.

What happens is this. When Mike first meets Pat (in the first ten seconds or at most, ten minutes, after they first set eyes on each other), Mike's Child senses exactly what Pat's Child is up to. But as quickly as possible, Pat's Child, with the assistance of his Adult and Parent, generates a thick smoke screen which, like a jinn, gradually takes on a human form as Pat's persona, or disguise. Mike then starts to ignore and bury his Child's intuitive perception in favor of acecpting Pat's persona. Thus Pat cons Mike out of his accurate perception and offers his persona instead. Mike accepts Pat's persona because Mike is just as busily throwing up a smoke screen to con Pat, and he is so intent on this that he forgets not only what his Child knows about Pat, but also what he knows about himself. I have discussed the first ten seconds in more detail elsewhere. People ignore their intuitive perceptions and accept each other's persona instead because that is the polite thing to do and plays along with the needs of their games and scripts. This mutual acceptance is called "the social contract" [7].

The script significance of sphincters is that each person seeks, and intuitively spots, someone who has a complementary script. Thus, to put it in the most basic terms, the person whose script calls for him to eat shit will seek out someone whose script calls for him to shit on people. They will hook into each other in the first ten minutes, spend more or less time disguising the sphincter basis of their attraction for each other, and if they continue beyond this point, eventually they will satisfy each other's script needs.

If this does not sound credible, consider the more flagrant cases where there is an immediate satisfaction of script needs. A male homosexual can go into a men's room or bar, or even walk down the street, and in ten seconds he can unerringly spot the man he is looking for, one who will not only give him the kind of sexual satisfaction he wants, but do it in the way his script calls for: in a semi-public place where the thrills of a game of "Cops & Robbers" are added to the sexual satisfaction, or in a quiet place where they may form a longer-lasting liaison which may (if the script calls for it) end in murder. An experienced heterosexual man walking down the right street in any large city can usually pick out unerringly just the woman he wants: one who will not only give the desired type of sexual satisfaction, but will also play the games that fit into his script. He can get rolled, paid, drunk, high, killed, or married, whichever one his script calls for. Many civilized or well-brought up people learn to ignore or suppress their intuitions, although these abilities can be unmasked and developed under proper conditions.

HOW TO LISTEN

In the first section we described some of the visual script signals. We now turn to the art of listening. The therapist can either listen to the patients with his eyes closed, assuring them at some point that he is not asleep, and rewarding them for their indulgence by telling them what he has heard, or listen to a tape recording of a group meeting, again preferably with his eyes closed so as to shut out visual distractions. One of the scripty things taught to almost all children, along with not looking at people too carefully, is not to listen with their eyes closed, lest they hear too much. This injunction is not always easy to overcome—mother wouldn't like it.

Even if he has never seen the patients, and initially knows nothing about their previous histories, an experienced script analyst can learn an enormous amount from a ten- or twenty-minute tape run of a treatment group. Starting with zero information he should, merely by listening to an unknown patient talk for a while, be able to give a quite detailed account of his family background, favorite games, and probable destiny. After thirty minutes, the returns diminish because of fatigue, and no tape ought to be played for more than a half-hour at one sitting.

There is always room for improvement in knowing how to listen. This is a kind of Zen proposition, since for the most part it depends on what is going on in the listener's head, rather than on what is taking place outside. The useful part of the listening is done by that aspect of the personality known as "The Professor," the Adult in the Child. The Professor commands the power of intuition [8], and the most important aspect of intuition concerns transactional sphincter behavior: What sphincter does the other fellow want to use on me, and which one does he want me to use on him? Where do these desires come from, and where are they headed for? By the time this archaic or "primal" information filters through to the Adult of the listener, it may be elaborated into something more specific: information about the patient's family background [9], his instinctual strivings [10], his occupation, and his script goal. What is necessary, then, is to know how to free the Professor to do his job most effectively. The rules for this are as follows:

1. The listener should be in good physical condition,

having had a good night's sleep,* and should not be under the influence of alcohol, medications, or drugs which impair his mental efficiency. This includes both sedatives and stimulants.

2. He must free his mind of outside preoccupations.

3. He must put aside all Parental prejudices and feelings, including the need to "help."

4. He must put aside all preconceptions about his patients in general and about the particular patient he is listening to.

5. He must not let the patient distract him by asking questions or making other demands, and should learn harmless ways of warding off such interruptions.

6. His Adult listens to the content of what the patient says, while his Child-Professor listens to the way he says it. In telephone language, his Adult listens to the information, and his Child listens to the noise [11]. In radio language, his Adult listens to the program, and his Child listens to how the machine is working. Thus, he is both a listener and a repairman. If he is a counselor, it is enough for him to be a listener, but if he is a therapist, his most important job is making repairs.

7. When he begins to feel tired, he stops listening and starts looking or talking instead.

BASIC VOCAL SIGNALS

After he has learned how to listen, he must learn what to listen for. From the psychiatric point of view there are four basic vocal signals: sounds, accents, voices, and vocabulary.

Breathing Sounds

The commonest breathing sounds and their usual meanings are as follows: coughs (nobody loves me), sighs (if only), yawns (buzz off), grunts (you said it),

* This probably means REM sleep. Often a therapist who has lain awake tossing all night will find his intuition sharper than usual the next morning. The hypothesis would be that his Adult is tired from lack of NREM sleep while his Child is in extra-good shape from plenty of REM sleep.

and sobs (you got me); and various kinds of laughs such as jollies, chuckles, snickers, and titters. The three most important types of laughs, known colloquially as Ho Ho, Ha Ha, and He He, will be discussed further on.

Accents

Culture has very little to do with scripts. There are winners and losers in every layer of society and in every country, and they go about fulfilling their destinies in much the same way all over the world. For example, the prevalence of mental illness in any large group of people is pretty much the same all over [12], and there are suicides everywhere. Every large group in the world also has its leaders and its rich men.

Nevertheless, foreign accents do have some meaning for the script analyst. First, they make possible educated guesses about early Parental precepts, and that is where culture does come in: "Do as you're told" in Germany, "Be quiet" in France, and "Don't be naughty" in Britain. Secondly, they indicate the flexibility of the script. A German who has been in this country for twenty years and still speaks with a thick accent probably has a less flexible life plan than a Dane who speaks good American after only two years. Thirdly, the script is written in the native language of the Child, and script analysis is swifter and more effective if the therapist can speak that language. A foreigner living out his script in America is the equivalent of putting on *Hamlet* in Japanese in the Kabuki theater. A great deal is going to be lost or misunderstood if the critic does not have the original at hand.

Native accents are also informative, particularly if they are affected. A man who speaks with a Brooklyn accent but throws in a few Boston or Broadway broad *a*'s clearly shows the influence of a hero or a parental person he is carrying around in his head, and that person must be tracked down, because his influence is probably widespread, even if the patient denies it. "She passed a remok, or I should say an epigram," or "We left oily, but didn't get to the game until hof time," clearly indicates a split in the Parental directives.

Voices

Each patient has at least three different voices, Parent, Adult, and Child. He may keep one, or even two of them carefully hidden for a long time, but they will slip out sooner or later. Usually a careful listener can hear at least two of them in any fifteen-minute period. The patient may say a whole Parental paragraph with only one Child whine, or a whole Adult paragraph with only one Parental scold, but an alert listener will pick up the key phrase. Other patients change voices from one sentence to another, or even use two or three voices in a single sentence.

Each of the voices reveals something about the script. A Parental voice, speaking to another person, uses Parental slogans and precepts, and duplicates what father or mother would have said in the same situation: "Doesn't everybody?," "Look who's talking," "You've got to keep your mind occupied," "Why don't you try harder?," "You can't trust anybody." An unswerving Adult voice usually means that the Child is being suppressed by Parental command in favor of some humorless pedantic pattern perhaps loaded with a few "official" or anal jokes. This indicates that the Child will therefore find devious ways of expression or periodically explode, giving rise to the nonadaptive behavior and waste of energy which makes a loser. The Child voice indicates the script role: "Cute Kid," "Little Old Me," "Clinging Whine," for example. Thus, the Parental voice tells the counterscript, the Adult voice gives the pattern, and the Child voice takes the script role.

Vocabulary

Each ego state may also have its own vocabulary. Parental words, such as "bad," "stupid," "coward," and "ridiculous," tell what Jeder is most afraid of being, and tries hardest to avoid. A persistent Adult technical vocabulary may be simply a way of avoiding people, as is common in engineering, aviation, and finance, under a script directive of "Do great things but don't get involved personally." The Adult "helpnik" vocabularies (PTA, psychology, psychoanalysis, social science) may be used in an intellectual Rite of Spring, where the victim's dismembered psyche is left scattered over the floor on the theory that he will eventually join himself together and be more fertile afterward. The story line of this script reads: "I'll tear you apart, and remember I'm only trying to help you. But you'll have to put yourself together, since nobody else can do it for you." Sometimes the patient is his own favorite Ritual victim. The Child vocabulary may be the obscene words of revolt, the clichés of compliance, or the sweet phrases of charming innocence.

A typical triad often found in the same person is Parental marshmallow-throwing, Adult dissection, and Child obscenity. For example: "We all have our ups and downs; I think you're handling it beautifully. Of course you have to split off your autonomous ego from your identification with your mother. After all, it's a shitty world." This script comes right out of Dante's *Inferno:* "How to keep smiling while reading a textbook when you're up to your neck in sewage."

CHOICE OF WORDS

Sentences are constructed jointly by the Parent, Adult, and Child, and each one reserves and exercises the right to insert words and phrases according to its needs. In order to understand what is going on in the patient's head, the therapist must be able to break the finished product down into its significant components. This is called transactional parsing and is somewhat different from grammatical parsing.

Parts of Speech

Adjectives and abstract nouns are name-calling. The correct response to a person who says that he suffers from "passive dependency" or that he is "an insecure sociopath" is "What names did your parents call you when you were little?" Action euphemisms such as "aggressive expression" or "sexual intercourse" should be eliminated by asking "What did you call that when you were little?" "Expressive aggression" is a pure artifact and means that Pat has gone to a modern dance class or been wrestled by a Gestalt therapist, while "intercoursal sex" means that he attends meetings of the Sexual Freedom League.*

Adverbs are a little more intimate. Thus "I sometimes feel sexual excitement" is over there in the vague distance, while "I sometimes get sexually excited" is over here. The precise psychological significance of adverbs, however, remains to be clarified.

Pronouns, verbs, and concrete nouns are the most real parts of speech, and "tell it like it is." Telling it like it is may mean that the patient is ready to get well. Thus, a woman who is afraid of sex often stresses adjectives and abstract nouns: "I had a satisfactory sexual experience." Later on, she may emphasize pronouns and verbs: "We really turned on." One woman went to the hospital the first time to have "an obstetrical experience." The second time, she went to have a baby. Patients "express hostility against authority figures." When they become real people, they just swear or tear up the papers. On the therapist's side, the one who reports: "We initiated the interview by exchanging positive greetings. The patient then related that he had expressed hostility by performing an act of physical aggression against his wife," is having a harder time than the one who says: "The patient said Hello and told me that he hit his wife." In one case the therapist maintained that a boy "attended a residential school setting in the private area," while the boy said that he merely "went to boarding school."

The most important single word in script language is the particle "but," which means "According to my script, I don't have permssion to do that." Real people say: "I will," or "I won't," or "I won," or "I lost," while "I will but . . ." "I won't but . . ." "I won but . . ." or "I lost but . . ." all are scripty.

---

* "Noun adjectives" ending in "ic," such as hysteric, sociopathic, psychopathic, are usually put-downs applied to patients. "Verb adjectives" ending in "ive," like punitive and manipulative, are more neutral, and can be applied to patients and staff members alike.

O.K. Words

The rule for listening to tape recordings is: If you can't hear what the patient is saying, don't worry about it, because usually he isn't saying anything. When he has something to say, you'll hear him, no matter how noisy or poor the recording is. Sometimes a poor tape recording is better than a good one for clinical purposes. If every word can be heard, the listener may become distracted by the content, and lose the more important script indices. For example: "I met a man at a bar and he made a pass at me. So after he got too fresh I said to him, I said 'Whom do you think you are anyhow, so he could see I was a lady, but he kept on so after a while I told him off.'" This is a rather dull, uninstructive, and commonplace tale. It is much more revealing on a poor recording, where it comes out: "Mumble mumble mumble PASS AT ME mumble mumble FRESH mumble mumble mumble SEE I WAS A LADY mumble mumble TOLD HIM OFF." Here the audible words are "the O.K. Words." This patient is under instructions from her mother to TELL MEN OFF, thus proving that SHE IS A LADY, providing she can collect enough trading stamps or PASSES to justify herself (as a lady) in becoming angry. The instruction reads "Remember LADIES get angry when men make passes at them." Father throws in helpfully: "There are lots of FRESH guys at bars. I ought to know." So she goes to bars and sets about proving that she is a lady.

After she has been in psychoanalytic therapy for a while, her tape goes: "Mumble mumble mumble SADISTIC MAN mumble mumble mumble MY MASOCHISTIC SELF mumble mumble. Mumble mumble mumble EXPRESSING MY USUAL HOSTILITY mumble mumble." She has replaced the old O.K. Words with some new O.K. Words. If she transfers to a transactional analyst, the tape goes: "Mumble mumble HIS CHILD mumble mumble mumble MY PARENT mumble mumble played 'RAPO.'" But a month later there are no more mumbles even on a poor and noisy tape, and what comes through clearly is "I've met some awfully nice men since I stopped going to bars."

O.K. Words tell the story much better than the story itself. It might take months of conventional therapy to unravel the details of a hard-luck story told in the clear by a female graduate student, but if the tape goes "Mumble mumble mumble STUDIED HARD mumble mumble GOOD GRADES BUT mumble mumble TERRIBLE AFTERWARD," the loud O.K. Words that come through tell the story of her life right there: "You're supposed to work hard and succeed except that something is supposed to go wrong so you'll end up feeling terrible." The O.K. Words state her script directives loud and clear.

The O.K. Words referred to in the last section come from the Parental precepts, patterns, and threats. Precepts such as "Be a lady," "Study hard," give Lady and Study as O.K. Words. The threat "Otherwise something awful will happen" gives Something Awful as an O.K. Word. When a patient gets couchbroken, the therapist's vocabulary becomes O.K. Words, and indeed, this is one of the signs that the patient is couchbroken. She says masochism, hostility, Parent, Child, etc, because at this stage the therapist becomes a substitute parent, and his O.K. vocabulary replaces the original one learned in childhood. O.K. Words are those approved by the Parent part of the patient's father, mother, therapist, or other parental person.

Script Words

We remember, however, that many of the script controls are given by the Child part of the father or mother, and these rely on a whole other vocabulary of Script Words and Phrases, which are usually quite different from the O.K. Words. Some of them, indeed, may be in direct contradiction. A woman who uses very ladylike O.K. Words when she is in her antiscript may use very foul language when she is in her script. Thus, she may call her children "my lovely teen-agers" when she is sober, and "those shitfaces" when she is drunk. Script words give important information regarding script roles and script scenes, both of which are important in trying to reconstruct the script world, or the kind of world the patient's Child is living in.

In men's scripts, the commonest roles for females are girls, ladies, and women. In women's scripts, males becomes kids, men, and old men. More specialized are "little girls" and "dirty old men." These two attract each other, especially in bars. The man refers to the women he meets as "nice little girls." The woman refers to the men she meets as "dirty old men." He needs a little girl for his script and she needs a dirty old man for hers, and when they meet the action begins and they know what to say to each other after they say Hello. Various women live in worlds populated by wolves, beasts, charmers, cats, creeps, suckers, and pricks, and their menfolk see them as dishes, bitches, grooves, chicks, broads, whores, and cunts. All these are script words which emerge in the course of conversation or group treatment.

The script scenes are usually centered around one or other room of the house: the nursery, the bathroom, the kitchen, the living room, and the bedroom, and these are located in such expressions as "plenty to drink," "all that crap," "a regular feast," "all those people," and "sock it to them." Each of these rooms has its own vocabulary, and the person stuck in any of these chambers will use the appropriate expressions over and over. Equally common is the workroom, signified by "Get your ass over there."

Counterscript words can also be detected in people who are fighting their scripts. Jack became a professional baseball player, partly because it was his thing and partly because he was boxed into it by his uncle. As Dr. Q listened to him one day, he noticed for the first time a tremendous power behind the word "not," which Jack said frequently, and a lesser but still striking impact whenever Jack said "something else." He immediately sensed intuitively the meaning behind these two terms. Whenever Jack said "not," he was pitching, and whenever Jack pitched his Child was saying "not" —"You're *not* going to hit it!" Whenever he said "something else," he was throwing to first base, and whenever he was throwing to first base, he was saying "something else"—"If I can't strike you out we'll try something else." Jack not only confirmed these intuitions, but related how a pitching coach had told him the same thing in different language. "Relax! If you throw every pitch that hard, you're going to get a bum shoulder!" Which Jack eventually did. Like Dr. Q, the coach had perceived, on the basis of his intuition and experience, that Jack was pitching in anger, and he knew that was no good.

Jack's antiscript was to succeed as a baseball player, and behind his professional pitching was a great rage against his father and uncle for commanding him to be a loser. Thus, every time he threw the ball he was fighting his script and trying to smash his way out of his bag into success. This gave him tremendous speed, and his antiscript gave him superb control. The only thing he lacked was the ability to cool it and fit his pitches into the context of the batting order and the state of the game. In the end, his nonadaptive rage brought about just the payoff he was trying to avoid, and he had to quit the game. The intuitive perceptiveness of the Adult in the therapist's Child, The Professor, is his most valuable therapeutic instrument. The acute sensitivity of a properly attuned Professor is demonstrated by the fact that Dr. Q knew all this in spite of the fact that he had only been to one professional baseball game in his whole life, although he had pitched in many sandlot softball games.

Metaphors

Closely allied to script words are metaphors. Thus, Mary had two different and separate vocabularies of metaphors. In one, she was all at sea, couldn't fathom anything, could hardly keep her head above water, had stormy days, and waves of feelings. At other times, life was a feast, she could eat her words, she had lots of goodies, or she might feel sour or bitter because that was the way the cookie crumbled. She married a sailor and complained of obesity. When she felt at sea, all her lingo was maritime, and when she was overeating, it was culinary. Thus she fell from the ocean to the kitchen and back again, and the therapist's problem was to get her feet on the ground. Metaphors are an extension of the script scene, and a change in metaphors means a change of scene. In her case, the stormy waters turned out to be a sea of anger.

Security Phrases

Some people have to go through certain rituals or make certain gestures before they begin to talk, in order to protect themselves or apologize for speaking. These rituals are addressed to their Parents. We have already cited the case of Abelard, who always slid his hands under his belt before he began to talk. It was evident that he was protecting his testicles from some inner assailant who was scheduled to attack him when he was off guard bcause he was speaking to somebody, so he always took care of that danger before he ventured to speak. In other cases these security measures are incorporated into the sentence structure. There are various degrees of protection in answering a question like: "Did you ever get mad at your sister?" "*Maybe* I did" implies a Parental order "Never commit yourself." "I *think maybe* I did" implies two Parental orders: "How can you be sure?" and "Don't commit yourself." The first usually comes from father, the second from mother. "I *think maybe* I *might* have" contains a triple protection. Security phrases are chiefly of prognostic value. It is much easier for the therapist to penetrate one layer of security measures than three. "I think maybe I might have" is similar to the Berkeley Subjunctive, and is likewise designed to protect and conceal a very young and very apprehensive Child who is not going to let anybody in very easily.

The Subjunctive

The subjunctive, or as it is called colloquially, the "Berkeley (California) Subjunctive," comprises three items. First, the phrases "if" or "if only"; secondly, the use of subjunctives or conditionals such as would, should, and could; and thirdly, the noncommitment words such as "toward." The Berkeley Subjunctive is most highly developed on college campuses. The classical phrase is "I should, and I would if I could, but . . ." Variants are "If only they would, I could, and I think I probably should, but . . ." or "I should, and I probably could, but then they would . . ."

This subjunctive attitude becomes formalized in the titles of books, theses, papers, and student assignments. Common examples are "Some Factors Involved In . . ." (= if only), or "Toward a Theory of . . ." (= I would if I could, and I know I should). In the extreme case, the title reads: "Some Introductory Remarks Concerning Factors Involved in Gathering Data Toward a Theory of . . ."—a very modest title indeed, since it is plain that it will take about two hundred years before the theory itself will be ready for publication. It is obvious that this man's mother told him not to stick his neck out. His next paper, presumably, will be: "Some Intermediate Remarks Concerning . . . etc." and then "Some Final Remarks Concerning . . . etc." Having disposed of Remarks, presumably the titles of his succeeding papers will get shorter and shorter. By the time he is forty, he will have the prolegomena shaved off and will come out with number six, "Toward a Theory Of . . ." but the actual theory is rarely forthcoming. If it is, and the seventh paper is the theory itself, then there will be an eighth entitled: "Oops, Sorry. Back to the Old Computer." He is always on the way, but never gets to the next station.

This is not amusing for the therapist who undertakes to treat a man who is writing a paper with such a title. Pat will also be complaining of not being able to finish his thesis, inability to concentrate, sexual and marital problems, depression, and suicidal impulses. Unless the therapist can find a way to change the script, the treatment will follow exactly the eight stages outlined above, each phase taking six months to a year or more, with the therapist writing the final paper (the Oops one) instead of the patient. In script language, "toward" means "don't get there." Nobody asks "Does this airplane go toward New York?" or would many people want to travel with a pilot who says: "Yes, we're going toward New York." He either goes *to* New York or you take another airplane.

Sentence Structure

Besides the subjunctivists there are other people who are forbidden to finish anything or come to the point, so when they talk they "run off at the mouth." Their sentences are strung out with conjunctions: "Yesterday I was sitting at home with my husband and . . . and . . . and then . . . and . . . and then . . ." Often the directive is "Don't tell any of the family secrets!" so they go all around the secret and play with it as long as they can without giving it away.

Some speakers are careful to balance everything: "It's raining, but the sun will come out soon." "I have a headache, but my stomach is better." "They're not very nice, but on the other hand, they look cheerful." The directive in this case seems to be "Don't look at anything too closely." The most interesting example of this type was a man who had been a diabetic since the age of five, and had been taught to balance his diet with the utmost care. When he spoke, he weighed every word with similar care, and balanced each of his sentences very cautiously and precisely. These precautions made him very difficult to listen to. All his life he had been in a rage against the unfair restrictions imposed on him because of the disease, and his speech became very unbalanced when he was angry. (The implications of this for the psychology of diabetes must await further study.)

Another type of sentence structure is the dangling point, with free use of "and so forth" and "et cetera." "Well, we went to the movies and so forth, and then I kissed her and so forth, and then she stole my wallet and so forth." Unfortunately, this often conceals a deep anger against the mother. "Well, I'd like to tell her what I think of her, et cetera." "What is 'et cetera?' " "What I'd really like to do is cut her to pieces." "Et cetera?" "No, no more 'et cetera.' That's the et cetera." Sentence structure offers a fascinating field for study.

THE GALLOWS TRANSACTION*

Jack: I stopped smoking. I haven't had a cigarette for over a month.

Della: And how much weight have you put on, heh, heh, heh?

Everyone smiled at this sally except Jack and Dr. Q.

Dr. Q: Well, you really are getting well, Jack. You didn't fall for that one.

Della: I want to get well, too. I could have bitten my tongue off for saying that. That was my mother talking. I was trying to do to Jack exactly what she does to me.

Don (a new member): What's so terrible about that? Just a little joke.

Della: My mother came to see me the other day and she tried to do it to me again, but I wouldn't let her. It sure made her mad. She said "You're sure putting on weight again, ha ha." I was supposed to laugh, too, and say "Yeah, I'm overeating, ha ha." But instead I said "You're kind of heavy yourself." So then she changed the subject and said "How can you live in a run-down shack like this?"

It is pretty clear from this that for overweight Della, keeping mother happy = putting on weight and laughing about it, the tragedy of her life, and that not laughing about it is impudent and makes mother unhappy. She is supposed to hang herself while they have a good chuckle over it.

The gallows laugh is the dying man's joke, or famous last words. As already noted, the crowds of spectators at the Tyburn or Newgate hangings in the eighteenth

* Berne, always scrupulous in crediting others for their contributions, must be forgiven if in this instance he failed to remember his own initial opposition to the idea of the gallows laugh and transaction when I first presented it at a meeting of the San Francisco Transactional Analysis Seminar. Laughter was something Eric's fun-loving child enjoyed and when I pulled it apart by critical analysis it made me, in Eric's view, something of a party-pooper, a role he thoroughly disliked. The fact that he later embraced the idea and made it his own is perhaps the best compliment a teacher may pay his disciple.
—C. S.

century used to admire people who died laughing: "I was the capper, see," says Daniel Then. "We had the cull all set up and then something went wrong. The others got away but I got nabbed, ha ha ha!" And "Ha, ha, ha," roars the crowd in appreciation of the jest as the trap is sprung, "the damber died game." Danny seems to be laughing at the wry joke fate played on him, but deep down he knows who is responsible, and he is really saying: "Well, mother (or father), you predicted I'd end up on the gallows, and here I am, ha ha ha." The same thing happens in a minor way at almost any group-treatment session.

Danny Now was one of four children, none of whom had permission to succeed. The parents were both a little dishonest in socially acceptable ways, and the children each carried this tendency a little further. One day Danny told about his troubles at college. He was falling behind in his work, so he had paid a ghost writer in advance to do his thesis. The group listened with interest as he described his negotiations with this man, and told how the ghost writer had also undertaken to write theses for some of Danny's friends, all of whom had paid in advance. The other members asked questions, here and there, until finally Danny came to the point. The writer had absconded to Europe, taking all the money he had collected, and without leaving any theses behind. At this, the group broke into uproarious laughter in which Danny joined.

The others said they thought the story was funny for two reasons: first, the way Danny told it, as though he expected them to laugh, and would be disappointed if they didn't; and second, because it was the sort of thing they expected, or perhaps even hoped, would happen to Danny because of the complicated way he went about doing things instead of carrying out his obligations in a straightforward, honest way. They all knew that Danny was supposed to fail, and it was amusing to see how much effort he put into it. They joined in Danny Now's laughter the same way the crowd had joined in Danny Then's. Later they would all be depressed about it, Danny most of all. His laugh said "Ha, ha, ha, mother, you always loved me when I failed, and here I go again."

The Adult in the Child, The Professor, has had the task from earliest years of keeping mother contented so that she will stay with him and protect him. If she likes him and expresses the liking with a smile, he feels safe even when he is actually in trouble or even in dire peril of death. Crossman [13] discusses this in more detail. In normal mothering, she says, mother's Parent and Child both like kids. So when mother smiles both her Parent and her Child are pleased with her offspring, and things will proceed smoothly between them. In other cases, mother's Parent smiles at her son because she is supposed to, while her Child is angry at him. He can get on the good side of her Child, and get a smile that way, by behavior which her Parent might disapprove of. For example, by demonstrating that he is "bad," he may get a Child smile because he has proven that he is not-O.K., and that pleases the Child in mother— what we have previously called "the witch mother." From all this, Crossman concludes that both script and antiscript can be considered attempts to evoke mother's smile: the antiscript for the approving smile of mother's (and father's) Parent, the script for the smile of mother's Child, who enjoys the baby's pain or discomfiture.

The gallows laugh, then, occurs when Danny "finds himself" with the rope around his neck, and his Child says: "I didn't really want to end up this way. How did I get here?" Then Mother (in his head) smiles, and he realizes that she has conned him into it. He then has the choice of either going crazy, killing her, killing himself, or laughing. At such moments he may envy the brother who chose instead to go to the mental hospital, or the sister who elected to kill herself, but he is not ready for either of those—yet.

The gallows laugh or the gallows smile occurs after a special kind of stimulus and response called the "gallows transaction." A typical example is an alcoholic who has not had a drink for six months, as everyone in the group knows. Then one day he comes in and lets the others talk for a while. When they have gotten all their troubles off their chests, so that he has the stage to himself, he says: "Guess what happened over the weekend?" One look at his slightly smiling face and they know what happened. They get ready to smile, too. One of them sets up the gallows transaction by asking: "What happened?" "Well, I took one drink and then another, and the next thing I knew"—by this time he is laughing and so are they—"I went on a three-day bender." Steiner [14], who first described these phenomena clearly, says it thus: "In the case of the Alcoholic, White tells the audience about last week's bender while the audience (including, perhaps, the therapist) beams with delight. The smile of the Children in the audience parallels and reinforces the smile of the witch mother or ogre who is pleased when White obeys the injunction ('Don't think—drink'), and in effect tightens the noose around White's neck."

The gallows laugh (which results from a gallows transaction) means that if the patient laughs while recounting a misfortune, and particularly if the other group members join in the laughter, that misfortune is part of the catastrophe of the patient's script. When the people around him laugh, they reinforce the payoff, hasten his doom, and prevent him from getting well. In this way, the parental come-on is brought to fruition, ha ha.

TYPES OF LAUGHTER

It can be fairly said that script analysts and their groups have more fun than anybody, even though they do refrain from laughing at the hanging or when someone gets his feet dirty. There are several kinds of laughs which are of interest in script analysis [15].

Scripty Laughs

a. "Heh Heh Heh" is the Parental chuckle of the witch mother or ogre father who is leading someone, usually his own offspring, down the primrose path of derision and defeat. "How much weight did you put on, heh heh heh?" (Sometimes written "ha ha.") This is the scripty laugh.

b. "Ha Ha Ha" is the Adult's chuckle of rueful humor. As in Danny's case, it signifies a superficial insight. From his recent experiences, Danny had learned not to trust ghost writers, but he had not learned much about himself and his own weakness, which would again and again lead him into similar traps until the final one was sprung. This is the gallows laugh.

c. "He He He" is the Child's laugh when he is going to pull a fast one. He is really getting into a game of "Let's Pull a Fast One on Joey," a true con game where he is enticed into thinking that he is going to fool somebody, but he himself ends up being the victim instead. For example, Danny Now said "He He He!" when a ghost writer explained how they could pull a fast one on the English professor, but then Come to Find Out, Danny ended up as the victim. This is the gamy laugh.

Healthy Laughs

d. "Ho Ho Ho" is the Parent's laugh at the Child's struggle to succeed. It is patronizing, benevolent, and helpful, at least as far as the immediate problem is concerned. It usually comes from people who are not too heavily involved and can turn over the final responsibility to someone else. It demonstrates to the child that there are rewards for nonscripty behavior. This is the granddad or Santa Claus laugh.

e. There is another kind of "Ha Ha Ha" which is much more hearty and meaningful. This signifies true insight on the part of the Adult as to how he has been conned, not by external figures, but by his own Parent and Child. It is similar to what psychologists call an "aha experience" (although I personally have never heard anyone except a psychologist say "aha" on such occasions). This is the laugh of insight.

f. "Wow Wow" is the Child laugh of sheer fun or the belly laugh of older people who have bellies. It only comes to people who are script-free or can put their scripts aside for the occasion. This is the spontaneous laugh of healthy people.

GRANDMOTHER

No one who has ever known his grandmother is an atheist, even if she herself was one, for all grandmothers, good or evil, are watching somewhere out there, usually on pass from Heaven. During group meetings (and often during poker games as well) she hovers in the corner of the room by the ceiling. If a patient's Child does not have complete confidence in his Parent, in time of need he usually feels that he can still trust grandmother, and he will gaze up at the ceiling in her direction to get protection and guidance from her invisible presence. It should be remembered that grandmothers are even more powerful than mothers, although they may appear but seldom on the scene. But when they do, they have the final say. This is well known to readers of fairy tales, where the old crone can put a blessing or a curse on the baby prince or princess, and the bad fairy or the fairy godmother cannot take it away, but can only tone it down. Thus, in "Sleeping Beauty" the old crone condemns the princess to die. The good fairy modifies this to sleeping for one hundred years. That is the best she can do, for as she says: "I have no power to undo entirely what my elder has done."

Thus grandmother, for good or evil, is the court of last appeal, and if the therapist succeeds in breaking the curse put on the patient by her mother, he still has grandmother to reckon with. A good therapist, therefore, must learn how to deal with antagonistic grandmothers as well as with mothers. In therapeutic situations, grandmothers always think they are right, and justified. The therapist has to talk firmly to them: "Do you really want Zoe to be a failure? Do you really think your complaint will be well received at Headquarters if you tell them the truth? The truth is that I am not seducing your granddaughter into bad ways, but I am actually giving her permission to be happy. Whatever you tell them, remember that psychiatrists come from Headquarters, too, and will also be heard there.

Zoe cannot speak for herself against you, but I can speak for her."

In most cases, it is grandmother who decides which cards Jeder will get when he plays poker. If he keeps in good with her he will certainly not lose, and will usually win. If he offends her by thought or deed, he is bound to lose. But he must remember that the other players have grandmothers, too, and they may be just as powerful as his. In addition, they may be in better standing with their grandmothers than he is with his.

TYPES OF PROTEST

The main types of protest are anger and weeping. These are highly regarded by the majority of group therapists as "expressing real feelings," while laughter is for some reason not so highly thought of, and is sometimes lightly dismissed as not expressing a "real feeling."

Since about ninety per cent of anger is a "racket" encouraged by the Parent, the real question is "What good does it do to get angry?" It seldom accomplishes anything that cannot be done better without it, and the price is hardly worth paying: four to six hours of disturbed metabolism, and possibly several hours of insomnia. The crucial point in the after-burn of anger occurs when Jeder stops saying to himself or his friends: "I should have . . ." (using the past tense) and switches into "I'd like to . . ." (using the present tense). This staircase anger is nearly always misguided. The rule for staircase anger is the same as the rule for staircase wit. "If you didn't say it on the spot, don't go back to say it afterward, as your intuition was probably right in the first place." The best policy is to wait until the next occasion, and then if you are really ready to do better, you will.

The phase of the present tense ("I'd like to . . .") is usually short-lived, and the future tense soon takes over: "Next time I'll . . ." This signifies a shift from Child to Adult. I am firmly convinced (without any chemical evidence) that the shift from past to future coincides with a shift in metabolic chemistry, and is merely a slight change in some small radical of some complex hormonal substance—a simple process of reduction or oxidation. This is another assault on the illusion of autonomy. As the person shifts from past to future in his indignation, he thinks "I am calming down," or someone says: "Now you are being more sensible." But in fact he is neither "calming" nor "being" and is simply reacting to a trivial chemical change.

Nearly all anger is part of a game of "Now I've Got You, You Son of a Bitch" (NIGYSOB). ("Thank you for giving me an excuse to get angry.") Jeder is in fact pleased at being wronged, since he has been carrying around a bag of anger since early childhood and it is a relief to vent some of it legitimately. ("Who wouldn't get angry under such conditions?") The question here is whether abreaction is beneficial. Freud long ago said it didn't do the job. Nowadays, however, for most group therapists it is the mark of a "good" group meeting, and leads to lively staff conferences. Everybody is delighted and exhilarated and relieved when a patient "expresses anger." Therapists who encourage patients to do this, or even demand it from them, feel very supercilious toward their less trippy colleagues and have no hesitation in saying so. The *reductio ad absurdum* of this attitude is in the following statement by an imaginary patient: "I took public transportation toward my occupational area and resolved that today I would really communicate with authority figures by expressing real feelings. So I screamed at my boss and threw my typewriter through the window. He was very happy, and said, 'I'm glad that we're finally communicating and that you're freely expressing your hostility. That's the kind of employee we like to have around here. I note that you have liquidated a fellow employee who happened to be standing under the window, but I hope this will not arouse hampering guilt feelings in you that will interfere with our interpersonal interaction.'"

The distinction between racket anger and genuine anger is often easy to make. After NIGYSOB anger the patient may smile, whereas genuine anger is usually followed in the group by weeping. In any case, the patients should understand that they are not permitted to throw things, or assault or strike each other in the group. Any attempt to do so should be physically restrained, and, except in special cases, a patient who does either of these things should be dropped from the group. There are, however, some therapists who contract to let patients express their anger physically, and have proper facilities and personnel for handling the possible complications.

Weeping is also a racket in most cases, or may even be a dramatic put-on. The response of the other group members is the best way to judge this. If they feel annoyed or overly sympathetic, the tears are probably spurious. Genuine weeping usually results in a respectful silence and genuine responses of Aristotelian tragic pity.

THE STORY OF YOUR LIFE

One of the most instructive tales ever written for the script analyst is *The Strange Life of Ivan Osokin,* by P. D. Ouspensky, the well-known mystic. Ivan Osokin is given a chance to relive his life, and the prediction is that he will make the same mistakes all over again, and that he will repeat all the behavior he regrets. The hero replies that this will be no great wonder, since he will be deprived of the memory of what he has been through and will therefore have no way of avoiding his errors. He is told that quite to the contrary, and against the usual policy in such cases, he will be permitted to remember everything and will still make the same mistakes. On these terms he accepts, and sure enough, even though he can foresee each disaster that he brings on himself, he does repeat his previous behavior, as Ouspensky skillfully and convincingly demonstrates. Ouspensky attributes this to the force of destiny, and the script analyst will agree with him, adding only that that destiny was programed into him in his early years by his parents, and did not come from a metaphysical or cosmic force. The script analyst's position, then, is the same as Ouspensky's: every individual is compelled by his script to repeat again and again the same patterns of behavior no matter how much he re-

grets their consequences. In fact, the regret is itself a
motive for repeating them, and they are repeated, in
fact, just in order to collect regrets.

This picture can be rounded out by including another
tale: "The Strange Case of M. Valdemar," by Edgar
Allan Poe. M. Valdemar is hypnotized just before his
death, and survives for a long time. Eventually, he is
brought out of his hypnotic trance, and immediately,
before the gaze of the horrified onlookers, he turns into
a putrefying corpse, in just the state he would have
been in if he had died on the day he was hypnotized.
That is, he "caught up with himself." In script terms,
this is also an everyday occurrence. The child is, in
effect, hypnotized by his parents into carrying out a
certain life pattern. He will show all the signs of vitality
as long as it is humanly possible for him to continue,
until his script destiny is completed. After that he may
fall apart very rapidly. In effect, many people are
"propped up" by their scripts, and as soon as the script
is completed, they deteriorate. That is the fate of many
old or "retired" people all over the world, as I have
noted. (Not only in "our society," as is commonly
claimed.)

The script itself is under the protection of the Greek
Goddess of Necessity, "the sublime *Ananke*," as Freud
calls her. In psychoanalytic language, it is driven by the
repetition compulsion, the compulsion to do the same
thing over and over. Thus, a short script may be repeated over and over in the course of a lifetime (a
woman marries one alcoholic after another, on the
premise that each time it will be different; or a man
marries one invalid wife after another, thus under-
going a whole series of bereavements). Furthermore,
in a diluted form, the whole script may be repeated
every year (Christmas depressions due to disappointment) within the larger framework of the lifetime script
(eventual suicide due to a very big disappointment).
Also, it may be repeated every month within the year
(menstrual disappointments). And beyond that, it may
also be repeated every day in a smaller version. Even
more microscopically, it may be run through in an
hour: for example, the whole script, in watered-down

form, may occur in the course of the weekly group meeting, week after week, if only the therapist knows where to look. Sometimes a mere few seconds of activity may reveal the "story of the patient's life." I have given an example elsewhere of the commonest form of that, which may be called "Rush and Stumble"—and "Quick Recovery" [16].

"Mrs. Sayers stretched her arm out across Mrs. Catters's chest to reach for an ash tray on the end table. As she drew her arm back she lost her balance and almost fell off the settee. She recovered just in time, laughed deprecatingly, muttered 'Excuse me!' and settled back to smoke. At this moment, Mrs. Catters took her attention away from Mr. Troy long enough to murmur: 'Pardon me!' "

Here, condensed into a few seconds, is the story of Mrs. Sayers's life. She tries to be careful but does things in an awkward way. She almost comes to grief but is rescued just in time. She apologizes, but then someone else takes the blame. One could almost visualize her ogre father telling her to fall over, or pushing her (script), and her mother rescuing her in the nick of time (counterscript). After that, she apologizes politely for being clumsy. (She learned in childhood that it paid to be clumsy if she wished to keep her father's love, because that was the way he wanted it; furthermore, it gave her an excuse to apologize, and that was one of the few times when he listened to her and acknowledged her existence.) Then comes the script twist, which makes the whole episode into a drama rather than a mere catalogue of misfortune: someone *else* takes the final blame and apologizes even more sincerely. Here we have a classical illustration of the Karpman triangle for categorizing scripts and theatrical dramas ([17]), Figure 10, page 210.

THE SCRIPT SWITCHES

According to Karpman, all dramatic action can be summarized as switches between three main roles: Victim, Persecutor, and Rescuer. These switches occur at varying speeds and may go in either direction. In the drama Rush and Stumble—and Quick Recovery, we have a very rapid set of switches. Mrs. Sayers starts off with Father (in her head) as Persecutor ("pushing" her), Mother in her head as Rescuer ("rescuing her from falling"), and herself as Victim. That is the way the triangle stands in her head, the skull script. In the action script, she makes herself the Persecutor by brushing against Mrs. Catters, who thus becomes her Victim. She apologizes for this, but Mrs. Catters in turn (in accordance with the needs of *her* script) pulls a very quick switch, and instead of behaving like a Victim, apologizes as though *she* had done something wrong, thus taking the role of Persecutor.

In this condensed set of transactions we learned a great deal about the story of two lives. Mrs. Sayers ordinarily came on like a plaintive victim; it is now clear that she can switch into the role of Persecutor providing it is "accidental" and she apologizes for it. The goal of the Rush and Stumble script is to be relieved of responsibility by getting the Victim to apologize. She has found a complementary script figure in Mrs. Catters, whose script is evidently called something like "Hit Me and I'll Apologize," or "I'm Sorry My Face Got in the Way of Your Fist"—the typical script of the wife of an alcoholic.

Danny, the young man without a thesis, also ran through the drama story of his life in recounting his experience. As already noted, the name of his favorite game, which is also the title of his script, is "Let's Pull a Fast One on Joey." Danny meets a friendly neighborhood Rescuer who offers for a fee to help him pull a fast one on his Victim, the professor. Danny ends up holding the bag as the Victim, and his friendly Rescuer turns out to be a better crook or Persecutor than Danny is. The professor, who, unknown to himself, was originally slated to be the Victim, now has to play the part of Rescuer to Danny who comes to him for help in order to graduate. That is the story of Danny's life. He gets outsmarted in his attempts to pull a fast one and ends up being a martyr; but since everyone can see that he arranged his own downfall, instead of sympathy he gets laughter. He not only fails to accomplish his task, he even fails at being a martyr. That is one thing that keeps him from attempting suicide. He knows that if he tries, he will either bungle it in some laugh-provoking fashion, or if he succeeds, something will happen that will make the whole sacrifice seem humorous. Even his attempts at psychosis are unconvincing and just make the other group members laugh. What his mother has given him is a benevolent trap for a script. "Look," she has instructed him, "you're going to fail in everything. It's no use beating your head against the wall, because you'll even fail at going crazy or killing yourself, so go on out there and try it for a while, and when you're convinced, come back to me like a good boy and I'll take care of everything for you."

This is one reward for the group therapist if he watches every movement of every patient at every moment during the session. He may observe one of his patients going through his script in condensed form in the space of a few seconds. Those few seconds may break the case wide open by telling him the story of the patient's life, which he might otherwise have to spend laborious months or years in digging out and clarifying. Unfortunately, there is no rule to pass on about how to know when this is happening. It probably happens with every patient at every group meeting in some form or other, more or less heavily disguised or coded. Its detection then depends on the therapist's readiness to understand what is happening, and that depends on his intuition. When his intuition is ready not only to understand what the patient is doing, but also to communicate that understanding to his Adult, then he will be able to recognize the patient's script when he sees it, including the roles he and the other group members play.

REFERENCES

1. Berne, E. *Principles of Group Treatment*. Oxford University Press, New York, 1966. Grove Press, New York (Paperback), 1968.

2. The Child's perceptions often occur in dreams as day

residues, caricatures, or symbols: perceptions which the Adult was not aware of but which nevertheless registered. Such perceptions are the basis for intuitive judgments. See Berne, E. "Concerning the Nature of Diagnosis." *International Record of Medicine* 165: 283-292, 1952. Also refs. 6, 8, 9, 10, and 11.

3. Feldman, S. S. *Mannerisms of Speech and Gestures in Everyday Life.* International Universities Press, New York, 1959.

4. Deutsch, F. "Analytic Posturology." *Psychoanalytic Quarterly,* 21: 196-214, 1952.

5. Zeligs, M. "Acting In: Postural Attitudes Observed During Analysis." *Journal of the American Psychoanalytic Association,* 5: 685-706, 1957.

6. Berne, E. "Primal Images and Primal Judgments," *Psychiatric Quarterly,* 29: 634-658, 1955.

7. Berne, E. *The Structure and Dynamics of Organizations and Groups.* J. B. Lippincott Company, Philadelphia, 1963. Grove Press (Paperback), New York, 1966.

8. Berne, E. "Intuition VI. The Psychodynamics of Intuition." *Psychiatric Quarterly* 36:294-300, 1962.

9. Berne, E. "The Nature of Intuition." *Psychiatric Quarterly* 23: 203-226, 1949.

10. Berne, E. "Intuition V. The Ego Image." *Psychiatric Quarterly,* 31: 611-627, 1957.

11. Berne, E. "Concerning the Nature of Communication." *Psychiatric Quarterly* 27: 185-198, 1953.

12. Cf. Berne, E. "Difficulties of Comparative Psychiatry: The Fiji Islands." *American Journal of Psychiatry,* 116: 104-109, 1959.

13. Crossman, P. "Position and Smiling." *Transactional Analysis Bulletin* 6:72-73, July, 1967.

14. Steiner, C. M. "A Script Checklist." *Transactional Analysis Bulletin* 6:110-114, April, 1967.

15. Grotjahn, M. *Beyond Laughter.* McGraw-Hill Book Company, New York, 1957.

16. Berne, E. *Transactional Analysis in Psychotherapy.* Grove Press, New York, 1961, pp. 123ff.

17. Karpman, S. "Fairy Tales and Script Drama Analysis." *Transactional Analysis Bulletin* 7:39-43, April, 1968.

THREE

○○○

Group Dynamics

Introduction

Eric Berne's interest in group dynamics preceded his development of Transactional Analysis. It was actually his first interest in life which he exhibited as a little boy who asked other little boys in his neighborhood to join him in an Agamemnon Club, the dynamics and flaws of which he analyzed many years later in his book *The Structure and Dynamics of Organizations and Groups*. This book appeared years before *Transactional Analysis in Psychotherapy* and is extremely dense with information and therefore quite difficult to excerpt. Instead of excerpting it we have taken his summary of the group dynamics information which he wrote up for students in psychiatry in *Principles of Group Treatment*. We do include some sections from the original group dynamics book which refer to leaders of organizations. This particular aspect of Berne's writings is very poignant to me because it appears to be a vision of his own future. Speaking of the dead primal leader he seems to be setting up his role in the organization that he built, The International Transactional Analysis Association. He felt that an organization which honored its *euhemerus* (dead primal leader) would be a strong and cohesive group. His knowledge and skills in group dynamics helped him to lay the foundation for that organization which has grown steadily since its inception and which at this point counts 10,000 members.

Eric Berne's interest in group dynamics was primarily in relation to group psychotherapy, although he also wanted to develop a theory which was helpful to the therapy of whole groups rather than just individuals in groups. In addition to the section on group dynamics we include a section of pieces which bear on the dif-

ferent aspects of group psychotherapy. The contract,
the therapist, preparing the scene, and the first three
minutes are all interesting and innovating contributions
to the field of group psychotherapy.

—C.S.

21. Group Dynamics

A sound knowledge of group dynamics is as important to a group therapist as a knowledge of physiology is to a physician. The two classical concepts that are currently stressed in this area, provocative though they are, are not sufficient equipment for a scientific therapist: the principle of identification with the leader, first outlined by Freud [1], and its corollary, the therapy group regarded in the transference sense as a kind of "family." The identification concept, even in its competent and detailed elaboration by Scheidlinger [2], does not serve to explain adequately many aspects of the relationship between the therapist and his patients; in fact, since one desirable effect of therapy is to release the patient from the bonds of such an identification when it exists, it is also necessary to understand what happens in a group when the members are not identifying with the leader. As to the concept of the group as a "family," this is often applied in a naive and uncritical way, which offers only a rudimentary approximation to the clarification of the actual clinical occurrences.

With this conventional equipment alone, the therapist will be confronted repeatedly with situations for which he is unarmed and theoretically unprepared. It is therefore necessary for him to acquire a more comprehensive, consistent, and pragmatic approach to group dynamics if he wishes to deal effectively with all the vicissitudes that will arise in his daily work. Such an approach, which has proven its practical value, is offered below. The terminology is taken from the writer's book *The Structure and Dynamics of Organizations and Groups* [3], and what is offered here is a summary applied specifically to small therapy groups of not more than ten members.

In some institutions, therapists are confronted with the necessity of dealing with larger groups running from ten to two hundred members. At present there is no theory competent to determine the rational handling of such congeries, since in effect the members become divided into two classes, performers and audience. In order to approach such situations with any degree of precision, it would be necessary to have a reasonably rigorous theory of audiences, and that is not yet available. Hence the conduct of such larger groups is mostly an empirical art and will remain so pending further theoretical developments. In the meantime, as a stop-gap, some of the principles given below can be profitably extrapolated to larger groups, albeit with some loss of confidence.

In order that the analysis of group situations in the following scheme be practical and realistic, it is necessary that for each aspect an appropriate diagram be drawn giving the actual details as found in the situation being studied.

THE SEATING DIAGRAM

Every presentation or discussion of a problem in group therapy or group dynamics should be accompanied by a seating diagram such as that shown in Figure 15 (p. 317). A simple gauge of its value is the number of times the members of the audience will glance at such a diagram during the course of the discussion if it is drawn on the blackboard—and the discussant should make sure beforehand that a blackboard is available. Nothing leads to straying thoughts and unproductive comments as much as trying to keep track of John, Jane, Tom, Mary, Dick, Debbie, Harry, and Holly (or Mr. A, Mr. B, Mrs. C, Mr. D, etc.) without such a visual aid. A long pointer should be used, particularly if a tape-recording is being presented, and the presenter should point to the speaker (including himself) *every* time the speaker changes. A seating diagram answers automatically dozens of questions which would otherwise take up valuable time if they had to be answered orally. It also eliminates questions

arising from sheer confusion in trying to keep track of
who is who without visual aid. A common example is
trying to remember who the spouses are in a marital
group. This can be indicated definitively by simple arrows on a seating diagram, with no strain on anyone's
memory or attention.

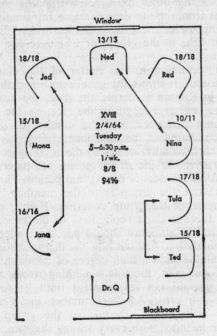

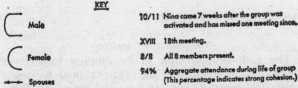

KEY

Male	10/11 Nina came 7 weeks after the group was activated and has missed one meeting since.
Female	XVIII 18th meeting.
	8/8 All 8 members present.
Spouses	94% Aggregate attendance during life of group (This percentage indicates strong cohesion.)

Figure 15. A seating diagram. A diagram like this is drawn
on the blackboard whenever a treatment group is discussed.

The central feature of the diagram, the seating arrangement itself, answers many questions of group-

dynamic or clinical interest: the relative positions of men and women, and of spouses (if any); it tells who sits near the therapist or near the door, and who far away from either or both, and who sits opposite in the therapist's direct line of vision; who likes an isolated seat; and, if a table is used, who prefers to sit away from it. Many other examples will occur in special situations from time to time. Various informative items can be appended next to each seat: age, diagnosis, length of time in the group, or whatever else may be pertinent.

The information in the center of the diagram is equally useful. It shows the serial number of the group meeting in Roman numerals, the date, the day of the week, the hour and length of the meeting, the number of meetings per week, and the number of members present compared to the total membership (as a fraction). The percentage refers to the total aggregate attendance over the life of the group compared to the total possible attendance during that period. This shows how attractive the group is to the members and, in effect, measures the group cohesion. If it is over 90 per cent the attraction (cohesion) of the group is superior, and the audience should pay close attention to the presentation to find out how the therapist succeeded in maintaining such a high degree of cohesion; if it is under 70 per cent, there is something wrong and the therapist should not rest content until he finds out where he is in error. All these numbers and figures together constitute the schedule of the group, which should be included with every seating diagram.

THE GROUP AUTHORITY

The Authority Principle

The authority principle in its simplest form is as follows: each member of an organizational hierarchy feels constrained to comply with the wishes of those above him. This compliance in practice takes the form of playing the organizational game. At the Adult level the therapist attempts to meet the formally stated terms of his therapeutic contract in its administrative and professional aspects. At another level, however, he is careful to preserve certain unstated but recognized conditions. Experience has shown, for example, that in a public agency which plays "I'm Only Trying to Help You" the worker is expected to discharge a small proportion of his patients as improved, but if he goes beyond the permissible minimum he will be challenged, and sometimes fired. This phenomenon is familiar in industry, where in certain situations workers who exceed their quotas are looked upon with disfavor; there the restriction is overtly stated, however, and may even be part of the written contract, while in social agencies its covert influence may be indignantly repudiated. It is evident, however, that a worker in such an organization who is too efficient threatens to disturb the administrative and budgetary plans of the agency, and must be slowed down on some pretext or other. Usually the brakes are applied at the level of the staff conference, where the zealous worker may be told that he is discharging patients or clients too quickly because they have "only intellectual insight" or because "their basic problems are still unsolved"—even when the stated purpose of the agency may only be to find jobs for its clients, which has nothing to do with insight or "basic problems."

More commonly, there may be a strong tendency to stick to conservative methods of treatment in order to avoid unusual occurrences that would require special reports, since these are equally upsetting, although in a different way, to superiors. None of these restrictions, perhaps, would be explicit, but they would have some implicit influence on the therapist's behavior, particularly in times of stress during the course of the therapy.

In effect, the therapist imputes to his superiors a set of unstated expectations and restrictions which he feels obliged to adhere to. He might not be conscious of these most of the time, but under certain emergency situations they might come vividly to mind. If for example a patient in such an agency should climb up on the window sill several stories above the street and threaten suicide, the therapist would become acutely aware of some of the possible consequences if the patient were to jump: the report to his superiors, the report of the superiors to the agency head, the agency head's report to state or national headquarters, and so on. It might even occur to him that the incident could become a political issue reaching into the highest echelons of government under pressure from influences he is familiar with in his daily work: taxpayers' associations and veterans' organizations, for example. If he rebels frequently against these stated or unstated constraints, he may be labeled a "psychopath," "paranoid," or "troublemaker"—the last, perhaps, justifiably.

In drawing an authority diagram, such as those shown in Figures 16a and 16b (pp. 321 and 322), the chain should be taken right up to the highest echelon. In a state agency, that would be the governor. If the agency receives federal funds, the chain ends with the President. This may seem like carrying matter to an extreme, but it is not as pedantic as it looks at first sight. Most patients and clients in government-supported agencies know that they have the privilege of writing letters of complaint to the highest headquarters, and some of them do. The experienced therapist is well aware of this possibility, and naturally prefers to avoid it. Thus, whether he likes it or not, or whether he faces the fact squarely or not, every therapist in a public agency is potentially limited to some degree by ill-defined restrictions based on organizational factors. Since these restrictions do not apply to therapists in private practice to any appreciable extent, there is a qualitative distinction between group therapy in a public agency and that in private practice which every organizational therapist had better face rather than attempt to ignore.

In order to understand these influences as thoroughly as possible, it is necessary to investigate four different aspects of the organizational authority: the personal, the organizational, the historical, and the cultural.

The Personal Authority

The therapist's feeling of freedom and his willingness to take risks depend to some extent on the personalities of his superiors. An administrator with little interest in psychodynamics might take an intransigent view of an untoward incident, and his staff might feel apprehensive about any departure from the most conservative, or even stereotyped, forms of group therapy. A supervisor with a more sympathetic attitude toward therapeutic problems might encourage his staff in new ventures and make them feel that he would stand behind any sincere attempt to improve their proficiency. Hence the therapist's estimate of his personal standing in the hierarchy and his assessment of the expectations of his superiors are strong influences in determining the boldness and freedom of his therapeutic approach. In both cases he should recognize that his superiors are vulnerable to the press and to the budgetary authorities, but his approach to his patients will be different if he is restricted by fear of the administration than if he is motivated by consideration for it.

These influences are set up and discussed in the personal aspect of the authority diagram, which answers

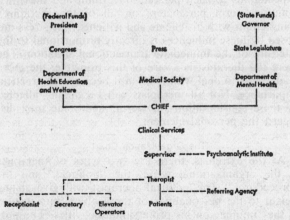

Figure 16a. A formal authority diagram of a treatment group

the question "Whom do you have to deal with?" In this connection, the authority principle may be stated in its more extended form as follows: each individual in an organizational hierarchy imputes a special set of

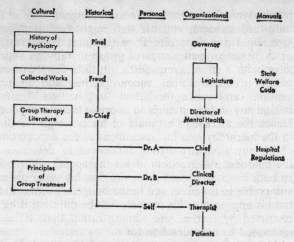

Figure 16b. An informal authority diagram.

expectations to each person above him, and these imputations form parameters on all of the therapist's transactions with his clients and patients. The stress imposed by these influences is directly proportional to the intensity of the immediate transactional situation. The more the therapist is aware of this principle, the more ready he is to deal with it when it becomes of practical importance. Not all therapists will be equally affected by these considerations, however, and some may disregard the personal element.

The Organization Chart

At the extremes, there are two types of therapists in the organizational sense, the "political" and the "procedural." The political therapist will give strong weight to the personalities of those above him insofar as they impinge on his professional activities. The procedural therapist will do what he thinks is right and justify himself according to the rules without regard to the personalities of his superiors. Each therapist should try to decide on a basis of past behavior to which side he leans. The political therapist should familiarize himself with the personal aspect of the group authority, while the procedural therapist should pay special attention to the formal organization chart in order to have a clear idea of his "official" position in the hierarchy and his organizational relationships with the other members. Then if acute difficulties arise in the course of therapy, each will be prepared beforehand to answer for the consequences in one way or the other. This will diminish his "organizational anxiety" and enable him to deal better with the matter at hand.

The Historical Aspect

Precedent, of course, is always important when stress arises in social situations. A therapist's knowledge of his predecessors may serve as a useful guide for his own behavior; on the other hand, it indicates what kinds of difficulties he may run into if he wishes to introduce a technical innovation. The staff of a clinic founded by a psychodramatist may take a different view of an attempt to introduce gestalt therapy than the staff of one founded by an orthodox analyst. A traditionally experimental clinic will take a different view of LSD than a traditionally conservative one will take.

The Cultural Aspect

The written word is the first appeal of the procedural therapist and the backstop for the political therapist. The cultural aspect of the authority diagram lists the canonical works that guide the activities of the organization. Professionally, these may be the works of Sigmund Freud, or perhaps those of one of his dissidents or opponents. Administratively, they may include the welfare code of the state, where the aims of the organization may be explicitly stated in legal terms. At the local level, there may be a manual for the guidance of clinic or agency personnel. The therapist should make sure that he is familiar with the contents of all these canonical writings.

THE GROUP STRUCTURE

Small therapy groups usually have a simple structure, consisting of an external boundary that separates the members of the group from the rest of the population, and a single major internal boundary that separates the therapist from the patients.

Complex Leadership

There may, however, be a minor structure within the leadership, including a co-therapist or assistant therapist. As noted previously, it is often difficult to state clearly the purpose of having more than one therapist, and experience shows that in most cases it is a handicap. This can easily be tested by starting the group with two therapists and continuing afterward with one. The reasons usually given for co-therapy are of an institutional nature and remain unconvincing to contractual therapists. Teaching, however, may be a legitimate reason for having an assistant therapist.

The Structural Diagram

The structural diagram of a simple treatment group is shown in Figure 17 (p. 325). This structure has a defect not occurring in more highly organized groups. It does not distinguish between the leader and his executive arm, the group apparatus; a distinction which is of paramount dynamic importance, and which must be clearly grasped. When functioning as a therapist, the therapist is an activity leader. When he is performing other duties, such as answering the telephone, opening and closing the door, arranging the furniture, announcing the time of the next meeting, and keeping internal order, he is functioning as his own group apparatus. It is essential that in his own mind he separate these two functions, which are as different as those of a judge and a bailiff in a courtroom. In more highly organized groups, the leader has a staff to do the work of the apparatus. When he is dealing with pressures from outside the therapy chamber, the therapist is the external apparatus of his group; when he is keeping order among his patients, he is the internal apparatus. Only when he is engaged in transactions directly related to the therapeutic work is he a leader. If these distinctions are not clear in his own mind the patients may become confused as to his function and the therapeutic situation may be fogged.

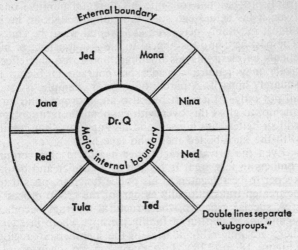

Figure 17. Structural diagram of a treatment group.

This is most clearly brought out in certain types of public agencies and in correctional work, where the leader works not only as a therapist, but also as a delegate of the group apparatus of the organization as a whole. A social worker may control the funds allotted to the patients in her group; there are agencies where a therapist to needy mothers has the task of rehabilitation combined with the duty of conducting "night raids" if someone suspects that a client is not really eligible for benefits; in correctional work, the parole or probation officer may carry handcuffs and have the authority to imprison members of his therapy groups who transgress the conditions of their liberty. Where such punitive functions are combined with those of therapist, it is particularly important for the therapist to clarify his two roles to himself and his clients. Sometimes the roles are so irreconcilable that the situation cannot be resolved and therapy proceeds at best in a tentative, limping, opaque style, with therapist and patients always on trial with each other.

Briefly, the difficulty lies in the fact that the therapist can be provoked at any juncture into swinging from his Adult professional role into his Parental punitive one. Even if his actual ego state is Adult throughout, he is almost inevitably perceived as Parental when he shifts. The best he can do is appeal to the Adult aspect of his clients by clarifying his dilemma, and to do this effectively may require considerable courage in facing it squarely himself. A parole officer, for example, is after all not only a therapist but also an informer, and any attempt to gloss this over with euphemistic terminology will sit better with himself and his superiors than it will with the hard-boiled men who face him.

Even the private practitioner has to resolve certain conflicts in this area. Is his job as a cashier and book-keeper to be relegated to his police function, or is it to be treated transactionally as part of the group process?

A special aspect of the structural diagram becomes significant in marital or family therapy, where in effect there are minor boundaries in the membership region (Figure 18, p. 328). In a marital group, each couple functions as a separate entity in situations of stress, so that the therapist is then dealing with four subgroups rather than with eight individuals. Similarly in a family group, the parents may function as a subgroup forming a united front against the children, who in turn function as another subgroup. The therapist should carefully distinguish in such situations when the members are acting as individuals, in which case he is dealing with a simple group, and when they are split into conflicting or allied subgroups, in which case he is dealing with a compound or complex group.

THE GROUP DYNAMICS

The External Group Process

The dynamics diagram considers the forces acting on the major group structure, that is, the external boundary and the major internal boundary. In the external group process (comprising transactions between the group and the external environment), external pressures are met by the group cohesion. Usually this aspect of the process is latent during most of the life of a therapy group, and plays little part in the proceedings. If the external environment becomes turbulent, however, the group must begin to mobilize to prevent disruption. If an agency is in a state of change or upheaval, both therapist and patients may recognize that at any moment external pressures may terminate the existence of the group. This creates special situations which are interesting to study. For the most part, however, external pressures can be ignored in the ordinary course of therapy.* It should be noted that external pressure may be either positive or negative. An executive order terminating group therapy in the agency and a party of people talking loudly outside the door while waiting to use the meeting room, both constitute positive external pressure; a holdup in the applications of new patients while there are vacancies in the group constitutes negative external pressure.

The Major Internal Group Process

The action in the group centers on the major internal group process at the major internal boundary, comprising transactions between the members and the therapist. Here the group cohesion, represented by the leadership, meets agitation from the membership, as shown in Figure 18 (p. 328). The patients exhibit their individual proclivities in action for or against the therapist. This may be regarded in transactional terms as between the Child in each patient and the Parent or Adult of the therapist; in psychoanalytic terms, as an interplay of transference, therapeutic maneuvers, and countertransference.

The Minor Internal Group Process

Transactions which pit individual proclivities of patients for or against each other constitute the minor internal group process. In a more formal sense, the membership may be conceived of as divided into

* In the Southern states, the current governmental demand for integration constitutes an external pressure which may override all the other dynamic forces in the group.

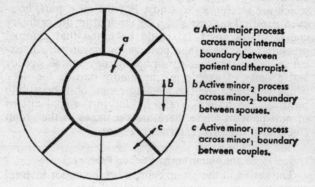

Figure 18. A dynamics diagram of a mixed marital group.

regions, with the boundaries labeled $Minor_1$. The $Minor_1$ process then consists of transactions across these boundaries. If each region is occupied by only one individual, then no further classification is necessary. If some or all regions are occupied by subgroups such as married couples, however, then those $Minor_1$ regions have internal boundaries labeled $Minor_2$. In that case transactions involving one couple with another constitute the $Minor_1$ process, and transactions between spouses comprise the $Minor_2$ process.

It is of some interest and profit to sort the proceedings of a group meeting into those which are part of the major internal process (direct or indirect transactions between the therapist and the patients); and those in the minor group process (transactions between patients which do not involve the therapist); and where indicated, the minor process should be broken down into $Minor_1$ and $Minor_2$. This offers a useful and fairly rigorous framework for discussing such problems as how much the therapist should talk, and what happens when spouses do or do not sit near each other.

The relationship between the various aspects of the group process is expressed in the principle that the external, the major internal and the minor internal group processes are to some extent mutually exclusive, so that energy employed in one aspect is taken from the reservoir available for the other aspects. The complete equation would read: External + Major + Minor + Group Activity = K (group cohesion at a given moment).

THE GROUP IMAGO

The organizational structure (formal role relationships) of a small therapy group is simple, consisting of two roles, therapist and patient, typically with one slot for therapist and eight slots for patients. The individual structure (the roster of people present) can be directly observed, since the entire personnel are assembled in one room. The private structure, that is, the group as seen through the eyes of each member, is found in the group imago of the member. This private structure is the most decisive structural aspect for the outcome of the individual's therapy.

Differentiation

The variables in the group imago are both qualitative and quantitative. The qualitative aspects concern the transactional, functional, and libidinal roles which the other members fill for the subject, and the nature of the slots activated by and for them in his imago. These qualities are historically determined, and their investigation is a matter of careful and systematic analysis of the psychodynamics of his transactional stimuli and responses. There are four general types of slots found in the imago of every member of a group, as illustrated in Figure 19 (p. 330), each type having certain cathectic peculiarities. The leadership slot will be invested with the same libidinal characteristics that would be involved in the transference if the patient were formally psychoanalyzed; thus the leadership slot is a "transference" slot. The self-slot may be characterized psychodynamically as a narcissistic slot. Differentiated slots correspond psychodynamically to "extra-analytic transferences." Undifferentiated slots form a reservoir for further differentiation.

The basic quantitative variable is differentiation, inferred from behavior and confirmed by free association, introspection, and dreams. Sometimes dreams indicate a greater degree of differentiation than is otherwise manifest; in such cases, differentiation of certain group members is referred to as "latent" or "repressed." A group may be under-differentiated, fully differentiated, or over-differentiated in the imago of a given subject. Under-differentiation may occur when there are more members than there are differentiated slots in a patient's group imago. If, as is in Figure 19, there are five differentiated slots: the leadership slot, the self-slot, and three membership slots; then the other four members may be relegated to the undifferentiated slot, where they are colloquially known in transactional terms as "these other good people," "the rest of you," or "these other jerks." The slots now occupied by Dr. Q, Red, Mona, and Jana, may already have been activated in Jed's group imago at the time he entered the group (his provisional group imago), and may be cathected according to early experiences, say with his father, a brother, his mother and a sister.

Such an imago can become fully differentiated in two ways. The four "others" may be distributed between

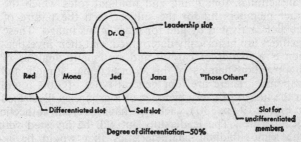

Figure 19. A group imago.

the four slots already activated, so that Jed behaves toward three or four of the women as though they were mothers or sisters, and toward three or four of the men as though they were fathers or brothers. The imago is then homomorphically differentiated. Or Jed may activate new slots as time passes; son and daughter slots, teacher, nursemaid, and grandparent slots, etc., depending on his early family history and his present attitudes. This is heteromorphic differentiation; the previously undifferentiated members are put into newly activated slots.

Now let us suppose that the patient whose imago is fully differentiated heteromorphically, so that he has nine active slots (including the self-slot), is transferred to a new group with only four members. He then has the option of either shutting down four slots (usually the least significant ones) or of assigning some or all of the members of the new group to more than one slot. In the latter case, the new group will be over-differentiated in his imago. This will be manifested by his behaving transactionally in different ways at different times toward the same member; he may shift from treating her like a mother to treating her like a sister and back again, which she and the other members of the group, including the therapist, may find incomprehensible and disconcerting if they do not understand the principle involved.

ANALYSIS OF TRANSACTIONS

The analysis of single transactions may constitute a definite phase of group therapy, in which case it is advisable to draw transactional diagrams such as that shown in Figure 20 (p. 332). The detection and rectification of crossed transactions is of particular importance, and in the major process they constitute transference and countertransference actions * and re-

---

* The passive tendency of much conventional psychotherapy is illustrated by the implication at many conferences and in much of the literature that the patient's sole right is to "react." A patient who reacts is usually diagnosed neurotic or psychotic, and that is OK. A patient who acts, instead of reacting, may

actions. The principle at stake here is one of the rules of communication. If a crossed transaction occurs, communication will be broken off unless and until the crossing is rectified; conversely, if communication is broken off, it can be resumed when the crossed transaction is found and rectified.

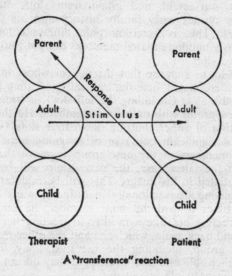

A "transference" reaction

Figure 20. A transactional diagram: crossed transaction type I.

be called a psychopath or sociopath and that is not-OK. In transactional analysis, the patient is considered without prejudice equally as an agent and as a respondent. He acts when he offers a transactional stimulus, and he reacts, or responds, when he offers a transactional response. The conventional statements are "The patient's reaction was . . ." and "My reaction was . . ." Conventional therapists are sometimes startled at transactional conferences to hear: "The patient acted," or "I acted." The notion of a therapist acting (rather than merely intervening) is disconcerting to some people, and the notion of a patient acting instead of reacting is threatening or reprehensible. The commonest fallacy is a failure to distinguish Adult "action" from archaic "acting out."

SUMMARY

In summary, then, for a group therapist to consider himself competent, he should have some background in group dynamics and in particular should be familiar through practice and experience with the use and significance of the six basic diagrams mentioned above. He should always have sufficient information about his group to be prepared to draw any of these diagrams when occasion arises or when it would be helpful in understanding what is going on in therapy. The advantages of such diagrams, and the principles they represent, are listed below.

1. The seating diagram offers the considerable pedagogical advantages of a visual aid. It discourages hypothetical questions and emphasizes the uniqueness of each situation in the here and now.

2. The authority diagram uncovers covert influences on the operations of the therapist which he might prefer to ignore. The authority principle states that the therapist tends to be influenced by expectations which he imputes to those above him in the hierarchy.

3. The structural diagram emphasizes the advantages of structural simplicity if the therapist wishes to maintain a continuous grasp of the significance of the proceedings. The principle here is to make a clear distinction between disparate functions.

4. The dynamics diagram helps the therapist sort out the proceedings in a meaningful way. The principle is that the external, the major internal, and the minor internal group processes are to some extent mutually exclusive, and that energy employed in one aspect is taken from the reservoir available for other aspects.

5. The group imagos are constructed from perceptions of "real" personalities. They serve to clarify the more cogent relationships underlying the institutionalized and banal transactions and self-presentations which are common in therapy groups. The principle at stake is that of differentiation.

6. Transactional diagrams help to clarify problems

of communication. The principles at stake are the rules of communication.

REFERENCES

1. Freud, S. *Group Psychology and the Analysis of the Ego.* Hogarth Press, London, 1940.

2. Scheidlinger, S. *Psychoanalysis and Group Behavior.* W. W. Norton & Company, New York, 1952.

3. Berne, E. *The Structure and Dynamics of Organizations and Groups.* J. B. Lippincott Company, Philadelphia, 1963. Grove Press, Inc., New York, 1966. (Chap. 2, ref. 4.)

22. The Group Authority

THE LEADER

The group authority consists of two sectors: the leadership and the group canon. These fit together so that a member can appeal from the leader's decision to the canon, from the judge's verdict to the body of laws; or he can appeal from the canon to the leader, from the legal punishment to the Governor's pardon.

There are three kinds of leadership, corresponding to the three aspects of the group structure. The responsible leader is the front man, the man who fills the role of leader in the organizational structure. The effective leader, who makes the actual decisions, may or may not have a role in the organizational structure. He may be the man in the back room, but he is the most important person in the individual structure. The psychological leader is the one who is most powerful in the private structures of the members and occupies the leadership slot in their group imagoes. All three types of leadership may be invested in the same individual, but there are all sorts of combinations. Thus, in the British Government, the Prime Minister is the responsible and effective leader, and the monarch is the psychological leader. In certain of our cities, the mayor is the responsible and psychological leader, and the ward boss is the effective leader. In certain criminal groups the front men are the responsible leaders, while another man who has no fixed role in the organizational structure is the effective and psychological leader.

The distinction between the three kinds of leadership is not always easy to make. For example, the psychological leader, who belongs to the private structure (which is often unconscious), can sometimes only be identified by psychiatric methods. But since the private structure usually comes out into the open in times of stress or over the long term, the psychological leadership may become clearer in historical situations. For example, in the case of the British Empire, it is quite certain that Queen Victoria, even when she was not constitutionally responsible or effective, was psychologically supreme. No matter how distinguished her prime ministers were, this period is still known as the Victorian era, and the Queen was very likely the most influential person of her time.

The effective leader can be distinguished by studying the group in action. He is the one whose questions are most likely to be answered or whose suggestions are most likely to be followed in situations of stress. There is some resemblance between effective leaders and the so-called "subleaders" found in various types of experimental groups. "Subleaders" have been carefully studied in experiments with soldiers and college students. They are members who attract attention because they are dominant, popular or show a special interest in the group activity. One object of these experiments is to study the personality characteristics of such influential people as an aid to selecting officer candidates, executives or student leaders. However, in judging such experiments, it is often overlooked that the effective leader of an experimental group is usually the experimenter himself.

The responsible leader is the individual who is going to be called to account by higher authority if things go wrong—the experimenter in an experimental group and the executive in a business group. Since in many organizations the responsible leader is only a front, it is here that dominance, popularity and helpfulness find their usefulness. A man who possesses these qualities may be attractive to the members and thus serve the purposes of the effective leadership.

The psychological leader of a group occupies a special position, whether or not he is also the responsible and effective leader. The members demand certain qualities of the psychological leader, the one who is likely to survive in the group tradition as a euhemerus.

And these are the qualities of a god. The leader is supposed to be omnipotent, omniscient, immortal, invulnerable, irresistible, incorruptible, unseducible, indefatigable and fearless. These are the same qualities that were attributed in ancient times to emperors such as "the unequalled, almighty, invincible, unwavering Assur-nasir-pal." If a leader in real life fails in any one of these respects, there will always be those who will criticize him for it. For example this happens if an American president shows weakness, ignorance, sickness, touchiness, corruptibility or fear. The effects soon begin to show in the stock market, the political cartoons and the letters to the editor. Even a group therapist is supposed to have most of these qualities. In many groups, the members will become uneasy if he so much as has a cold. He will be teased, some patients will say that they feel insecure because he got sick, and some of them will ask how he can cure them if he gets sick himself.

It will be noted that the qualities required of a psychological leader already resemble the attributes of a euhemerus. The ancient emperors who expected to be treated like gods while they were still alive were actually insisting that they be euhemerized before they were dead, as shown by the inscription about Assur-nasir-pal.

In addition to classifying leaders according to the three aspects of leadership, it is also desirable to classify them according to their positions in the group. The one who first establishes the group is the primal leader. Leaders who follow in his footsteps may be called executives. Subsequent leaders who change the constitution are to that extent again primal leaders. The actual living leader at any given moment may be called the personal leader. Leaders who have certain independent powers but are answerable to higher authority for other decisions may be called subleaders. Leaders who are answerable for everything are personal leaders in their subgroups, but, in relation to the whole group, they may be called delegates. A practical test of leadership is the power to make decisions that are not subject to revision or veto by anyone else present; most convincingly, decisions concerning the group structure, such as who is allowed to remain in the group, when the meeting ends and when another meeting will be held. If no one else can override an individual's authority in such matters, then that individual is the leader of the group. If the so-called leader plays the king but someone else can play the ace (to paraphrase Eugene Field's epigram), then he is more a subleader or delegate than a true leader.

Leadership is most strongly confirmed by existential reinforcement. Historically, great leaders have always been able to kill or be killed and to take responsibility for everything, including death. In our own country the three most euhemerized presidents, Washington, Lincoln and Roosevelt, were all war presidents and were all able to take the responsibility for killing. Assur-nasir-pal, Cheops, Pericles, Mahomet, Ataturk, Hitler and Stalin were all able to order bloodshed; Socrates and Jesus were men who knew how to die. Under more civilized conditions banishment replaces killing, and a good leader must have the ability to enforce this when it is required. Thus Freud banished agitators who tried to twist his theories, and every good professor must be able to fail a student when circumstances require it. So the basic tests of leadership are the responsibility and the right (organizationally) to apply sanctions and give rewards, and the ability (individually) to do so irrevocably. In a small way, even the chairman of a PTA meeting must be ruthless so that he can keep people from getting out of hand.

THE GROUP CANON

After the death of the primal leader, the course of the group work is regulated by the canon that he has established. As already mentioned, the canon consists of three parts: the constitution, the laws based on it and the culture. The basic canon follows that of the mother group; but each group develops its own peculiar departures from the mother canon, and it is these departures which distinguish the canon of one group from that of another in the same society.

The main features of a typical constitution are: First, there is the naming of the group, the existential provision that gives it its responsibility toward other groups and toward society in general. Secondly, there is a statement concerning the activity, the teleologic provision which gives the group its goal. Thirdly, the structure is described in the structural provision. Fourthly, the process is regulated by the regulatory provision. And fifthly, the changing of the constitution itself is authorized by the autotelic provision.

The first canon is made by the primal leader, who through his authority is able to establish a tradition of behavior which in some respects is different from what the members are accustomed to outside the group. This is the primal canon and has a very forceful appeal for the members in later generations. Anyone who changes, adds to or subtracts from the primal canon is himself to that extent a primal leader. The appeal to the traditional canon in times of doubt is nearly always made in a personal way by bringing up the name of the appropriate euhemerus. Thus, we have, "Confucius said," "Lincoln said," "Freud said," "Lenin said." That is the way in which the euhemerus exerts his authority on the posterity of his group. Ataturk and Lenin were typical primal leaders. They set up new constitutions and new cultures with organizational and personal relationships radically altered from the old ways of their mother groups. Constitutionally, both of them changed the form of government, and culturally, both of them changed the relationships between men and women, for example.

Because the euhemerus and the primal canon have a sacred quality in even the most "irreligious" groups, a good executive rarely tries to become a primal leader. Instead, he changes the canon according to his needs or the demands of the times in such a way that he appears to be interpreting it rather than changing it. In this way he lessens the risk of a diminished cohesion. However, if he wishes to form his own group in a revolutionary operation, he must boldly attack the old canon and often weaken the authority of the old euhemeri as well. But he must carefully consider how far he can go safely. A simple way out is to attack the personal leader without attacking the euhemeri, to overthrow Emperor Nicholas without derogating Peter the Great, to depose Abdul Hamid without destroying the prestige of Sultan Achmet, to attack Kennedy without attacking Lincoln.

As noted, the object of the canon is to regulate the group work, and particularly the internal group process, which consists of operations meant to change the organizational, the individual or the private structure of the group. The roles in the organizational structure are maintained by the constitutional contract, which reads: "I promise to support the constitution of this group." The rest of the internal group process is regulated by the social contract, which reads: "You respect my persona, and I'll respect yours." The social contract is enforced by the group etiquette, but each group develops certain relaxations in the etiquette, and these relaxations form part of the group character.

Since the social contract is the most important influence in the group culture, its meaning should be clearly understood. The way in which an individual chooses to present himself to a group is called his persona. The social contract states that his presentation must be accepted courteously at face value, according to the group etiquette. Every group must find its own ways of legitimately violating the social contract; otherwise life would become intolerably dull. These departures from strict etiquette belong to the group character.

This can be illustrated by comparing the culture of news photography in the Soviet Union with that in America (in 1956). The material aspects, the equipment and the technic are similar in both countries. But in the Soviet Union the persona is protected by a strict etiquette. For example, athletes and political figures can only be photographed while they are engaged in their official occupations, and, to make certain that the photographers abide by the social contract, they must get permission beforehand in both cases. Thus, Soviet news photography tends to be dull. In America, it is much more lively because it is full of character. There is hardly any etiquette, and every possible exception to the social contract is taken full advantage of. In fact, our photographers delight in playing with the personas of their subjects: taking pictures of athletes at nightclubs and of bankers with midgets on their knees.

In the culture of police activity, the situation is reversed. It is the Soviets who disregard the social contract, and the crudest violations of personas by their secret police apparatus are (or were) tolerated by the membership and even encouraged by the leadership. In America there is a strict legally controlled etiquette that forces the police to observe the social contract, and violations are not tolerated except by the lowest elements. Thus, in the U.S.S.R., in the culture of press photography the etiquette predominates with strict adherence to the social contract, while in the culture of police activity, character predominates to permit gross insults. In the American group culture, it is the other way round.

It should be noted that the culture does not change with the individual but with the group he is in. For example, a husband may be quite unrestrained toward his wife at home, but he must treat her differently at a PTA meeting. It is the individual who adjusts to the culture and not vice versa, except in the case of a primal leader.

THE GROUP CULTURE

For a practical understanding of organizations and groups it is necessary to have a workable theory of group culture, since the culture influences almost everything that happens in a social aggregation. The following approach has been found to be the most useful in dealing with ailing groups.

Culture is divided into three segments—technical culture, group etiquette and group character. The technical culture is used principally in the work and the combat groups and includes all sorts of useful (and decorative) artifacts, from quartz chips to space ships; all sorts of practical technics for changing the environment, from daubing pigments to making plutonium; as well as all sorts of practical intellectual operations, from counting reindeer to programing computers. It includes those aspects of culture that require the use of a logical mind directed toward reality, that part of the personality which later will be called the Adult.

The group etiquette is based on the general social etiquette and includes all items of etiquette which are different from the general etiquette but are acceptable in the given group. Etiquette deals with standards of behavior and ways of presenting an acceptable persona or of reinforcing or guiding the personas of others. What makes people comfortable socially is to feel that other people see them as they want to be seen. Most people want to be seen as generous, intelligent, courageous, sincere and loyal—in general, acceptable according to the standards of the group. Each group has its own special standards and its own favored ways of presenting or reinforcing a persona. There is a different standard and a different approach for presenting oneself as courageous at a scientific meeting, at a revival meeting or in a group of skin-divers. And there is a different etiquette for acknowledging courage in each of these situations. Etiquette is usually traditional and in most cases only changes slowly or under special conditions. This part of the group culture originates from that aspect of the personality which later will be called the Parent.

The group character includes departures from the social contract which are established as legitimate in a particular group through relaxations of the group etiquette. Sometimes these freedoms are surprising to outsiders. For example, Bell, Cuppy and J, being inexperienced spiritualists, were a little startled to find that it was all right to tease some of the spirits and to laugh at certain times. The social contract was relaxed with Ruby, but no liberties were permitted with Dr. Murgatroyd.

Character is more "primitive" than etiquette. Etiquette requires a restraint, an understanding and a knowledge of social behavior that an infant, for example, does not have. Character is a more direct expression of instinctual life. It includes many things that infants can do, such as laughing, singing and weeping. The group character is chiefly an expression of that aspect of the personality which later will be called the Child.

The usefulness of this three-pronged view of culture can be illustrated by analyzing some items of group behavior which are often thought of as typically "cultural."

1. Circumcision may be regarded as an initiation rite, i.e., a constitutional requirement for membership. When the constitution is a written one, as in the Old Testament, for example, the primal canon can be found in its original form. Rituals surrounding the operation then would be part of the group etiquette—the etiquette of circumcision. In many localities the ceremonies include a feast where more relaxed expressions of feeling are permissible as part of the group character.

2. The organizational structure of the United States of America provides a slot for the Presidency. The man who occupies this slot is known officially as the President or Mr. President, and unofficially by his surname and nickname. As the President, his role cannot be attacked, under the constitutional contract, except by constitutional means. If there are changes to be made in the manner of his election or the maximal number of terms that he can serve, this must be done by due process, and the changes then apply not to any specific individual but to whoever fills the Presidency slot in the role of President.

However, the incumbent at any moment presents himself as an acceptable person with a certain kind of courage, generosity, sincerity and loyalty in regard to certain specific problems, such as racial integration and interstate commerce. Mr. President can be attacked on the floor by marshalling facts against his viewpoint, but these facts must relate to the matter in hand, and the personality of the President must not be brought into the argument; his deed can be scrutinized courteously, but his persona must not be questioned, as this would be considered a breach of etiquette. Thus, it was regarded as rude when, several years ago, the head of another state referred to Mr. Eisenhower as insincere. One of the official manuals for this etiquette is *Robert's Rules of Order*. In unofficial reports, the President's title is replaced by his surname, which belongs to the individual structure.

However, in accordance with the American group character, Ike the personality could be teased in a decent way about his golfing and criticized for some of his friendships. But there were definite limits as to how far this could go publicly, and to transgress them was an insult. These aspects of the canon relating to the Presidency are shown in Table 1.

Table 1. Canon of the American Presidency

STRUCTURE	CANONICAL PROVISION	ASPECT	CONTRACT	REQUIRE- MENT	VIOLA- TIONS
Organiza- tional	Constitution	Role: The President	Constitu- tional	Due Process	Revolution
Individual	Etiquette	Persona: Mr. Presi- dent, Eisenhower	Social	Courtesy	Breach of Etiquette, Rudeness
Private	Character	Personality: Ike	Social	Decency	Insult

While there is often a manual or authority concerning a group's etiquette, the character comes so naturally and is so plastic that it is difficult to pin down or formulate in words. The political cartoonist carries his Rules of Satirical Order mostly in his head. The distinction between rudeness and insult should be noted. Rudeness is a mere neglect of etiquette or an exhibition of character ("familiarity") when etiquette is called for. An insult goes beyond even the latitude allowed by the group character.

3. Secret societies, primitive or otherwise, with their elaborate concern over dignity, are good examples to consider. They are boring to many people because they have so much etiqutte and so little character; i.e., everyone has to take everyone else very seriously. But in many of them, if a member breaks a rule, it is legitimate to attack him, and this is where the character comes out and the fun begins. For example, some American service clubs derive much of their fun from

fining members 10 cents each time they use a swear word.

The psychological aspects of culture as outlined here may be summarized as follows. The technical culture, what one has to do, is based on an objective, realistic, "adult" approach to the environment. The group etiquette, what one is supposed to do, is a matter of tradition, dealing with behavior standards and their maintenance, and is passed down from one generation to another, being learned from the parents, as it were. The group character deals with what one might like to do, and, with proper restraint, allows the expression of more archaic aspects of the personality. The culture of clothes in our society illustrates the integration of these three aspects. Women wear clothes to protect themselves from the weather, which is a rational or Adult view; for reasons of modesty, which is a traditional or Parental view; and to decorate themselves and make themselves appear more interesting and sometimes provocative. Thus, clothes are a part of the technical culture in being useful, part of the etiquette in being modest, and part of the character in allowing self-expression even when this conflicts with the persona of modesty. From the organizational point of view clothes are also worn for constitutional reasons; i.e., in most places they are required by law.

This approach to culture has two advantages. On the one hand it is based on the personality of the individual, and on the other it fits into the dynamics of the group as a whole. Thus, it has a natural place in the consideration of what happens between specific individuals in any particular group.

SUMMARY

The following hypotheses are offered:

1. The proceedings of any group are regulated by two authorities: the leadership and the group canon.

2. There are three kinds of leadership: the responsible leader, the effective leader and the psychological leader.

3. The members demand certain absolute qualities

of their leaders so that fundamentally every successful leader is a charismatic leader.

4. The culture of a group can be divided into three aspects: the technical culture, the group etiquette and the group character. The last two are based on an implicit contract that the members will respect each others' personas. Each group evolves its own standards of behavior, its own ways of reinforcing the contract and its own ways of violating it in certain respects.

5. Each of the three aspects of a group culture is derived from a special aspect of the members' personalities: the technical culture from the realistic (adult) aspect; the group etiquette from the traditional (parental) aspect; and the group character from the emotional (archaic) aspect.

23. Group Treatment

THE FIRST THREE MINUTES

The Therapeutic Attitude

As the group therapist takes his seat before the assembled patients, his first concern should be to compose his mind for the task which lies before him. He should make a point of starting each new group, and ideally each new meeting, in a fresh frame of mind. It is evident that if he conducts his groups this year just as he did last year he has learned nothing in the meantime and is a mere technician. For the sake of his own development and self-esteem he should not allow such a thing to happen. He may set as a goal (which he may not always be able to attain) to learn something new every week—not something new out of books, nor some interpretive sidelight, but some more general truth which will increase his perceptiveness.

Physical Condition. The first requisite for this fresh frame of mind is a physiological one which takes literally the word "fresh." The group therapist, like any physician, owes it to his patients to keep in good health, to get sufficient sleep during his work week, and not to arrive in his treatment room under the influence of medication, alcohol, fatigue, or a hangover. He should have a healthy and regular sex life such as marriage provides. Regular outdoor exercise will give him more respect for the benefits of physical vitality and for the health of the body, which is the only known vessel for the human psyche. He should not allow the skepticism of his more self-indulgent or lazier colleagues to interfere with this old-fashioned and healthful regime.

Psychological Attitude. Psychologically, as the patients on their part compose themselves for the session with uneasy rustle, the therapist clears his mind of everything that has gone before in the way of preparation, of all that he knows about the patients, of all his personal problems, and of everything he has learned about psychiatry and psychotherapy. At his best, he becomes like an innocent new-born babe who has passed under the arch of his office doorway into a world he never made. Then on the *tabula rasa* of his unencumbered mind should appear three ancient slogans.

Therapeutic Slogans

Primum non nocere. The first concern of all healing arts is not to injure, to cut only when and where necessary, but then to cut cleanly and with clear knowledge of what is being cut into. The group therapist, then, must become aware of the possibilities of damaging his patients by bruising them, by misleading them (especially sinful and wicked toward the young), by opening up areas of pathology without proper preparation, or by losing them in such a way that they will be unable afterward to avail themselves of the services of other psychotherapists. Specifically, he should wield the interpretive knife gently, though firmly and steadily; he should avoid entering sequestered areas of psychosis until the patient has been fully prepared to meet face to face what he has so long sequestered; and he should be careful not to agree too quickly with derogatory statements of a patient concerning a parent or spouse. He should not poke into any traumatized areas until he is ready to finish what he begins and feels assured that the patient can survive the procedure. His first task, therefore, is to locate such areas and estimate their extent, in order to avoid them until the time has come for them to be explored.

Vis medicatrix naturae. The patient has a built-in drive to health, mental as well as physical. His mental development and emotional development have been obstructed, and the therapist has only to remove the obstructions for the patient to grow naturally in his own direction. This means, among other things, that there is no such thing as a "weak ego," but only weakly cathected egos. The therapist's second task, therefore, is to locate the healthy areas in each patient's personality so as to nurture them and strengthen their potential.

Je le pensay, et Dieu le guérit. The therapist does not cure anyone, he only treats him to the best of his ability, being careful not to injure and waiting for nature to take its healing course. There is no need for false humility, but only for facing the facts: we treat them, but it is God who cures them. Hence in practice "curing the patient" means "getting the patient ready for the cure to happen today." We can be persistent, industrious, devoted, conscientious, and acute, but we must not be ardent. The professional therapist's job is to use his knowledge therapeutically; if the patient is going to be cured by love, that should be left to a lover. When the patient recovers, the therapist should be able to say, "My treatment helped nature," and not "My love overcame it"—a statement which should be reserved for the patient's intimates.

These are the first thoughts which run through the therapist's head as the patients wait for him to give them instructions, or begin to talk by themselves.

The Therapeutic Relationship

Basic Questions. His next step should be to ask himself some fundamental questions about the real meaning of the therapeutic relationship. He may never be able to answer these definitively, but each time he asks them of himself he may come a little closer to a signicant answer.

First, in regard to his own development, he should ask himself: "Why am I sitting in this room? Why am I not at home with my children, or skiing, or skindiving, or playing chess, or whatever else my fancy might dictate? What will this hour contribute to my unfolding?"

In regard to his patients and their motivations, he should ask: "Why are they here? Why are they not home with their children, or doing what their fancy dictates? Why did they choose psychotherapy as a solution? Why not religion, alcohol, drugs, crime, gambling, or automobile racing? What will this hour contribute to their unfolding?"

Then in regard to his duties toward them and their expectations of him: "Why did they choose to come to me rather than to some other equally qualified person? What do they think I can do which someone else could not do as well or better? What makes them think I can do more for them than an experienced clergyman or scoutmaster could? Why did I get a doctor's degree? Of what value here are the hours I spent studying the surgical anatomy of the hand, the cross-section of the spinal cord, the pituitary hormones, the way of a rat in a maze, or the ethics of the slums?"

The Therapist's Assets. During the time these questions are running through the therapist's mind, the patients have perhaps become restless. His preoccupation has prevented him from making premature interventions which might help them conceal their anxieties. Now when he turns his attention to the other people in the room, they are already, without unnecessary delay, offering samples of their behavior which may be significant and useful. At this point, after a few minutes have elapsed since he sat down, the therapist can give himself a partial answer to the question of what a well-trained group therapist has to offer that other types of group leaders do not: his special powers of observation, his willingness to be looked over without prejudice, and his ability to structure the group to the best therapeutic advantage. Against the background of his philosophical questionings and reservations, his clinical qualities now come to the fore: observation, equanimity, and initiative. He prepares to use these three interdependent faculties, based on his whole previous clinical training and experience, for the maximum benefit of his patients.

Observing and Listening

Like any good clinician, the group therapist should ideally use all five senses in making a diagnosis, assessing the situation, and planning the treatment: sight, hearing, smell, touch, and taste. As previously noted, he should sit in such a position that he can easily observe all his patients at all times, so that as far as possible not a single movement in the room escapes him; with enough experience, he can develop useful eyes in the back of his head. Similarly, his ears should be selectively open so that he misses no sound emitted by any patient, no matter what sounds of traffic and construction penetrate into his office. Good odors and bad odors should be noted, and this may require the resurrection of a sense of smell which has been severely suppressed by social training, especially in America. Generally speaking, touching patients is poor technique except for naturally exuberant people; but even the most reserved therapist should permit himself an occasional handshake, which may yield useful information. The sense of taste has become even more unfashionable as a clinical intrument than the sense of smell, even for diagnosing diabetes, and in group treatment there is seldom an occasion to use it unless the patient offers the therapist a candy, which may turn out to be sour or bitter.

Visual Observation. Observation is the basis of all good clinical work, and takes precedence even over technique. Any well-read student or properly programed computer can make correct interpretations, given properly weighted findings; the real skill lies in collecting and evaluating data. Observations in group treatment should be made on a physiological basis, although their interpretation will be psychological. The therapist should be aware of the probable physiological state of every one of his patients during every moment of the session. He should know when to look directly at a patient, when to be content with peripheral vision, and when to sweep the whole group with his gaze. He should note not only overt blushing, palpitation, sweating, tremors, tension, excitement, rage, weeping, laughter, and sexuality, but should also be able to detect each of these in their incipient stages before they come out into the open. In order to do this he must observe carriage, posture, movements, gestures, facial mimicry, twitches of single muscles, arterial pulsations, local vasomotor and pilomotor phenomena, and swallowing.

Facial Expressions. The most subtle and challenging of these manifestations are the semi-voluntary expressions of facial mimicry and gestures. There is a rule of facial mimicry which has played an important part in determining the destinies of individuals and even of nations. The therapist meets this in day-to-day practice if he becomes drowsy during an interview. He does his best, he thinks successfully, to conceal his condition from the patient facing him, but almost invariably he will find that the patient is fully aware of what is going on. The rule is as follows: the visual impact (on the onlooker) of small movements or small changes of the facial musculature is greater than their kinesthetic impact (on the subject). Very small movements of certain muscles such as the levator palpebrae superioris, which may seem insignificant to the subject or escape his attention altogether, may be very obvious to an onlooker. This can be easily tested by drooping the eyelids to what seems kinesthetically a negligible extent, and then examining the effect in a mirror. The experiment may be repeated by contracting the risorius or the orbicularis oris just a few millimeters. There is a surprising difference between the small kinesthetic impact of such minimal excursions, and the visual impact of the facial expressions they produce. Few people are aware of the visual extent of the changes in the chin muscles produced by putting the tip of the tongue between the teeth and the upper or lower lip; in this case the changes spread even to the zygomaticus and temporalis.

When people are preoccupied with other matters, they may be unaware of even more extensive changes in their facial expressions. This means that people (including parents and children) are continually giving themselves away without knowing it; sometimes when the therapist or another patient points out an inconsistency between verbal content and facial expression, the patient finds it hard to believe that he has made his "hidden" feelings so obvious. For a lesson in keenness of observation in such matters, Darwin's wonderful book *Expression of the Emotions in Man and Animals* should be consulted—it is worth missing a month of newspapers and journals in order to read it.

Gestures. Another science which the group therapist should cultivate is that of pasimology, the science of gestures. For his purposes, gestures may be classified descriptively as symbolic, emphatic, exhibitionistic, or functional. A symbolic gesture is a conventional sign which is not directly related to the subject matter, such as the circle made with the thumb and forefinger that symbolizes "OK." An emphatic gesture is one which emphasizes a point and is in effect a nonverbal exclamation, such as knee pounding, finger-pointing, head-nodding, and simpering. An exhibitionistic gesture is one which the speaker is more conscious of than he is of the content of what he is saying; for example, a woman who raises her leg in a group to show a run in her stocking is often evidently more interested in how the men react to seeing her legs than she is in the condition of her stocking. Most interesting are the functional gestures. These are of an archaic nature and form a counterpoint to what the person is saying. They are characteristically idiosyncratic with the speaker, so that in order to understand them it may be necessary to inquire why certain gestures accompany certain words, since they do not seem to be directly related. Such cases give the effect of two messages coming at once, the verbal content and the more primitive and picturesque gestural accompaniment.

Some gestures are sex-linked and constitute "trade secrets," as it were, which the other sex is not a party to. Few men would intuitively know the meaning of a woman snapping a side-curl of her hair with her forefinger, but a friendly female confides that this indicates she is tired of the man she is talking to or associated with, and is ready for a change.

Sometimes it is the gestures rather than the facial expression which reveal the "hidden" thoughts by their inconsistency. A woman who smiles happily when she says she has an "extremely happy" marriage may meanwhile be twisting her wedding ring or tapping her foot impatiently. It is evident that the triad words-expression-gestures offers several variations to be studied and clarified through clinical experience. If all three are consistent, the personality may be termed "well-organized." In less well-organized personalities, words + expression may be inconsistent with gestures, or words + gestures may be inconsistent with expression. In poorly organized personalities, all three may be inconsistent: typically, the Adult ego state may say one thing in words, the Child ego state may say another through facial expressions, and the Parental ego state may convey its sentiments through gestures. Physiological, each of the triad may be regarded as a final common pathway. In the well-organized personality, the messages from each pathway reinforce each other; in the less well-organized personality, there are inconsistencies between them. The significant point is that in social behavior there are at least three final common pathways, each arising from a separate system or ego state, and these systems are often inconsistent with each other. It may be intuitively surmised, and experience bears it out, that in the long run the destiny of the individual will more likely be determined by the systems which control his facial expressions and his gestures, than by the one which puts his sentences together.

Mimicry and gestures are vast and fascinating fields for the group therapist to learn about, and if he learns well there will be few "hidden" feelings (or "real feelings," as they are called nowadays) that will not be revealed to his private gaze.

Listening. There are several kinds of listening. While the therapist is maintaining his visual observation he may at the same time note the grosser aspects of auditory clues, such as coughing, gasping, weeping, laughing, talking, and the content of what is said. If he wants to listen for more subtle indications, he may have to suspend visual observation, lower his head, and sometimes close his eyes as well, to concentrate on the pitch, timbre, rhythm, intonation, and vocabulary of the speakers. Sometimes it is only in this way that he can become aware of the functional aspects of verbalization, whose diagnosis may be largely intuitive: e.g. patients who are primarily talking to themselves rather than to the group, patients who are talking as their parents must have talked, and patients who are talking the way a child of a certain age does.

The careful listener, besides noting inconsistencies such as childlike or dialectic pronunciations by well-educated grown-ups, clear thoughts delivered in a shaky voice, and slips of the tongue contaminating otherwise good delivery, will also observe sooner or later that each of his patients has more than one voice. Under stress or varying circumstances there will be well-marked changes in the timbre, speed, and rhythm of talking, as well as a switch in enunciation and vocabulary. A psychiatric resident had a consistently measured delivery at staff conferences and supervisory interviews. One day he received a telephone call during an interview with the chief. It was an intimate friend, and the resident's manner of talking was quite different from that which he employed professionally. When he hung up, the chief remarked: "I've been waiting almost a year to hear you talking like that to somebody. Now I know you."

Vocabulary is the simplest vocal variable to study without special preparation. In general, there are three types of vocabularies, corresponding to different ego states. 1. Borrowed (Parental) vocabularies are often striking when they are highly mannered. A man who habitually spoke with an Edwardian vocabulary, manner, and syntax readily recognized that this form of speech was borrowed from a respected grandfather and was supposed to have the same effect on the contemporary listeners as his grandfather's talk had on him when he was a little boy. 2. Vocabularies learned as conceptual frameworks and mannerisms for dealing with external reality are classified as Adult. Social scientists and their disciples among PTA members, for example, are notably given to using "this" instead of "that" as an indicative pronoun. Such a tendency, according to the consensus of several therapy groups, implies an over-objectivity and a lack of commitment. "I do this (past action) often," for example, is a kind of apology, an exhibition of "proper" objectivity, even a plea for forgiveness, and at the same time somehow an evasion of full responsibility. "I do that often" has a more authentic ring. The historic "this" is as much of an intellectualism for a social scientist as the use of the historic present tense is for the person given to action. Whether or not such generalizations prove to be valid, they illustrate the kind of thing group therapists can be thinking about. 3. The most dramatic of the Child vocabularies are those motivated by rebelliousness, consisting of expletives and "tough talk." These often alternate, particularly among women, with baby-talk or sugary words of over-compliance. In effect, the therapist who studies his patients carefully will find in each of them at least three different systems of voice, rhetoric, and vocabulary.

Proper listening is manifested by giving the right response, or at least knowing what response would be most gratifying to the speaker. This must be differentiated from the response the speaker has learned to expect. For example, some so-called supportive groups are set up so that a speaker learns to expect as a response what is called in transactional analysis "a marshmallow" or "gumdrop." There may be a continual interplay of outstretched psychological hands as stimuli, and marshmallow throwing as responses. This merely indicates that no one has really listened to anyone else, since the responses become stereotyped and have only a superficial relationship to the content of the stimuli. Anyone who wants people to listen to what he is really saying and to get a really pertinent answer in such a situation is likely to be disappointed.

The therapist should not be beguiled by the currently fashionable talk about nonverbal communication into forgetting the fact that it will take years of study for him to master the subtleties of verbal communication.

Being Looked Over

Since the patients will be noting everything the therapist does, in an attempt to size him up, he can make it easier for them and himself by behaving in a naturally dignified way instead of trying to hide behind a professional poker face. If he says a few words occasionally during the first hour, that will not seriously impair the patients' ability to distort his image in accordance with their needs. He will do no harm by presenting himself as a reasonably courteous, alert, interested, and enthusiastic person, but behind these spontaneous superficial characteristics a certain reserve should be maintained. His responses, however, should be from his own volition and not forced by pressure from the patients.

His conduct should be guided by aesthetics, responsibility, and commitment, all of which may be novelties to those of his patients who come from unsatisfactory homes; nor will his attention to such criteria impair his standing with those who come from more stable environments.

Aesthetics. It is evident that most clinical psychopathology is unaesthetic. Schizophrenics, manics, and depressives may be physically untidy. Many neurotics are preoccupied with untidy bedroom, bathroom, and kitchen fantasies. Psychopaths and delinquents often live in an untidy atmosphere of county jail cells, broken windows, and bloody sidewalks. Since aesthetic standards, so seldom mentioned in psychotherapy, have a strong appeal for many patients and offer an attractive motivation for recovery, the therapist may set an example by being clean, decently groomed and dressed, and graceful though not pedantic in his manners and speech.

Responsibility. The therapist can make it implicitly clear that he knows at all times to whom he is responsible and for whom he is responsible, and also that he feels a responsibility to and for himself.

Commitment. Most important of all perhaps is commitment. He should set an example to his patients of someone who has a job to do and will let nothing interfere for very long with the progress of his task. This may cause consternation and wonder in a number of patients who have perhaps never before met anyone who knew what he was doing and went about doing it in a systematic and constructive way regardless of enticements, and who could not be inveigled into abandoning his goal.

The Therapist's Idiosyncracies. Within this matrix, the therapist is bound to exhibit all sorts of idiosyncracies which the patients will be looking for and will think about and frequently exploit. He should, however, never underestimate their ability to appreciate honest effort and estimable characteristics. The therapeutic situation is better if the patient says of the therapist, "He reminds me of my nice grandmother, and he is actually decent, responsible, and committed," than if he says, "He reminds me of my nice grandmother but actually he is a slob."

In general it is more important for the group therapist to know what to do, and to let the patients see that he knows what to do, than to do nothing. For him to act as though group treatment were formal individual psychoanalysis is a pretense. They are different procedures and require different approaches.

Structuring the Group

The natural structure of the group should be accepted at face value: that is, the patients are coming to the therapist because he knows more about something than they do. Democracy has many meanings, and the best of them is that of common courtesy. Beyond this, there is no use pretending, as some therapists do, that the therapist and patients are equal in the group—if only for the obvious reason that he is getting paid for being there and they are not, and they expect and are entitled to some services while he does not have a right to expect the same from them.

If he sets up rules, he should remember that for many people in treatment groups, as in other groups, rules are there for the purpose of being circumvented. Explicit rules should be kept at a minimum, since each of them is for one-third of the patients unnecessary, for another third an opportunity for ingratiation, and for the remainder a challenge. On the other hand, without any explicit regulations, the patients will be avidly seeking from the very first hour to find out what is OK and what is not-OK in the society in which they find themselves. He will soon reveal his predilections, in spite of any efforts not to, and a formal statement will only detract from the smooth running of the group. For the greatest effectiveness, he should indicate in one way or another that what is OK is whatever furthers the therapeutic program, and what is not-OK is whatever impedes it.

The Therapist's Responsibility to Himself

In summary, then, during the first three minutes the therapist is composing himself for a unique experience, for nothing just like the impending meeting has ever happened before, and nothing just like it can ever occur again; that is, unless he allows his groups to fall into utter banality, and it is precisely to prevent such an outcome that he pays attention to what is discussed in this chapter. After clearing his mind of extraneous matters, and reminding himself of some basic principles of the healing arts, he then tries to penetrate the reality of the situation in which he finds himself. Finally he mobilizes the capacities he has carefully cultivated through years of training and experience, and sets about to exercise them to the utmost, with prudent initiative, for the maximum benefit of his patients.

In a broad sense, this is a most important chapter in this book, and a few existential remarks will serve to emphasize that its implications are even more significant than its explications so far as the decisive factor is concerned: the therapist's responsibility to himself.

The difficulty that the group therapist runs into if he wishes to become an authentic individual arises from the fact that almost anything that can be called a "therapy group" is inherently beneficial to its members. A respectable percentage of them will improve regardless of or even in spite of what the "therapist" does. Under these conditions, the "therapist" who is willing to accept consensus as a substitute for authenticity can gather with his colleagues of like mind and exchange "observations" and "technical procedures."

Therapists who allow themselves to accept such a spurious situation as their destiny are suffering from the same disability in self-confrontation as the lottery winner. All over the world, able-bodied men are sitting under trees year after year, each of them with an ever-renewed lottery ticket in his pocket, waiting for fortune to smile upon him. When one of them wins, there is a strong tendency for him to feel that it is his skill and intelligence which brought him his windfall, and many of his less lucky neighbors will concur in this opinion. The authentic professional is not content merely to accept such gifts of fortune. He wants to win every time; he is a "compulsive winner." The dilettante is not bothered in the same way as the authentic professional by his losses, that is, by patients leaving, getting worse, or staying in treatment without any visible progress. For the group therapist to be the master of his own destiny requires a commitment which misses no opportunity to learn, uses every legitimate method to win, and permits no rest until every loss has been thoroughly analyzed so that no mistake will ever be repeated.

The Therapist

The conscientious group therapist will prepare himself in two ways: professionally and personally. Professionally, he will not undertake therapeutic programs for which he is not qualified, unless he is under adequate supervision. He will not, for example, attempt psychoanalytic therapy, transactional analysis, or psychodrama unless he has had approved training in those fields* or is able to find a qualified supervisor. Personally, he will examine his motives and fortify himself against temptation or exploitation of his weaknesses.

Education. Ideally he will have had preliminary training in psychoanalytic theory and practice, transactional analysis, the principles of group therapy, and group dynamics. The training in group dynamics should come from a competent source, since this is the area in which most clinicians are weakest. It is a current fashion to consider that a knowledge of individual psychodynamics and some experience with therapy groups somehow qualifies people as group dynamicists. This is not so.

---

* If he lives in a remote area where none is available, he is reduced to assiduous reading and prudent experiment until he can take time off to obtain the necessary education.

Group dynamics is a special branch of science requiring serious study in order to attain the degree of understanding necessary for the effective leadership and control of a therapy group. In this area neither the assumptions current in clinical literature nor the basic principles of Freudian group psychology are sufficient equipment for clinical competence. Unfortunately, the modern "research" approach of social psychology and sociology is of limited value for the group therapist. Far more pertinent and realistic is the work of the older thinkers (1500–1800) as summarized by Otto Gierke in 1883.* For a more thorough clinical preparation, he should also have some acquaintance with existential therapy, gestalt therapy with its laudable emphasis on observation, modern Jungian psychology, psychodrama, and the ideas of Trigant Burrow.

Self-Examination. Optimally, the therapist should have had not only didactic training, but also personal experience as a patient in both individual and group therapy. These are the best preparations for attaining the degree of self-awareness necessary to have a full grasp of what is happening in his groups. Why it is, for example, that the same patients are more excitable or impulsive with one therapist than with another? Even if the therapist has not had an opportunity for extensive personal therapeutic experience, however, he can prepare himself if he subjects himself to a sufficiently ruthless self-examination. In fact, personal analysis or group therapy is not enough and must be supplemented by a more specific appraisal.

This specific preparation will consist of an examination of his motives for starting group therapy. First, he should be clear as to why he is using the group instead of individual therapy for his patients. It is good practice for him to write down three reasons for this choice. In most cases, these will be appropriate and convincing, and constitute the rational or Adult aspect of his motivation. Once this is settled, he should write down a fourth and fifth reason. These may be more revealing of important influences which might not otherwise be

* The present writer's book on group dynamics is also directly relevant to the problems of group treatment.

brought into the open. Some beginners discover that they are dazzled by the prospect, or that it is an act of compliance or bravado, or that it offers a unique arena for therapeutic ardor. Ambitious and "parental" drives should be dissected out as forming the Parental aspect of his motivations. Finally, he should search assiduously for archaic needs which he is "unconsciously" (in reality usually preconsciously) planning to satisfy through manipulation and exploitation. These form the Child aspect of his motivations, which is not only the most difficult to get at, but is the most important because it in the long run will usually determine the outcome of his therapeutic efforts.

Self-Correction. The Parent and Child aspects of his motivations influence the therapist much more systematically and pervasively than he may realize. It may take him several months to perceive that he is consistently acting like a jerk, a slob, or worst of all, a sulk, in his interventions. It may take even longer to become clear that almost everything he says has the exploitative quality that is characteristic of a game leading to a masked ulterior goal. In any case, the more productive question is not "Am I playing a game?" but rather "What game am I playing?" When it is discovered through supervision, for example, that a group therapist is engaged in a particular set of subversive maneuvers, this should not be a matter for surprise nor should it be taken to mean that he is unusual; rather it should be taken as a challenge and a matter for concern if a given therapist's game cannot be unmasked quickly so that self-corrective measures can be applied.

The therapist's attitude in this regard should be that of the professional rather than the amateur. He should not assume that until proven otherwise his behavior will be irreproachable, but should find out ahead of time in what respects it is likely to depart from the ideal, so that he can correct for them from the beginning. His position is analogous to that of a navigator: it is only the amateur who expects his compass to point due north; the professional assumes that there will be a deviation and wants to know what correction he should apply every time he takes a reading. In this sense the therapist, before undertaking group therapy, should "calibrate" himself so that at all times he knows in which direction he should make corrections.

Types of Therapists

As already mentioned, each therapist has his favorite game which it is his duty to become aware of and take steps to avoid during his therapeutic operations. Beginners, however, do not always have sufficient insight to do this properly. Every supervisor becomes familiar with certain typical game-like attitudes prevalent among psychiatric residents and psychology and social work trainees. A descriptive characterization of some of the commoner ones is given below. The descriptions are of extreme cases, but most residents have a little of each of these in them, and it is a good idea to break up these tendencies in the second or third year so that the underlying talents can begin to manifest themselves free of such hampering attacks.

*Phallus in Wonderland.** This man approaches his patients as though they were exotic creatures from another planet, and is continually astonished because they behave the way the book says they will. He is a staunch admirer of his own skill and perspicacity, and if nothing really happens with his patients he knows that his public will understand. He is a devoted disciple of Freud, and as one of the sorcerer's chosen apprentices he is fascinated by the strange antics of parapeople and their interesting reactions to his incantations. It takes a ruthless supervisor to shatter his dreamy world by telling him that patients are people too, and that in fact he may be the paraperson and they the real ones.

The Delegate. This man knows the answers, and if his patients do not get better no one can criticize *him*. He has the whole weight of the psychoanalytic traditions behind him. Although Freud has not yet sent him a personal message to that effect, he knows that the old man would not find fault with anything he has

* The writer first heard this expression under the most poignant circumstances from E. H. Erikson.

done. If he runs into misfortune with a patient, he is sure that his sympathetic colleagues would agree that sometimes it is like casting pearls before swine. The supervisor has to tell him that it is more like doing twirls without a spine.

The Smiling Rebel. This man is late for conferences and appointments, but it does not bother him, so why should it bother anyone else? He is doing his own thinking. His teachers are parapeople who are so preoccupied with their own square ideas that they miss things obvious to him. Some day he will be grown-up like them, and then the public will listen to what he has to say. In the meantime he can quietly carry on his experiments, throwing in a word occasionally to let people know he has something cooking without necessarily telling them precisely what it is. Someone has to tell him that he is already grown-up and must be punctual. He really ought to tell his supervisor about the experiments.

The Patient Clinician. He is never flustered and never raises his voice. Psychotherapists are parapeople, but they are entitled to laugh occasionally just like real people—only for a few seconds, however, and then they must get back to work. He says what he has to say calmly and deliberately, but often his colleagues are not as rational as he is and do not follow his advice. Patients usually follow it, but if they do not they must be gently persuaded to see the error of their ways. He gets along well with alcoholics and in fact has often thought of taking a drink himself. Since he will probably get along in his own way, it is perhaps best for his supervisor to listen and say nothing.

The Jargon Juggler. Nobody knows the homosexual sadistic Oedipal incorporation resistance better than he does. His patients are wonderously transistorized robots with human bodies just like his own, and they are completely unaware of their underlying motivations. The one who says, "Hello, I just came from work and I'm sort of tired, do you have a cigarette?" does not realize that he has initiated an interview, traveled from his place of employment, complained of fatigue, and attempted to manipulate the therapist. Naturally, after his phallic drivenness, the patient regresses to hypochondriacal self-pity, sucking on a breast-baby-feces symbol cigarette borrowed because of maternal transference. All this may be very true, but the beginning therapist is only guessing. The supervisor has to tell him to take one thing at a time, not to guess, and above all to try to say it in Anglo-Saxon words of no more than two syllables.

The Conservative. The man knows better than to break a silence, or to interrupt when a patient may be about to prepare to express affect. His patients often complain that the group sessions are boring, but they do not realize what a serious matter psychotherapy is. He himself is not bored because he is too busy gripping the arms of his chair or keeping his back muscles tense. There is nothing exactly wrong with his staff presentations but somehow they lack impact. No one criticizes him because there is nothing to criticize, and besides they have all made more mistakes than he has. The supervisor has to encourage him to experiment: break a silence occasionally and see what happens, or take the initiative away from the patients maybe just once every two or three sessions, and observe the effect.

The Hypochondriac. He cannot try anything new because it makes him uncomfortable. It does not occur to him that he is not there to be comfortable, but to treat his patients. He rationalizes his neophobia on the grounds that he cannot do a good job if he is uncomfortable. When he was on surgery (one assumes), gloves and gowns made him uncomfortable, and he explained to the chief that he could not do good surgery unless he was comfortable. Perhaps the chief said, "Oh, my, I wouldn't want one of my residents to be uncomfortable, do come into the operating room bare-handed in your street-clothes." More likely the chief said, "If you're uncomfortable with surgical techniques, perhaps you had best transfer to some other branch of medicine, such as psychiatry." The supervisor should tell him that if he is not comfortable with the best possible technique, he should either get comfortable, or else transfer to some other branch of medicine, such as surgery.

PREPARING THE SCENE

The Contracts

The group therapist is subject to the same two types of contracts as the practitioner in any field of treatment: one referring to organizational practice, the other to private practice. The complexities of organizational practice will be considered first. The organizational therapist has a double responsibility—on the one hand to his organization and on the other to his patients. Each of these aspects should be clarified separately before a synthesis is attempted.

The Administrative Contract. If the therapist or his organization proposes to do group therapy, the first step is to have an understanding as to the occasions for and purposes of the project and the organizational goals. In some agencies these are stated in writing and perhaps set forth by law. During the preliminary discussions, the law or other directives should be read aloud in the presence of all those interested in furthering the project. A personal, detailed knowledge of all pertinent directives may avoid later difficulties with supervisors or higher authorities. If there are no written directives, then the supervisor should be persuaded to make a formal, unequivocal statement of the purpose of the project. This basic discussion may employ terms which are essentially sociological, such as "rehabilitation" and "remission," and the local understanding of those terms should be elucidated. There should also be a clear understanding and firm commitments concerning problems of finance, personnel, facilities, and equipment.

The Professional Contract. After the administrative aspects are settled, the next problem is the professional goal of the therapy, which will be stated in psychiatric terms such as "symptomatic cure," "personality reorganization," "social control," " reorientation," or "psychoanalysis." The local meaning of such terms should again be agreed upon even at the risk of appearing pedantic, for this is preferable to being vague at this point.

The Psychological Contract. This concerns personal needs of supervisors, superiors, and colleagues, of which they themselves may or may not be aware, but which it is within the professional province of the therapist to assess. It is of decisive importance for the therapist to formulate these factors to himself, drawing upon his personal knowledge of the individuals concerned, but he must not of course refer aloud, even jokingly, to this aspect, except to people who are fully competent and fully prepared to understand its significance. The meaning of the psychological contract will be clearer later after the reader becomes familiar with some of the "games" commonly played by the staff members of clinical agencies. For the present, a provocative paradox will serve to illustrate the point. A very effective therapist who discharged his patients much more rapidly than any of his colleagues did, might be disappointed to find that instead of being congratulated on all sides, he was regarded as a "controversial figure," even though the administrative and professional contracts explicitly encouraged effective therapy. They might treat him as though he had broken some unspoken "gentleman's agreement" which was different from and perhaps even in conflict with the stated goals. As one hard-headed therapist put it: "My problem is, how effective can I be without getting fired?" By this he meant that in his new job the unstated psychological contract must be considered along with the stated "job description."

Organizational Needs. In this area also lies the problem of how conservative or daring the therapist should be in his therapeutic efforts in a given organization. If he is too daring, he may have a high withdrawal rate and more "incidents," and this may arouse uneasiness in his superiors, and bring censure on himself, even though he might get quicker and better results with a larger proportion of patients than his more conservative colleagues do.

The Authority Diagram. In order to consider systematically these three aspects of the organizational contract—the administrative, the professional, and the psychological—the therapist should draw an informal "authority diagram," including everyone inside the organization and as much of the external hierarchy (the Mother Group) as possible. For example, a complete authority diagram of a federal agency would start with the elevator operators and receptionists (who might be giving various patients friendly advice from time to time), go up through the medical staff and director, and then jump to the hierarchy in Washington right up to the President (to whom a patient might appeal by letter or through an interested organization). In the case of a state hospital, the authority diagram should include the state department of mental health, and above that, the governor. The therapist should surmise which aspects each person in this hierarchy would consider the therapist's responsibility, and what each of them would (and would not) expect from the group therapy program. He should then formulate plans for meeting or dealing with these expectations.

While at first sight such thoroughness might seem to be superfluous, anyone who recalls vividly the many sensational occurrences and investigations in mental health agencies in recent years will appreciate its value. Any unfortunate happening in a public agency may be subjected to pitiless and often unsympathetic scrutiny by a crusading press. A certain type of oversight on the therapist's part, taken together with other oversights in other programs of the same agency, might result in someone in the hierarchy losing his job. The therapist must therefore consider all these possibilities and clarify for himself where his responsibilities lie and what compromises he is willing or unwilling to make in balancing rapid therapeutic progress against other factors.

The Therapist-Patient Contract. The therapist's contract with the patients will have the same aspects as the organizational contract—administrative, professional, and psychological. At the administrative level, he should explain to the patients the relationship between himself, the organization, and themselves. He should consider not only what he intends to convey to them, but also how they are likely from their side to understand his organizational role and responsibilities.

At the professional level, the most acute question is

whether the therapeutic goals will conflict with the patient's understanding of the administrative contract, particularly if he is receiving material aid from the agency or from some other agency. He may be in a dilemma between getting better and losing the material aid, or staying sick in order to continue receiving it. This dilemma strongly influences the psychological aspect of the therapist-patient contract, the "games" which are likely to be played in the group. There are often good grounds for doubting whether the patients will be able to adhere consistently to their declarations of good faith. This dilemma may require a frontal attack before therapy can proceed. Similar considerations apply in hospitals and clinics of the armed services, where the question of returning to duty, whether hazardous or not, becomes a decisive consideration in the patient's mind; and obversely, in correctional institutions where the patient's release is the critical item.

It is, therefore, important in such situations that the therapist-patient contract be clarified realistically, first in the therapist's mind and then with the patients. The therapist's commitment to them ("My job here is to . . .") and their commitment to him ("My reason for coming to this group is to . . .") should be stated unequivocally, so that any shilly-shallying on either side can immediately be brought into question as a possible breach of good faith, with the focus on the hidden ambiguities which now stand revealed. If such clarification is made a bilateral obligation, the therapist may be pleasantly surprised at how much he can learn about his own motivations under the critical scrutiny of patients who are thus put on their mettle.

Unless all three aspects of these two contracts—that with the organization and that with the patients—are considered beforehand, the therapist may find himself taken by surprise at a later date, with the loss of a considerable investment of time and energy. At this initial stage, above all, there is no place for naiveté and uncritical acceptance of unspecific assurances of good will. The therapist should stand skeptically, even cynically, aloof until he has used his clinical knowledge to assess the real goals of all the parties concerned, including himself. Only after he has attained full awareness of the possibilities can he afford the luxury of being a good fellow.

Private Practice. In private practice the situation is different. There the responsibility of the therapist is almost exclusively to the patient; the possible impact of authorities external to the group itself is so unlikely that no reasonably circumspect practitioner need take them into account under ordinary conditions. There is essentially no organizational contract beyond that contained in his Code of Ethics, unless fees are paid by an outside organization, in which case their regulations may prove hampering in some respects. In such cases, the contract with the intruding organization should be treated like any other organizational contract. In "pure" private practice, the contract with the patient is favorably influenced by the fact that the patient is seeking treatment on his own initiative, and his overt motivation at least—the alleviation of his suffering—is usually in good faith.

Even in "pure" private practice, however, the therapist should examine the contractual situation carefully. If the patient's bills are being paid by another individual (as in the case of minors, for example) or he comes for treatment under pressure (as is frequent in cases of impending divorce or excessive drinking), the therapist may find himself involved in a "three-handed game" in which he may end up holding the busted hand and lose not only the patient but his fee as well. He should therefore make sure that all parties directly concerned understand clearly both the practical demands of the therapeutic situation (the administrative contract) and the limitations and potentialities of what his treatment has to offer (the professional contract). In this way the therapist is least likely to be hurt professionally and financially and is more free to devote himself to the psychological aspects of the contract which become part of the therapeutic struggle.

Conclusion

This last section is a catalogue of useful Bernian information. A complete bibliography of Berne's writings, a biography, and a glossary of Transactional Analysis terms. It is our hope that having read this collection of Eric Berne's writings the reader will have a well-rounded understanding of his contribution. Some readers will wish to read on. We believe that those who do should go to the original sources. Either way we hope we have managed to represent Eric Berne fairly and completely. Eric Berne's contribution goes far beyond what could possibly be included in an anthology of this sort. His writings were only part of his work. He also founded and organized a large movement which includes the International Transactional Analysis Organization by which by now reaches into every corner of people's consciousness in this country.

Eric Berne has changed the face of psychiatry in the United States; the concepts of contracts, strokes, transaction, games, and script have become common parlance in the field and the whole theory is now given serious consideration by established training institutions. His work could possibly in the future change the face of psychiatry all over the world. His views, which are becoming more and more accepted, have established in the minds of people the possibility that all emotional disturbance can be cured because everyone is basically OK. His contribution along with the contributions of other of his contemporaries, such as Carl Rogers, Abraham Maslow, Fritz Perls, and R. D. Laing, have humanized the practice of psychotherapy and advanced it toward being truly a service to people.

—C.S.

Eric Berne: Annotated Bibliography

Prepared by
ROBERT M. CRANMER, B.A., B.A.

1939A BERNSTEIN, E. LENNARD "Psychiatry in Syria." *Am. J. Psychiatry* 95: 1415-1419, 1939. Describes in detail the limited psychiatric treatment facilities and lack of trained personnel in 1938-39 Syria and Lebanon.

1939B ———— "Psychiatric Aspects of Porencephaly." *Am. J. Psychiatry* 96: 723-731, 1939. Seven epileptic cases admitted to the psychiatric clinic at Yale School of Medicine proved to have unsuspected lesions. Diagnosis of porencephaly should not be ruled out in any case of epilepsy.

1940 ———— "Who Was Condom?" *Human Fertility* 5: 172-176, 1940. What was the origin of the name? Most probably an English Col. Condom. The legends attached to him are researched with humor and wit.

1941 BERNSTEIN, ERIC L. and FEITELSON, NORMAN "Apprehension and Pain: The Practical Introspections of a Psychiatrist." *J. Am. Dental Assoc.* 28: 1129-1132, 1941. Berne and his dentist explore the psychological effects of the dentist's drill and present some ideas which may help the dental profession.

1944 BERNE, ERIC "The Problem of Masturbation." *Diseases of the Nervous System*, V: 3-7, 1944. Information is offered therapists in the following areas: 1) What constitutes normal masturbatory practices; 2) Determination of whether patient needs further treatment; and 3) How to treat various anxieties stemming from masturbation.

1946 Capt. BERNE, E., Lt. Col. STILES, MERRIT H.,

and Maj. PIKE, GEORGE M., Med. Corps., AUS. "Diagnosis of Acute Porphyria." *Northwest Medicine*, Seattle, 45: No. 3, 166, 1946. (Unavailable for annotation.)

1947 BERNE, ERIC *The Mind in Action.* Simon and Schuster. New York, 1947. Berne's first book. Revised in 1957, it became *A Layman's Guide to Psychiatry and Psychoanalysis;* third edition published 1968.

1949A ——— "The Nature of Intuition." *Psychiatric Quart.* 23: 203-226, 1949. The initial article in Berne's series of six on intuition. Describes the process, gives various examples of his successful use of intuition, and summarizes his knowledge of it.

1949B ——— "Some Oriental Mental Hospitals." *Am. J. Psychiatry* 106: 376-383, 1949. This is a detailed, objective description of staff, treatment, physical conditions, patients, and results of treatment in mental hospitals in Manila, Hong Kong, Bangkok, Singapore, Colombo, Madras, Bombay, Yeravda, and four in Turkey.

1950 ——— "Cultural Aspects of a Multiple Murder." *Psychiatric Quart. Supp.* 24: 250-269, 1950. A Filipino "ran amuck" and killed five men. Why? The case is studied in terms of the murderer's ancient tribal customs, childhood experiences, environment, and religious instruction.

1952 ——— "Concerning the Nature of Diagnosis." *Int. Rec. Med.* 165: 283-292, 1952. No. 2 in the Intuition series. Diagnosis is dependent, to some definite degree, on the use of intuition. Examples of the use of intuition in diagnostics are given and the intuitive process is further analyzed.

1953A ——— "Concerning the Nature of Communication." *Psychiatric Quart.* 27: 185-198, 1953. No. 3 in the Intuition series. Any emission of energy which affects an organism may be called a communication, provided it is understood by the receiver. "Noise" often tells more to the receiver than does the "information."

1953B ——— "Principles of Group Psychotherapy." *Indian J. Neurol. & Psychiat.* 4: 119-137, 1953.

(Annotation at this time not possible due to un-availability of publication.)

1954 ———— "The Natural History of a Spontaneous Therapy Group." *Int. J. Group Psychother.* 4: 74-85, 1954. This reports on Berne's second major experience in formal group therapy, following 18 months of group therapy in the Army. "Spontaneous" means members started the group without referral from a doctor. Berne reflects on this successful 5-year-long group experience.

1955A ———— "Intuition IV: Primal Images and Primal Judgment." *Psychiatric Quart.* 29: 634-658, 1955. The primal image and the primal judgment defined. Primal images are sometimes activated in interpersonal relationships and are related to the information of basic judgments concerning people encountered. The clinical value of using primal judgments is discussed.

1955B ———— "Group Attendance: Clinical and Theoretical Considerations." *Int. J. Group Psychother.* 5: 392-403, 1955. This unpremeditated study contradicted almost all of Berne's impressions concerning attendance at therapy groups. The tabulations reveal some remarkable consistencies among 5 groups studied.

1956A ———— "Comparative Psychiatry and Tropical Psychiatry." *Am. J. Psychiat.* 113: 193-200, 1956. Comparative psychiatry defined as the study of psychiatric problems in one group as compared to those in another group. Results of such studies indicated that illness and treatments are similar in various parts of the world.

1956B ———— "The Psychological Structure of Space With Some Remarks on Robinson Crusoe." *Psychoanalytic Quart.* 25: 549-567, 1956. Interests in exploration, measurement, or utilization of space are sublimations, respectively, of oral, anal, and phallic attitudes.

1957A ———— *A Layman's Guide to Psychiatry and Psychoanalysis.* Simon and Schuster, New York, 1957; third edition published in 1968. Originally published as *The Mind in Action*, 1947.

1957B ———— "Ego States in Psychotherapy." *Am. J.*

Psychother. 11:293-309, 1957. Structural analysis is presented as a new psychotherapeutic approach.

1957C ———— "Intuition V: The Ego Image." *Psychiatric Quart.* 31: 611-627, 1957. The ego image refers to an ego state. Berne gives clinical examples of the value of ego states as guiding influences in therapy, recognizing the importance of separating "adult" from "child."

1957D ———— "The Mythology of Dark and Fair: Psychiatric Use of Folklore." *J. Amer. Folklore* (1957?) Analysis of racism; "White is good—black is evil." Black and white are contrasted in the many ways this myth has affected our lives since 3066 B.C. A case is presented of a Spanish-American woman who suffered severely from having dark skin.

1958A ———— "Transactional Analysis: A New and Effective Method of Group Therapy." *Am. J. Psychother.* 12:735-743, 1958. First published appearance of the term, "transactional analysis." A seminal article.

1958B ———— "Group Therapy Abroad." *Int. J. Group Psychother.* 8:466-470, 1958. Evidence tends to show the nature of psychiatric disorders and the response of patients to various forms of treatment is uniform throughout mankind. The therapeutic value of group therapy appears to be one of these universals.

1959A ———— "Principles of Transactional Analysis." *Indian J. Psychiatry*, pp. 215-221, received for publication August 1, 1959. Berne wrote this as a corresponding member of the Indian Psychiatric Society.

1959B "Psychiatric Epidemiology of the Fiji Islands." In *Progress in Psychotherapy*, Vol. 4. Grune & Stratton, New York, 1959: pp. 310-313. Statistics tend to indicate "the stress of modern life" does not increase the tendency to seek psychiatric hospitalization.

1959C ———— "Difficulties of Comparative Psychiatry: The Fiji Islands." *Am. J. Psychiatry* 116:104-109, 1959. Certain interpretations of Fiji Island psychiatric data which tend to give false conclusions are discussed in detail.

1960A BERNE, E., STARRELS, R. J., and TRINCHERO, A. "Leadership Hunger in a Therapy Group." *AMA Archives of General Psychiatry*, 2:75-80, 1960. In an experimental situation the absence of the leader for three consecutive meetings caused deterioration of the group performance and indicated profound psychological dependence on the leader.

1960B BERNE, E. " 'Psychoanalytic' Versus 'Dynamic' Group Therapy." *Int. J. Group Psychother.* 10:98-103, 1960. Psychoanalysis and group therapy are two different therapies and need to be understood as such, especially by group therapists. Call group therapy "psychodynamic" or "dynamic," but not "psychoanalytic."

1960C ———— "The Cultural Problem: Psychopathology in Tahiti." *Am. J. Psychiatry* 116:1076-1081, 1960. The tendency to relate so-called "cultural factors" to mental illness is open to question.

1960D ———— "A Psychiatric Census of the South Pacific." *Am. J. Psychiatry* 117:44-47, 1960. The prevalence of South Pacific psychiatric disorders and the incidence of hospital admissions are discussed.

1961A ———— *Transactional Analysis in Psychotherapy.* Grove Press, New York, 1961. The first book devoted entirely to TA.

1961B ———— "Cultural Factors in Group Therapy." *Int. Ment. Health Res. Newsletter.* 3:3-4, 1961. (Annotation not possible at this time due to unavailability of the publication.)

1962A ———— "Intuition VI: The Psychodynamics of Intuition." *Psychiatric Quart.* 36:294-300, 1962. Internal conditions within an individual promote or interfere with the workings of the intuitive process.

1962B ———— "In Treatment." *Transactional Anal. Bull.* 1:10, 1962. Treatment proceeds in 3 stages for the patient: 1) Child assesses therapist as potential Parent; 2) Child divorces therapist's Parent, accepts therapist's Adult; 3) Child accepts own Adult as substitute for therapist's Adult.

1962C ———— "Teaching Group Therapy." *Transactional Anal. Bull.* 1:11, 1962. In the Berne advanced Seminar, single transactions, one single stimulus and one ensuing response, are played on the tape recorder; members then make predictions and deductions about the agent and respondent.

1962D ———— "The Obesity 'Problem.'" *Transactional Anal. Bull.* 1:11, 1962. "Obesity" is like "Alcoholic"; it is a four-handed game with one who is It plus three others who are Persecutor, Patsy and Rescuer, respectively.

1962E BERNE, E., BIRNBAUM, R., POINDEXTER, R., and ROSENFELD, B. "Institutional Games." *Transactional Anal. Bull.* 1:12, 1962. In social agencies if clients are rehabilitated too quickly the case load drops to a threateningly low level. The question asked by an eager worker is "How efficient can I be without getting fired?"

1962F BERNE, E. "Classification of Positions." *Transactional Anal. Bull.* 1:23, 1962. The four basic OK-Not OK positions are presented for the first time in published form.

1963A ———— *The Structure and Dynamics of Organizations and Groups.* J. B. Lippincott Co., Philadelphia, 1963; Grove-Evergreen Press, 1966, New York. The second major book of TA theory and practice.

1963B HAIBERG, G., SEFNESS, W. R., and BERNE, E. "Destiny and Script Choices." *Transactional Anal. Bull.* 2:59-60, 1963. Each individual has four destiny choices which correspond to the four basic positions.

1964A BERNE, E. *Games People Play.* Grove Press, New York, 1964. World-famous best seller describes the games Berne had observed and classified up to this time.

1964B ———— "The Intimacy Experiment." *Transactional Anal. Bull.* 3:113, 1964. Two persons with valid TA clinical experience sit in chairs facing each other, their faces less than 20 inches apart. A referee with similar TA knowledge is on hand. Withdrawal, rituals, pastimes, activities and games must be avoided. Will intimacy result? This experience has been "unforgettable" in some cases.

1964C ——— "More About Intimacy." *Transactional Anal. Bull.* 3:125, 1964. This follow-up on "The Intimacy Experiment" described in 1964B goes into more detail regarding the experiment methods and the kinds of communication considered legitimate.

1964D ——— "Trading Stamps." *Transactional Anal. Bull.* 3:127, 1964. Transactional trading stamps are introduced for the first time in published form.

1964E ——— "Pathological Significance of Games." *Transactional Anal. Bull.* 3:160, 1964. Games are pathological. For every game there is a healthy (Adult) alternative. How the transactional analysis approach can effect a stable "cure" for a game remains to be demonstrated.

1964F ——— "Principles of Transactional Analysis." In *Current Psychiatric Therapies,* Vol. IV, pp. 35-45, Grune and Stratton, New York, 1964. This article, essentially a simple outline of TA, was adapted from a paper presented at the APA annual meeting in St. Louis, 1963.

1964G ——— "Review: Four Books on Group Therapy." *Am. J. Orthopsychiat.* 34:584-589, 1964. In this detailed review, parts of each of these books are considered by Berne to be valuable additions to the therapist's knowledge.

1966A ——— "The Public Eye." *Transactional Anal. Bull.* 4: 81, 1965; 5: 101-102, 1966; 5: 132, 1966. The book *Games People Play* put Berne in the public eye. In this three-part article he discusses three hazards for the benefit of others who may find themselves in a similar position.

1966B ——— "Recent Advances in Transactional Analysis." In *Current Psychiatric Therapies,* Vol. VI, 1966. Also in *Transactional Anal. Bull.* 6: 27, 1967. Having used TA for a number of years Berne now defines new discoveries in the areas of personality structure, transactions, games and rackets, scripts, and therapy.

1966C ——— *Principles of Group Treatment.* Oxford University Press, New York, 1966. Berne's most recent book on TA theory and practice. Paperback available from Grove Press, New York, 1966.

1967A ———— BERNE, E. and others as discussants. "Characterological Aspects of Marital Interaction." *Psychoanalytic Forum*. 2: 7-29, 1967. The writer compares the simple language of TA with the long words and obscure psychological terms used by the author of the article being discussed. It is clearly shown how the TA approach provides a way to understand and help solve marital problems.

1967B ———— BERNE, E., and others. Symposium on Game Theory and Theater. *Tulane Drama Review*. Vol. II, No. 4 (Summer Issue), 1967. (Unavailable for annotation.)

1968A ———— "Staff-Patient Staff Conferences." *Am. J. Psychiatry* 125: 286-293, 1968. Describes a procedure whereby, following a ward meeting or group therapy session, the staff holds its professional conference—including treatment planning—in the presence of the patients. If certain listed rules are followed and each member of the staff speaks frankly and to the point, patients of all ages and diagnostic categories are almost unanimously appreciative. A few staff members find this procedure distasteful while others find it congenial, stimulating, and therapeutically valuable.

1968B ———— "History of the ITAA: 1958-1968." *Transactional Anal. Bull.* 7:19-20, 1968. These first 10 years saw the spread and growth of TA as an international therapeutic method.

1968C ———— *The Happy Valley*. Grove Press, New York, 1968. A children's book about a python named Shardlu who earns a living by being nice to people on Tuesday night and Friday morning. Berne's first children's book.

1968D ———— *A Layman's Guide to Psychiatry and Psychoanalysis*. Simon and Schuster, New York, Third Edition, 1968.

1969A ———— "Editor's Page." *Transactional Anal. Bull.* 8: 7-8, 1969. There are two crusades to undertake: 1) Lower the infant mortality rate and 2) Increase our esthetic standards.

1969B ———— "Introduction to Reparenting in Schizophrenia." *Transactional Anal. Bull.* 8: 45-47, 1969. One element in curing a schizophrenic was missing from the TA approach of transactional analysis, game analysis, and script analysis—namely *re-parenting*, using boldness, theoretical clarity, and devotion. "This the Schiffs have done."

1969C POINDEXTER, W. RAY and BERNE, ERIC, "Games Prevent Social Progress." In *Hemmende Structuren in der heutigen Industriegesellschaft.* ("Inhibiting Structures in Today's Industrial Society.") Buchdruckerei. Schuck Sohne AB, Rusch-likon ZH; Switzerland, 1969, pp. 153-170. Mr. Poindexter presented this paper in English at an international symposium, Zurich, Switzerland, on March 7, 1969. The book has been published only in German.

1969D BERNE, ERIC. "Reply to Dr. Shapiro's Critique." *Psychological Reports*, 25: 478, 1969. Accepted for publication Sept. 4, 1969. Berne replies to a paper by Shapiro critical of TA (1969). He clarifies the concepts of ego states, inner dialogue, and "growth" in a sharp, effective reply.

1970A ———— "Eric Berne as Group Therapist." *Transactional Anal. Bull.* 9: 75-83, 1970. Transcription of taped therapy session conducted by Berne at a closed ward of McAuley Neuropsychiatric Institute at St. Mary's Hospital, San Francisco, 1970. The observer method is used with two groups alternating as "patients" and "observers."

1970B ———— *Sex in Human Loving.* Simon & Schuster, New York, 1970. Published November 1970, serialized in the *Ladies Home Journal* beginning October 1970. Based on the Jake Gimbel Sex Lectures, Univ. of California Medical Center, San Francisco, 1966.

1971 ———— *What Do You Say After You Say Hello?* Grove Press, New York, 1972. The biggest book on TA theory and practice Berne wrote; features a comprehensive discussion of scripts and how they function.

Eric Berne: Biographical Sketch
by WARREN D. CHENEY, M.A., M.A.

EARLY LIFE AND EDUCATION

Born May 10, 1910 at his family home, 73 Saint
Famille Street in Montreal, Eric Berne was the son
of general practitioner David Hillel Bernstein, M.D.,
and Sarah Gordon Bernstein, a professional writer and
editor. There was one sibling 5 years his junior, a sister
named Grace, now Mrs. Arthur Rose.

Both Eric's mother and father graduated from Mc-
Gill University; Dr. Bernstein practiced as a physician
with an office on the ground floor of his house (no
longer standing).* Eric was very close to his father,
spoke fondly of days as a small boy when he was
allowed to make rounds with his father, house-to-house,
in a sleigh in the snow. When the doctor died at 38 of
tuberculosis, Eric, 9 years old, took the loss very hard.
Sarah Gordon Bernstein took over support of her two
young children, earning the living working as an editor
and writer. She became very ambitious for Eric, encouraged him to enter medicine, which he did, receiving his B.A. at age 21, his M.D. and C.M. (Master of
Surgery) at 25, from McGill in 1935.

PRE-WAR YEARS

At this point Eric turned his sights toward America,
went to Englewood Hospital, Englewood, New Jersey,

Copyright © 1971 The International Transactional Analysis
Association, Inc. Reprinted by permission of the ITAA.

* Dr. Bernstein was a successful and compassionate Jewish
physician, who, in order to serve the poor, founded and devoted his life to a free clinic in a Jewish neighborhood.

—C. S.

to intern. In 1936 he started psychiatric residency in the Psychiatric Clinic of Yale University School of Medicine where he worked for two years. His first appointment was at Mt. Sinai Hospital, New York City, with the title, Clinical Assistant in Psychiatry, a post he held from 1941 to 1943, when he went into the Army Medical Corps.

Although exact dates for two major changes in his life are lacking at this writing, we know he became an American citizen sometime during 1938–1939 and soon thereafter shortened his name, Eric Lennard Bernstein, to Eric Berne.

By 1940 he had established private practice in Norwalk, Connecticut, where he met and married his first wife by whom he had two children, Ellen and Peter. He also practiced concurrently in New York City, 1940–43, commuting from his home in Westport where Ruth (now Mrs. Ruth Manning), still lives.

In 1941 he began training as a psychoanalyst at the New York Psychoanalytic Institute, became an analysand of Paul Federn. During the war years he began thinking analytically, critically about psychiatry and psychoanalysis and started making notes for his first book, *The Mind in Action,* a critical survey of those two subjects, which was published in 1947.

MEDICAL CORPS, AUS

The demand for army psychiatrists during World War II led him to enter the AUS Medical Corps where he served from 1943 to 1945, rising from 1st Lt. to Major. During the latter two years he began practicing group therapy, with civilians, at Ogden, Utah, in addition to conducting group therapy in the psychiatric wards of Bushnell General Army Hospital.

The year 1946 marked more than one significant change, more than one major step in the professional career. Upon release from uniform, bachelor Berne decided to relocate in California and chose seaside Carmel as the town, an area he had fallen in love with during the days when he was stationed at nearby Fort Ord. Before the year was out he had completed the manuscript of *The Mind in Action* and signed a contract for its publication with Simon and Schuster of New York. The same year marked resumption of training in psychoanalysis, this time at San Francisco Psychoanalytic Institute. In 1947 he became the analysand of Erik Erikson, with whom he worked for two years.

FAMILY LIFE IN CALIFORNIA

The choice of Erikson for his analyst, totally satisfactory professionally, turned out to be something less than pleasurable personally inasmuch as soon after Eric got started with the famous man, he met a lovely divorcee named Dorothy De Mass Way and almost immediately decided to marry her. "No," said the analyst, "not until you have finished your didactic analysis with me!" So it was not until 1949 that Eric and Dorothy exchanged vows and bought a roomy house on Carpenter Street in Carmel. Dorothy brought three children to the marriage, Robin, Janice and Roxanna. In 1952 she and her husband had their first son, Ric, and in 1955 a second son, Terry, which made a total of five children in the Berne family. In addition Ellen (now Mrs. Victor Calcaterra) and Peter started coming to Carmel during vacations, making seven.

Eric loved the pater familias role, relished the large group of offspring, and tended to be, if anything, overly permissive, a nurturing parent more often than an authoritarian one. But he knew how to protect the writing operation. He had a small isolated writer's study built at the far southern end of the large garden, well out of earshot of seven healthy youngsters. It was in that little study where most of his writing was done between the years 1949 and 1964 when he and Dorothy divorced, on the friendliest of terms.

During these years Eric set a demanding pace for himself. He took an appointment in 1950 as Assistant Psychiatrist at Mt. Zion Hospital, San Francisco, and simultaneously began serving as a Consultant to the Surgeon General of the U.S. Army. In 1951 he added the job of Adjunct and Attending Psychiatrist at the Veterans Administration Mental Hygiene Clinic, San

Francisco, these three appointments being carried out in addition to private practice both in Carmel and San Francisco.

As a result, Eric's work week virtually from the outset of his Carmel days began on Mondays and ended on Sundays. For example, Monday morning he saw patients in his Carmel office, Monday afternoon he traveled to San Francisco. Tuesday morning he spent at St. Mary's Hospital there, Tuesday afternoon he saw patients; and beginning in 1950–51 he spent Tuesday evening conducting his seminar. Wednesday he was back in the hospital, or during the 1960–70 days, lecturing at Langley Porter, University of California School of Medicine. Wednesday afternoon patients, Wednesday evening teaching the TA 101 course, Thursday morning at Stanford or working with private patients, traveled back to Carmel Thursday afternoon. Thursday evening he conducted the Monterey TA Seminar. Friday he wrote, Friday evening beginning in 1951, poker at his house, every week without fail. Weekends were devoted to writing. The winter of 1969–70 he was working on six books at once.

BREAK WITH PSYCHOANALYSIS
AND THE CREATION OF TA

The development of Berne's iconoclastic thinking and the breakaway from orthodox psychoanalysis is a fascinating story. Probably the most significant traces of transactional analysis' origins are contained in the first five of the series of six articles Berne wrote on intuition. (Berne 1949A, 1952, 1953A, 1955A, 1957C. See the article "Eric Berne's studies of Intuition," by Dusay.) The first article, "The Nature of Intuition," reveals the subject was originally dealt with in a paper read before the annual joint meeting of the San Francisco and Los Angeles Psychoanalytic Societies, October 1947. Already, at that early date when he was still working hard to gain the status of psychoanalyst, he was daring to defy a rigid Freudian concept in stating "the word *subconscious* is acceptable since it includes both the pre-conscious and the unconscious" (Berne 1949A, p. 1).

When Berne began training in 1941 at the New York Psychoanalytic Institute he must have been convinced that gaining the title "psychoanalyst" was a goal thoroughly worth reaching. After the war when he resumed psychoanalytic training at the San Francisco Psychoanalytic Institute he still deemed the goal worth striving for, and strive he did for another ten years. Yet in the end that coveted title was withheld, his 1956 application for membership turned down with a verdict to the effect that he was not yet ready, but, perhaps, after three or four more years of personal analysis and training he might apply again.

An individual who was intimate witness to Eric's reaction to the turn-down, namely Mrs. Dorothy Berne, reported that the rejection was devastating but cathartic, spurring him to intensify the long-standing ambition to add something new to psychoanalysis. Almost at once he set avidly to work, determined to develop a new approach to psychotherapy by himself, without benefit of blessings or support from the psychoanalytic fraternity.

The speed with which he accomplished that feat is astonishing. Before 1956 was out he had written two germinal papers based on material read earlier that year at the Psychiatric Clinic, Mt. Zion Hospital, San Francisco, and at the Langley Porter Neuropsychiatric Clinic, U.C. Medical School, viz. "Intuition V: The Ego Image" (Berne 1957C, written before 1957B), and "Ego States in Psychotherapy" (Berne 1957B).

Using references to Paul Federn, Eugen Kahn and H. Sliberer, Eric in the first article indicated how he arrived at the concept of ego states and where he got the idea of separating "adult" from "child." In the next article he developed the tri-partite schema used today, namely *Parent, Adult* and *Child*, introduced the three-circle method of diagramming them, showed how to sketch contaminations, C-A, and P-A, labeled the theory "*structural analysis*" and termed it "a new psychotherapeutic approach." The third article, written a few months later, was first presented at the

Western Regional Meeting of the American Group Psychotherapy Association, in Los Angeles, November 1957, by invitation, carrying the title, "Transactional Analysis: A New and Effective Method of Group Therapy." With the publication of this paper in the *American Journal of Psychotherapy*, October 1958, the name of Berne's new method of diagnosis and treatment, *transactional analysis*, became a permanent part of the psychotherapeutic literature.

Thus, in little more than a year after resolving to part company with psychoanalysis, Eric Berne had created a substantially new kind of analysis, transactional, a term directly descriptive of what psychotherapy is all about, viz., transactions between people. In addition to re-stating his concepts of *P-A-C, structural analysis* and *ego-states,* the November 1957 paper added the important new features of *games* and *scripts*. TA by then was already 90-percent complete, more than 13 years ago. From that time on there could be no further conflict with psychoanalysis as it became clear that TA was bigger in structure and concept. TA offered no quarrel with psychoanalysis; rather, TA embraced it.

THE SEMINARS

It is significant to remember that important TA testing grounds had been brought into use by Eric beginning in the early fifties in the form of clinical seminars at Monterey which he ran faithfully every Thursday evening. In 1950-51 he had also started a clinical seminar Tuesday evenings at his San Francisco home which in 1958 became the San Francisco Social Psychiatry Seminars, Inc., incorporated in order to handle funds required for the publication of the *Transactional Analysis Bulletin* that first appeared in January 1961, with Eric as editor.

In 1964 he bought the house at 165 Collins Street where the seminars continued until his death. (However, the seminars did not cease in 1970. Rather, the very active group which had met with Eric every Tuesday evening elected to continue meeting at the office and home of Dr. Jack Dusay, 2709 Jackson Street, San Francisco. In honor of Eric, the group changed its name to the Eric Berne Seminar of San Francisco.)

That Eric regarded the seminars as highly valuable to the growth and development of TA is clear from introductory acknowledgments printed in each one of his TA books, where he lists the names of various clinicians who stimulated him the most. He also never failed to thank his patients for what they had taught him. The San Francisco seminar soon became the major Bay Region advanced training course, a 202 Seminar for those who sought to reach ITAA Clinical Member status.

It was also 1964 when Eric and his San Francisco seminar colleagues plus those from the Monterey TA Seminar decided to create a TA association, naming it the International Transactional Analysis Association in recognition of the growing number of TA professionals who resided outside the USA. The new body was then designated successor to the San Francisco Social Psychiatry Seminar as publisher of the *TA Bulletin* and the San Francisco seminar changed its name to the San Francisco Transactional Analysis Seminar in recognition that it should be considered from then on merely as one of the branches of the ITAA.

The breadth of Eric's interests was extraordinary. One of them was a lifelong interest in how psychiatry was practiced in other nations of the world. His first published paper, for instance, was a report on mental hospitals in Syria and Lebanon (Bernstein, 1939A). In 1948 he made a trip around the world, visiting 17 mental hospitals in the Philippines, Hong Kong, Singapore, Ceylon, India and Turkey. Between 1957 and 1960 he traveled summers annually, making a personal study of mental illness in the South Pacific, including New Guinea and New Ireland, Fiji and Tahiti (Berne 1959B, 1959C, 1960C, 1960D). He was also deeply concerned with the problems of racial discrimination, wrote a brilliant analysis on the subject long before racism became a popular concern (Berne 1957D). His interest in the parapsychological cropped up re-

peatedly, as witness his series of six articles on intuition, 1949 to 1962. Other travels took him to
Trinidad, Europe and the Mediterranean, to Vienna in
1968 where he presented transactional analysis to the
International Congress for Group Psychotherapy.

THE LAST YEARS

The years 1964 to 1970 were restless ones for Eric.
His personal life after divorce from Dorothy became
rather chaotic as he tried to find another mate. Frus-
trations in this area led him to work longer and longer
hours at his writing, but he still wanted female company. In 1967 he married the young Torri Rosecrans,
yet gave up none of his increasingly complex writing
commitments. By the fall of 1969 he and Torri were
living apart a good deal of the time and in early 1970
they were divorced.

Strangely, Eric was telling all his friends how well
he felt the two weeks before his heart attack. He had
just completed two books, *Sex in Human Loving*
(Berne 1970B) and *What Do You Say After You Say
Hello?* (Berne 1971), and he was pleased over the
way they had turned out. He actually was allowing
himself some weekends of pure play, no writing. But
on Friday, June 26, 1970, he suffered the first warning:
sharp pains that went through his chest and back.
Cautious, as was his habit in matters of health (he
had jogged every weekend and gone swimming often),
he asked to be taken to the hospital where a cardio-
gram, and because of back pains, chest X-rays were
made. For some unknown reason the EKG graph was
within normal ranges, the X-rays were clear. He was
told to go home and take it easy. By Sunday afternoon he felt all right again and was getting ready to go
to the beach when a heavy cardiac attack struck. He
was rushed to an intensive care unit where he was
kept heavily sedated for three days.

By the end of the first week of hospitalization Eric
began to improve, and so did the cardiograms. The
attending physicians and nursing staff were impressed
with his progress and unofficial reports leaked out

that he was going to pull through all right. Proofs of the *Sex in Human Loving* book were sent for, and he finished three hours of work on them while sitting in his hospital bed.

Due to the improvement he was allowed to move to a regular room on another floor from the ICU. EKG's continued to look non-critical. But Eric admitted several days before he died that he had begun to feel unusually tired, was noticeably discouraged when he called the San Francisco seminar the night of July 14, saying "the road ahead seemed full of curves." The next morning, shortly after having breakfast, he started choking, gasping for breath. The staff was unable to save him. An autopsy proved the original attack from coronary thrombosis had been so massive, virtually all parts of the heart had been hopelessly damaged. The date was Wednesday, July 15, 1970.

Glossary

Adaptation The alternation of a script to make the best use of the facilities at hand.

Adult An ego state oriented toward objective, autonomous data-processing and probability-estimating.

Antiscript The inverse of the script. The defiant opposite of what each directive calls for.

Archaeopsyche The hypothetical organ that deals with Child ego states.

Authentic Individual One whose signature on an act is free of external influences irrelevant to the act itself.

Authority Principle The principle that each member of an organizational hierarchy tries to comply with the presumed or fantasied wishes of those above him.

Boundaries Physical or psychological factors that separate relevant regions in the group structure.
External The boundary separating the group from the external environment.
Major Internal That which distinguishes the leadership from the membership.
Minor Internal Those which distinguish subgroups or individual patients from each other (Minor$_1$), or individuals within a subgroup (Minor$_2$). There may also be minor boundaries in the leadership if there is more than one therapist present.

Button An internal or external stimulus which turns on scripty or gamy behavior.

Child An ego which is an archaic relic from an early significant period of life. The adapted Child is influenced by Parental parameters. The expressive Child is more autonomous.

Clock-Time A period measured by clock or calendar.

Come-on A provocation or seduction into nonadaptive behavior.

Commitment An operationally ratified decision to follow certain principles of action in order to attain a certain goal.

Confrontation The use of information to disconcert the patient by pointing out an inconsistency.

Consensus An explicit agreement of several people without a serious examination of motives.

Contract, Administrative The statement between the administration and the therapist concerning the occasions, purposes, and goals of a treatment group, usually in sociological language.

Contract, Organizational The agreement concerning group treatment between the therapist and his organization.

Contract, Professional A statement of the technical goals of a treatment group, usually in psychiatric language.

Contract, Psychological The therapist's assessment of the ulterior motives of the administration that will influence the fate of his treatment group in the organization.

Contract, Therapist-Patient Administratively, this concerns the relationships between the therapist, the patients, and the organization. Professionally, it states the goals of the therapy. Psychologically, the therapist (inwardly) tries to anticipate which games the patients are likely to play in the group.

Conviction A firm opinion about the OKness or not-OKness of oneself on the one hand, and the rest of the world on the other.

Counterscript A possible life plan based on parental precepts.

Cowboy A relaxed therapist who knows how to make himself understood by the patient's Child.

Curse The script injunction.

Cut-off A script release from without.

Cut-out A script release from within.

Death Decree A fatal script payoff.

Decision A childhood commitment to a certain form of behavior; the basis for character formation in the form of a verb absolute.

Demon (a) Urges and impulses in the child which apparently fight the script apparatus, but in reality often reinforce it. (b) The whispering voice of the Parent urging the Child on to nonadaptive impulsive behavior. The two usually coincide in their aims.

Despair The failure of a dialogue between the Adult and the outside world.

Diagram, Authority 1. A diagram showing the relationships of all individuals, particularly superiors, who might influence the therapist's attitude or determine the scope or fate of his group. 2. A diagram showing the four aspects of the group authority:

The Organizational Aspect is shown on the Organization Chart, which gives the administrative relationships of those in the hierarchy.

The Personal Aspect is shown on the Personnel Chart, which gives the name of each individual filling a slot on the Organization Chart.

The Historical Aspect gives the names of past leaders whose influence is still felt.

The Cultural Aspect names the canonical books and manuals that regulate the workings of the organization.

Diagram, Dynamics A diagram that demonstrates the forces acting on the major and minor group boundaries.

Diagram, Seating A diagram showing where each member of a group sits in relation to the others and in relation to the furnishings and layout of the treatment room.

Diagram, Structural 1. One which shows the internal structure of a group. 2. One which shows the ego-state structure of a personality.

Differentiation The assignment of slots in a group imago to the actual individuals in a group. Thus a group may be under-differentiated (more people than slots), fully differentiated (each individual assigned to a special slot), or over-differentiated (more slots than people). Heteromorphic differentiation corrects under-differentiation by activating new slots; homomorphic differentiation, by assigning several members to the same slot.

Drama triangle A simple diagram showing the possible switches of roles in a game or script. The three major roles are Persecutor, Victim, and Rescuer.

Earthian One whose judgments are based on preconceptions rather than on what is actually happening. A square.

Earthian Viewpoint One which is obscured by preconceptions learned from other people, usually in early
childhood.

Ego State A consistent pattern of feeling and experience
directly related to a corresponding consistent pattern
of behavior.

Electrode The Parent in the Child. When activated, it
brings about an almost automatic response.

Engram A trace left by an early experience, influential
in later relationships.

Exteropsyche The hypothetical organ that deals with
Parental ego states.

Family Culture The chief interest of the family, particularly in regard to bodily functions.

Family Drama A dramatic series of events which occurs
repeatedly in each family, and which forms the protocol
for the script.

Gallows Laugh The laugh or smile which accompanies
a gallows transaction, and which is usually shared by
the others present.

Gallows Transaction A transaction which leads directly
toward the script payoff.

Game A series of transactions with a con, a gimmick, a
switch, and a crossup, leading to a payoff.

Game Formula The sequence of events occurring in a
game, expressed as a formula by means of letter symbols:

$$C + G = R \rightarrow S \rightarrow X \rightarrow P.$$

Gamy Behavior Behavior which seems more calculated
to get an eventual trading-stamp payoff than to accomplish its declared purpose.

Gimmick A special attitude or weakness which makes a
person vulnerable to games or scripty behavior.

Goal Time A period terminated by the attainment of a
goal.

Group Apparatus Those people who preserve internal
order in a group (internal apparatus) and those who
deal with the external environment (external apparatus).

Group, Heterogeneous One to which the patients are assigned with whatever degree of randomness is available.

Group, Homogeneous One in which the patients are

selected because they have a common characteristic.
The homogeneity may be a matter of organizational
planning, for patients with the same syndrome, symptom, or condition; or it may be a matter of personal
policy, according to idiosyncrasies of the therapist.

Group Imago A mental image of the dynamic relationships between the people in the group, including the
therapist; idiosyncratic for each individual present.

Group Process Transactions that are not directly concerned with the group activity.

External Transactions between the group and the external environment.

Major Internal Transactions between the members and
the therapist.

Minor Internal Transactions between patients not directly involving the therapist; or transactions between
therapists not directly involving the patients.

Group Treatment 1. The treatment of several psychiatric
patients simultaneously by meeting in a room for a
specified period of time with a small number of them
for the declared purpose of alleviating psychiatric disabilities. 2. The treatment by a trained psychotherapist
of more than one patient at a time with the object of
relieving symptoms or effecting psychodynamic changes
in the patients' personalities.

Group Work. 1. Guidance in group experience without
systematic focus on the psychiatry of specific psychopathology. 2. A form of group activity in which the
leader guides or manipulates the members according to
psychodynamic principles without revealing to them the
basis for his actions.

Illusion An unlikely hope which the Child clings to and
which influences all his decisive behavior.

Injunction A prohibition or negative command from a
parent.

Institution A set of transactions standardized by consensus and containing elements irrelevant to the material aim of the set.

Institutionalization The introduction of irrelevant elements into a procedure, or their retention after their
usefulness is past and their maintenance by consensus
without serious examination of their relevancy and truth.

Interpretation An operation designed to de-confuse the Child.

Interrogation A question designed to document a clinically decisive point of information.

Intervention A therapeutic operation that intervenes in the conflict between two ego states.

Intimacy A game-free exchange of affective expression without covert exploitation.

Life Course What actually happens.

Life Plan What is supposed to happen according to the script.

Life Sentence A negative but not fatal script payoff.

Loser Someone who does not accomplish a declared purpose.

Magic Orb The mythical reward which the Child spends his life hoping for.

Marshmallow An overly sweet or affected response of encouragement or approval.

Martian One who observes earthly happenings without preconceptions.

Martian Viewpoint The naivest possible frame of mind for observing earthly phenomena, leaving the intellect free for inquiry without the distraction of preconceptions.

Mortgage An optional obligation undertaken to structure long periods of time.

Neopsyche The hypothetical organ that deals with Adult ego states.

Nonwinner Someone who works hard just to break even.

Observer One who observes a group without active participation or duties.

Ogre Father The Child ego state of the father, which forms the Parent of his daughter's Child ego state and directs the tragic script. In a productive script, this is called the Jolly Giant.

O.K. Words Words rewarded by parental approval.

Palimpsest A later version of script arising from new

potentialities as the child enters later phases of development.

Parent An ego state borrowed from a parental figure. It may exert itself as an indirect influence, or be directly exhibited in parental behavior.

Pastimes Semi-stereotyped sets of transactions, usually of a multiple-choice, sentence-completion structure.

Pattern A style of life based on parental instruction or example.

Permission (1) a parental license for autonomous behavior. (2) An intervention which gives the individual a license to disobey a parental injunction if he is ready, willing, and able, or releases him from parental provocations.

Persona A masked presentation of self. It usually is at an eight- to twelve-year-old level.

Position A predicate absolute that justifies a decision.

Prescription A set of precepts offered by a nurturing parent.

Private Interview Time spent with an individual patient immediately following a group session, usually extemporaneously at the patient's initiative.

Procedure A set of operations all of which are relevant to, and necessary for, the stated aim.

Program The lifestyle which results from all the elements of the script apparatus taken together.

Protocol The original dramatic experiences upon which the script is based.

Provisional Fantasy (Provisional Group Imago) The patient's fantasy of what will occur when he enters a group.

Provocation Nonadaptive behavior encouraged or demanded by a parent.

Racket The sexualization and transactional exploitation of unpleasant feelings.

Ratification The demonstration in operation that a contractual commitment will be carried through in spite of difficulties and unforeseen eventualities.

Release, External An outside intervention which releases the individual from the demands of his script. A cut-off.

Release, Internal A condition built into the script whereby the individual is released from it. A cut-out.

Re-Parenting Cutting off early Parental programing and

substituting a new and more adaptive program through regression, especially in schizophrenics.

Rituals Stereotyped sets of transactions.

Role A set of transactions played out in any of the three ego states according to the demands of the script.

Role Playing An imitative form of behavior, not all of which is procedural, designed to meet institutionalized requirements.

Santa Claus The illusory source of the illusory gift which the Child spends his life waiting for.

Script A life plan based on a decision made in childhood, reinforced by the parents, justified by subsequent events, and culminating in a chosen alternative.

Antithesis A command which directly contradicts the parental injunction; a therapeutic intervention which brings about temporary or permanent release from the demands of the script. An external release.

Can Script One stated in positive terms.

Can't Script One stated in negative terms.

Controls The payoff, the injunctions, and the provocations which control the individual's scripty behavior.

Currency The medium that leads to the script payoff: words, money, or tissues are examples.

Directives Controls, patterns, and other script equipment.

Driven Of a person who has to accomplish what his script calls for at any cost, but may have fun on the side.

Episcript An excess of parental programing. *See* Overscript.

Failure If the script cannot be carried through, it leads to despair.

Hamartic One with a self-destructive, tragic ending.

Matrix A diagram showing the parental directives which form the basis of the script.

Outbreak (or Outbreak of Script) shifting from more or or less rationally controlled behavior into a scripty scene.

Overscript An excess of parental programing which is passed from one person to another, as from parent to child. Whoever has this "hot potato" at any given moment is overscripted. An episcript.

Payoff The ultimate destiny or final display that marks the end of a life plan.

Primal The earliest version of the script, based on the infant's interpretation of the family drama.

Ridden Of a person who must concentrate on his script at the expense of everything else.

Set The dreamlike setting in which the Child plays out the script.

Sign A special item of behavior which gives a clue to a patient's script.

Signal A movement or mannerism which marks scripty behavior.

Space The space within which the decisive transactions of a script take place.

Theme Love, hate, revenge, or jealousy are the commonest.

Velocity The number of role switches occurring in a script in a given unit of time.

World The distorted world in which the script is played out.

Scripty Behavior Behavior which seems more motivated by a script than by rational considerations.

Self-Correction The therapist's duty to be aware of what games he is likely to be tempted to play in the group, and to apply appropriate corrections to his own behavior at all times.

Sequestration To cut oneself off from society, by going to an institution or by partial or complete social isolation.

Slot A place in a script to be filled by any person who will respond according to its demands.

Slots Elements of an Organization Chart or a Group Imago.

Spellbreaker An internal release, built into the script.

Stopper A script injunction or prohibition.

Stroke The unit of recognition; e.g. "Hello."

Structural Analysis Analysis of the personality into its constituent Parent, Adult, and Child ego states.

Sweatshirt A life motto which is apparent from the person's demeanor.

Switch 1. A switch from one role to another in game or script.

2. A manner which forces or induces another person to switch roles.

3. An internal or external stimulus which turns off adaptive behavior.

Therapeutic Hypothesis A hypothesis concerning the value of a planned therapeutic operation.

Totem An animal which fascinates the individual and influences his behavior.

Trading Stamp An incident "collected" for the purpose of justifying pathological feelings or behavior.

Transaction A transactional stimulus plus a transactional response. In a *complementary* transaction, the vectors are parallel. In a *crossed* transaction, they are crossed. An *ulterior* transaction is effective at two levels, the social and the psychological. An ulterior transaction may be *angular* involving three ego states, or *duplex*, involving four.

Transaction, Autistic A transaction carried out mentally rather than overtly. It may be adapted or unadapted.

Transactional Analysis 1. A system of psychotherapy based on the analysis of transactions and chains of transactions as they actually occur during treatment sessions. Its principal phases are structural analysis, transactional analysis proper, game analysis, and script analysis. 2. A theory of personality based on the study of specific ego states. 3. A theory of social action based on the rigorous analysis of transactions into an exhaustive but finite number of classes based on the specific ego states involved. 4. The analysis of single transactions by means of transactional diagrams. This is transactional analysis proper.

Vis medicatrix naturae The healing powers of nature.

Winner Someone who accomplishes his declared purpose.

Witch Mother The Child ego state of a mother, which forms the Parent of her son's Child ego state and directs the tragic script. In a productive script, this is called the Fairy Godmother.

Withdrawal Unexplained, unannounced, or merely plausible termination.

World View The Child's distorted view of the world and the people around him, upon which his script is based.

Learn to
live with somebody...
yourself.

EVERYTHING YOU'VE ALWAYS WANTED TO KNOW ABOUT EVERYTHING

Ballantine's Comprehensive Reference Books